The Critical Philosophy
of
Hermann Cohen

SUNY Series in Jewish Philosophy
Kenneth R. Seeskin, editor

THE CRITICAL PHILOSOPHY
OF
HERMANN COHEN

(La Filosofia Critica DI Hermann Cohen)

ANDREA POMA

Translated by
JOHN DENTON

STATE UNIVERSITY OF NEW YORK PRESS

Originally published as Filosofia critica di Hermann Cohen,
© Copyright 1988 Ugo Mursia Editore, Milan, Italy

Published by
State University of New York Press, Albany

For information, address State University of New York Press,
State University Plaza, Albany, N.Y., 12246

Production by Marilyn P. Semerad
Marketing by Fran Keneston

Library of Congress Cataloging in Publication Data

Poma, Andrea.
  [Filosofia critica di Hermann Cohen. English]
  The critical philosophy of Hermann Cohen / Andrea Poma :
translated by John Denton.
    p.   cm. — (SUNY series in Jewish philosophy)
  Includes bibliographical references and index.
  ISBN 0–7914–3185–1 (hc : alk. paper). — ISBN 0–7914–3186–X (pb :
alk. paper)
  1. Cohen, Hermann, 1842–1918.   I. Title.   II. Series.
B3216.C74P6613   1997
193—dc20
                                                      96–30131
                                                      CIP
10 9 8 7 6 5 4 3 2 1

Contents

Preface

—————

Die Kerls wollen glücklich sein!
(Hermann Cohen)

There is no doubt that an essential, indispensable conviction of the adherents of critical philosophy is that philosophy is rational. This conviction is one of the reasons why critical philosophy has been included in contemporary criticism of the presumption of many schools of thought that reason is omnipotent. In our century rationalism has been analyzed in its various forms and frequently condemned because of its various errors. Thus, both the all-embracing claims of absolute reason and the arrogant pragmatism of instrumental reason have been rejected. In both cases it was pointed out that reason was a principle of overwhelming control, threatening to smother any creative expression of the freedom of mankind. The reasons for the condemnation and subsequent neglect of critical reason lie, rather, in its abstract nature and inability to take account of reality. It has also, on various occasions, been associated by its opponents with absolute reason, pragmatic reason, Hegelian idealism, or positivism. The result has been that it has been condemned either to neglect, or, at most, to the cold storage of history.

Cohen's case is of particular interest. His reputation as a philosopher was greatly damaged by the judgments of those, such as Martin Heidegger and Julius Ebbinghaus, who accused him of limiting philosophy to science and of having joined the ranks of positivism, and by those, such as Georg Lukács, who dismissed him as a representative of outdated bourgeois philosophy. Subsequently, many others accepted these views, reiterating them, often without further discussion.

Taking a new look at Cohen's critical thought today, establishing an ideal link with those who shared his aims and, more generally, with a new, growing interest in critical reason and its tradition, can mean more than a mere attempt at historical conservation. Today the needs and demands of critical idealism and rationalism may well attract renewed attention, both because the violent opposition to rationalism in the name of the immediate values of life and feeling is now a thing of the past and because the balance sheet of the errors of totalitarian reason is now practically complete. Both phenomena are preconditions for a more serene, dispassionate discussion of critical philosophy, as a specific, different position.

However, certain positive reasons can, be added to these negative preconditions. Critical philosophy could attract attention and be a source of inspiration in the reproposition of the rights and duties of reason in philosophy, and, in general, in the interpretation of reality, thus becoming a stimulating interlocutor in contemporary philosophical debate. With its valiant defense of reason, carried on within the context of "limits," and grounded in its 'purity,' critical philosophy does differentiate itself from, or rather opposes, the concepts of all-embracing and instrumental reason, but opposes every kind of irrationalism even more vigorously.

As regards the more specific and interesting accusations of abstractness and inability to understand reality brought against critical philosophy, I have, in this book, tried to present the development and enrichment of critical philosophy in Cohen's thought, in order to show, in this especially meaningful example, its potentiality in the face of these important, unavoidable demands of our century. It is certainly true that, for chronological reasons, it is impossible to find specific answers in Cohen's works to those twentieth-century thinkers who made the above objections against Kant's critical philosophy. However, what can be found in Cohen are the needs of his own time, which encouraged him to investigate thoroughly and discuss critical philosophy in different directions, especially in its capacity for the interpretation and foundation of concrete scientific, moral, political, historical, and religious reality.

Thus, this book, though attempting to approach the many specific subjects with which it deals analytically, attaches most importance to a unified view of Cohen's philosophy as a development of the principles and potentiality of critical philosophy. It is my conviction that it is in this perspective that Cohen's thought can be really understood, both as a whole and in detail, this being its most interesting and rewarding aspect for representation today.

First of all (chapters 1–3) I shall follow the route along which Cohen reinterpreted Kant's critical philosophy, modifying and enriching it by means of his encounter with the tradition of "critical idealism" (especially Plato and Leibniz). After defining (chapter 4) the essential traits of critical idealism, which Cohen adopted as his own philosophical position, as a result of the tradition he inherited, in opposition both to what he termed more or less appropriately "romantic idealism," and to materialism, I shall follow the developments of Cohen's critical thought in the parts of his philosophical system (chapters 5–7). Finally (chapters 8–11), I shall pay particular attention to Cohen's last, religious works, showing that he did not abandon his critical approach, but developed and enriched it, enlarging on the aspect of thought on the limit of reason, which is an essential, necessary complement to the aspect of thought *within* the limit of reason. Without this, critical philosophy would be seriously curtailed, while, with it, it is able to put forward ideas which are important for the supreme problems of religion and history.

The cornerstones of Cohen's critical philosophy, in his dedication to the foundation and interpretation of the concrete reality of mankind and history, are certainly faith in the truth and rejection of the eudemonist foundation of morality and history. In connection with these two themes, the consideration of suffering also deserves particular attention. One of the most interesting aspects of contemporary philosophy is its interest in the dramatic reality of suffering shown by many modern thinkers (some of whom are indebted to the rediscovery of biblical, traditional, and contemporary Jewish thought). It is precisely for this reason that I believe that there is some value in offering a confrontation with the critical thought of Cohen to the many thinkers now showing interest in this reality. Cohen's thought is certainly Kantian, but it goes beyond Kant on this point. It is also Jewish, but it is different from the more usual models of Jewish thought. Far from banishing the problem of suffering, he made it the climax of his moral and religious reflections and the central problem of history, in the very name of rationalist and critical idealism, where rationalism proves itself to be capable of reaching the limit and maintaining its position over it, not omnipotent in theoretical control over it, but anything but impotent in accounting for practical loyalty toward it.

Acknowledgments

I wish to thank those whose help made the completion of this book much less difficult and much more stimulating: Prof. Giuseppe Riconda, who followed the development of my work at every stage, offering encouragement, advice, and criticism. Our friendly, fruitful philosophical discussions kindled my enthusiasm for philosophy in general and the values of the critical school in particular; Prof. Helmut Holzhey, director of the Cohen-Archiv in Zurich, Switzerland, who not only was generous enough to allow me access over the years to his archive's bibliographical resources and to his own research, but also carried on a friendly, detailed series of discussions on the theme which is of interest to both of us, providing me with extremely useful advice and opinions. This personal and philosophical dialogue has proved to be of great value. I should also like to thank Prof. Luigi Pareyson for accepting the Italian edition of this book in the series he edits.

It is with great pleasure that I make my book on Hermann Cohen available to American readers, in the hope that it will contribute to more widespread knowledge of his philosophy. I should like to take this opportunity of remembering the late Prof. Steven S. Schwarzschild, a sincere friend, who suggested that I have this book translated and encouraged me from the outset. For this reason I am honored to dedicate it to his memory.

I should also like to thank Prof. Kenneth R. Seeskin, who kindly accepted this translation for publication in the series under his editorship, following the project through with understanding and patience.

My further thanks go to Dr. John Denton, who translated the text both accurately and with a fine sense of style, on more than one occasion expressing better in English what I had written in Italian.

Last but not least, I am grateful to the State University of New York Press, and am proud to see one of my books included in their prestigious catalog.

1

The Interpretation of Kant

1. Neo-Kantianism

The problem of Cohen's reception of Kant should first be placed, briefly, within the context of the widespread Kantian movement which flourished in German philosophy in the second half of the nineteenth and early decades of the twentieth centuries. The confines, contents, and articulation of this movement have been, and still are, the subject of extensive discussion among historians of philosophy.[1] Here, I do not intend to give either a complete account of the matter, or an exhaustive historiographical judgment. I shall limit myself to those aspects which are essential for our problem.

The urgent need for a return to Kant, expressed by Zeller[2] in 1862 and by Liebmann[3] in 1865, was part of a particularly critical cultural situation for philosophy: the "collapse of the Hegelian system"[4] and, with it, that of the whole of philosophy (which for a long period had been bound up with speculative idealism and Hegel's system in particular) had left a gap in philosophical culture. A particularly fruitful time for science (physiology, biology, anthropology, etc.) had shifted interest and expectations in the direction of empirical research and the inductive method, and had contributed to mistrust and a feeling of "nausea"[5] for philosophical speculation. The need was still certainly felt for a general synthesis, for a fundamental response to philosophical, ethical, social, and religious problems.[6] What were forthcoming, however, were theories that were often crude and superficial, in their reliance on naive naturalistic objectivism and an illusory empirical method, taken over from

1

scientific research. The *Materialismusstreit* controversy of 1850 through 1860 appeared to have come to an end with liberation from all metaphysical illusions and with the definitive establishment of materialistic dogma. Books such as *Köhlerglaube und Wissenschaft* (published in 1854 and reaching its sixth edition by 1856!) by Karl Vogt,[7] and especially *Kraft und Stoff* (1855, twenty-first edition by 1904!) by Ludwig Büchner[8] appeared to have opened up a new, more "scientific" conception of reality and man. Materialistic prejudice crossed the boundaries of specialization to take on the role of popular philosophy.

Neo-Kantianism came into being as a tentative response and critical alternative *both* to idealist metaphysics *and* to naturalistic materialism. Certainly, the need for a "return to Kant" did not grow out of the conviction that he had been forgotten, but, in a way, from the very opposite view. Continual reference to Kant had been the cause of distortion of his authentic thought by his followers, who had always emphasized its less valid aspects (thing-in-itself), neglecting more and more his truly valuable contribution (the transcendental). I am here referring to the central thesis of the book by Liebmann, *Kant und die Epigonen.* The author, however, was only joining a larger group of thinkers, which included Benecke,[9] Weisse,[10] Haym,[11] and Zeller,[12] who had shown the same intentions. The rediscovery of the "real" Kant had a twofold meaning: "the real, historical Kant, the essential, meaningful Kant."[13] The twofold nature of this "return to Kant" clearly shows that the need for a historical reconstruction of the real Kant was not limited to a kind of Kantian neoscholasticism, but was in search of a sound point of reference for the "reconstruction of philosophy" in this real Kant.[14] Natorp expressed the attitude shared by a large number of Neo-Kantians, with great clarity: "Kant, who saw philosophy as critique, as method, certainly wished to teach us to philosophize, but not to teach 'one' philosophy. Anyone who understood otherwise would be a bad disciple of Kant!."[15] One could add that, if the first aspect, that is the historical reconstruction and faithful exegesis of Kant's thought, left a great deal to be desired, at least in the initial stages of Neo-Kantianism, a true *Kant-Philologie* only coming into being in the 1880s (with Arnoldt, Adickes, Erdmann, Paulsen, Vaihinger, etc.), as far as the originality and creativity of Neo-Kantian thought is concerned, it is sufficient to take note of the variety and diversity of philosophical work stimulated by the "return to Kant."

However, the "return to Kant" was not merely a warning against the speculative systems of the first half of the nineteenth century, but also, and perhaps even more (or at least more immediately), a rebellion of idealism against the dull naturalistic objectivism of materialism, and an attempt to bring together philosophy and science from a critical standpoint, as opposed to the arbitrary, superficial theorizings of "vulgar materialism" (*Vulgärmaterialismus*). The protagonists of the first phase of Neo-Kantianism, so-called "physiological" Neo-Kantianism, were scientists (Helmholtz)[16] and philosophers (Lange,[17] Liebmann[18]), who recognized that the real conceptual framework within which to react against materialistic objectivism and empiricism was the correspondence between the theories of Johannes Müller's *Synnenphysiologie* and Kant's a priori. If physiology was able to demonstrate that it is not possible to explain all the phenomena of the world and of existence with the properties or movements of matter, without the help of a guiding principle of reason, as Büchner would have us believe, but that it is necessary to have recourse to "innate laws," peculiar to the psychophysical "organization" of the subject, as presuppositions of every experience of natural objects, and if these results of scientific research corresponded to what philosophy had already stated in the Kantian a priori, then science and philosophy found themselves allies in a critique of objectivism on the basis of a theory of knowledge formulated by philosophy and confirmed by science. "Enquiry into sense perceptions leads us to that knowledge already discovered by Kant: that the proposition 'No effect without a cause' is a law of our thought, given before every experience." Thus Hermann Helmholtz, in his 1855 lecture, *Über das Sehen des Menschen*,[19] lent all the weight of his recognized scientific prestige to the conciliation between philosophy in decline and triumphant science. This pact, continued Helmholtz, can be easily recognized, provided that one compared the recent achievements of science (especially those of Johannes Müller's physiology) not with "certain new philosophical systems," but with "the exceptional progress made by philosophy through Kant."[20] What was seen in Kant then was the model of a well-founded philosophical method, in close contact with science and thus credible (in contrast with the unacceptable speculative constructions of romanticism), but also the departure point for a return to the idealist and subjectivist conception of reality and knowledge, which met with scientific support, for example, in Johannes Müller's psychophysiology.

If I have dedicated some attention to this early "physiological" phase of Neo-Kantianism, even though it was soon definitively refuted and became obsolete, both as an interpretation of Kant and as a general philosophical conception of knowledge (Cohen's criticisms were certainly one of the first and most fundamental refutations of this position),[21] my purpose was to point out that it played an important role, despite its inadequacy. It not only contributed to the renewal of German philosophy and to the opposition of idealism and subjectivism to naturalistic objectivism and the empiricism of materialism and positivism, but also to the resumption by philosophy of the critical function which was correctly recognized to have originated with Kant. The physiological position was basically inadequate because its opposition to naturalistic objectivism, which, in any case, it substantially resembled, was illusory. The psychophysical organization of the knowing subject, which was made to correspond to Kant's a priori, was only an aspect of the natural, objective reality to be established. Subjectivism could no longer be the correct way of refuting materialistic objectivism, or, indeed, discredited metaphysical or only apparent psychophysiological objectivism. However, the antiobjectivist requirement persisted, and it remained part of Cohen's Neo-Kantianism.

Cohen understood the need for abandoning the subjectivism-objectivism alternative, and for finding a new direction which would lead beyond, not only speculative metaphysics and materialism, but also psychophysiological subjectivism. He found the solution in the "return to Kant," that is transcendental philosophy. The opportunity for Cohen to follow this new route was provided by the Trendelenburg-Fischer dispute.

2. The Trendelenburg-Fischer Dispute

In 1871, with his essay *Zur Controverse zwischen Trendelenburg und Kuno Fischer*, Cohen intervened in the famous "Homeric"[22] struggle between Trendelenburg and Fischer.[23] In this essay Cohen did not take sides, postponing his confutation of Trendelenburg's thesis to a "more detailed work" (which he had, in fact, already finished writing,[24] and which was to be published in the same year). Having thus avoided the fundamental question: "Did Trendelenburg demonstrate that Kant, in his arguments in favor of the exclusive subjectivity of space and time, had left a gap?" (*S I*: 231),[25] Cohen only examined the controversial aspect of the dispute: "Did Kuno Fischer demonstrate that the gap claimed to exist by Trendelenburg was not, in fact, present in Kant's arguments?" and "Did Trendelenburg demonstrate that Kuno Fischer had introduced non-Kantian elements into his exposition of Kant's theory?" (*S I*: 231).

Cohen's decision in favor of Trendelenburg was influenced by personal reasons, over and above the latter's merits, which are dealt with in detail in the essay. Trendelenburg was a very influential person on the Berlin academic scene, to which Cohen belonged. According to Ollig, the Lazarus/Steinthal group,[26] which included Cohen, and whose journal (*Zeitschrift für Völkerpsychologie und Sprachwissenschaft*) had published his essay, was closely connected to Trendelenburg. Cohen himself was

influenced by Trendelenburg,[27] who had already praised one of the former's youthful works.[28] However, Cohen had no academic or ideal ties
with Fischer. In fact, when he had the opportunity of listening to
Fischer's classes, he expressed a very negative view of them.[29]

The occasional nature of this essay would reduce its interest, if it
were not for a number of important general considerations. Toward the
end, in his discussion of Trendelenburg's and Fischer's methodological
ideas about the history of philosophy, Cohen makes some interesting
observations.[30] In Cohen's view of the history of philosophy as the history
of problems which are investigated with ever increasing depth, their
solutions following, one after the other, it is an important task of the historian to separate the new from the old in each author. However, the
new—that is the particular author's original contribution to the history
of a philosophical problem—can only be discovered if one isolates the
"fundamental thought," the "point of origin" (*Springpunkt*), around
which all his philosophy is organized.[31] In order to isolate this original
nucleus of Kant's thought, "*the historian should be a philosopher. The historian should not hesitate to place himself between the contending par-
ties*" (*S I:* 272). When the interpreter is directly involved in philosophical
problems, any claim to interpretative objectivity becomes illusory, if we
understand this as the product of a detached, disinterested attitude.
Genuine objectivity is rather the product of the meeting between "the
possibly impartial assumption of the outsider and one's own rigorous
development." It is grounded in the "many-sided, solid" development of
subjectivity (cf. *S I:* 272). This is why Fischer's approach to Kant's philosophy, "not from the point of view of an advocate, but only from that of a
writer of history of philosophy (*philosophischer Geschichtsschreiber*),"[32] is
mistaken. It is only by starting from present problems that a *critical* study
of history is possible:

> So if an age allows itself to be dominated by the trend of history, it will
> soon find its full satisfaction in the fulfilment of this trend, and the longer
> this state of affairs lasts, the less will it be affected by the question: what
> will be?, and even less by the even more urgent question: what *must* be?
> But these levers of the future are, at the same time, the gages of the past.
> The historical link with the old must only be established with what in the
> old was also the new, and only in this regard will historical knowledge of
> the old come about. We are still closely tied to the new in this sense, and
> we must take its side as advocates of truth, if our result is to be real history.
> (*S I:* 274–75)[33]

Now, in the case of Kant, what is the "new," the "*Springpunkt*," the "fundamental, effective thought" (*wirksame Grundgedanke*) (*S I:* 270), which

will act as a starting point? What philosophical approach must the researcher adopt in order to be able to understand Kant? To what present philosophical need does Kant offer an answer? Cohen's answer is clear: "If one does not adopt the critical approach in philosophy, in historical exposition, he will not be able to avoid rebuking *Kant* himself for his 'a priori *magic*,' his '*fantastic* concepts' and other like objectivities, supplying the corresponding information" (*S I:* 272). However, the development of this keypoint was postponed to the future "more detailed work." Despite this, it already seems clear that Cohen did not view the dispute between Trendelenburg and Fischer as being restricted to Kant's conception of space and time, but as covering "all the efforts of philosophical investigation" (*S I:* 229). What is at stake here is the choice between gnoseological subjectivism and objectivism: "Is the nature of things grounded in the conditions of our mind? Or must and *can* our thought be confirmed by the law of nature? The question of the meaning and value of Kant's theory of space and time can be valid as another expression for the question of the principles of knowledge" (*S I:* 229). Furthermore, the very conception of philosophy is at stake: "But one can start off from the physiology of the senses, or from pure psychology, from metaphysics in its ancient meaning, or from *that* metaphysics which is known as the theoretical science of nature. Anyone who does not feel at home in Kant's *Transcendental Aesthetic* will lose his bearings at speculative crossroads" (*S I:* 230).

If philosophy, once it has abandoned the speculative illusion of embracing all theoretical knowledge, including the sciences, is inclined to challenge the claim of the positive sciences to confine it to a "psychological (Mach, Avenarius) or conventionalist (Poincaré) foundation of the exact sciences,"[34] or to an irrational *Weltanschauung* (Fechner, Haym, Strauss, Lotze),[35] or to reduce it, as historicism would like to, to mere history of philosophy,[36] if philosophy wishes to rise up again as a science among sciences, it must begin again from the function of transcendental theory of knowledge given to it by Kant, from the "clearcut boundary line [. . .] drawn by Kant for all future metaphysics, and *thus for all psychology*" (*S I:* 229), it must recover its fundamental, essential, critical character.

3. THE FIRST EDITION OF *KANTS THEORIE DER ERFAHRUNG*

The study of Kant, announced by Cohen, soon appeared and represented a decisive stage in the evolution of his thought, but also a turning point in the history of the interpretation of Kant. The work went ahead rapidly. In a letter, probably dating from mid-July 1870, Cohen wrote: "I am getting on with my writing. The whole thing is there alive in my head; it just has to be put down in writing."[37] Cohen approached Kant's thought following the hermeneutic principles already set out. On August 2, 1870, he wrote to his friend Hermann Lewandowsky: "My Kant is there facing me, and I am trying to penetrate his gaze. It is a fine thing to enter the mind of such a man, and observe all possible developments from his point of view."[38] At last, in the previously quoted letter dated October 3, 1870, Cohen was able to announce that the work had been completed. Cohen's decision to take on the role of "advocate" of Kant frequently led him to formulate his interpretation as a "metacritique" (*KTE*[1] v), that is as a critique of the criticisms of Kant. Cohen himself recognized that this was not only a controversial stance, but that it really corresponded to the route he had followed in his rediscovery of Kant:

> My aim in this book was to establish Kant's theory of apriority on a new basis. My conviction that it was true did not grow directly out of my reading of Kant's works. It developed and was consolidated, rather, during my battle against the attacks to which it had been subjected. Like most young people who dedicate themselves to the study of philosophy, I too had been accustomed to the idea that Kant had become outdated, that he now belonged to history. Thus, when the idea that those attacks left Kant unscathed first came to me, I was inclined to believe current opinion and put this idea aside. However, the more I immersed myself, to the best of my abilities, in the opinions which were the cause of those negative judgments, the more tenacious that doubt became. Nevertheless, I thought it incredible that Kant, to whom everyone wishes to trace their origins, could be understood in a different way, in a fundamentally, essentially different way, from that in which those who are leaders in the field interpret and teach him [. . .]. But I felt the urgent need to present the historical Kant again, and to defend him from his opponents in his genuine physiognomy, as far as I was able to understand it. In this drudgery (literally "cart driver's job" *Kärrnerarbeit*), which I enjoyed, I became more and more aware, as it proceeded, that his opponents had not really got to grips with Kant as he appears in the documents; that their conception could be confuted simply by making quotations. (*KTE*[1] iii–iv)

Cohen's letters also contain, in connection with the development of his new interpretation of Kant, frequent criticisms of Kant's interpreters.[39]

Cohen's first idea for the title was to include in it the subjects dealt with: *Raum und Zeit im Zusammenhange der Kantischen Metaphysik und Psychologie, ein Beitrag zum Verständnis des Kantischen Idealismus*[40] (later Cohen was to widen the scope of the work, also taking into consideration transcendental logic, and, as a consequence: "the title will probably be:

"*Raum, Zeit und Kategorien etc.*"[41]). In the end, however, Cohen chose to state Kant's "fundamental thought" directly in the title, since it was around this that he intended to build up his interpretation: the *Critique of Pure Reason* is, in essence, the "Kantian theory of experience" (*Kants Theorie der Erfahrung*): Kant's critical idealism is above all a new theory of experience.

Although I do not intend to provide the reader with a complete description of the contents of this work here, I am obliged to refer to some of the fundamental aspects of Cohen's interpretation of Kant, so as to highlight the object of my research: the meaning of critical philosophy for Cohen in this phase of the development of his thought. As Mariano Campo has rightly pointed out, the type of interpretation of Kant carried out by Cohen "is now common knowledge, and it can be found in all textbooks. However, one should not forget Cohen's contribution to making it obvious, including his trimming of the thick forest of the debate over Kant's legacy."[42]

As is well known, faced with the classical problem of whether our representations are innate (Leibniz) or acquired (Hume), Kant reformulated it in an entirely novel way: "There can be no doubt that all our knowledge begins with experience. . . . But though all our knowledge begins with experience, it does not follow that it all arises out of experience."[43] "In these words experience is propounded (*aufgegeben*) as an enigma. The solution to this enigma is the content of Kant's philosophy. *Kant discovered a new conception of experience*" (*KTE*[1] 3). Experience cannot be considered to be a "datum," in the empiricist meaning of a "prolix series of perceptions" (*KTE*[1] 7), facing which the subject is purely passive: "On the contrary the object is given only because it is intuited" (*KTE*[1] 15–6). Kant's "Copernican Revolution" confirms the principle that the necessary, universal character of knowledge as a science derives from the fact that it "*produces its experience*" (*KTE*[1] 12), i.e.: "we can know a priori of things only what we ourselves put into them."[44] Thus, the task of critical philosophy is an investigation of a priori elements of experience.

Kant began by considering space, which, in our mind, precedes every sensation and "is at the base" of outer phenomena. This, according to Cohen, is the *first degree* of the Kantian a priori: the *a priori as primary origin* (*Ursprünglichkeit*) (cf. *KTE*[1] 88). Therefore, the discovery of the a priori came about in Kant through a reflection on a "fact" of consciousness. However, this psychological method led to an initial result that is not psychological, but metaphysical. The a priori is characterized, not as "initial" (*anfänglich*) as regards experience, but as "originative"; it is what "is at the base" of outer phenomena.

Nevertheless, with this result, transcendental investigation had not even begun. If empirical consciousness isolates space as an originative element in its own experience, it does not justify its apriority for this reason, nor will it ever be able to do so by means of an empirical psychological procedure. Demonstrating the "possibility" of the apriority of space is the task of transcendental investigation:

> If a type of knowledge is called transcendental inasmuch as a priori it must be possible, then the a priori itself is indicated as possible only inasmuch as it is known in a type of transcendental knowledge. And this is truly how it is. The knowledge that a concept is a priori is called *metaphysical* by Kant. This metaphysical knowledge can, however, only come about empirically, by consulting inner experience. . . . In what sense, though, this a priori is *possible*—only this manner of knowledge is transcendental. (*KTE*[1] 36)

Thus, the transcendental question concerns the possibility of the a priori, not its existence. As regards space, it can be formulated as follows: "How is it possible for such a *pure* intuition, an intuition within ourselves, to provide a priori concepts of objects?" (*KTE*[1] 37). Kant's answer, in the *Transcendental Exposition of the Concept of Space*, is well known: "Manifestly, not otherwise than in so far as the intuition has its seat in the subject only, as the formal character of the subject, in virtue of which, in being affected by objects, it obtains *immediate representation*, that is, *intuition*, of them; and only in so far, therefore, as it is merely the form of outer *sense* in general."[45]

This, in Cohen's view, is the *second degree* of the a priori: the *a priori as form* (cf. *KTE*[1] 90). Kant's concept of 'form' should be, however, precisely defined, to avoid the mistaken interpretation of it as "organ," which had weighed heavily on the interpretation of Kant. As is well known, Herbart had criticized the Kantian concept of "a priori form," understood as a hypostatized organ, countering it with his own theory of psychic processes.[46] This mistaken conception of form did not elude the difficulties of innateness. Several of Kant's interpreters had identified the a priori with the innate. Cohen, on the contrary, also intended to avoid the high degree of subjectivism which had characterized physiological Kantian interpretations (Helmholtz, Lange, etc.), which, precisely on the basis of the identification of the a priori with the psychophysical organization of the subject, intended to counter materialist objectivism. Finally, the subjectivist interpretation of the a priori would not be able to elude Trendelenburg's objections. Thus, with his interpretation of Kantian form, Cohen went to the heart of the disputes over Kant and established the basis for the new interpretation of the Kantian concept of 'experience.'

Kant distinguished between form and matter solely with reference to the phenomenon. These concepts are, thus, in no way to be hypostatized, but, quite the opposite, to be considered correlative with reference to knowledge (cf. *KTE*[1] 44). The form of intuition is, therefore, for Kant, "the very act of intuition" (*KTE*[1] 46), being considered independently of its content; so much so that he also called it "pure intuition."

However, if form for Kant is always form of the phenomenon, pure form is an abstraction, and transcendental investigation cannot stop at this point, without running the risk of a subjectivist conception of the a priori, which will not be able to account for the objectivity of knowledge, as Trendelenburg argued. But Kant's authentic "Copernican" turning point consisted in demonstrating that the objectivity of knowledge is assured precisely on the basis of the subjective a priori. To reach this, however, Kant had to render explicit a *third degree* of the meaning of the a priori: the *a priori as a formal condition of the possibility of our experience* (*KTE*[1] 93). With this last and fuller meaning of the a priori, all accusations of subjectivism or adherence to innateness were overcome: "Space is an a priori intuition, after this clarification, now means: space is a *constitutive condition of experience*. It does not appear a priori because it is innate, but appears innate because it is an a priori condition of possible experience" (*KTE*[1] 94).

In this way the "enigma" of experience began to find a solution. First of all, transcendental investigation does not deduce experience from a priori forms, but on them founds "possible experience," or rather "the possibility of experience." Thus we are dealing with a formal, not an ontological, foundation. Second, however, experience is thought of as the set of phenomena, and not as things in themselves, outside and independent of the subject. Thus the "formality" of transcendental justification is not an empty but a ground breaking formality: "The a priori is only conceivable in the form, and the form only with reference to the phenomenon. Thus the a priori now builds up an experience, which desires nothing more than to be *a combination of phenomena*. The foundation of that new type of idealism founded by Kant, and deduced by him from the theory of space and time, resides in the a priori" (*KTE*[1] 58).

This is transcendental idealism, founded on the empirical reality and transcendental ideality of space and time.

However, this meaning of the a priori cannot be totally understood within the context of the *transcendental aesthetic*, since what is missing is an investigation of the act of "synthesis," which alone constitutes experience, and of the categories, the a priori conditions of the unity of the synthesis (cf. *KTE*[1] 81, 98). Therefore, Cohen greatly emphasized the complementary nature of the *transcendental aesthetic* and the *transcendental logic*, showing that he opposed the widespread trend of his time, which favored the *aesthetic* in Kant's *Critique*. Cohen believed that the *aesthetic* needed to be complemented by the *logic*, partly because the theory of the empirical reality and transcendental ideality of space and time is not sufficiently well grounded without clarification of the difference between phenomenon and noumenon, and the limitation of the noumenon to its negative meaning, which can only take place within the *logic*.

Cohen also returned, for the apriority of the categories, to the Kantian distinction between metaphysical and transcendental meanings. First of all, they were inferred by psychological-logical means[47] from the Table of Judgments, as "primary concepts of understanding,"[48] and this enabled Cohen to demonstrate that Kant had already resolved the a priori forms in psychic processes, as required by Herbart. However, this first step, had to be overcome by further investigation, in transcendental deduction, highlighting their character as formal conditions of possible experience, since they are conditions of the synthesis. By emphasizing the formal character of the a priori, Cohen concentrated its meaning in the concept of 'synthesis': "The synthesis is the common tie, which guarantees the same apriority, in the forms of intuiting and thinking" (*KTE*[1] 104–5). Thus, Kant's intention was not to build up a closed system of the a priori with his table of categories. The categories are formal conditions of possible experience; that is, they establish experience in respect of its formal possibility, not its content. Since the formal possibility of experience consists in the synthetic unity of the manifold in it, the meaning of the categories is resolved in their function as unity of the synthesis:

> For our conception, the essential point of the a priori lies, solely, in the fact that it contains the formal condition of experience. As a consequence we only uphold "*synthetic unity in the connection of the manifold*" as an a priori category. For experience in general is not possible without this. By means of it, the "rhapsody of perceptions" becomes "synthetic unity of the phenomena." *This is the reason why we uphold, not so much the apriority of the categories, but that of the category.* . . . For the single categories are a priori altogether, even if they might not be necessary forms of thought in their logical capacity, *inasmuch as they contain a synthetic unity in the connection of the manifold.*" (*KTE*[1] 101)

In the above context, Cohen's conclusion that the apriority of the categories is nothing other than the synthetic unity of apperception is wholly coherent:

> Although not a Kantian expression, it can be in the spirit of Kant to observe: how space is the form for outer intuition and time that for inner intuition; thus transcendental apperception is the *form for the categories*. Self-consciousness is the transcendental condition under which we pro-

> duce the pure concepts of understanding. Synthetic unity is the form
> which, as a common element, is at the base of all the single types of unity
> thought in the categories. (*KTE*[1] 144)

In this way the "transcendental self" also entirely loses its ontological or anthropological character and turns into a pure "transcendental
form," the constitutive condition of the possibility of experience (cf.
KTE[1] 141, 184), while the content of the synthesis is "given" in the inner
sense. Only through the distinction and correlation in the synthesis
between transcendental and empirical apperception is it possible to formulate a "healthy psychology" (*KTE*[1] 146, 164).

The very transcendental character of the a priori forms of sensibility and understanding, which has been clarified up to this point, implies
that the separation of the two "sources" of knowledge be regarded as the
result of an abstraction. Transcendental investigation starts from the fact
of experience as a synthesis of the phenomena, only to return to the a
priori conditions of the possibility of such a synthesis in sensibility and
understanding, which therefore co-operate in the foundation of experience. Thus, after separate analysis of the two sources, they must be
joined together in the construction of experience; inner sense being the
intermediary: "The a priori form of space: a chimera, which does not
combine with the pure forms of understanding in the synthesis of the
phenomena, of which experience above all consists for us! However, this
synthesis - and this is where we reach the most important point, where
the inseparability of logic from aesthetics becomes clear - this synthesis is
only possible in the *inner sense*" (*KTE*[1] 84).

Thus, in the *Analytic of Principles*, and in the theory of schematism,
the true meaning of the transcendental a priori is finally given full
expression. The transcendental method, whose point of departure is the
fact of experience and whose aim is to find the a priori conditions of its
possibility, does not allow any misunderstanding about the pre-eminence of the transcendental over the metaphysical a priori, and thus of
the principles over the judgments and categories:

> Now the sense of metaphysical deduction will no longer be misinter-
> preted. The pure forms of thought are not intended to be discovered a pri-
> ori! Our intent is to discover the necessary forms of given experience. Our
> path will not lead to them, but will take them as its point of departure. As is
> very well known, it is not by proceeding from the category of causality that
> we establish through it the second analogy of experience. Our question,
> rather, concerns the possibility of the latter. What is available to us is the
> synthetic *principle*, which, together with those similar to it, must be clari-

fied. This procedure is indeed clearly indicated in the Prolegomena, but also in the Critique. (*KTE*[1] 206-7)

4. COHEN AND THE DISPUTES OVER THE INTERPRETATION OF KANT

The "new foundation" of the Kantian a priori, discussed above in its essential outline, allowed Cohen to formulate decisive answers to some problems and objections concerning Kant brought up by his interpreters. It should not be forgotten that Cohen began his interpretation of Kant with the intention of contributing to the "restoration (*Wiederaufrichtung*) of Kant's authority" (*KTE*[1] vi), against the mistakes and objections of the latter's interpreters and critics.

First, Cohen was finally able to to reply to Trendelenburg's objections; the reply which in his essay on the dispute between Trendelenburg and Fischer had been postponed. The new theory of Kant's experience now invalidated the problem of the relationship between subjectivity and objectivity in the terms in which it had been posited by Trendelenburg. The way proposed by the latter—to consider space and time both subjective and objective forms, and thus to presuppose harmony between subject and object, which would ensure the objective value of knowledge[49]—had not been neglected by Kant (as Trendelenburg argued), but rejected and overcome with the new meaning of the a priori. Experience is a priori synthesis of the phenomena for Kantian transcendental idealism, and the principle of this synthesis is that "the conditions of the *possibility of experience* in general are likewise conditions of the *possibility of the objects of experience*, and that for this reason they have objective value in a synthetic *a priori* judgment."[50] The objectivity of knowledge consists of its necessity and its universality, which are founded exactly by the a priori in the subject: "we can know a priori of things only what we ourselves put into them."[51] The subjective character of space and time thus did not leave a "gap"[52] in the Kantian theory of knowledge, since it is precisely, in its transcendental meaning, the formal condition of the possibility of experience and of its objectivity: "The transcendental question does not regard the possibility of an a priori intuition, in the sense of an intuition *prior* to the objects; but at the same time of such an intuition that 'the *concept* of the latter (i.e. of the objects) can be *determined* a priori in it.' The a priori, whose possibility as a type of knowledge the transcendental question concerns, does not simply precede objects, but constructs them" (*KTE*[1] 48-9).

A further problem of interpretation, extensively dealt with by Cohen in the first edition of *Kants Theorie der Erfahrung*, was the question of the discovery and justification of the a priori. While Herbart, as we have already seen, believed that it was necessary to recognize a psychological foundation for the a priori, but criticized Kant for his conception of the a priori as a faculty of the soul, Fries complained that Kant had rejected a psychological foundation. In this criticism he was joined by Beneke and Schopenhauer, while Helmholtz and Lange interpreted Kant's a priori in psychophysiological terms. Besides, a well-established tradition in the interpretation of Kant, which began with Reinhold and through the idealists reached Ulrici and Fischer, was of the opinion that the a priori should be discovered and justified exclusively through deduction, without turning to experience at all. A schematic view could reduce the problem to the question of whether the discovery and justification of the a priori comes about in turn a priori or a posteriori. Then the book by Jürgen Bona Meyer, *Kants Psychologie,*[53] which emphasized this contrast and followed the line taken by Fries, had been published in 1870.

His investigation of the transcendental meaning of the a priori, and of the relationship between metaphysical and transcendental deduction, allowed Cohen to take up an exact position on this subject. First, he rejected the thesis of the a priori discovery of the a priori. The very first words of the *Critique of Pure Reason*—"There can be no doubt that all our knowledge begins with experience"—exclude any interpretation of this kind. The consequence of Kant's transcendental method is that the departure point of any investigation will always be experience. Fischer,[54] argued that if one admits that the categories are the object of a psychological investigation, then they are made objects of experience and cannot be necessary and universal, thus raising a difficulty that derived solely from confusion between "empirical knowledge" and "knowledge of the empirical."[55] The a priori is to be discovered by "psychological thought, or, to use Kant's terminology, the Analytic of Concepts" (*KTE*[1] 120), which does not identify objects of experience, but the conditions of its possibility; psychological thought, therefore, which discovers metaphysical concepts. Cohen considered this misunderstanding of Kant particularly serious, since this disregard of the transcendental method forced speculative idealism to accept intellectual intuition, radically distorting the meaning of transcendental idealism: "But this is really incredible: that Kant could be so completely misunderstood! The a priori is *discovered* not only in the concepts, but above all in sensibility. In this way *intellectual* intuition becomes impossible" (*KTE*[1] 243).

When elucidating the role of metaphysical deduction, Cohen underlined its complementarity with psychological discovery. Empirical deduction prepares the way for metaphysical deduction. On the one hand, the investigation can only *begin* with experience; on the other, thought cannot reach the a priori if it remains within the area of experience; *thought* is a necessary stage between psychology and metaphysics:

> Metaphysical deduction, which shows the a priori in the forms of consciousness as well as in spatial representations, or in the functions of unity in judgments, makes empirical deduction appear to be a "waste of time." . . . But this proposition should not be misunderstood. Metaphysical deduction certainly presupposes empirical deduction, i.e. psychological reflection . . . in metaphysical deduction, correctly considered, it is only the concept of empirical deduction that is enhanced: through comprehension of the difference between the constitutive parts of experience. (*KTE*[1] 121–22)

However, Cohen did not entirely accept the views of Fries and Meyer. If the a priori is discovered by empirical means, it cannot be justified by the same means. The a priori is not justified up to the point of being left with its originative metaphysical meaning, and even less so in its psychological meaning. Only in transcendental deduction can it find its full meaning, and its full justification as the "formal condition of the possibility of our experience." Cohen accused Meyer of having reduced the transcendental to the psychological, following the lead of Fries (cf. *KTE*[1] 123). Transcendental logic is not only an "unusual name" with which Kant "baptized" empirico-psychological induction:[56] "No! It is not simply the 'unusual name,' but it is the unprecedented thing which was born under that name: that the forms found in empirical thought are not simply psychological categories, but the *gnoseological conditions (erkenntniss-theoretisch) of the possibility of experience*" (*KTE*[1] 124).

Finally, concerning the problem of the thing in itself, *the* classic problem in Kantian interpretation, Cohen limited himself, in the work under review, to a minimal, reductivist conception, which was certainly unsatisfactory, but was to be further developed and extended in successive works. In the first edition of *Kants Theorie der Erfahrung*, Cohen restricted his considerations to the "noumenon in the negative sense." Here he demonstrated how critical philosophy excludes once and for all both the object in itself and the subject in itself, thus radically opposing empirical materialism and idealism (cf. *KTE*[1] 82, 246ff.). Even the Kantian 'idea,' which was to play a crucial role in the further development of Cohen's idealism, was only treated in its negative sense in the first edition of *Kants Theorie der Erfahrung*. "The result of the Transcendental Aesthetic was the noumenon as a limiting concept. 'The theory of sensibility is at the same time the theory of the noumenon in the negative sense.' Something similar can be said of the Transcendental Logic: the theory of the categories is at the same time the theory of ideas in the negative sense" (*KTE*[1] 269).

It is certainly not by chance that one of the most important additions Cohen made to the second edition of *Kants Theorie der Erfahrung* was precisely the development of the role and meaning of the idea. By that time he had arrived at a more mature, detailed standpoint on critical idealism, through further important reflection, which even went beyond Kant.

5. KANT'S CRITICAL PHILOSOPHY

Before singling out the characteristics of critical philosophy as they emerge from the first edition of *Kants Theorie der Erfahrung*, for this was my objective in summarizing its contents, I am obliged to begin with the consideration that his first Kantian interpretation is not the best place to identify Cohen's conception of critical philosophy. This work only examined the *Critique of Pure Reason*, not the whole Kantian critical system. Even within the first *Critique*, the whole of the *transcendental dialectic* was practically ignored (except for the chapter on the antinomies, which, however, only treated them with reference to spatio-temporal problems, rather than those of ideas). As we have already seen, in the first edition of *Kants Theorie der Erfahrung*, Cohen's principal aim was to intervene in contemporary disputes over the *transcendental aesthetic* and the theory of the a priori, rather than to develop the potential of critical philosophy as a whole.

It has already been noted that Cohen had originally intended to entitle his essay: *Raum, Zeit, und Kategorien im Zusammenhang der Kantischen Metaphysik und Psychologie, ein Beitrag zum Verständnis des kritischen Idealismus*. However, in the previously quoted letter to Hermann Lewandowsky, dated October 3, 1870, where Cohen announced the completion of his essay on Kant, we have documentary proof that he had deliberately not gone into critical idealism in depth:

> I am not going to write the last chapter on critical idealism, because, otherwise, I would have to present my program. The chapter can be my next work. The present essay goes no further than the defense of Kant, opposing the main attacks on him. Don't you see my point? What I have done is to illustrate the meaning of the theory of space and time for Kantian psychology and metaphysics and examine the objections against it. That is enough. What further meaning Kant's idealism may have and what its rela-

tionship is with that of Plato, Descartes and Spinoza, what influence it ought to have on present day philosophy, what direction idealism has followed in modern natural science; these are all very fine things, but they are not strictly relevant to this theme, and since, otherwise, I would burn my mouth (*ich mir den Mund daran verbrennen*), I am going to restrict myself to this.[57]

The following points clearly emerge from these few lines: 1) Cohen was of the opinion that his essay on Kant's theory of experience responded to the needs which gave rise to it, and that it justified itself even though restricted to the "defense of Kant, opposing the main attacks on him"; 2) he believed that, in order to approach the theme of critical idealism, without the risk of "burning his mouth," Kant's thought had to be included in a wider-ranging critical tradition (Plato, Descartes and Spinoza),[58] and the influence of Kantian idealism "on present day philosophy" and its application to "modern natural science" evaluated: it was these two needs that were to prove decisive for the orientation of Cohen's thought in the years that followed, and were to lead to interesting, new developments in his interpretation of Kant and his conception of critical philosophy; 3) Cohen was aware of the fact that further, satisfactory investigation of critical idealism would have required him to present his own philosophical program ("because, otherwise, I would have to present my program"). This third point is especially interesting. Here Cohen showed that he was conscious of the fact that an interpreter of Kant had to go beyond Kant, if he wanted to bring out the full consequences of critical idealism. Cohen was certainly not inhibited by scholastic-type scruples. Rather, on the one hand, he was aware that, to go beyond Kant, he would have to expand his historical knowledge, by exploring the thought of other philosophers more deeply (his studies of Plato and Leibniz were to be decisive, as we shall see) and investigate the critical role of philosophy as regards the natural sciences. On the other hand, though he himself had formulated the principle that—"it is impossible to express any judgment on Kant, without, on every line, betraying the world which one has in his own head" (*KTE*[1] v), he seemed to want to restrict the contribution of the individual interpreter—to place greater emphasis on the need to "present the historical Kant again, and to defend him from his opponents in his genuine physiognomy, as far as I was able to understand it" (*KTE*[1] iv). He felt the need, then, on the one hand, to restrict himself to the reconstruction of the historical Kant, while, on the other, he was aware of not being ready to approach the theme of critical idealism in all its aspects.[59] Both these reasons originated in Cohen's conviction that an exhaustive analysis of critical idealism could not remain within the confines of a pure reinterpretation of

Kant. Bearing in mind this proviso, it is, nevertheless, possible to analyze the characteristics of critical philosophy as they emerge from the first edition of *Kants Theorie der Erfahrung*.

The first, fundamental characteristic of critical philosophy is the *transcendental method*. For Cohen this method was the everlasting legacy of Kant's philosophy. This conviction was to remain unchanged, not only in the whole of Cohen's thought, but also in that of his school.[60] The transcendental method is the methodological consequence of the above-mentioned Kantian principle, according to which "all our knowledge begins with experience, but it does not follow that it all arises out of experience." Philosophy, like all knowledge, must start off from experience; however, it must investigate the conditions of the possibility of experience, and these cannot be found within experience itself. In this way, critical philosophy overcomes both dogmatism, whose analytic method proves to be insufficient for the foundation of knowledge which goes beyond concepts and includes the phenomena, and empiricism, which by limiting itself to the field of experience is unable to grasp the latter's a priori conditions. The transcendental method can be schematically presented under three fundamental headings: 1) Philosophy must take the "fact" of experience as its starting point; 2) it must return to the a priori conditions of this fact; 3) the meaning of the a priori lies wholly in its function as the formal condition of possible experience.

First, the reflective character of philosophical thought, which requires its starting point to be a "fact," is the lesson which critical philosophy draws from empiricism, and which opposes it to all purely speculative and deductive metaphysics. As we have seen, all claims that the a priori is also "discovered" a priori are incompatible with critical philosophy. Philosophy acquires the value of scientific knowledge only inasmuch as it is a reflection on science. As a matter of fact, in the first edition of *Kants Theorie der Erfahrung*, the identification of Kantian "experience" with natural science, which Cohen was to underline in the works that followed, though still "latent,"[61] does come through.[62] In the works that followed, Cohen was also to use the transcendental method for critical reflection on cultural areas outside natural science (moral sciences, art, and religion) and was to continually recall the need to take a "fact" as the point of departure, in order to investigate its a priori conditions, even though the scientific nature of the fact was not always obvious.

Second, if philosophical knowledge must begin with experience, it must, however, identify the *nonempirical* principles of its possibility. This allows critical philosophy to go beyond empiricism and skepticism. The route for the a priori is, as we have already seen, reflection on experience with the aim of identifying its formal principles. This route, which is explicit in the *transcendental aesthetic*, where the point of departure for the identification of its a priori forms is sensibility, is hidden in the *transcendental logic*, where Kant proceeds from the judgments to the categories, ending up with the principles. Cohen re-established the primary role of the principles, reversing the order of succession of the logical a priori:

> So now we can present the progress of the Kantian system. First of all the question on the *principles* (*Grund-sätze*) was posed. Their number was unknown, but their apriority was deemed to be present in the concepts alone. Therefore, subsequently, fundamental *concepts* (*Grund-begriffe*) were admitted. If an exhaustive compendium had to be achieved for the former, in the case of the latter such a compendium needed to be created. Thus he reached the Table of Judgments, and, from there, the table of fundamental concepts and principles he was looking for. (*KTE*[1] 209–10)

Third and finally, the a priori must in no way be hypostatized, either in a metaphysical substance or in an organ or faculty of human physiological structure. The particular attention which Cohen devoted to the difference between metaphysical and transcendental deduction allows a rigorous definition of the purely functional or "formal" meaning of the a priori. If the a priori is understood, in the transcendental sense, as a formal condition of experience,

> experience itself becomes a concept, which we must build up in pure intuition and pure thought. The formal conditions of its possibility, space, time and synthetic unity, now count as a priori, because we *build up experience* with them, because they are the formal constituents of experience. Now it is no longer necessary for the formal foundation of the possibility to be innate even for spatial intuition. Space is a priori, because it is a formal condition of experience. We are not at all concerned about whether it be innate or not. We build up a concept of experience as synthetic unity of experiences, according to transcendental principles. What we need for the creation of this synthetic unity, these necessary *constructive elements*, we call a priori. (*KTE*[1] 104)[63]

It is from this single mistake, the hypostatization of the a priori, that the ontological and psychophysiological interpretations of Kant derive. Critical philosophy must rigorously maintain a purely functional definition of the a priori itself.

Kant's critical philosophy had, then, a second meaning for Cohen, consisting in the conception of knowledge as synthesis. By giving sensibility a position of full respect within knowledge, Kant went over the limit common to intellectualism and sensualism, that is the unbridgeable separation between subject and object. With the well known Kantian theory of the empirical reality and transcendental ideality of space and time and the necessary addition of the negative meaning of the noumenon, critical theory finally abandoned ontology and presented itself as transcendental idealism. The distinction between and complementarity of sensibility and understanding, inner sense and transcendental apperception, phenomenon and law, are the basis of the possibility of experience. It is this new concept of experience that sums up the originality of Kantian critical philosophy. What differentiates transcendental idealism from empirical idealism is the fact that the a priori does not only consist in the concepts of understanding, but also in the forms of sensibility; indeed *"the very synthesis of understanding requires an apriority of intuition!"* (*KTE*[1] 163). Therefore, transcendental idealism is "formal idealism,"[64] and thus empirical realism: "The category alone does not make the object; sensible intuition must be added. And the latter has exactly the same rights to be a formal condition of experience. It is formal idealism which differentiates transcendental from empirical idealism and makes empirical realism of it" (*KTE*[1] 244–45).

Therefore, transcendental method and formal idealism are the two qualifying characteristics of Kantian philosophy: "Thus, transcendental idealism is completed and confirmed in the theory of the negative noumenon, critically according to the method, formally according to the content" (*KTE*[1] 252). In the further development of Cohen's thought, these two aspects of critical philosophy were to evolve differently. While the transcendental method was to maintain a central role, the complementarity of understanding and sensibility in knowledge was to be abandoned by reducing sensibility to understanding and increasing the role of pure thought. In the first edition of *Kants Theorie der Erfahrung*, however, these two aspects were still undivided, as inseparable characteristics of critical philosophy.

What was missing in Cohen's first Kantian interpretation was the systematic meaning of critical philosophy, which could not be approached without taking into consideration all three of Kant's *Critiques*. Above all the problem of the "limit" in critical philosophy was not dealt with. The fact, which has already been mentioned, that Cohen limited consideration of the noumenon to its negative meaning, and the absence of an analysis of the positive meaning of the Kantian idea (which was to be rectified in the works that followed) explain the failure of the meaning of critical philosophy to develop in this sense and thus require that further investigation of critical idealism which Cohen had postponed to a later stage in his reflections. Therefore, the definition of idealism which concludes the first edition of *Kants Theorie der Erfahrung*—"To resolve the diversity between things into distinctions between ideas: this is the secret of idealism" (*KTE*[1] 270)—required further investigation to acquire its full critical meaning.

2

The Interpretation of Plato

1. THE INITIAL PSYCHOLOGICAL INTERPRETATION

Cohen's "further investigation"[1] of Kant's critical idealism by way of his reading of Plato began with the brief but intense 1878 essay *Platons Ideenlehre und die Mathematik*. Cohen had been showing interest in Plato since the beginning of his philosophical studies. His first unpublished work, which won him the Breslau University Philosophy Faculty prize in 1863 bears the significant title *Über die Psychologie des Plato und Aristoteles*. In the following years, after moving to Berlin, Cohen took part in another competition with an essay on the concepts of '*casus*' and '*contingens*' in Aristotle, which earned the praises of Trendelenburg,[2] even though it was not awarded the prize. On the strength of a new version of this essay, however, Cohen was awarded a university lecturing license by the University of Halle in 1865.[3] An important part of this dissertation is devoted to the interpretation of Plato (cf. *S I:* 18-21). The last of the theses presented in the final part of the essay, "*Platonis Convivium post Phaedonem scriptum esse*" (*S I:* 29) shows that Cohen's investigation of Plato was already philologically oriented. In 1866 he published his first work dealing exclusively with Plato: *Die platonische Ideenlehre psychologisch entwickelt.*

Nevertheless, even if Cohen's interest in Plato can be documented from his very early philosophical studies, his critical-idealist approach to Plato cannot be traced back to a date earlier than 1878, the year *Platons Ideenlehre und die Mathematik* was published. With the sole exception of the 1876 article, *Friedrich Albert Lange*, which already contains an impor-

tant theme in Cohen's new interpretation of Plato—the idealist interpretation of Greek philosophy, particularly of the line of thought from
Democritus to Plato, which will be dealt with later—Cohen's previous
writings show his attachment to the *Völkerpsychologie* of Lazarus and
Steinthal. These writings, therefore, deal with problems unrelated to
critical idealism and posit theses that were either to be abandoned or
considerably modified from the 1878 essay onward.

Some commentators consider *Die platonische Ideenlehre psychologisch
entwickelt* and *Platons Ideenlehre und die Mathematik* to be components of a
coherent interpretation of Plato. This was especially true in the years in
which the Marburg school's work on the interpretation of Plato was still
in full swing, a fact which made a neutral, comprehensive examination
of its development more difficult.[4] E. Hohmann,[5] when criticizing the
unilateral nature of Natorp's exclusively logical, nonontological interpretation of Plato's ideas, wrote that, though Cohen was the "father" of
this kind of interpretation, he was less radical than Natorp, since in his
1866 essay he recognized that Plato did develop, however negatively, in
the direction of a substantialist conception of ideas.

If we want to see matters in a correct historical perspective and have a
clearer theoretical idea of Cohen's thought, it is better to think of *Die
platonische Ideenlehre psychologisch entwickelt* as a youthful work, which was
superseded to all intents and purposes by his later studies, and which is
of negligible interest from the standpoint of critical idealism. One striking example of Cohen's early outgrowing his initial interpretation of
Plato is the fact that in the 1866 essay he recognized an ontologically oriented development of Plato's theory of ideas, which was stressed by
Hohmann, while this recognition is nowhere to be found in his subsequent works. This does not mean, of course, that Cohen had necessarily
abandoned this view,[6] but that, from 1878 onwards, his interpretation of
Plato's ideas changed radically. He was no longer interested in investigating the birth and psychological development of the theory of ideas in
Plato's mind, but turned to the analysis of the logical, transcendental,
and critical meaning of these ideas, as Plato's truly significant contribution to critical idealism.

Die platonische Ideenlehre psychologisch entwickelt was published in the
Zeitschrift für Völkerpsychologie und Sprachwissenschaft co-edited by
Lazarus and Steinthal. It was conceived and written entirely under the
influence of the idea of the shared identity of philosophy and psychology that characterizes Cohen's early thought.[7] This is true for at least two
reasons: principally, because interest in Plato is justified by the recognition of the latter's role as the originator of "psychological philosophy" (*S
I*: 39); second, because the interpretation of the birth of Plato's theory of

ideas as an original "discovery" (*Entdeckung*), for which the way was prepared by earlier and contemporary Greek culture and philosophy, but which really sprang from a psychological process in a genius' mind, is an excellent example of the "psychological" historiographical method theorized by Cohen in the same essay (cf. *S I:* 30 ff.).

There are two themes in this essay that deserve special attention, not so much because they were to be taken up again in later works, but because they were to undergo substantial changes during this development and thus become valuable yardsticks in the evaluation of Cohen's outgrowing his early interpretation of Plato. These two themes, which I shall now briefly discuss, are the distinction between εἶδος and ἰδέα and the relationship between Plato and Kant.

In his 1866 essay Cohen tried to show that it is possible to identify a clear distinction between Plato's use of the terms εἶδος and ἰδέα, starting from the dialogues of the second period.[8] The first term, often used in the plural, corresponds to the Socratic concept and is synonymous with γένος, δύναμις, φύσις, and οὐσία. The second term, which is only rarely used in the plural, is the truly original, creative concept discovered by Plato, meaning the act of intuition, the "vital intellectual activity of contemplation (*Schauen*)" (*S I:* 61), which is capable of grasping the essence of things. Plato's Idea, which has a close etymological connection with the act of contemplation, is thus the transposition, into the field of general knowledge, of the intuitive act of immediate understanding of essence, which Plato had seen in the work of the artist:

> So when this question arose: what is the Socratic concept, the essence of a work of art, of a table, of the beautiful? Plato's answer was: what I contemplate as this essence, the image revealed to me in contemplation, that which the artist observes in his creation, and the carpenter or mechanic in his making a chair or shuttle. Did he ask: what is it that attracts us in Phidias' statue of Zeus? Is there a being completely resembling it in the world of bodies? No. Then is it perhaps a purely spiritual essence, a product of Eastern speculation? No, it is the image of the art of genuine Greek sculpture. But if it is neither body nor spirit, what is it then? It is the true union of both, which we grasp during contemplation, it is the vision (*Gesicht*), to use Biblical language, the intuitive sign of a harmonious union between these two extremes, which in discursive thought never again will allow themselves to be united. In the harmonious fusion of the everlasting with the ephemeral, of the necessary with the contingent, of the spiritual with the bodily, of what is spaceless with what is in space, this vision is the true essence of the work of art we all admire. (*S I:* 53–4)

Ideas as εἴδη are therefore none other than the hypostatized result of the act of spiritual contemplation, from which the object of contemplation has not yet been isolated as a separate substance. This act is the authentic, original meaning of the Platonic ἰδέα. Each substantialization of an idea, then, is a distancing from and distortion of the original meaning, "which alone can allow access to knowledge of the real sense" (*S I:* 65), of the Platonic Idea. This distorting process had already begun in Plato's own works, in particular in *Parmenides* (cf. *S I:* 65ff.).

Distinguishing εἶδος from ἰδέα is also a permanent feature of Cohen's subsequent interpretation of Plato. However, at least in one fundamental respect, there was a significant change in its meaning. In the 1866 essay the close association of Idea with the psychic act of contemplation is not only a metaphor, but an identification, which led Cohen to think of the Platonic Idea as a forerunner of Fichte's concept of intellectual intuition:

> Socrates interpreted essence, the concept as the thing it is (*das Seiende*), but left one question open: how do we know this essence, this concept? Plato answered the question, with the conditional originality of the discoverer, by pointing to contemplation as the activity peculiar both to thinker and artist, as the phenomenon of all creation, whether it be at a high or low level. Thus he is the original forebear of intellectual intuition, of transcendental idealism.(*S I:* 53)

It is interesting to note how transcendental idealism is grounded in intellectual intuition, at this stage in Cohen's development. However, in the 1878 essay, he found important new features in Plato's theory of ideas: in the first instance, the function of mathematics and the meaning of Idea as hypothesis. This was to bring about a radically new interpretation of the difference between εἶδος from ἰδέα. The idea of contemplation is now only thought of as the psychic origin of Idea, or as the occasion of its discovery by Plato, or even as an image inspired by the word's etymology, but in reality misleading, owing to its subjective nature.[9] For Cohen, the Platonic ἰδέα is still a further development of the Socratic εἶδος not as intellectual intuition, but rather as logical foundation: Idea is hypothesis, that is, critical foundation of the concept.[10] In a passage in the *Ästhetik des reinen Gefühls* there is an interesting description of the development of Plato's reflection on the meaning of Idea:

> We have known since the *Logik der reinen Erkenntnis* that Plato established Idea as *hypothesis*. As regards the meaning of the word, he saw Idea in contemplation, and thus, in the guise of *vision*, it earned its place in the history of cultural problems. However, when his scientific knowledge reached maturity, Idea was no longer limited to vision. The initial psychological origin of Idea, qualified by *contemplation*, moved on in the direction of an objective, profound, systematic realization, in relation to *mathematics*. Thus Idea was not limited to vision, but became *foundation*. (*ARG I:* 243)

This passage is more of a reflection of Cohen's progress in interpreting Plato's ideas than of development in Plato's own thought. Moving on from the conception of Idea as a psychic-metaphysical act of the knowledge of essence to that of Idea as the logical foundation of concept denies any kind of legitimacy to intellectual intuition. In fact, Cohen now recognized that the latter is a distortion of the Platonic Idea, and was responsible for the metaphysical deviations in the subsequent history of philosophy:

> Intuition springs from idealism: it is probably the most effective constituent feature of Plato's Idea. Therefore, it may seem that it could have no better references. But it is well known that so far no agreement has been reached on the meaning of Idea. It is thus only too understandable that this ambiguous feature of the concept of Idea has become the fundamental reason behind a kind of idealism, whose falsity is revealed in its hostility to rationalism. Idealism is logically grounded scientific rationalism. If, on the other hand, intuition (*Intuition*) is not to activate pure contemplation, which is identical to pure thought, if it is to go beyond scientific thought, invalidate it and make it suspect, then the ambiguity of the intuitive moment (*Anschauung*) manifests itself in this intuition, which is irreconcilably opposed to the truthfulness of Idea. (*LRE* 500)[11]

After this clarification of the meaning of the Platonic Idea, we can now form a more precise picture of the limits of the relationship between Plato and Kant posited by Cohen in his 1866 essay. Cohen placed Plato on the same line as Kant, inasmuch as the conception of Idea as intuition inevitably leads on to the recognition of reality as a phenomenon. However, if such a development is coherently followed, it will lead on beyond Kant to Fichte. If things *are* inasmuch as they communicate ideas, and ideas are nothing other than intuitive acts of the subject, then this subject of intuition must be recognized as "that which only exists" (*alleinseiend*) (cf. *S I:* 68). As can be seen, Cohen had not only identified a Plato-Kant line, but also a Plato-Kant-Fichte line. Indeed, the interpretation of Plato in this essay is conditioned more by reference to Fichte than to Kant, as the interpretation of Idea as intellectual intuition and the special meaning attributed to transcendental idealism, to which I have already referred, confirm.[12] In subsequent works, especially *Platons Ideenlehre und die Mathematik*, Cohen developed further the tenuous links between Plato and Kant discovered in 1866. This time the direction was not Fichte oriented but led toward scientific and critical idealism. Particular attention was devoted to Plato's role as a forerunner in the establishment of the transcendental doctrine of knowledge, the discovery of the transcendental a priori, and the evaluation of the function of mathematics.

2. Plato in The History of Idealism

The new interpretation of Plato in *Platons Ideenlehre und die Mathematik* consists, in the first place, of a realignment of his position in the history of philosophy. He is now presented as the founding father of critical idealism. This historiographical act, which, as we shall see, has important theoretical implications, was nothing more than an initial response to the need for expanding the historical roots of critical idealism already felt by Cohen when preparing the first edition of *Kants Theorie der Erfahrung*. There are no traces of this new history of critical idealism in Greek philosophy in the 1866 essay, which followed the completely different historiographical line of the development of "psychological philosophy" (cf. *S I*: 45-53).

The undoubted source and point of reference for Cohen's reconstruction of the history of ancient idealism was Lange's *Geschichte des Materialismus*. One piece of documentary evidence for this connection is provided by Cohen's obituary of *Friederich Albert Lange* written for the *Preussische Jahrbücher* in 1876. The obituary contains critical discussion of Lange's book and the first references to Cohen's new historiographical approach, before those in *Platons Ideenlehre und die Mathematik*. Further evidence can be seen in Cohen's clearly antithetical position vis-à-vis Lange in many parts of his discussion.[13] Lange considered Democritus to be the real founding father of materialism. It was the latter who, with his atomism, had opened up the road of science, freeing knowledge from the fallacious poetics of myth and religion. He was the first to provide a rigorous definition of matter (cf. ibid., p. 8). He replaced teleology with a mathematical, mechanical explanation of reality (cf. ibid., p. 13). He provided a materialistic interpretation of the soul (cf. ibid., pp. 19ff.). He formulated a eudemonist morality which was entirely coherent with his theoretical materialism (cf. ibid., pp. 21f.). The theories of Socrates, Plato and Aristotle, which Lange believed to be part of a coherent whole,[14] were a "reaction" (ibid., p. 38) of religious and poetic idealism against Democritus's scientific materialism and Protagoras's sensualism, which complements it gnoseologically. The only point in favor of this idealism is its claim that the human spirit has the right to free itself "in a poetic upward thrust above the rough, defective edifice of scientific knowledge" (ibid., p. 60),[15] but, from the point of view of the progress of scientific knowledge and of rigorous thought, it was a "great revolution which, for thousands of years, misdirected the world into the maze of Platonic idealism" (ibid., p. 42).

In his 1876 obituary Cohen showed that he was already aware of the decisive importance of substantially correcting this interpretation of

Greek philosophy, not only for historical reasons, but also, from the theoretical point of view, in the name of a correct definition of genuine idealism as critical idealism:

> Here there is a historical error, which led Lange to a systematically mistaken view. Did Kant, who put an end to materialism, invent idealism from nothing? Perhaps what Lange considered materialism *before* Kant was in fact idealism, in the same way as he admitted that there was an element of materialism in Kant himself. In short, how did Lange treat idealism in *Plato?* This question is of fundamental importance, both for a systematic solution and historical understanding. Though Democritus' work was written before Plato, all subsequent materialism depends on the latter. Was Plato cured of materialism? Did not Democritus depend on the Eleatic philosophers, whose speculations he rendered consequent in his own way? Is not the Eleatic theory one of Plato's main sources? Thus a clear view of the sources of idealism is crucial for a work adopting this approach. Following it, the traditional picture of philosophical viewpoints could be subjected to detailed revision. Judgment on the regulative factor in conflicting world views seems to depend on their delimitation on the basis of a historical appreciation of Platonism. It must be admitted that the meaning and value of Platonism is unacknowledged in this work. (*S II:* 378–79)

It was the significance of Democritus and his relationship with Plato that was crucial for this reinterpretation of Greek philosophy: "Democritus was the ancient philosopher who lay behind Lange's mistaken view of Plato. And the understandable prominence he accorded to Democritus had the result of overshadowing Plato, though objectively this need not necessarily have been the case" (*S II:* 380).

In Cohen's view, an opposition between materialism and idealism limited to the dogmatic appropriation of matter and spirit, two opposing principles of reality, was too superficial. In this sense one should recognize spiritualism, not genuine idealism, as the opposite of materialism:

> Materialism is in no way the opposite of idealism. The two concepts are not mutually exclusive. Lange was well aware of this, and demonstrated the fact with regard to several historical figures. However, he never managed to formulate precisely the inexactitude of the traditional opposition, because he failed to acknowledge either the historical origin of this opposition, or the significance of Platonism. Materialism maintains that matter is the sole concrete reality, the only explanatory principle of every specific real being. In view of this, it is not entirely true to say that idealism posits Idea as corresponding to matter. It is more exact to say that idealism is in search of the meaning of concrete reality, while materialism, starting off from sense perception, places reality in something, for which the senses

cannot satisfactorily vouch. Idealism asks a question about the *value* of reality (*Wirklichkeits-Wert*), of that something, of that matter. On the other hand, there are certain presumed forms of idealism which, to no lesser extent than materialism, dogmatically appropriate an equivalent something, the so-called spirit, as the location and organ of ideas. This deceptive name must be denied those attempts, and, on the basis of their teaching, the term spiritualism should be used to describe them. This is the natural opposite of materialism. (*S II:* 382–83)

However, critical idealism was the genuine idealism, in the light of which the philosophy of Democritus and Plato was to be interpreted. This rational method of foundation provides the basis upon which the concepts of 'matter' and 'spirit' can and must be philosophically justified:

> On the other hand, idealism, in its classic forms in Plato, Descartes and Kant, is a method, not a doctrine. Its results, both positive and negative, are the consequences of a gnoseological critique. If idealism does acknowledge matter, this is a gnoseologically verified concept, i.e. a concept which has been investigated in its relationship with the conditions on which the certainty of knowledge is founded. If it groups together certain phenomena, considering them to be spiritual, since they would receive a false common name without such delimitation, idealism does not become spiritualism, even if it professes a noumenon: as long as this is verified on the basis of its cognitive value, or, rather, on the basis of its degree of validity. In this case, however insignificant its invitations to carry out such elaborations, one could ask where true opposition to idealism is located in philosophical practice. I know only one answer: in all thought that does not proceed gnoseologically, whether or not it starts off from faith in outer objects or rational things (*Vernunftdinge*). Immanent idealism is mathematical investigation of nature, if this is not an ambiguous expression. This criterion proves useful indeed for understanding the great historical forms, including materialism. What Lange admired in Democritus is certainly not simply materialism, but a gnoseological endeavor. (*S II:* 383)

In *Platons Ideenlehre und die Mathematik*, Plato's theory of ideas is presented as a synthesis of multiple trends in previous thought, and, at the same time, as the original reworking of results achieved into a new line of thought (cf. *ERW* 97). The Platonic theory of ideas, for the first time in the history of thought, by positing the problem of knowledge, had established idealism.[16] In Cohen's view idealism had existed before Plato, but it had reached maturity, and therefore its true meaning, in the Platonic theory of ideas. Plato was the meeting point of three trends in Greek thought. Two of them had already been developed and summed up in Democritus. Democritus, on the one hand, was the heir of the

Eleatic philosophers, inasmuch as he took over the principle of the identity between being and thought: "There is no other being than that of thought" (*S I* 337). However, while Parmenides's 'being which is thought' was still the sensible being of the cosmos, and only its changeable, illusory appearance, its becoming, denied, Democritus put aside the being of things and reinstated the being of pure thought, the void, the nonbeing (μὴ ὄν) as the true being (ἐτεῇ ὄν). He was able to achieve something Parmenides had not achieved, because he made use of the mathematical thought of Pythagoreanism and thus filtered off all sensible content from being: "Now there is a being which the Eleatics consider a non-being; this is the true being! This true being consists of mathematical concepts, not only as regards atoms, but also the abstraction of a separator, in the thought of an interval (*Zwischen*), or of a distance (*Abstand*), in which sensible beings are no longer present" (*S I:* 340–41).

Cohen did not accept Lange's view of Democritus as the founding father of materialism. For him: "*Eleatic thought regarding being passed from atomism and underwent an idealist transformation*" (*S I:* 340–41).

Democritus went beyond the synthesis he had achieved of Eleatic and Pythagorean thought. His achievement was taken over by Plato and grafted onto the Socratic tradition, with important new results. Once having put aside the thesis that the Platonic Idea is to be identified with the Socratic concept, Cohen did not even accept the conception of the Platonic Idea as a substantialization of this concept: "it would only be an Eleatic concept applied to the Socratic being; the result would then be the opinion, recently expressed with fruitful frankness, that the theory of ideas in no way represents Plato's specific philosophy" (*S I:* 343).

Plato's starting point was the fundamental requirement of "skeptical idealism" (*S I:* 343) (or perhaps it would be better to use the term *critical idealism*), that is, the problem of error, which any critical theory of true being must face: "*How can it come about* that the Eleatic being, the validity of οὐσία should suit this Socratic εἶδος, this thought, defined γένος," while sensible phenomena become and change, as Heraclitus showed in his teaching on the cosmos? How can one understand that genuine being consists of something withdrawn, inasmuch as it is withdrawn, from any sensible corroboration?" (*S I:* 343).

In Plato's theory of ideas this "critical constituent feature" (*S I:* 344) is at the same time a further investigation of the Socratic theory of concept and a decisive step forward. The Socratic concept is put to the test: Idea is the established concept, or, to put it better, the very foundation of the concept; it is thought justifying itself. Thus Plato passed from mere reflection on thought to the very formulation of the problem of knowledge (*S I:* 341) and consequently can be considered the initiator of genuine idealism, that is, of "gnoseologically founded" idealism (*S I:* 342).

3. THE THEORY OF IDEAS

Cohen's intention, in his interpretation of the Platonic theory of ideas in *Platons Ideenlehre und die Mathematik*, was to deny the validity both of the ontological and of the psychological interpretations. If so many interpreters, over such a long period, had viewed Platonic ideas as separate entities, this was due to the fact that Aristotle's views on the subject had undeservedly carried too much weight. He must take responsibility for the outset of a distorted ontological interpretation of these ideas, which was to dominate the later history of philosophy. It was Aristotle who attributed separation (χωρισμός) between the world of ideas and the sensible world to Plato (cf. *S I:* 344), as well as the view of ideas as substances (cf. *S I:* 347), and the placing of mathematical concepts at a lower level than ideas, at a halfway stage between the latter and sensible things (cf. *S I:* 342).[17]

Cohen also rejected the psychological interpretation of Plato's ideas as mere νοήματα in the mind of the thinking subject, while he had accepted it in *Die platonische Ideenlehre psychologisch entwickelt* (cf. *S I:* 66):

> If ἰδέα is to be viewed correctly as being conditioned by thought, as in *Parmenides*, where it is at least mentioned as νόημα ἐν ψυχαῖς, this state is not to be understood in the sense that Idea thus becomes the chimera of skepticism. Plato rejected this consequence in no uncertain terms. It is the following meaning of current opinion that is to be accepted without hesitation: that all that is known in pure thought was seen by Plato as genuine being. The opinion that the outcome of this pure thought, that what is revealed during its progress, when released from the illusion of the senses, is the creation of thought itself, instead of being the archetype with which the contemplating, reminiscing spirit complies and which it imitates—this phase of subjective idealism would be impossible to find in Plato. It is not even worth considering whether such a conclusion can be attributed to Plato at all. (*S I:* 345–46)

Cohen's new interpretation thus saw Plato's theory of ideas as a genuine forerunner of Kant's transcendental theory of knowledge. It is true that ideas are the object of thought (νοήματα), but by going beyond the Eleatic tradition, which identified thought with being, and that initiated by Democritus, which recognized true being in nonbeing, Plato concluded that ideas, precisely because they are thought, are the true being (ὄντως ὄν), since they are the truth of things: "The beautiful and the good, the rectilinear and the equal—all these ὄντα are ὄντως ὄντα, and are all conditioned by thought, inasmuch as they are νοητά. Since they are thought, are not grounded in perception and cannot trace their origin in completion or expansion of the latter, they are thus ὄντως ὄντα, having the value of οὐσία, inasmuch as they are νοήματα" (*S I*: 346).

The route Plato followed to arrive at this conception of ideas, and at the consequent establishment of knowledge as science (cf. *S I*: 349), was reflection on mathematics: "The necessary mediation is to be found in Plato's investigation of *mathematics*, in the essential direction for the modern gnoseological conception, where such a mediation can become a certainty, when it takes mathematical method and objects as its starting point. But this is how Idea itself takes on a new meaning, which reconciles the above mentioned alternative between οὐσία and νόημα" (*S I*: 351).

The passage in Plato's *Republic* (523ff.) where Socrates makes a distinction between sensations which induce intellectual investigation and those which do not were, in Cohen's view, of crucial significance. By pointing out that the *Republic* singles out mathematics as the type of intellectual investigation stimulated by certain sensations, he was led to the conclusion that Plato had regarded mathematics as the mediator between sensibility and understanding. This was the means by which investigation reached the heights of pure thought from humble empirical beginnings: "Just as, on the one hand, the object of mathematical thought is linked to the sensible of ordinary perception, on the other hand, it also sets up a relationship with the cognitive value of ideas, and can thus be a mediator between the two extremities of being, between ὄν and ὄντως ὄν" (*S I*: 353).

Thus, by way of mathematics, Plato, like Kant, had reached the fundamental discovery of Kantian critical idealism, that is the a priori of sensibility itself,[18] even if "in Plato's view, the senses in themselves certainly do not contemplate the νοητόν, but contain the impulse for this other kind of knowledge. This logical character distinguishes *the types of perception* from one another" (*S I*: 353). However, in Plato's view, mathematical objects, despite their role as mediator, are in every sense ideas, inasmuch as they are objects of pure thought. In this sense, mathematical investigation already belongs to dialectic: "Thus Plato is shown to have considered the entire cosmic world, at whose apex is situated the complex labyrinth of patterns in the heavens above, as mere *examples* for the problems of mathematical investigation. And there can be no doubt that those who devote their attention to the contemplation of mathematical 'ideas,' *in this very activity at the same time engage in dialectic"* (*S I:* 357).

Cohen did not try to avoid Plato's well known distinction between νόησις and διάνοια;[19] in fact he made use of it to proceed to hypothesis, a second, fundamental component of the meaning of ideas. Plato was correctly identified as the originator of analysis as a scientific method.[20] The essential truth of his theory of ideas consists in establishing knowledge as critical method, and in the meaning of Idea as hypothesis:

> It is clear that this method of taking what is sought for as found, only to re-encounter it by means of deductions and connections between them, is highly productive for philosophical problems. This is why Plato himself advises and has recourse to imitation. However, this analogy is not only effective when single problems are to be dealt with. The fundamental concept of his specific philosophical method - he uses the term μέθοδος when treating the theory of ideas—springs from this characteristic of geometrical thought, at least *for its gnoseological legitimation. Idea itself is thought as hypothesis.* (*S I:* 361)

Thus the theory of ideas manifests itself as the critical method of foundation: Idea "gives account" of the concept. In this sense the theory of ideas further investigates the Socratic theory of concept and constitutes the ultimate response to the fundamental question which was Cohen's starting point for his investigation: why should the value of *οὐσία* be attributed to the being which is thought, the Socratic *εἶδος*, when it is denied to sensible phenomena (cf. *S I:* 343):

> Idea, revealed in the guise of hypothesis by documentary evidence, is not only better understandable from the psychological point of view; it has been seen to be the *spur to gnoseological criticism.* From now on it is possible to understand how Idea, inasmuch as it is νοητόν, must, at the same time, be οὐσία, and νοητόν, inasmuch as it is οὐσία: *the two constituent features of idealism are intertwined in hypothesis.* Only that which is thought as an adequate presupposition of being corresponding to the law is thought as Idea, just as this presupposition can only become productive in the methodical connection of thoughts, as their root. (*S I:* 362)

Mathematical concepts are ideas, in the sense of hypotheses, in all respects, and the mathematical method is analytical, that is, grounded in hypothesis. However, it is not the ultimate degree of pure thought, since it cannot "be more than its hypotheses." Mathematics takes hypotheses as principles of its reasoning, but indulges in no further discussion of the a priori establishment of these principles. Returning to the foundation of hypotheses to track down "that which is adequate for itself"[21] in the absolute principle, in ἀνυπόθετον,[22] in the idea of good, goes beyond mathematics as a way of thinking; this is the "dialectical" process of the ἐπιστήμη; but both "mathematics and thought of ideas" "remain subsumed under pure rational thought (νόησις)" (*S I:* 365).[23]

4. PLATO'S CRITICAL PHILOSOPHY

It has often been said that the Kantian interpretation of Plato by Cohen and the Marburg school in general is unacceptable. As a matter of fact, Cohen himself, when defending his interpretation (cf. *E* 25ff.), does not disavow this opinion at all. Nevertheless, this objection needs re-examining and correcting. Admittedly, Cohen does stress those aspects of Plato's theory of ideas that point forward to Kant's views, and also places Plato at the outset of the history of critical idealism, in which Kant's role is fundamental. Furthermore, I would suggest that Cohen's reading of Plato be seen in the light of his brand of Kantianism. As we have already seen, his interpretation of another philosopher centered on questioning him from the standpoint of the interpreter's present concerns. There is no doubt that in 1878, at the time of writing *Platons Ideenlehre und die Mathematik*, Cohen saw everything from a Kantian viewpoint. However, the differences Cohen brought out between Plato and Kant are far more significant than the similarities. What is more, these differences led Cohen to investigate critical philosophy further and revise his interpretation of Kant, which implied that a considerable critical distance from Kantian philosophy was set up, even to the extent, perhaps, of authorizing us to speak of Cohen subsequently reading Kant in a "Platonic" light.[24]

We have already seen that one of the most important "Kantian" motifs that Cohen unearthed in Plato was the identification of the a priori in sensibility, connected with the mediating role of mathematics between thought and sense perception. Admittedly, however, on this point Platonic theory, *in Cohen's interpretation of it*, contrasts decisively with Kant's, even though this is missed by Cohen himself in his 1878 essay. In Plato's view sense perception is merely a "stimulus" (ἐγερτικόν, *Weckmittel*) to "pure mathematical thought" (*S I:* 353): phenomena are simply examples (παραδείγματα, *Beispiele*) "for mathematical tasks" (*S I:* 358), but the latter are an integral part of pure thought (νόησις) (*S I:* 365). Mathematical thought is thus seen as a model and an integral part of knowledge, *inasmuch as it is pure, nonrepresentative thought*.[25] It is to this nonrepresentative character of thought that the interpretation of ideas as hypotheses is linked. Plato's critical theory of knowledge is not only the grounding of the object in hypothesis, of being in nonbeing, identified with thought, but also the production of content by pure thought. It is only thus that Democritus's μὴ ὄν, as Cohen interprets it, is fully realized in Plato.

This conception of hypothesis as origin (*Ursprung*) and of the Platonic method of knowledge as method of purity (*Methode der Reinheit*) is clearly still not explicit in the 1878 essay. However it is potentially present, and it can be said that Cohen stops short of drawing all the conclusions from his reading of Plato. But when, in his later writings on Plato, after he had already developed his theory of origin and pure thought, Cohen stresses the meaning of the Platonic hypothesis, and sees it as a forerunner of his theories, this should not be seen as a modification of the views expressed in the 1878 essay, but as a coherent development of themes already to be found there, which have freed themselves from an earlier, cautious approach and been taken to their logical conclusions.

The final point to note is the absence of an enquiry into the critical meaning of the idea of good in *Platons Ideenlehre und die Mathematik*. Cohen only briefly refers, without further development, to the critical function that the idea of good, as ἀνυπόθετον, can exercise, both in the ethical and in the logical fields (cf. *S I*: 365). Undoubtedly this negligence is partly due to the limitations imposed by the subject of the essay. Nevertheless, when dealing with Plato, Cohen found his greatest difficulties with the interpretation of the idea of good. In 1878 Cohen was still a long way from a clear conception of this idea and from a satisfactory solution to his difficulty. When, several years later, he was to find one, it would bring about a partial break with Plato.[26]

5. The Interpretation of Plato's Theory of Ideas in The Post-1878 Works

The meaning of the Platonic Idea as hypothesis was further investigated by Cohen in the works that followed *Platons Ideenlehre und die Mathematik*. It became the fundamental historical point of reference for the "method of purity," theorized in Cohen's philosophical system.[27]

The Platonic Idea is a development of the Socratic concept, which, in its formulation as the question What is it? (τί ἐστι), is a clear assertion of the primacy of thought over being, but not yet the authentic grounding of being in thought. Thought can be the truth of being, that is the being of thought is true being, protected from error, only inasmuch as it is critically grounded in thought itself. Idea as hypothesis is the concept that gives account (λόγον διδόναι, *Rechenschaft geben*) of itself. The Platonic

Idea is not merely ground (*Grundlage*), since thought would then only account for itself relatively and the founding hypothesis would in turn be without foundation. Rather, it means the very "method" of "foundation" (*Grundlegung*). Therefore, the Platonic Idea as hypothesis is identical to critical knowledge, in which science is grounded.[28] For this reason, although, on occasion, he identified the Platonic Idea with scientific knowledge (cf. *KBE* 27f.), Cohen, elsewhere and more important, showed that this identification is unsatisfactory and that Idea has a deeper originative nature.[29] What is ἐπιστήμη?—considering the ambiguity of the Greek word which means both "knowledge" and "science,"—was for Cohen the crucial Platonic question, which provided its own answer: true knowledge is science, that is, well founded knowledge, for which ideas as hypotheses are the foundation: "We already have our answer here: *ideas* as *foundations* make up the content of knowledge, a treasure which can be forever increased by means of new foundations, even if all of them might turn out to be developments of older ones" (*E* 18).[30]

On the basis of these developments in the meaning of Idea, Cohen now identified the Platonic conception of mathematics with the model of pure thought, rather than with mediation between thought and perception:

> This is one of the most profound and daring thoughts in his [Plato's] methodology: that he *detects a reason for thought in sensation itself.* Thus *numbers* are posited as "stimulators" and "provokers of thought," which are already at work in sensation itself. Nevertheless, he clearly goes too far in his inclination to play down the conflict between thought and sensation. It was his predecessor Pythagoras who stressed the sense of substance in numbers. Plato also believed that the doctrine of numbers is a science of everlasting entities. Therefore, numbering is nothing other than thinking. However thinking is thinking unity. So producing unity is thinking, not only producing the number two, as in Plato's example. But he certainly believed that it is the moment which starts off this thought that is part of sensation. He did not believe that thinking numbers takes place within sensation. (*LRE* 472–73)

It is not contentless thought that is "pure" (cf. *LRE* 5), but thought that produces its content by itself: "after Plato's καθαρῶς, for any entity appearing in itself and for itself, pure signifies rather the means of scientific production by which the entity as such is realized."[31] Thought is therefore the true being inasmuch as it is being of the being. Pure thought is certainly not separate from knowledge, in the sense of being contentless; on the contrary, it is inseparably tied to knowledge: pure thought is the thought of knowledge.

However, the conclusion is to be drawn that real knowledge is pure thought, since the true foundation of the being is grounded in thought, which produces its content in the process of self-foundation:

> *Idea became the justification of concept,* in the sense that thought laid its own foundation on it. *"Giving account"* (λόγον διδόναι) and *laying foundation* (ὑποτίθεσθαι) *become synonyms.* Logos is the same concept. But when it becomes logos by itself, then it becomes self-foundation. And this foundation of Idea means and guarantees the true being. There is no truth, no knowledge, no being beyond this, just as on this side there is no being and no science. (*LRE* 211)

It is not difficult to realize how such reflections had already led Cohen far from Kantian transcendental philosophy, as he had interpreted it in the first edition of *Kants Theorie der Erfahrung.* Plato's pure thought is the opposite of representative thought, and scientific knowledge is the grounding of the object entirely in thought; in fact it is production of the object by thought: "In his critique of knowledge Plato's task was to bring about such a drastic separation as to put the thought of knowledge entirely on one side, while he put *representation* on the side of sensation. One ought to believe that representation also partakes of thought, or rather thought of representation. But Plato makes a clean divide and, to all intents and purposes, assigns representation to sensation" (*ERW* 113).

Cohen now saw the essence of scientific idealism, that is, critical idealism in Platonic pure thought, rather than in the Kantian a priori synthesis. It was Plato who had moved on from Socratic rationalism to idealism, by way of the critical meaning of ideas,[32] since Plato's theory that "*all laws are only foundations,* can only be foundations . . . is the *principle of every idealist method* and thus of all true idealism and rationalism. *Foundation is the criterion of reason*" (*ARG I:* 88).

3

The New Interpretation of Kant and the Definition of Critical Idealism

1. FROM THE FIRST TO THE SECOND EDITION OF *KANTS THEORIE DER ERFAHRUNG*

The second edition of *Kants Theorie der Erfahrung*, which was published in 1885, is far more than a mere revision and correction of the 1871 version. It contains the results of additional historical and theoretical investigations, carried out by Cohen in the intervening years. In this way he reached a deeper, more detailed understanding of critical idealism, which was to go beyond Kant, in the direction of an original philosophical system. The second edition of *Kants Theorie der Erfahrung* cannot be seen as the culmination of Cohen's research, since it is still situated at a provisional stage in the formation of his philosophy. Nevertheless, it does collect his results up to that point, even though they are still subject to interpretation of, and comment on, Kant's *Critique of Pure Reason*. Although his efforts to harmonize further investigation of critical idealism with the *Critique* prevented Cohen from following up all the consequences of his new research, they did result in a more fruitful reading of Kant. In this second edition, Kant's work is subjected to a more exhaustive analysis. The parts Cohen had neglected in the first edition (especially the theories of ideas and of the thing-in-itself) are considered here.

37

He also substantially revised his interpretation of the theory of principles (especially the principle of the anticipations of perception), and, as a consequence of this, the whole theory of knowledge, with special attention to the relationship between thought and intuition. The work ends with the chapter on critical idealism that Cohen had not written for the first edition and which he now felt able to write, after carrying out further historical and theoretical investigations, the need for which he had already acknowledged in 1870.

The opinion expressed by Franz Staudinger, one of the book's reviewers, seems to me to be particularly well formed: "The first edition, as would be expected from the title, contains an explanation of Kant's theory of experience. This edition is rather the author's foundation of transcendental idealism, closely linked to Kant's philosophy."[1] In addition, it should be pointed out, as mentioned above, that the foundation of critical idealism posited by Cohen in the second edition of *Kants Theorie der Erfahrung* cannot as yet be seen as definitive. Therefore, the final chapter, "Das System des kritischen Idealismus," should not be considered conclusive, but rather a starting point, the opening up of a more original philosophical perspective, independent of the literal interpretation of Kantian philosophy.

My aim, then, in this chapter is to foreground the main novelties in the second edition of *Kants Theorie der Erfahrung* as compared with the first edition[2] and connect them to some of the works written between 1871 and 1885. I shall concentrate here on three points: 1) the placing of Kant in a well-established historical tradition of critical idealism, the most important figures being Plato and Leibniz. (In this regard Cohen returned to his previous analyses, in the 1878 work, *Platons Ideenlehre und die Mathematik* and in that of 1883, *Das Prinzip der Infinitesimal-Methode und seine Geschichte.*); 2) the reinterpretation of the principle of the anticipations of perception, and, closely connected to this, of the concepts of 'intensive magnitude' and 'reality,' besides the problem of the thought-intuition relationship and, consequently, of the wider-ranging problem of the critique of knowledge. (Cohen, in this instance, revived, in general terms, the research already carried out in *Das Prinzip der Infinitesimal-Methode und seine Geschichte.*); 3) the new consideration of the theoretical meaning of the thing-in-itself and of ideas, which Cohen developed starting from the analyses carried out in 1877, in the first edition of *Kants Begründung der Ethik*. Finally, I shall attempt to highlight the fundamental aspects of the meaning of philosophy as critical idealism, in the light of the last chapter of the second edition of *Kants Theorie der Erfahrung.*

2. THE INTERPRETATION OF LEIBNIZ

The first novelty the reader encounters in the second edition of *Kants Theorie der Erfahrung*, as compared with the first edition, is a substantial historical introduction, which assigns Kant his place in the history of philosophy, both by showing how his thought differs from the Aristotelian-empiricist tradition,[3] and by reconstructing the idealist tradition of which he is a part. The idealist tradition is closely linked to the development of scientific thought, Cohen having, by this time, identified science as the object of philosophy. For Cohen critical idealism now meant scientific idealism (*PIM* 6). Plato and Leibniz are seen as the leading thinkers in the history of critical idealism leading up to Kant.[4] Plato's role has already been examined in the previous chapter. Here it is worthwhile to devote some space to Cohen's opinion of Leibniz's contribution to the history of scientific idealism.

In Cohen's view, Leibniz's importance lies in his reflections on the problem of infinity, which were not limited to mathematical aspects, but also embraced physics, and what is more important, philosophy in general.[5] Cohen glosses over Leibniz's indecision as to the choice between a purely logical-mathematical consideration of infinity using the limit method and the metaphysical alternative using the infinitesimal method[6] and highlights the latter option. It is true that Leibniz's starting point for his reflections on infinity is mathematical, but the relationship he posits between the concept of 'infinity' and the principle of continuity paved the way for wider, more important applications of the infinitesimal method. By subordinating infinity to the principle of continuity, Leibniz opened up a new perspective in the conception of the relationship between thought and being:

> *Continuity became the higher concept, from which infinity derives.* Together with this change, however, the change in the *correlation* of those concepts that concern the distinction between *being and thought*, which is more important from the systematic point of view, was also given. Now it was possible to consider the question about the sense in which infinity, although not existing in itself, nevertheless, and precisely for this reason, is valid in nature. For the *being* of infinity is now grounded in the *thought* of continuity. Continuity, inasmuch as it is *idea*, and inasmuch as it is *law*, is now a principle both of *reason* and of *nature*. (*PIM* 57–8)[7]

However, it was not in its application to problems of algebra and geometry that the infinitesimal method in Leibniz reached its full potential, but in its application to problems of mechanics. It is here that this method is revealed as a principle of the reality of nature. If Descartes is to be credited with the merit of removing material reality from the subjective criterion of sense perception, he had still grounded it in geometric intuition, identifying it with extension, and he had thus thought of it as still belonging to the province of the given, as opposed to thought, that is, to *res cogitans*. Leibniz overcame this distinction and also grounded extension in thought (cf. *KTE* 57), making use of the infinitesimal method and the concept of 'intensive magnitude.'[8] Extensive magnitude cannot be considered a founding principle in the absolute sense, since it is nothing other than a "*comparative magnitude* . . . which, in its arbitrary unity as in its origin in co-ordinates appears to be grounded in convention and sensible relativity" (*PIM* 70). A nonextensive principle should thus be sought as the ground of extensive magnitude, which can account for the reality of the being given in intuition. This principle, not in the simple negative nonextensive definition, but rather in the positive intensive one, which Leibniz took over from Galileo, is precisely the infinitesimal, which cannot be the object of sensible imagination, but rather is a pure concept of thought, which is, however, valid as a productive principle of extended reality: "Thought from now onwards can no longer be equal to evidence, to sensible intuitability (*Anschaulichkeit*)" (*KTE* 55).

Intensive magnitude constitutes the origin and authentically valid meaning of Leibniz's monadology: "If the monad had been exclusively thought as such a moment of thought and as a definition and condition, which is purely deducible from thought, of matter, and, in it, of the object of the science of nature, then Leibniz would have been far in advance of his predecessors" (*KTE* 55).

But Leibniz did not stop here. His critique of Descartes's concept of extension led him to underestimate sensible knowledge as "confused" knowledge, and to "overestimate logic" (*KTE* 57; cf. *PIM* 4), for which "the inalienable right of sensibility is obscured" (*KTE* 58): thought passes over its meaning as the transcendental ground of knowledge and slides into ontological indeterminacy. Therefore, in Cohen's view, Leibniz's ontology is no alternative to his logic, but is rather the product of an overestimation of it, so much so that logic loses contact with the science of nature and mathematics, which is its essential mediator, taking flight, like Kant's "dove," into the deceptively free space of ontological speculation.

The contradictions of Leibniz's monadology originated in the block attribution of the concepts of 'reality,' 'substance' and 'simplicity' to the monad (cf. *KTE* 545). The law of continuity is for Leibniz an "ideal metaphysical law" (*PIM* 55), even though it has the value of a law of nature, inasmuch as natural phenomena can only be made understandable by this rule (cf. *PIM* 58f.). However, Leibniz did not show sufficient clarity in his critique of knowledge (which Kant alone would achieve), to enable him to make a clear distinction between idea and category, between *Prinzip* and *Grundsatz.*[9] It is only with such clarity that he would have been able to make a clear distinction between idea and category, as Kant was to do in the theory of the antinomies, between infinity understood as the "simple," considered as idea, and continuity as a principle of reality, and thus of experience. In the latter view, "the question about the infinitely small can only have the sense of a question about its character, *about its validity, as idea producing reality;* but not about its character as existence in the world of sensible things" (*PIM* 55). Leibniz, however, moving from gnoseology to ontology, invested the monad with substantial reality, considering it as a simple substance, as an "atom":

> In this way, however, the originary view of the monad is shifted: since it is realization that above all should have been founded through it. However, instead of realization, it is extension, specifically as *composition* that is explained through the simplicity of monads. Now the simple can certainly be extensionless, seeing that the extended has become the composed. *But the monad should have been the principle of the realization of things, not that of the phenomenalization of space.* Thus the monad now becomes *de facto* the auxiliary instrument of the *phaenomenon bene fundatum,* not the ground of reality. (*PIM* 54)

Although Leibniz recognized and partially developed the meaning of the infinitesimal for the critique of knowledge, his limitations were in his lack of a clear command of the terms of transcendental discourse and in his consequent moving over to an ontological conception of the monad, through his underestimating sensible knowledge and "overestimating logic." It is clear that this estimate of Leibniz's merits and limitations led Cohen to see Kant, at least as regards the critique of knowledge founded by the latter, as an advance on Leibniz and the originator of the correct grounding of being in thought by means of the concept of intensive magnitude.

3. THE PRINCIPLE OF INTENSIVE MAGNITUDE IN KANT

It is only in Kant that the concepts of the infinitesimal and of intensive magnitude were developed in their fundamental meaning as a gnoseological principle.[10] From his predecessors Galileo and Leibniz, Kant took over the concept of the infinitesimal as intensive magnitude (he did not think it necessary to justify the "identity" of the two concepts, since it was already widely accepted in contemporary philosophical debate (cf. *PIM* 14; *KTE* 545, 548), but he developed the principle-of-reality function, which Leibniz had not been able to establish satisfactorily, since he had discussed it ontologically, rather than gnoseologically, working it out in the concept of the simple, of the monad (cf. *KTE* 548). However Kant freed the concept of intensive magnitude from that of simple substance and returned it to its originary grounding in the principle of continuity, thus making it suitable for setting up as one of the fundamental principles of the possibility of experience: the principle of the anticipation of perceptions (though Cohen preferred to use the terms *principle of intensive magnitude*, or *principle of reality*, "or more exactly of realization by means of intensive magnitude" [*KTE* 543]). Cohen argued that Kant followed two investigative directions in his analysis of this principle, each objectively entailing the other. But Kant overturned their relationship and order of priority, thus distancing himself from a correct transcendental analysis.

The principle of the axioms of intuition, which grounds the possibility of mathematics in the concept of 'extensive magnitude,' does not work out all the grounding requirements of the object connected to the concept of magnitude, since extensive magnitude is a "comparative relation" (*Vergleichungsrelation*) (*KTE* 538), where the unity is compared with other unities by means of the number schema. But comparison supposes that there is an object to compare. The relative unity which comes up for comparison is "fictitious" and "hypothetical" (*PIM* 107–8), if it is not further grounded: Kant grounded it, no longer in a metaphysical substance, such as Leibniz's monad, but rather in a principle, a fundamental law of thought, that is in the concept of intensive magnitude, which, through the schema of continuity, constitutes the principle of reality. Intensive magnitude does not only have a relative meaning, like extensive magnitude; it is "absolute unity" (*KTE* 547) or rather "productive magnitude" (*Erzeugungsgrösse*) (*KTE* 547), since it is "the origin . . . from which every extensive magnitude starts off, in which it has its "ground" (*Fundament*)" (*KTE* 545).

The principle of intensive magnitude represents the "triumph of thought," since, inasmuch as it is a principle, it grounds the reality of the object in sensibility and in the understanding, ensuring a decidedly leading role for the latter:

> This productive type of magnitude is not a category either, but a principle. However, it is thought that causes all the comparative magnitudes to be overcome. Thus reality is the category, which, in this role, fills the forms of space and time at the initial stage with the content that prepares the math-

ematical object for its future as a physical object. But this can be termed "the triumph of thought": that in its effort towards realization it overcomes sensible conditions; that it is the latter which need thought, to be able to build up their own products positively with what is offered. Thus reality, that by virtue of continuity constitutes intensive magnitude, is the pivot of critical idealism, where space and time exhibit their negative meaning and category its positive meaning. (*KTE* 547)

Therefore, intensive magnitude is "first of all" (*KTE* 546) "ground and origin" (*KTE* 758) of extensive magnitude. In this connection, however, sensation must also be mentioned. The need for going beyond simple relative magnitude, considered by pure intuition, cannot come from intuition itself. Rather, it is aroused by sensation, "another element of scientific knowledge" (*KTE* 539): "It is to sensation that I turn when the magnitude of intuition is not enough for me, when it appears to me that, being distorted in intuition, it is only a comparative magnitude, which lacks ground. Sensation seems to incorporate this ground" (*KTE* 540).[11]

Unfortunately, Kant did not posit the relationship between sensation and reality correctly. His formulation of the principle of the anticipations of perception, in the first edition of the *Critique of Pure Reason*: "In all appearances sensation, and the *real* which corresponds to it in the object (*realitas phaenomenon*), has an *intensive magnitude*, that is, a degree,"[12] credits sensation with intensive magnitude, but, notes Cohen,

> Sensation is nothing other than the expression of a relationship of consciousness with its content, just as intuition is another such expression, and thought another. However both intensive and extensive magnitudes, being content of a principle, can alone be called upon to determine an object. Sensation is not in itself an object, but only a type of relationship of consciousness with its content, whose aim is the determination of this content as an object. (*KTE* 553)

Kant's new formulation, in the second edition of the *Critique of Pure Reason* ("In all appearances, the real that is an object of sensation has an intensive magnitude, that is, a degree"[13]), is still ambiguous, since it seems that the real has intensive magnitude only *inasmuch as* it is an object of sensation. Thus the a priori foundation of the reality of the object makes room for an a posteriori foundation of sensation. This mistake influences the whole demonstration of the principle and schema of intensive magnitude and obscures its transcendental character (cf. *KTE* 554): "Instead of going on from the *reality of grounding*, which lies beyond extensive intuition, to sensation, Kant started from sensation and grounded reality in it, as a *degree* of sensation. Thus the transcendental center of gravity was shifted in favor of the principle" (*KTE* 540).

Cohen re-established the correct relationship between reality and sensation, foregrounding the fact that the grounding of reality in the object does not lie *in* sensation, but *for* sensation, in the principle of intensive magnitude, and thus in thought (cf. *KTE* 558).

4. THE THING-IN-ITSELF AND IDEAS

Even before the second edition of *Kants Theorie der Erfahrung*, Cohen had been devoting careful attention to the problem of the thing-in-itself, the most classic of the problems in any interpretation of Kant, since the first edition of *Kants Begründung der Ethik* in 1877. Gottfried Martin accused Cohen of having, to all intents and purposes, removed this problem from his interpretation of Kant, as had German idealism and Neo-Kantianism in general, arguing that, though Cohen had kept the term *Kantianism*, he had drained it of its meaning and of the problems connected with it.[14] In one sense, Martin's criticism is certainly legitimate, since Cohen, true to his idealist reading of Kant, rejected any sense of the thing-in-itself belonging to the general conception of naive or metaphysical realism. However, in another sense, Martin's criticism is unacceptable, since Cohen, far from seeing the thing-in-itself as the most ephemeral and incoherent aspect of Kant's philosophy, as did many Neo-Kantians,[15] attempted an interpretation and reappraisal of this much-debated Kantian concept, turning it into a fundamental element in Kant's idealism and critical philosophy.

As already mentioned, Cohen rejected any realistic interpretation of the thing-in-itself, which could not be reconciled with the idealist formulation of Kant's philosophy. The fundamental principle of all idealism, including the Kantian variety, is that true reality is situated in the idea, and thus the world of the senses is only real because, and inasmuch as, it shares in idea. Therefore, if the ground of the reality of the phenomenon is to be sought for behind the phenomenon, this ground will be found, not in an indistinguishable and thus illusory thing-in-itself, but rather in the idea, that is in Kantian terms, in the "law." It is the law that invests the phenomenon with objective validity, and thus with reality. In Kantian philosophy, as in Platonic philosophy before it, the law is the true thing-in-itself:

> It is precisely ideas that designate and guarantee that real that common sense believes that it sees in things, that it possesses in things. So things are not? And is idealism skeptical as regards all that is sensible? No! Things are, because and inasmuch as they are ideas.

Things are phenomena. Are they, therefore, appearance? No! Phenomena *are* because and inasmuch as there are *laws* in which they take on being, in which the flux of phenomena takes on subsistence. The law itself is thus the most direct expression of the thing-in-itself that dogmatism, camouflaged as skepticism, desires. (*KBE* 26–7)[16]

However, Cohen did not restrict himself to this statement of the idealist principle, which would be a mere limitation of the thing-in-itself to the ground of the objective value of the phenomenon, and thus of the law, and also a reduction of its specific meaning as regards the principles of intellectual knowledge (cf. *KBE* 38). The law "is only one of the *meanings* of the thing-in-itself" (*KBE* 38). The specific role of the thing-in-itself in Kant was grounded by Cohen in the recognition of the "intelligible contingency" (*intelligible Zufälligkeit*) of experience. The principles of understanding establish the need for possible experience, which Cohen identified with the mathematical science of nature. However, this "possible experience," though necessarily grounded within it, is "entirely contingent,"[17] not only in the sense that the concept of experience depends on science (cf. *KBE* 39), but also, and above all, since the need for experience is grounded in the validity of principles. However, the latter "do not have their strength in themselves alone, but exclusively in their relationship with 'possible experience.' The latter has been recognized as 'entirely contingent.' Therefore, it is a question of the need for that which is contingent" (*KTE* 639).

Thus, it is precisely a critical need that drives reason to overcome the limits of experience, in order to establish experience itself, seen in its entirety as a thing-in-itself: "Experience itself, therefore, becomes the thing-in-itself that was being sought" (*KTE* 641). The thing-in-itself, though it cannot be given, is of necessity an object of critical thought, inasmuch as it posits the problem of the "limit" of experience. This is the meaning of Kant's "limiting concept": a requirement that Cohen, following Kant, considered essential for critical philosophy and a distinguishing feature of it as regards skepticism (cf; *KBE* 39ff.; *KTE* 645f.). The thing-in-itself, inasmuch as it is an object of thought that cannot be given in intuition, that is inasmuch as it is a noumenon, thus has a limiting function as regards experience, and therefore a transcendental meaning: it is Idea, in the sense this word already had in Platonic idealism: "a thing that is not intuitable, but only thinkable, that in its function fulfills its validity" (*KTE* 643). Like the Platonic Idea, Kant's idea is not the "absolute," the object of merely intellectual knowledge, but "a tool for the knowledge of objects, a tool that the synthetic principle, all the laws of nature, can neither offer nor make useless" (*KBE* 44–5). It is a task (*Aufgabe*). It was precisely in his further investigation of the transcendental meaning of idea, with which he now identified the thing-in-itself, that Cohen returned to and further developed certain of Kant's concepts, which are connected to that of idea: the unconditioned, the regulative principle, purpose.

Idea as the unconditioned, in its transcendental function, means the totality of conditions (cf *KBE* 79). Having abandoned the possibility of considering the unconditioned an object of knowledge (this is the negative outcome of the transcendental dialectic as "a critique of understanding and reason in respect of their hyperphysical employment"),[18] what is required is a definition of the transcendental meaning of ideas as the task of reason, as regards the knowledge of nature. Cohen identified this meaning principally in the role of the unconditioned in the syllogism, which, as is well known, is the proper logical form of reason, just as judgment is the proper logical form of understanding. Idea as the major premiss of the syllogism determines the "tendency" to extend the concepts of experience in the direction of that totality of conditions, which, though, is never a given, but rather an infinite yet essential task (cf. *KTE* 666f.). The old skeptical objection that the major premiss of the syllogism is a *petitio principii*, is groundless if the principle itself, within the major premiss, is considered a *petitio*, that is an infinite task, a line of systematic research (cf. *KTE* 665).

Cohen's observations, which set up an insurmountable barrier between critical and absolute idealism have an immediate, notable consequence in the strictly logical field, since they allow only the apparently antagonistic methods of deduction and induction to be taken as a unit. Partaking of a vigorous debate, in the German as well as in the Anglo-Saxon sphere, explicitly debating the theses of John Stuart Mill (cf. *KBE* 76; *KTE* 666), Cohen remarked that "*in the critical-cognitive sense, the distinction between syllogism and induction no longer exists*" (*KBE* 76),[19] since "every induction is a syllogism" (*KBE* 76), inasmuch as it is guided by the principle of the unconditioned as the totality of conditions. So idea takes on the role of a hypothesis, which Cohen had already acknowledged in the Platonic Idea. This role is the theoretical meaning of idea as a task. Thus idea fully reveals its transcendental function as a logical maxim, that is as a subjective principle, for which, however, a fundamental regulative function is acknowledged in respect of the systematic character of the objective knowledge of nature.

Finally, the concepts Cohen grouped together as multiple, complementary articulations of a single line of discourse—thing-in-itself, noumenon, limiting concept, idea, unconditioned, principle of syllogism, regulative principle—are brought to completion and achieve their essential meaning in the idea of end (or goal). The difference between the presentations of Kant's theory of ideas in *Kants Begründung der Ethik* and in the second edition of *Kants Theorie der Erfahrung*, which do not differ in most essentials, concerns the varying degree of importance Cohen attributes to the theoretical meaning of teleology in Kant's writings. Although he does point out the role of teleology in the theoretical field, in *Kants Begründung der Ethik*, Cohen sees his main task as demonstrating how Kant's ideas, inasmuch as they are unconditioned, and thus inasmuch as they are teleological principles, are the justification for the necessary passage from the area of causality to that of freedom, that is from the logic of science to ethics. He explicitly states that his aim is to demonstrate "*that the teaching of experience not only does not preclude ethics, not only does it leave a possibility open for it, it even requires ethics*" (*KBE* 17).[20] In the second edition of *Kants Theorie der Erfahrung*, however, Cohen's fundamental aim in his interpretation of Kant's theory of ideas is to demonstrate how essential the idea of end is for a complete theory of experience, and how necessary it is to integrate the "theory of nature" and the "description of nature" in a "system of nature." On the basis of Cohen's conviction that there is a strong tie between teleological judgment and theory of experience in Kant, the second edition of *Kants Theorie der Erfahrung* contains an analysis of the theory of teleological judgment, formulated by Kant in the *Critique of Judgment*. Cohen was backed up by the authority of Kant himself in this decision. It is well known that Kant, in his *Preface to the Critique of Judgment*, wrote, that teleological judgment consisted of: "logical estimates according to concepts (from which no immediate conclusion can ever be drawn to the feeling of pleasure or displeasure) having been treated, with a critical statement of its limitations, in an appendage to the theoretical part of philosophy."[21]

In the second edition of *Kants Theorie der Erfahrung* the meaning of the contingency of experience as a limitation for the mathematical science of nature is emphasized. Contingency of experience, in the first place, means its inability to understand nature as an organism, a set of qualitatively differentiated forms, only by means of its principles. Therefore, systematic knowledge of nature must include descriptive science, which, however, cannot be grounded in a mechanistic interpretation. It must be "guided" by a teleological principle, of which the different ideas of reason are "versions and expressions" (*KTE* 657). Thus the totality of experience is, as we have already seen, the true thing-in-itself, in the sense that it is the task in whose direction the systematic knowledge of nature moves. Ideas, as regulative principles of such knowledge, are nothing other than specifications of the idea of end, in their transcendental function as conditions of the possibility of the knowledge of nature as a system. One should not, therefore, speak of a teleological idea as such, since the end is the transcendental meaning of every idea, of the idea inasmuch as it is idea: "Idea as such is the idea of end" (*KTE* 707).

Kant himself, in Cohen's view, though he had emphasized the meaning of the teleological idea and faced the problem of the relationship between teleology and mechanism, did not reach all the necessary conclusions for a theory of experience, owing to a defect in his method:

> While he [Kant], starting from the improved formulation of the problem in the Prolegomena, addressed the transcendental question to the possibility of mathematics and of the pure science of nature, he did not turn to the fact of science for the transcendental validity of ideas. Instead, by analogy, he ought to have posited the question of the possibility of the description of nature. Even this defect in his presentation is understandable, since, in his view, ideas go far beyond the teleological principle of the descriptive science of nature. They reach the supersensible, and only really delimit experience in it. What he should have done is split the treatment of the idea of end, so as to attribute one of its areas to experience and take hold of the other as the area of ethics. (*KTE* 658)

The evolution of the meaning of critical philosophy in Cohen's thought now enabled him to go further than Kant by interpreting him. Having, however briefly, presented some of the fundamental aspects of Cohen's new interpretation of Kant,[22] it seems worthwhile collecting them together to provide an organic picture of the resulting new conception of critical philosophy.

5. THE NEW MEANING OF CRITICAL PHILOSOPHY IN KANT

Cohen had already identified the transcendental method as the essential element in Kant's critical philosophy, in the first edition of *Kants Theorie der Erfahrung*. His further investigation of the meaning of Kant's critical philosophy confirmed this. Cohen was able to modify and extend the other aspects of critical philosophy substantially, on the basis of this confirmation and development of Kant's transcendental method. The transcendental method starts from a "fact" in order to identify the a priori conditions of its possibility. The first, fundamental novelty in the second edition of *Kants Theorie der Erfahrung*, as compared with the first edition, is the precise, definitive identification of the "fact" that theoretical philosophy takes as its starting point. Cohen identified experience, the object of philosophy, with the science of nature.[23] As Edel succinctly put it: "Critique of reason now means: *critique of objectified reason in sci-*

ence."[24] This clarification is crucial, above all because it represents a crucial distinction between Cohen's interpretation of Kant and other interpretations he did not accept, but which only now could be definitely put aside, on the basis of the identification of experience with science. It now became clear that Cohen's interpretation was radically opposed to the subjectivist interpretation of Kant's philosophy as a philosophy of consciousness *in all its forms*. First of all, Cohen's interpretation is radically opposed to the "physiological" interpretation, which identifies Kant's philosophy of knowledge with a theory of the psychophysical structure of the knowing subject. Second it does not accept Fichte's interpretation of Kant's philosophy as a philosophy of consciousness capable of establishing a "scientific teaching," inasmuch as it systematically deduces all the objective content of knowledge from consciousness. Such an attitude is still the result of a psychological, not a transcendental, reading of Kant. In Cohen's view philosophy can become scientifically valid, not because, in the guise of a scientific teaching, it takes science's place and deduces the object from consciousness, but because, as a critique, it takes the fact of science as its starting point and justifies its possibility. Philosophy as a critique contains two meanings, two distinct but not separate functions: a) it is different from mathematical and physical science, since it does not produce objects but only "understands" how objects are produced in sciences following laws: critical philosophy is reflective; b) besides, in such an investigation, a critique discovers that the production of the objects of scientific thought is possible on the basis of, not only dynamic, mathematical, and philosophical laws, as is clearly shown by the example of the principle of intensive magnitude: critical philosophy is productive (cf. *KTE* 734 f.). Critical philosophy thus is valid as a science, since it is transcendental investigation of the conditions of the possibility of nature as an object of science, and also since, in such an investigation, it discovers that philosophical principles are part of the principles of science. Lehmann was quite right to observe that for Cohen "philosophy itself is only a science inasmuch as it has science as its object. But it has it as an object, not inasmuch as it reflects on science, but inasmuch as it is *the thought of science.*"[25]

The scientific value of philosophy, however, can in no way be interpreted in the way Fichte did, as a "scientific teaching," since the identification of philosophical principles of science can only be the result of a *critique* of science as a fact: philosophical principles cannot be posited as the ground of a metaphysical deduction of science, but can only be found and determined as conditions, by means of transcendental deduction. The productivity of logical thought is justified in its reflectiveness and not vice-versa. This is one of the two reasons why Cohen, already in

Das Prinzip der Infinitesimal-Methode und seine Geschichte and then in the second edition of *Kants Theorie der Erfahrung*, preferred to define philosophy as critique of knowledge (*Erkenntniskritik*), rather than as theory of knowledge (*Erkenntnistheorie*) (an expression he had used in the first edition of *Kants Theorie der Erfahrung*). The second reason lies in the slightly ambiguous character of the second definition, which could lead to its being invested with a psychological meaning (cf. *PIM* 5f.).

The initial result of the identification of experience with science, then, is this definition of Kant's philosophy as "critique of knowledge," which distinguishes critical idealism from any other form of idealism (cf. *PIM* 6). If Kant represents a step forward compared with his predecessors (Plato, Descartes, and Leibniz), it is because he was capable of shifting critical philosophy from the well-determined fact of Newton's physical-mathematical science. This was the necessary historical condition for a correct transcendental, and therefore critical, development of philosophy. However, it should not be thought, that Cohen limited the meaning of Kant's philosophy to a philosophical ordering of Newtonian physics. If science is the given in which philosophy has its starting point, this given is not limited to the form which has been historically determined by science, to which philosophy must, nevertheless, refer. It is rather an ideal, which is immanent in the historical forms in which it is realized, but is not resolved in any of them. Cohen and the whole Marburg school were unanimous on this point.[26] One of the widely recognized characteristics of Cohen and his school is the close critical attention they devoted to contemporary developments in the various sciences.

His identification of experience with the science of nature and confirmation of the centrality of the transcendental method caused considerable changes in other aspects of Cohen's reading of Kant's critical philosophy. First of all, the meaning of the distinction between intuition and understanding and that of their relationship in knowledge were re-examined in the light of a more radical interpretation of the transcendental. The theory of the three progressive meanings of the a priori, as origin, form, and formal condition of experience, formulated in the first edition of *Kants Theorie der Erfahrung*, was now re-examined, expanding the purely psychological-metaphysical, and thus temporary, meaning not only of the first but also of the second level, and developing the true transcendental meaning of the third. Space, time, and the categories are the formal conditions of experience; this means that they are the "methods" of the mathematical science of nature (cf. *KTE* 743). Intuition does not signal a vague faculty of knowledge, nor an unjustified given; rather, it signals the act, that is, the constructive method by which mathematics reaches its knowledge: "*A priori* space is not physical space, neither is it geometrical space, in the exact sense, but merely the process of production and formation of the latter. This is the meaning of space as pure intuition" (*KTE* 743). The same is true for the categories: "The concept of intensive magnitude represents a method, which bears the appropriate name of infinitesimal method" (*KTE* 744). Therefore, just as the term pure intuition signals the specific method of mathematics, the term pure thought should not be confused with thinking in general: "The concept of pure thought, inasmuch as it is represented by the categories, must be understood in a more exact, restricted sense. In the 'forms of thought' we are not dealing with thought in general, but only with thought at work in mechanics, including that thought already used in pure mathematics side by side with the methods of intuition" (*KTE* 744).

Thus, in their authentic transcendental meaning, pure intuition and pure thought, space, time, and categories are different methods that come together and reach fulfillment in science, or more precisely, in the words of Werner Flach, they are "the distinct moments of the ultimate foundation function of the methods that establish knowledge."[27]

At this stage in his intellectual development, when he still conceived philosophy as a *critique of knowledge*, Cohen had not yet reduced intuition to thought, as he was to do at a later stage in his *Logik der reinen Erkenntnis*. The two were still distinct, complementary methods. However, several clues to future development emerge, such as the conception of philosophical principles as immanent, originary principles of scientific knowledge, the conception of pure thought presented above, the triumph of thought over sensibility, so clearly highlighted in the case of the principle of intensive magnitude, and so on. All these are seeds that were bound to grow and prosper in the coherent, courageous ground of Cohen's philosophy.

The clear, concrete determination of the transcendental meaning of the a priori shed more light on several aspects that had not been satisfactorily worked through in the first edition of *Kants Theorie der Erfahrung*. The definition of a priori forms as methods allowed not only the difference between intuition and understanding, but also that between space and time, to be clearly determined beyond their vague, unsatisfactory psychological definition as forms, in the outer and inner senses respectively; space is the specific method of geometry, while time is the method of arithmetic and dynamics. Besides, from this new viewpoint, Cohen was able to make a transcendental deduction of the single categories as specific methods of the science of nature. Thus, after recognizing that it was "completely false" (*KTE* 319n), he put aside the theory he had posited in the first edition of *Kants Theorie der Erfahrung* (cf. *KTE*[1] 101)[28] of the apriority of the category as unity of synthesis, rather than of the single categories. The difference between the metaphysical a priori and the transcendental a priori was still not clear enough; the unity of synthesis was still a metaphysical meaning of the a priori (cf. *KTE* 323f.). At this point it is legitimate to face the question of whether Kant's transcendental deduction of the categories was still a metaphysical deduction in Cohen's view. Geert Edel, in my view rightly, underlines this fact.[29] Actually, what Cohen questioned now was the founding nature of the concept of synthesis: a further important symptom of how Cohen's critical philosophy was now open to new developments, that would lead on to the *Logik der reinen Erkenntnis*.

The true meaning of the a priori is thus concentrated in the synthetic principles. They are the "lever of experience" (*KTE* 518). Their central role, which had already been acknowledged in the first edition of *Kants Theorie der Erfahrung*, is actually attributed to them in the second edition. As a consequence, transcendental apperception is drained of any of the remaining psychological value, which it had retained in the first edition.[30] It is interpreted as a "principle," as a "unity of principles," as the "supreme principle" (cf. *KTE* 749ff.).

In his new interpretation of Kant's critical philosophy, Cohen filled the gap left in the first edition of *Kants Theorie der Erfahrung* in respect of the problem of the thing-in-itself, by highlighting a new feature of critical idealism, of decisive importance for future development, including the practical area. In 1872, Cohen had already written the following in a letter to Hermann Lewandowsky: "There [in Kant] every thought is rigorously carried on to the limits, and then the possibility of its being taken even further is examined, etc."[31] The investigation of the limits of experience is the other side of critical idealism, complementary to its role as a censor of dogmatism: it is indispensable, if critical philosophy really wishes to live up to its name and not be reduced to sterile skepticism:

> The characteristic of the meanings of the thing-in-itself, as a mechanical law and synthetic principle, or, otherwise, as an idea regulating end; here we have a summary of the content of critical philosophy. The system of transcendental idealism proves its worth in the custody of the limit of these concepts, both positively and negatively. It finds its unity in the connection of the two directions present in the task of the thing-in-itself: defense of science and justification of moral teaching. The system of critical idealism realizes the spiritual disposition of its author. The system originates in the distinction between the mathematical science of nature and the metaphysics of morality; it reaches fulfillment in the idea that the *asy-*

lum ignorantiae of the barrier (*Schranke*) can be turned into the place of knowledge of the limit (*Grenze*). (*KTE* 782–83)

Thus critical philosophy now clearly reveals its task: the defense of the finite, loyalty towards it, but also tension in the direction of infinity, which is still considered a limit and task of the finite. Further determination of this double task is given by particular translations of it and by original solutions to the specific problems present in it. Some of these specific traits of Cohen's critical philosophy have already emerged from his interpretation of Kant's critique of knowledge; others will emerge from analysis of Cohen's philosophical system.

4

Critical Idealism

1. FROM TRANSCENDENTAL TO CRITICAL IDEALISM

Apart from *critical philosophy*, Cohen also used the term *critical idealism* to define his thought. Bearing this in mind, it is worthwhile pausing to examine the category of *idealism*, to explain how Cohen used it to determine the fundamental characteristics of his philosophy and evaluate that of others. It is not my intention to present an exhaustive account of Cohen's critical idealism here, this being the objective of this whole book. What I shall try to do in this chapter is define the characteristics of Cohen's critical idealism in respect of the more general category of idealism.

Idealism has, on occasion, been taken to be one of the components of Cohen's thought, together with critical philosophy. This is the case, for example, with Joseph Klein,[1] in whose opinion an idealist tendency and interest for the philosophy of science coexist in Cohen's thought, the one component conditioning the other, so much so that the latter prevents the former from taking flight along the path of speculative idealism (this is the path taken up by Natorp, according to Klein, as a direct result of the former's setting aside any interest in science). In contrast, I shall attempt to demonstrate that idealism and critical philosophy are not simply two juxtaposed, extrinsic features, but two closely connected aspects, the result being that its critical character is the determining factor in Cohen's idealism, which differentiates it from, and contrasts it with any other kind of idealism.

Jacob Klatzkin wrote that *"as a philosopher, Hermann Cohen was the most rigorous idealist of his time."*[2] If we want to make this statement more precise, then we must further explore Cohen's idealism, investigating both the reason for its being superior to other kinds of idealism, and, above all, its "rigorous" character. Cohen's idealism is not a disciple's attempt at keeping fading German post-Kantian idealism alive, when it was under attack by scientism and triumphant materialism, and destined to collapse in the face of emergent new philosophical requirements, which were to find adequate replies in historical materialism, philosophies of life, historicism, nihilism, and existentialism. Cohen's idealism was not destined to be dragged down with post-Kantian idealism, because it did not originate there, but is rather the rediscovery of classical (Platonic and Kantian) idealism as opposed to the deviations and degenerations of romanticism.[3]

We have already seen that, in the first edition of *Kants Theorie der Erfahrung,* Cohen believed that the task of idealism was to "resolve the differences between things in distinctions between ideas" (*KTE*[1] 270). This vague definition is of little use, but it does appear at the end of a work, which, by means of analysis and justification of Kant's transcendental idealism, had already invested it with initial, significant content, by distinguishing between transcendental and (both dogmatic and problematic) empirical idealism, showing that it had the characteristics of empirical realism.

As will be recalled, Cohen then distinguished between two aspects of Kant's transcendental idealism: "as concerning method" it is "critical idealism," "as concerning content" it is "formal idealism" (cf. *KTE*[1] 252). We have already seen that, as his thought developed, Cohen gradually abandoned Kant's formal idealism and continued his further investigation of critical idealism. These are not two self-contained trends; it was just this coherent, ever more rigorous critical idealism that drove Cohen to dispense with Kant's conception of the relationship between object and forms of sensibility, which constituted the kernel of formal idealism. It is obvious that such a development could not be limited to Kant. Cohen was also influenced by his work on Plato and Leibniz. This passage from transcendental idealism to critical idealism was, on the one hand, the development of an essentially Kantian philosophical stance, and, on the other, a development beyond Kant, which Cohen saw as a purification of his idealism.

2. Scientific Idealism

Clearly, Cohen also recognized the pre-eminent role of Idea, albeit in the Platonic sense, as an essential characteristic of idealism: "idealism is the idealism of the *Platonic Idea.*"⁴ Now, as we have seen, the Platonic Idea, in Cohen's view, should not be interpreted as intellectual intuition, but as the hypothesis, by means of which reason gives account of itself, and founds itself. Therefore, idealism cannot be separated from rationalism, but is a development and further investigation of it. Just as the Platonic Idea is the methodical foundation of the Socratic concept, in the same way, true idealism is methodically grounded rationalism. The difference between false and true idealism ("scientific rationalism, the logically grounded type of rationalism" *LRE* 500) lies in the alternative between the interpretation of the Platonic Idea as an immediate vision of the being, which is transcendent with respect to reason, and its interpretation as a hypothesis and rational foundation of concept.

One of the fundamental characteristics of Cohen's critical idealism is its inseparable relationship with rationalism. This is also his sure criterion for distinguishing genuine from any kind of false idealism (cf. *BR* 30). Cohen's definition of idealism is "methodical rationalism" (*ARG I:* xii), since, in conformity with the meaning of idea as hypothesis, it is not so much in the content of idea, but rather in the method of critical foundation it represents, that the specificity of idealist thought can be identified: "*Idealism is characterized by idea, not by its manifoldness.* The value of ideas, inasmuch as they are, consists in the value of idea. *It is only by means of idea that purity acquires its methodical value*" (*LRE* 6).

We have already seen how fundamental for Cohen the role of Plato's reflection on mathematics and the scientific method was in the development of the meaning of the Platonic Idea as a foundation method. It was Cohen's view that idealism originated and developed as the foundation of the scientific method from Plato, and the entire Platonic tradition.⁵ Thus, critical idealism is, especially in the historical sense, scientific idealism, since it developed as the philosophical foundation of science, mathematics, and physics. From Plato's hypothesis to Leibniz's infinitesimal and Kant's transcendental, a tradition of thought developed, which Cohen called "classical idealism," and to which he considered his own philosophy was an heir. This is the tradition that formulated idealist thought in close connection with the problems of science, that started off from science, and to it applied its founding principles (cf. *LRE* 595ff.).

However, critical idealism is also scientific idealism in the theoretical sense, since it does not consist, like "any other kind of idealism," in simply identifying being with idea, but in considering every given as a problem, and in positing thought as methodical foundation of science, rather than metaphysical ground of being: "Idealism in general resolves things in phenomena and ideas. On the other hand, the critique of knowledge analyzes science according to *presuppositions and grounds,* that are admitted in and for its *laws*. Thus, idealism as a critique of knowledge has *scientific facts* as its objects, not things and events, *not even those of simple consciousness*" (*PIM* 6).[6]

Idea as hypothesis, that is, as a foundation method, the principle in accordance with which it is not a metaphysical ground of being that should be sought in idea but its gnoseological foundation, the ground for which lies exclusively in this foundation, makes critical idealism the true philosophical foundation of science, and, at the same time, a scientific philosophy itself: "Ground, in its essential formality, means the *twofold* direction of scientific idealism: *to recognize ground only in foundation; but also to be sure of ground in foundation*" (*LRE* 305). Furthermore, it is only the conception of idealism as the philosophical-scientific foundation of science that ensures philosophy has objective value (cf. *PIM* 126f.).

The vague definition of idealism in the first edition of *Kants Theorie der Erfahrung*, which is deliberately repeated and debated in the passage from *Das Prinzip der Infinitesimal-Methode und seine Geschichte* quoted above—"resolve the differences between things in distinctions between ideas" (*KTE*[1] 270)—corrected and better determined on the basis of the considerations offered up to now, can now be usefully applied to critical idealism. It is not so much a question of exclusively foregrounding the ontological pre-eminence of ideas over things, as one of the foundation methods of resolving things in ideas: pure thought as the method for the foundation of reality.

3. Materialism, Spiritualism, and Skepticism

The characteristics of methodical rationalism and scientific idealism that we have recognized as belonging to critical idealism place it in a position of radical opposition to any form of dogmatism. This is the case, both with dogmatic materialism and with absolute, dogmatic idealism. Critical idealism is opposed, above all, to that form of false idealism known as spiritualism, the exact dogmatic antithesis of metaphysical materialism. Critical idealism is the opposite of any metaphysics of the absolute, namely metaphysical materialism and metaphysical spiritualism. True idealism does not simply deny absolute material substance, but grounds matter itself, as a concept, in thought. Materialism is nothing other than dogmatic realism (cf. *KTE* 46). Critical idealism is opposed to it inasmuch as it is empirical realism.

The fundamental principle of critical idealism, since Plato, has been that of the *soul*. In Greek thought, matter was conceived as having a soul, inasmuch as it moves autonomously: "therefore materialism is only one episode in antiquity,"[7] Cohen asserted in disagreement with Lange. In the modern critical idealists, Leibniz and Kant, the concept of 'soul' evolved into, and was determined in, the fundamental concept of the '*unity of consciousness*.'[8] The transcendental unity of consciousness is the very principle of critical philosophy, inasmuch as it is the negation of substance being made dogmatically absolute (cf. *LRE* 606) and, at the same time, is the principle of its foundation as a concept of pure thought: "We must ask ourselves . . . what advantage is to be gained from the maxim of the soul as compared with 'soulless' materialism. The *unity of consciousness*, the fundamental term of critical philosophy, supplies an extremely clear answer to this question. Since every critical-cognitive foundation adheres to this principle, then *matter* is only a specific instance of consciousness, a 'type of representation'" (*KBE* 99).

However, in refuting materialism, Cohen was faced by a problem: its defense by his teacher Friedrich Albert Lange. Nevertheless, Cohen did not have any particular difficulty in integrating Lange's viewpoint with his own, after making the necessary corrections. Actually, this confrontation was useful in that it helped him to clarify his redefinition of the categories of materialism and idealism. Lange had already contrasted materialism as a fruitful, irreplaceable methodological principle of science, which reached its climax with Kant, with materialism as a metaphysical concept of post-Kantian philosophy, which Lange rejected as groundless. Clearly, on the basis of their common view of the work of Kant as a key stage in the history of philosophy (though glossing over the substantial differences between his and Lange's interpretations of Kant!), and of their different interpretation of ancient philosophy,[9] Cohen was able to re-examine Lange's theses and demonstrate that scientific materialism, to which the latter adhered, is none other than critical idealism.[10] In this way it was also demonstrated that "materialism and idealism are not opposites and are not mutually exclusive."[11] We have already seen that the true opposite of materialism is spiritualism, which, admittedly, is sometimes called "idealism," but is a false kind of idealism. Actually, the opposition between materialism and spiritualism is superficial; they are both the expression of metaphysical dogmatism, which posits an absolute without founding it and deduces all reality from it. In fact, spiritualism is itself a kind of materialism, since in it "idea is not seriously set against matter, but a material spirit in idea, even though, as *Kant* said, it is thought as superfine" (*ERW* 315): "*Spiritualism* is none other than the materialism of the absolute" (*LRE* 606). However critical idealism is the very method of foundation, for which matter can also find its justification in pure thought and thus become a valid concept for science.[12]

As mentioned in chapter 2, spiritualism for Cohen is a false kind of idealism; it is not really idealism at all, since its principle is the hypostatized *logos* and not idea as hypothesis (cf. *LRE* 6). Spiritualism originated in an erroneous development of Plato's principle of the soul. If the ancient concept of the soul is developed by critical idealism in Kant's concept of the transcendental unity of consciousness, it is made absolute, in spiritualism, in the concept of a metaphysical spiritual substance (cf. *KBE* 101f.). In this sense, Fichte's subjective idealism, grounded in the principle of self-consciousness, though drained of the mythical aspects of pre-Kantian spiritualism, is not very far from it either (cf. *KBE* 99). Self-consciousness, if it is not entirely resolved in its transcendental meaning, also remains a dogmatic, metaphysical principle (cf. *LRE* 416f.).

As far as skepticism is concerned, Cohen accepted Kant's view that it is not a serious concept,[13] though it is a necessary stage in opposition to dogmatism and in the passage to critical philosophy.[14]

In *Platons Ideenlehre und die Mathematik*, Cohen wrote:

> Idealism joins together two motifs, and its history proceeds in their intermingling. It contains: a *skeptical* stage, inasmuch as it highlights the nullity of the real of sense perception, and a *spiritual* stage, inasmuch as it teaches the reality of that which is in thought, of the spiritual. Plato's theory of ideas has both motifs. But neither the latency nor explicit action of these two motifs would turn the theory of ideas into the source of idealism *grounded in the theory of knowledge*, if the unification, the intermingling of these two opposite motifs were not demonstrably present in its development.[15]

Therefore, idealism is presented as the "unification" and "intermingling," not as the sum of spiritualism and skepticism. This means that the latter are not two components, but rather two unilateral degenerations of the profoundly unified concept of critical idealism. Thus, just as idealism, on losing its critical aspect, is dragged down into dogmatic spiritualism, so critical philosophy, unless it is enlivened by idealist content, remains sterile skepticism. This confirms that idealism and critical philosophy are not merely two different, juxtaposed matrixes in Cohen's thought, but two indissoluble aspects of a unified stance, critical idealism. If one is separated from the other, the result is degeneration and loss of identity. For Cohen there is no true idealism that is not critical, nor true critical philosophy that is not idealist, so what is the difference between skepticism and critical philosophy? It is adherence to science that distinguishes them, and we have already seen that idealism is con-

nected to this adherence, since a critical philosophy of science is necessarily a grounding of the phenomenon in idea as hypothesis.

4. IDEALISM WITHOUT A SUBJECT?

Cohen, the Marburg school, and Neo-Kantianism in general were
often criticized for being proponents of an "idealism without a subject."[16] This, together with all the problems associated with the transcendental subject, is a recurrent theme in criticism of Neo-Kantianism. In
Manfred Brelage's words: "Criticism of critical philosophy in the early
decades of this century mainly singled out its concept of the gnoseological subject. All the post critical philosophers, with whom we shall deal
[Husserl, Hönigswald, Hartmann, Heidegger], claimed the merit of having dispensed with critical philosophy's concept of the subject. Even if
the directions followed vary, criticism of Neo-Kantianism shared this
common enemy."[17]

In 1913, Sigfried Marck[18] looked into the problem of the subject in
the Marburg school, finding in it a development of Kant's transcendentalism, to the detriment of subjectivism. The latter is also present in
Kant, though continually threatening to turn into its opposite. Marck
identified three different problems in Kant's theory of consciousness:
the logical problem of the form-matter relationship, the gnoseological
problem of the relationship between subject and object of knowledge,
and the psychological problem of the relationship between concrete
consciousness and its contents. In Marck's view, in the field of logic,
Cohen accepted Parmenides's identification of thought with being and
of thought with what is thought, the former being preponderant, however. Thus, the *correlation* between thought and being actually becomes
identity, since it is in thought as the act of thinking that the content of
thought is constituted; content, therefore, is resolved in form itself.[19] In
the gnoseological field of the subject-object relationship, Marck also
identified an authentic orientation toward critical philosophy in the
Marburg school. This is to be seen in its genetic concept of knowledge,
where the object is the result of production of the subject, but not of its
emanation or creation. There is correlation, not identity, between subject and object, so much so that the object is an infinite task for the subject, that would be impossible in a philosophy of identity. However, even
here, the critical philosophy of the Marburg school hides deeper subjectivism, since the knowing subject is none other than a specification of
the transcendental subject, that is of thought as a producing act, an act
of positing the object. Thus the object is a problem for the knowing subject, albeit a self posited one: "Actually, the problem is determined as the

project (*Vorwurf*), the objective (*Gegenwurf*), worked out by the subject for itself."[20]

While Marck foregrounded the subjectivism lurking beneath the Marburg school's transcendentalism, Nicolai Hartmann[21] devoted more attention to the elimination of the subject (and the object as a thing-in-itself) in the school's logical idealism. In Hartmann's view, logical idealism is a route which "absolutely radicalizes the idealist thesis, and also resolves the last remaining realities (the thing-in-itself and 'subject in general') in ideal products."[22] In it "the real is *weakened in the ideal,* i.e. it is eliminated."[23] The subject is eliminated inasmuch as the *logos* is beyond the cognitive relationship between subject and object; subject and object are no longer present, only subjectification and objectification of the *logos*, which are secondary in respect of the *logos* itself. The object is no longer a function of the subject, but both are functions of the *logos*.[24] Actually, this viewpoint, according to Hartmann, ceases to be a kind of idealism; it is a kind of logicism that dispenses with the problem of knowledge. In fact, since this philosophy is resolved in the consideration of judgment and concept solely as functions of scientific thought, strictly speaking, it is not logicism at all, but rather a kind of scientism and methodology. Being becomes positing (being); the thing-in-itself becomes the infinite task. However, positing does not refer back to a positing subject, since thought itself, and not the subject, is the principle. Therefore, Hartmann accepted Marck's thesis on subjectivism being a characteristic of the Marburg school, as a consequence of thought prevailing over being, the thinking act over that which is thought, though explicitly revealing the paradox of "objectivism without a subject": "In opposition to empirical, transcendental subjectivism one can point to that of logical idealism as 'logical subjectivism.' It is the paradox of a 'subjectless subjectivism' and, in its consequences, must bear the entire inner split of such a paradox."[25]

In my view, Manfred Brelage usefully clarified certain fundamental points of the theory of the subject in Marburg school philosophy,[26] accurately restricting both its subjectivist character and its lack of a subject, while foregrounding its critical side. Brelage pointed out that the theory of the subject in critical philosophy is linked to the problem of the validity of knowledge. Even if its name is critical *idealism*, its interest is not in the subject but in the principles of the validity of our knowledge: "Critical idealism is not idealism of the subject, but of *idea*; it owes its name, not to Locke's 'idea' in its meaning as representation, but to Plato's Idea, in its interpretation as hypothesis, law, principle of validity (*geltender Wert*). This law—and not the spirit—is the absolute in which all knowledge is grounded. It is the 'subject' of all knowledge, which confers objectivity on the latter."[27] Critical philosophy dispenses with the problem of the relationship between subject and object, inasmuch as it rejects its originary character and posits the problem of knowledge at a previous level. Therefore, if the meaning of the subject of knowledge is the concrete subject in its factuality, then critical philosophy can legitimately be called "idealism without a subject." However, critical philosophy is not centered on this concrete ego, which is the subject both of valid knowledge and of error, but exclusively on the subject of valid knowledge, not that of error, on transcendental subjectivity as the ground of objectivity. Brelage rightly observed that:

> only if the connection with the question of validity is acknowledged, will it be possible to initiate intelligent criticism and dispense with the critical theory of the subject. Since every concept of subjectivity which is to take the place of the critical concept must fulfill the condition of at least *also* being capable of establishing the way in which the subject manages to be the subject of valid knowledge. What enables the concrete subject to produce universally valid knowledge cannot be a mere stage in its concreteness. The permanent merit of the critical theories of the subject could be its having attempted to work through a concept of the subjectivity which is the condition of the possibility of universally valid knowledge.[28]

Brelage identified two essential requirements for a theory of the subject from the point of view of the logic of validity: first, subjectivity must not restrict or eliminate the objectivity of knowledge; second, subjectivity can only be thought in connection with, and starting from, the logical-transcendental principles that reflection on the validity of knowledge determines apart from subjectivity. For critical philosophy, knowledge is not representation, but judgment, and thus the transcendental subject must be distinguished from the object of psychology: it must be the subject of valid judgments. The transcendental subject, Cohen's 'knowing' or 'scientific consciousness,' or Rickert's 'consciousness in general,' is therefore distinct from the concrete psychological subject; rather it is the *ideal*, the *norm* and *task* for the latter. In this sense it is a *principle.*

> Pure thought, consciousness in general, reason logos, or whatever terms critical philosophy used to analyze the network of principles in which the originary relationality of knowledge and its object are grounded, are a principle where gnoseological reflection encounters an ultimate ground. It is in these that all autonomy of knowledge is grounded. Inasmuch as it is made possible by them, knowledge does not refer to beings in themselves, but pure concepts and principles, which originate from it. Pure thought as an absolute principle of knowledge, this is the theme of critical philoso-

phy's transcendental logic. It is here that critical philosophy endeavored, above all, to ensure the absoluteness of this principle in a dual aspect. It highlighted, on the one hand, the independence of this pure thought from any presupposition of a being in itself, on the other, that of pure thought from concrete subjectivity. The assurance of the one was realized with its defense of the independence of transcendental logic from metaphysics, and that of the other with the defense of its independence from psychology.[29]

5. ETHICAL IDEALISM

Following on from Plato and Kant,[30] Cohen saw ethical idealism as an "expansion" of critical idealism.[31] It is extremely important to understand the meaning of this expansion in all its implications. It is undoubtedly an application of critical method to morality and moral sciences, outside the area of the knowledge of nature. Nevertheless, this expansion of critical idealism into the field of ethics is not only an extension of method, but it also reaches beyond being into what ought to be, from idea as hypothesis to idea as a task. Cohen acknowledged that both Plato and Kant had established a distinction between logic and ethics, at the same time joining them together in one system. He was to remain faithful to this essential principle of critical idealism.[32] Even before Cohen had identified the scientific fact, which is the starting point for ethics as critical philosophy, with the law (in his *Ethik des reinen Willens*), he was quite clear about the critical character of ethics:

> The critical viewpoint is also decisive for the inclusion of ethics in the system of idealism. There is certainly no science of moral problems which is equivalent to the fact of the mathematical science of nature. Nevertheless, the methodical analogy remains: that the moral philosopher cannot see his task as the production of the content of moral law, when he only has to determine its formula. Certainly his task is, at least initially, easier in the first instance than in the second. However, the moral philosopher must also restrict himself to positive and negative criticism. His task is to find the formula and value of moral law that can either be guessed at or is revealed by the facts of culture. (*KTE* 736)[33]

Ethics needs to be founded as knowledge (*Erkenntnis*) rather than as learning (*Wissen*),[34] on the same critical method as logic. This ensures that investigation is carried out critically and scientifically also in the field of ethics. Otherwise, it has to be left to the heteronomy of religion and politics.[35] Therefore, ethics too proceeds by way of the method of hypothesis and foundation; ethical idealism is also critical idealism in the methodological sense. Ethics "rests on the ground of logic. The fundamental law of truth has connected it with logic. Ethics, like logic is idealist. Both share the same foundation method. All problems must have a potential for legitimization in respect of this method, through which they must be examined and resolved. Thus *idealism* is methodically opposed to everything that usually comes under the heading of *metaphysics*" (*ERW* 428; cf. *ERW* 512). In this sense "ethics presupposes logic" (*ERW* 38; cf. *ERW* 23, 29, 43 *passim*).

Nevertheless, expansion of critical idealism at the hands of ethics is not restricted to an extension of the critical method. In it critical philosophy has far more than a methodological meaning. As we have seen, Cohen had already foregrounded the dual character of critical philosophy in Kant: the grounding of reason in its limits, and an inclination in the direction of the limit itself as an infinite task. The second aspect is that of ideas. The idea of end in Kant constitutes the limit of experience: if critical philosophy is unable to proceed beyond this limit, neither can it settle down quietly before it. The idea of end had already demonstrated its indispensability as a rule of knowledge, inasmuch as it is a system. However, this theoretical role still has a uniquely regulative meaning; it is in ethics that idea as end fully reveals its constitutive function in the broadening of the horizons of being (cf. *KTE* 658).

Plato's theory of ideas had identified the true being that also founds the being of things, with ideas and not things. But Plato posited the idea of good, what ought to be beyond being, as a supreme Idea beyond ideas. Kant also accepted this conception, while highlighting the transcendental character of what ought to be and translating Plato's transcendent idea of good into the ethical what ought to be, as the limit of being (cf. *KBE* 178). In this sense end is "an expansion of causality . . . *the idea of causality*" (*KBE* 105). If the true being of the law constitutes the ground of the possibility of the being of the existing, the what ought to be of the ethical idea constitutes the limit of being, and truth consists only in the infinite task of the unity of logic and ethics. In ethical idealism, the theme of not being, which is fundamental for critical idealism, is enriched with additional meaning: not being is no longer only the origin of being, but also what ought to be, that is, the task of being: "Since the task of ethics is to teach what ought to be, then it must teach what *is not.* Its task, therefore, is to dispense with the 'being' of experience, and, as there is no being beyond it to which our concepts of experience can refer, it must go further than experience. In practical philosophy it is thus not a case of 'positing principles of what ought to happen, *even if it never does happen*'" (*KBE* 14).[36]

At this level, all the problems connected to the metaphysical principle of the absolute can be faced again, once they have been separated from dogmatism. If metaphysical idealism associates all the aspects of the problems concerning the infinite with the dogmatic statement of an absolute in itself, critical idealism, on the other hand, separates them from this dogmatism, connecting them to idea as an infinite task. Thus ethics becomes "the metaphysics of the new age."[37]

The what-ought-to-be theme, however, does not satisfactorily characterize ethical idealism as critical idealism. Its fundamental principle is rather "the being of what ought to be" (*ERW* 13 *passim*). It is not simply a question of juxtaposing what ought to be and being, which could still merely represent a purely subjective aspiration. It is precisely the scientific method, taken over from logic, in which ethics is grounded, that facilitates the assignment of a priori objective validity, independent of experience, to what ought to be. In ethics, critical idealism very closely adheres to the fundamental principle that true being lies in idea. The idealist principle of the reality of idea, which in logic has a critical role as the foundation of experience, in ethics has a task involving action as its critical function. Idea as what ought to be is not deduced from experience; it refers to it and, therefore, is its principle of validity. So the accusation that Cohen's idealism is abstract, inasmuch as it invests ideas with too much power and does not give enough importance to facts is debatable.[38] The ethical maxim is never detached from empirical reality, inasmuch as it is a *task* and not a mere utopia. Inasmuch as it is an *infinite* task, it can never be denied by facts:

> We understand *truth*, the fundamental idea of *critical idealism*, as consisting in the *separation of idea*, as an infinite *task* for all the moral ends, both of the human race and the individual, of this *ethical* meaning of *idea*, from all *existing reality of nature*, and from all *historical experience*. Both are necessary: separation, but also *protection of both features* in their equal logical value, just as existing reality retains its value in the face of idea, and idea only grounds its meaning in the admonition and guidance with which it takes care of existing reality. This truth of idealism, which, at the same time, honors existing reality, ensures that all our thinking, investigating and acting be personally true.[39]

The transcendental apriority of what ought to be as idea in respect of empirical factuality is thus grounded in the a priori reality of idea, in the being of what ought to be, and therefore in the critical character (in the methodological sense) of ethical idealism. Genuine idealism "acknowledges no abyss, no opposition between the ideal and reality" (*E* 110), not because it posits, like Hegel, that ideal and real are identical, but because it posits idea as the infinite task of the existing real, grounded in the a priori reality of idea: "Not only must what the present offers in nature and the human sphere be real (*wirklich*), *but* what is not yet real, though foreseen in hope and required as reality in the *vision of hope, is* eminently *real. Hope, future, humanity go hand in hand.* They are a protest against the exclusive reality of the present in nature and history."[40]

Humanity, as an infinite task of ethics, is real in the future:

> The irreplaceable, very deep ground of the ethics of humanity can no longer lie in the prophetic *hope* of the future, but, in accordance with its method, in the *reality of the future.* This reality is ethical idea: the idea where the idealism of ethics separates from the utopia of a transcendent bucolic world, as *Jean Paul* once called the hereafter. . . . If ethical reality is an idea, then it is grounded in idealism, and therefore in knowledge. *The knowledge of morality needs the certainty of that future for humanity.*[41]

Correlation between idea and reality is not resolved in the past of identity, but thrusts itself into the real, not utopian, future of 'realization,' by means of 'action.'[42]

6. EUDEMONISM AND PANTHEISM

It should be clear by now that Cohen, like Kant, saw ethical idealism as opposed, first of all, to all materialistic and empiricist ethics. In Cohen's view this antagonism lay principally in eudemonism:

> What moral empiricism does not acknowledge is that a law is in force on the limits of nature, that in circumscribing nature a law originates establishing the certainty of the ethical, which gives birth to systematic connections of moral knowledge, just as all phenomena are only constituted as nature in all the laws, and, finally, that a similar *theoretical connection of being and what ought to be* exists. There is not even *theoretically* such an absolute what ought to be for eudemonism: it begins as sensualist materialism, and its quintessence is *individualism.* (*KBE* 200)

Plato's principle of the soul, protected from all metaphysical distortion by transformation into Kant's transcendental principle of the unity of consciousness, is the "best means of protection from materialism,"[43] both in the theoretical and in the practical fields. Acknowledging that man is not only an animal, and therefore substituting the ethics of pleasure and happiness with that of freedom and pure will does not imply ignoring the role of affectivity in human behavior, but simply not investing it with the value of a principle of morality. Eudemonism can be acknowledged as a positive, even essential, component in men's lives, but not as the ground of ethics (cf. *ERW* 295).

Thus ethical idealism is also opposed to any materialistic conception of history: "The materialism of historiography consists in the fact that it tries to deduce culture in its entirety, in all its products and endeavors, from the constraints of economic conditions. From this point of view purely spiritual forces lose their creative autonomy, and moral ideas become the products of economic needs and causes."[44]

Such an interpretation of history is not only mistaken, but it is also the very denial of history: "Thus this materialistic, naturalistic conception of history is, first of all, revealed to be *the elimination of history*. The history of man and his works and actions is the history of the spirit and ideas. Otherwise, there would be no universal history (*Weltgeschichte*), but only a history of nature (*Naturgeschichte*)" (*ERW* 39).

In this case too it is not a question of denying that material ends are legitimate for man. In fact, it is historical materialism that makes reaching these ends impossible. If the interpretation of history "sees *the economy* as the only originary force of culture, then not even this sector of culture will be improved, unless, in addition, there is a special effort in this direction. This effort is idealism, since materialism would continue to hold the opinion that this has always been the situation, that it is so today and will always be in the future."[45]

The other great adversary of critical idealism, and, in particular, of ethical idealism, is pantheism, with which Cohen associated all forms of monism, the philosophy of identity, and mysticism.[46] Pantheism is monism in origin and in essence. Its ultimate principle is the unity of being as identity.[47] The identity of God and nature necessarily implies the identity of being and what ought to be, even the reduction of what ought to be to being, and therefore the impossibility of ethics (cf. *ERW* 16). For this reason, pantheism is the very denial of idealism. Being and what ought to be are identified in it, and the critical function of idea annulled in the simple statement of being. Ultimately, it is still the metaphysics of the absolute that opposes critical idealism, even in pantheism. Whether the absolute is thought as substance, as in Spinoza,[48] or as idea, as in Hegel, it is still the absolute, which lacks the essential character of idea, that is, "giving account" of itself and of being, which is the critical function of a principle of foundation. Pantheism is always a philosophy of immanence. Admittedly, critical idealism also believes in the unity of being and what ought to be, but the ground of this unity is transcendent; it is real, though as an infinite task. This is the essential meaning of the fundamental law of truth and transcendence of God in Cohen's ethics.

However, where God and truth are immanent, what ought to be can no longer find a place. Good is no longer the infinite task of the realization of will, but is immediately identical to the real. Freedom becomes necessity, autonomy becomes heteronomy (cf. *ERW* 331f.).

The fundamental critical principle of ethical idealism, in accordance with which separation and unification of logic and ethics are equally necessary and complementary, is totally disregarded in pantheism. In the latter, ethics is restricted to logic, and both are depleted in the metaphysics of identity: "If, however, the idea of God means the unity of nature and morality, this cannot be confused pantheistically with identity. Rather, it means this unity of nature and morality as unification, as the harmonization of nature and morality" (*ERW* 462–63).[49]

Mysticism is also an illusion of unity with the absolute. It also implies separation from knowledge, the critical method, and rationalism. The ethics of freedom as autonomy and that of what ought to be as a task are drained of sense, because of a deceptive intuition of the absolute. In Cohen's view it is in mysticism that the relationship between pantheism and materialism is revealed: "Thus pantheism must be opposed to *rationalism* and *idealism*. It can only be arrived at surreptitiously, starting out from mysticism, where it remains concealed. But the overtures of mysticism are also accepted by *materialism*" (*BR* 28).

Where the identity of God and nature is posited, God is resolved in nature. Where trust is put in the immediate intuition of the absolute, there is a risk that the latter is resolved in the sensible intuition of the finite: "Where God and man or God and nature are seen in the same light, mysticism inevitably intervenes, making morality supersensible and the supersensible sensible. Mysticism also fanatically disturbs morality and superstitiously obscures the natural sensibility of the human world."[50]

Something similar also happens in the philosophy of history, where utopia, far from being the weakness of idealism, is the consequence of its being abandoned. Utopia is none other than the complementary aspect of the materialistic and eudemonistic conception of history:

> *The problem of the best State is also the problem of the best law.* Both are images, positive utopias. Justice does not provoke the image of a *future State*. A lawful State, as the future State, is part of the ideal of the State and law. An Ideal is forever an Ideal. It cannot be mistaken for a real image. In this way positive politics is mistaken for ethics, which directs its actions, but in which it is never resolved, because it never reaches the ideal. Therefore, ethics and politics cannot coincide. The future image of the best State is a eudemonistic utopia. *Utopia is the ideal of eudemonism.* The ethics of pure

will, of pure self-consciousness, separates from that of eudemonism in this relationship of the concept of the State with ethics. (*ERW* 601)[51]

When the reality of idea is abandoned, all that remains is restless drifting between what exists and what is wished for.

7. AESTHETIC IDEALISM

Cohen also approached aesthetics from an idealist viewpoint: "My intention is to deal with the relationship between aesthetics and the present time from the point of view of idealism" (*ARG I:* xii). Cohen looked back to the tradition of aesthetic idealism, from Winckelmann to Kant and Schiller. According to this tradition *form* is the constitutive principle of the beautiful:

> Kant's entire system was built up from the term "form," which, however, means *the law of the production of content* in aesthetics particularly, as well as in both logic and ethics. It is thus identified with the creative *a priori*, with the *idea of hypothesis*, and all existing reality receives its productive principle in it. Thus in *Schiller's* theory form is the creative idea concerned with the *materials* of art. It is in our acceptance of form as a principle of aesthetic idealism that we are the direct descendants of the Greeks, the heirs of Homer. Not only did *Winckelmann* rediscover *form in the plastic arts* and make it the sole link between German philology and Antiquity, but form, in its originary creative sense, was also the driving spirit of Greek *poetry*. Ultimately, then, form means the *immediacy* and *purity* of spiritual creation, neither of which are influenced by any further consideration of stimulus and effect.[52]

Pure feeling, the formal principle of art, is restored to the principle of purity, the qualifier of critical idealism in every area of culture, which ensures its well foundedness and objectivity (and its universality, in the case of aesthetics). If the aesthetics of pure feeling is thus placed beside the logic of pure thought and the ethics of pure volition in the system of critical idealism, it is also joined to logic and ethics in idealist reference to idea as a task. The regulative idea of end, as an idea of the system, constitutes the task of logic, as an idea of freedom, that of ethics, and, as an idea of aesthetic purpose (*Zweckmässigkeit*) posits an ideal task for art (cf. *KBE* 207f.).

Therefore, aesthetics makes a full contribution to the fundamental idealist and critical character of philosophy, both in the methodological principle of purity and in the direction of idea as a task. Thus Cohen's aesthetics is opposed to all naturalism, empiricism, and sensualism, on

the one hand, and, on the other, to all forms of pantheisim and panaestheticism. In his aesthetics he treats skepticism in the same way as in the
rest of his philosophy. Aesthetic skepticism can have a positive role to
play as a fundamental component of the critical approach, but, as
humor, it remains flawed and negative, if it degenerates into irony:

> When irony becomes a preparatory stage for humor it does not disturb the
> classical spirit. But if it gets stuck as irony, then it is taking the false route
> that leads to romanticism . . . criticism cannot become irony. It is only a
> half truth that all art is irony of the supersensible. Art should rise up to the
> supersensible, almost being elevated above itself. In religion the saying
> goes: you must make no images, while in art all that is eternal is nothing
> but a symbol.[53]

8. CRITICAL IDEALISM AND ECLECTICISM

So opposition to critical idealism came from various quarters.
While it retained and guaranteed the two complementary aspects of the
true being of idea (on the one hand, as hypothesis, as giving account of
the concept, as foundation, and, on the other, as the limit of being, as a
task), the same aspects were abandoned by any other direction taken by
philosophy. For this reason, all deviations from critical idealism are
blurred in a mixture, in which they coexist, since the critical meaning of
idea, which is the only genuine truth criterion, is missing. Thus the only
true contrast is between critical idealism and eclecticism:[54] "There are
really only *two opposites* in the whole of philosophy and science: *idealism
and eclecticism.* It is in the latter mixture, which is the inheritance of all
opposition to idealism, that absence of classicism is grounded.
Classicism requires and offers rigorous, pure unity. Thus, the forms of
idealism can also be isolated in accordance with their degree of separation from the mixture of styles" (*LRE* 595).

Genuine idealism, then, is to be evaluated by two main parameters.
First, the interpretation of idea as hypothesis and consequent reference
of being to thought in the sense of critical grounding of being in idea,
that is, the method of purity (cf. *E* 18). Second, rejection of any metaphysical absolute, understood as totality, and reference to the unconditioned, as an infinite task, as a limit, but never as an object, of science (cf.
E 36).

Therefore, Cohen's option for idealism should definitely not be
taken either for an attempted revival of romantic philosophy, or for an
adaptation of Hegel with corrections supplied by Kant's critical philosophy, as others had tried to do. Cohen did not offer a synthesis of Kant

and Hegel, but a choice between them. He aimed to recover the classical idealism of Plato, Leibniz, and Kant, that is, critical idealism, so as to contrast it with any philosophical deviation from it, including the false idealism of the romantics: "*Kant or Hegel*, for the continuation of German philosophy, this is not merely a question that concerns spiritual health, but in its truthfulness, it is absolutely vital for the German spirit."[55]

9. EXCURSUS: ROMANTICISM: FICHTE, SCHELLING, HEGEL

Cohen saw romanticism as the climax of false idealism and its various errors. In opposition to *classicism*, romanticism deviates from and abandons the fundamental principles of critical idealism. Romanticism, in this sense, is not only a historiographical category, but also that kind of philosophical thought, which, in the guise of idealism, betrays critical idealism, and ultimately philosophy itself. In Cohen's classification, even certain schools of thought that do not belong historically to romanticism, in the usual sense in which this term is understood, are labeled "romantic," such as Aristotle's philosophy (cf. *KBA* 338), certain aspects of medieval[56] philosophy, and some contemporary philosophers, especially Schopenhauer.[57] Certain similarities in content, then, forced romanticism to venture well beyond its historiographical limits, within which Cohen situated post-Kantian German philosophy, and especially its major representatives: Fichte, Schelling, and Hegel. Cohen identified the source of all the errors of romanticism with the abandoning of the fundamental principles of Kant's critical idealism: the relationship of philosophy with science and the transcendental method, on the one hand, and the distinction between being and what ought to be, between logic and ethics, and thus the correct conception of philosophy as a system, on the other.

Having left the vital link with science behind, romantic philosophy felt free to aspire to the elevated position of knowledge of the absolute, where consciousness is no longer the transcendental unity of the conditions of the possibility of experience, but metaphysical unity, which creates its own content. Thought and intuition are not seen as separate, complementary methods of scientific knowledge, but as organs of understanding and mystic union with the absolute. Pure intuition is no longer understood as a mathematical method, but as intellectual intuition. Productive imagination and pure thought do not owe their purity to the transcendental character of principles of the critical grounding of the empirical being in thought, but to the metaphysical character of organs of knowledge of the absolute being, beyond experience and thought of it (cf. *LRE* 11; *ARG I:* 13, 18, 25). All this led some romantic thinkers to abandon the critical area of logic and transcendental ethics, so as to make logic and ethics subservient to aesthetics, as the area of the direct contemplation of the absolute, of union with idea, which is the indistinct unity of God and nature, of subject and object, being and what ought to be. What is hidden in this romantic aestheticism is a revival of the medieval primacy of religion, of dogmatism and mythology, which represented a way forward, rather than an obstacle, for the pantheism of the romantics.[58]

However, the primacy of practical reason, as understood by Fichte, prepared the way for Schelling and Hegel's philosophy of identity, which is a revival of monism and pantheism. In the metaphysical absolute, dispensing with the distinction between logic and ethics, "the starry heavens above me" and "the moral law in me," between subject and object, spirit and nature, rational and real, being and what ought to be, God and the World, also makes building up a system impossible. Romanticism, by stating a unitary principle beyond Kant's dualities, believed it had made such a system possible. But it is precisely this unity, as an indistinct, identical principle, which drains the system of its authentic meaning as the unification of distinct features and turns it into a philosophy of identity, that is, pantheism.[59] Even if the romantics' absolute is not Spinoza's substance, but spirit or idea, it does still represent the unity of God and the world (*Deus sive natura*), and idealism, or rather spiritualism, takes up the effects of naturalism, as in Fichte's conception of consciousness (cf. *KBE* 291; *KTE* 750) or of a people (cf. *ERW* 254), or in mythology, as in Schelling (cf. *KBA* 338, 365ff.), or in historicism, as in Hegel (cf. *LRE* 416; *ERW* 252, 331).

a. Fichte

Cohen's opinion of Fichte deserves careful study.[60] First, Cohen acknowledged that, unlike other romantic philosophers, there were several positive features in Fichte's thought. Second Cohen's remarks on Fichte's errors are especially useful for identifying certain fundamental aspects of the former's critical idealism.[61] He acknowledged that Fichte had considerable "philosophical" and "idealistic" talents (*LRE* 416; *E* 66), and that he had recognized some of the cruxes of Kant's thought: the challenge to empiricism (cf. *KBE* 54; *KTE* 738, 754), the importance of the primacy of practical reason (cf. *KBE* 272, 292; *E* 38). He also praised Fichte's role in the formulation of the ideals of socialism and Germanism.[62] However, Cohen also considered Fichte "the founder of philosophical romanticism" (*KBA* 343), the thinker who "forged the instruments of romanticism in every field" (*LRE* 416).

One of the fundamental limitations of Fichte's philosophy was his failure to understand the authentic meaning of Kant's transcendentalism. In his attempt to dispense with the psychological subject for consideration of the transcendental subject, Fichte only arrived at the metaphysical subject, which, however, was unable to rid itself of its psychological determination, precisely because it had not been interpreted transcendentally. It will be recalled that Cohen saw the metaphysical a priori as a mere intermediate, provisional phase, "a pure *status evanescens*," in the words of Vuillemin,[63] between the psychological given and the transcendental a priori. If metaphysical apriority is not filled with its transcendental meaning as a condition of the possibility of knowledge, then its meaning remains that of a given, of an "in itself." Metaphysics is restored to psychology: "For Kant the transcendental means the criterion of the *a priori*; while, for Fichte, it means *selfconsciousness* in all its psychological ambiguity" (*KBE* 290).[64]

Since Fichte's philosophy had lost contact with Newton's science of nature, self-consciousness, Fichte's transcendental, was no longer a criterion, but an organ of the a priori (cf. *KBE* 291). In Cohen's view, this was why Fichte's subjectivism was a step backwards in respect of Kant, a return to Descartes's innate ideas (cf. *KBE* 55).[65] Limiting the transcendental to the metaphysical, and consequently to the psychological, is also responsible for the reduction of philosophical discourse to biography: "The ego is Fichte, and intellectual intuition is his science and his personal experience" (*KBE* 291). The biographical roots of Fichte's philosophy allow us to trace the ultimate origin of his thought, and thus of his errors; they reside in the practical interest by which the whole of Fichte's thought is conditioned (cf. *KBE* 289).

The problem of the relationship between nature and freedom and the primacy of practical reason are the most profoundly Kantian themes in Fichte's philosophy. However, they are also the origin of Fichte's departure from Kant and his deviation from critical philosophy. Fichte interpreted Kant's primacy of practical reason as recognition of freedom as a real principle establishing the laws of nature and morality:

> This is where one recognizes the true departure point of Fichte's philosophy, which allows us to avoid taking it for autobiography. The primacy of practical reason filled his head completely, occupied as it was with the problems of the historical being, almost to the extent of excluding the problems of natural knowledge. . . . Thus, just as the transcendental is not a criterion for him, in the same way neither is the *thing-in-itself* a problem, but rather an existence. Since practical reason has primacy, moral law, the thing-in-itself is the supreme requirement; t*he entire sensible world becomes its phenomenon* . . . . Thus Fichte's *theoretical idealism* originates in the idea of

the primacy of practical reason, which, therefore, intrinsically is and remains ethical idealism, since the overturning of transcendental critical philosophy originates in this primacy. (*KBE* 292–93)

Thus the distinction between being and what ought to be is eliminated and the thing-in-itself restored to philosophical discourse. The noumenon of freedom is not considered idea or task, but a real principle from which all the laws of nature and morality are to be deduced (cf. *KBE* 291). Thus the theme of the absolute and, consequently, the ontological perspective inevitably reappear in Fichte's philosophy. It was in this sense that Fichte prepared the arms of romanticism (*KBA* 364; *LRE* 416f.).

So an essential aspect of Cohen's critical idealism clearly arises from his critique of Fichte: the distinction between logic and ethics as a condition of their critical unification. Fichte had interpreted Kant's primacy of practical reason as the grounding of logic in ethics. Cohen, in opposition to Fichte, grounds ethics in logic, but not in the sense of simply overturning Fichte's position, by resolving ethics in logic. Ethics, inasmuch as it is knowledge, proceeds according to the transcendental method of purity, according to the method of idea as hypothesis. The historical and theoretical origin of this method is as a method of science, and thus as logic. If ethics rejects taking the method of hypothesis from logic, it gives up presenting itself as knowledge and loses its autonomy. But the problem of ethics goes beyond the natural being. It constitutes the limit of experience, the what ought to be to which being itself inclines to find an ultimate ground of its own validity.[66] It is just this transcendental, or rather limiting characteristic of what ought to be in respect of being that implies the impossibility of an identification of the problem of ethics with that of logic. The ethical idea is not only hypothesis, but also an infinite task which is always subsequent to the problem of logic. The unity between logic and ethics, in the philosophical system, is therefore only actual unity in the methodological sense, and, in this sense, primacy belongs to logic, not to ethics. From the point of view of content, the unity between logic and ethics is in the adaptation of being to what ought to be, as the realization of what ought to be. The ethical end is an infinite task, and it is in this sense that there is primacy of ethics over logic (cf. *BR* 36f.).

Unity of logic and ethics in method, distinction in content, the normative character of what ought to be in respect of being, and thus the unification of being and what ought to be as an infinite task are the essential characteristics of critical idealism. Where, as with Fichte, only one of them is put aside, the others are also ineffective. In this case critical philosophy becomes dogmatism and idealism becomes metaphysics.

b. Schelling

Fichte's elimination of the distinction between logic and ethics opened up the way for a return to "a general pantheistic leveling called *philosophy of identity*" (*LRE* 314) on the part of Schelling and Hegel. They considered Fichte's subjectivism partial and unsatisfactory and went beyond it by returning to the concept of the absolute as the identity of ideal and real, of knowing and being. The absolute is both the absolute object of knowledge and absolute knowledge (cf. *KTE* 754f., 762).

In Schelling the concept of the absolute as identity is developed in "aesthetically conceived pantheism,"[67] by means of the theme of the originary nature of the unconscious: for Schelling

> philosophy must again flow into poetry, which is its source. And poetry is the originary source of knowledge, since it is the originary strength of all consciousness. However it owes this originary strength to being the unconscious as regards all consciousness. All true consciousness, especially that of knowledge, is derived and mediated. Only art is originary, and therefore manifests consciousness in its fundamental form, i.e. as the unconscious. (*ARG I:* 125–26)

Cohen saw this panaestheticism as the preponderant characteristic and key to the understanding of all Schelling's philosophy: "We believe that Schelling's philosophy in general, not only his aesthetics, can only be understood by starting off from the idea that it was entirely aesthetic: that for him aesthetics is philosophy restored to its principle" (*KBA* 365).

For Schelling the subject's activity is aesthetic, and is unconscious in the production of the real objects of nature, and conscious in the production of the ideal world of art. But this conception, in Cohen's view, paradoxically, makes all aesthetic idealism impossible, since "if nature equals art, not only must the forms of nature be forms of art, which can be overlooked here, but, at the same time, the forms of art must be none other than the forms of nature. This is how the concept of the ideal comes under threat, since ideas are those forms which must be identical in nature and art" (*KBA* 366).

On this basis, however, not only aesthetic idealism, but idealism in general fails, since "ideas have now become gods" (*KBA* 367). Thus in Schelling's last works philosophy becomes mythology, and the intrinsic relationship between panaestheticism and pantheism is made manifest, which has famous precedents in the thought of Plotinus and Spinoza.[68]

c. Hegel

Hegel's philosophy of identity also arose as a consequence of the route followed by Fichte. Indeed,

> what was the point of Fichte proclaiming *moral law to be the ground of natural law?* After he had devalued theoretical reality, what good could his ethical idealism have done to its methodical roots? Ancient pantheism still appeared healthy as against such lack of respect for scientific reason. Thus the club foot introduced by this identification of idea and concept passed unnoticed. . . . So *Hegel* only brought a continuation to fulfillment when he developed the divinity of idea within the absoluteness of concept. (*LRE* 314)

Cohen identified two fundamental errors in Hegel's philosophy of identity: the elimination of the difference between concept and being, thought and reality, and the elimination of the difference between concept and idea, and thus the elimination of the difference between being and what ought to be, between reality and task, for the identity of concept with being.

Hegel saw being as nothing more than the self-transformation of concept; therefore, being is resolved in concept, while on the other hand, concept is being. This is a return to ancient ontology and logic becomes metaphysics (cf. *E* 39; *LRE* 416). Concept, *logos*, is the absolute, posited as a "pure being" at the outset of the system (cf. *KTE* 792) and identified with the totality of what is, at its end (cf. *LRE* 329). Thus, in Hegel, the metaphysics of *logos* takes the place of critical idealism: *logos*, concept, is identified with being, and ultimately with what is, while in critical idealism idea is posited as hypothesis and the task of being. Consequently, Hegel's philosophy of identity also eliminates the distance between being and what ought to be and absorbs ethics into logic, also draining idealism of this aspect of its meaning:

> We had already noted that Hegel, like Schelling, did not write any specific ethics. But even *Spinoza* only wrote an ethics including logic or metaphysics. *Thus Hegel's logic also had to include ethics.* Idea, the name of concept in its utmost fulfillment, develops as *absolute*. And this absolute means morality in its highest forms. . . . Idea is not the same as what ought to be, neither is concept the same as being. On the contrary, idea is only the development of concept. It therefore remains the focal point of being, which also includes what ought to be. Thus what is otherwise ethics becomes a product of the development of logic. *Deus sive natura.* That is

always the question. This is and remains the fundamental error of all pantheism, including that of the philosophy of identity . . . this is the naturalism of dialectical development. *Idea appears as a power of nature*, it is really a category of being. And it also appears as a power of nature to historical interest, which is at the same time speculative interest, since development, dialectical movement does not only unite the two interests, but identifies them absolutely. Therefore, it is ancient dogmatic metaphysics, only in modern historical garb, that takes the place of ethics here. (*ERW* 44–5; cf. *E* 39)

The result is a theory of historical justification that differs radically from the position of critical idealism, where idea is in a relationship with natural and historical reality, but with the critical role of a criterion of judgment and ideal:

The error in Hegel's introductory statement in his *Philosophy of Right* is not to be found in the second sentence: "That which is real is rational." This part of thought can be understood and justified in a historical-philosophical sense. . . . However, the first sentence says: "That which is rational is real." Here the error of heteronomy is obvious. In no way is existing reality the criterion and principle of moral reason. In no way does moral reason coincide with existing reality, moral law with the positive laws of the historical reality of right and the State. Here lies the enormous *difference between Hegel and Kant*. Indeed Kant would say: that which is rational is not real, but must become real. (*ERW* 331)

The difference between the authentic idealist interpretation of history and that of Hegel is especially evident in the conception of the state, which is the climax of Hegel's ethics, as it is of Cohen's, in which, however, the two conceptions are divided by the insurmountable distinguishing feature of critical idealism: "For Hegel the substance of morality lies in the State. Admittedly, he separates this concept of the State from the individual State, but it is still the factual reality of the State, to which the substance of morality is ascribed; and this reality does not mean the eternity of realization" (*ERW* 458).[69]

"Romantic" idealism, in all its forms, in Fichte's panethicism as in Schelling's panaestheticism or Hegel's panlogism, is always a revival of pantheism, because it is a metaphysics of the absolute and a philosophy of identity. "Romantic" philosophy thus abandons the critical character that alone guarantees the authenticity of classical idealism and, resolving thought, being and what ought to be in the identity of the absolute, makes philosophy as a system impossible: "Identity eliminates the system" (*LRE* 346).

5

Logic

1. FROM THE CRITIQUE OF KNOWLEDGE TO THE LOGIC OF PURE KNOWLEDGE

If one approaches the first volume of Cohen's philosophical system[1] with the aim of finding the characteristics of critical philosophy in it, the first thing that one cannot fail to notice is that, in this book, Cohen rejects his previous description of transcendental philosophy as a critique of knowledge, substituting it with a new formulation: logic of pure knowledge. This terminological change was the result of confrontation with Kant's work, thus being the first, most obvious result of that "drastic challenge . . . to the foremost features" of Kant's system, which Cohen saw more as a further investigation, rather than as a betrayal, of his Kantianism (cf. *LRE* xi f.).[2] Cohen's interpreters have underlined the fact that one cannot speak of a radical rejection of Kant's critical approach,[3] though there was a "break"[4] with his previous Kantian interpretations. Illustration of this point is my main purpose here.

As we have already seen, Cohen had identified two fundamental components of Kant's critical philosophy: the transcendental method and formal idealism.[5] In *Das Prinzip der Infinitesimal-Methode und seine Geschichte*, the second edition of *Kants Theorie der Erfahrung, Einleitung mit kritischem Nachtrag zu F.A. Langes Geschichte des Materialismus*, and other works written before *Logik der reinen Erkenntnis*, Cohen had already increasingly emphasized the transcendental meaning of critical philosophy to the detriment of formal idealism. The latter meaning is rejected

79

once and for all in *Logik der reinen Erkenntnis*, but the former is further investigated rather than rejected.

Cohen's starting point is the identification of experience with science, which can be found in previous works. From the opening pages of *Logik der reinen Erkenntnis*, he points out that the problem of the philosophy of knowledge is not knowledge in the common, generic meaning of the word, nor in the psychological sense of the cognitive process, but pure knowledge, identified with the principles of science: "We are going to start afresh. This means: we find ourselves again on the ground of the principles of the mathematical science of nature. They must again be indicated as pure knowledge and rediscovered in connection with logical reason" (*LRE* 11).

2. THE CONCEPT OF PURITY

Cohen's interpreters have often insisted on the fact that his use of the concept of 'purity' was substantially different from Kant's.[6] However, I believe it should be pointed out that, differences notwithstanding, there is continuity linking Cohen with Kant. In this way attention is drawn to the subtle dialectic between critique and investigation, originality and loyalty, which Cohen always saw as characteristic of his relationship with Kant's thought. As Holzhey rightly puts it, the meaning 'origin of' is prevalent in Cohen's concept of pure, but this cannot be separated from the meaning 'free from,' as a condition of the other. As regards the latter meaning, then, "the opposite of 'pure' is 'empirical,' which is perfectly in line with Kant."[7]

Thus, only knowledge whose origin is exclusively in thought is pure; so thought is pure, not only inasmuch as it has "no origin . . . beyond itself" (*LRE* 13), but also inasmuch as it is the origin of knowledge: "Pure thought in itself and only from itself must produce pure knowledge. Therefore, the theory of thought must become the theory of knowledge" (*LRE* 13).

The transcendental meaning of the method of purity also emerges in this way. Not only is pure knowledge not to be taken as empty of content, but the term pure content must also be used, in the sense of the content produced solely by thought in pure knowledge: "Nothing could be further from the truth than the layman's suspicion that 'pure' is empty, freed of its content. Impure content, which is not real content, is the sole opposite of 'pure'; and this is only the case in the sense of the extension of 'pure' to impure content, in order to turn it into pure content. This is the inevitable relationship of 'pure' with content. Without this 'pure' becomes senseless" (*LRE* 5).

3. LOGIC AND CRITIQUE

After clarifying the meaning of purity in Cohen, the reasons for his rejection of the Kantian term *critique* become clear. Kant had grounded knowledge in the pure principles of thought and sensibility. He had placed pure intuition next to pure thought, and, however much he tried to associate the former with the pure characteristics of thought, it remains a moment of sensibility. However, a theory of pure knowledge must ground knowledge solely in pure thought, so as to maintain loyalty to the transcendental character of principles and to show their productive aspect, to the exclusion of any previous given: "*So to thought preceding an intuition.* This is also pure, and therefore close to thought. But thought starts off in something *outside* itself. This is where the weakness in Kant's grounding lies. Here lies the reason for the early defections in his school. . . . Returning to the historical ground of critique, we will not allow a theory of sensibility to precede logic" (*LRE* 12–3).

It is not a question, then, as can be seen, of rejecting Kant's conception of critique as transcendental investigation of the pure principles of knowledge, but rather one of developing this investigation coherently, and *thus* rejecting Kant's conception of knowledge as the unification of understanding and sensibility (*LRE* 37f.). Once the *transcendental aesthetic* has been removed from Kant's *Critique*, all that is left is logic: critique is logic.[8] Thus Cohen also resolves space and time, Kant's pure intuitions, in categories of thought, mathematical thought to be precise,[9] grounding pure knowledge solely in the productive activity of thought.

In this way, Cohen's logic does not lose the critical meaning of philosophy, in the sense of thought being led "to face an examination, which no longer takes place within it" (*LRE* 403). Rather, this meaning is limited to the problem of the relationship between theory and research and is included as a specific chapter in *Logik der reinen Erkenntnis*. For Cohen "judgments of method" are "judgments of critique."[10] From this point of view, the relationship between logic and critique is overturned in respect of Kant's formulation. Logic is no longer part of critique; on the contrary, critique is part of logic, within the context, though, of transcendental philosophy, a distinguishing feature of the whole of Cohen's logic.

4. PRODUCTIVE AND REPRESENTATIVE THOUGHT

Cohen saw Kant's division in his *Critique* between transcendental aesthetic and transcendental logic as still being linked to the psychological conception of knowledge as representation. The conception of thought as representative activity, which has been widespread throughout the history of philosophy,[11] restores logic, as philosophy of knowledge, to psychology and drains thought of its purity, of its "creative strength" (*LRE* 23). Thought is only seen as a connection and association of concepts given to knowledge outside of it.

Cohen also saw Kant's concept of 'synthesis' as reflecting this same conception. By defining knowledge as the synthesis of thought and intuition and thought as the synthesis of the manifold given in sensibility, Kant did not identify the true synthetic character of pure thought. Cohen actually did not reject the synthetic character of thought, but interpreted it, not in Kant's sense of the unification of the manifold given in sensibility, but rather in a sense close to Plato's dialectic, as a process of separation and unification within the unity of thought. We shall return to this later.

It is symptomatic of the already noted special relationship of *Logik der reinen Erkenntnis* with Kant's teaching that, in order to sweep aside any psychological, representative interpretation of thought, which still held Kant in its grasp, Cohen used the Kantian term production (*Erzeugung*). Cohen did this, albeit by means of a "metaphorical expression," with the purpose of pointing out the "creative sovereignty of thought" (cf. *LRE* 28).

5. THE TRANSCENDENTAL CHARACTER OF COHEN'S LOGIC

As already noted, Cohen's transcendental formulation of his philosophy remained independent of these criticisms of Kant. Indeed, as I aim to show, it was reinforced by them.[12] Recognition of productive thought as the sole origin of knowledge and object, the fundamental theme of *Logik der reinen Erkenntnis*, can in no way be confused with the speculative construction systems of the object, belonging to romantic idealism, since, in Cohen's words, "thought is the thought of knowledge" (*LRE* 36), and knowledge is pure knowledge, identified with the principles of science; thus "*the thought of logic is the thought of science*" (*LRE* 19). The fact that thought need not presuppose a given in sensibility in no way means that logic need not presuppose the "fact" of science, so as to ground its possibility in the principles of pure knowledge. Cohen's logic is transcendental logic. The productive character of thought remains steadfastly within its reflective character, only keeping its legitimate meaning in this context.

This new, exclusively logical gnoseological formulation allowed Cohen to approach the transcendental question more radically than

Kant. Cohen had already expressed doubts over Kant's formulation of transcendental logic, which first claims to discover the categories systematically, starting from the identification of the unitary principle with the identity of thought and judgment, and then, however, justifies the validity of the categories on the basis of their transcendental meaning as principles of experience. As we have already seen,[13] the relationship between principles and experience posited by Kant was considered highly problematic by Cohen, inasmuch as the necessity of experience is grounded in principles, but only within the more general contingency of experience itself. In his writings on Kant, Cohen tried to resolve this problem by recourse to the interpretation of the thing-in-itself as idea.

In *Logik der reinen Erkenntnis*, Cohen also remarks on this discrepancy between Kant's "two points of view" (*LRE* 48) concerning the relationship between categories and judgments and that between categories and principles (*LRE* 48). Cohen's logic of origin aimed to establish the conditions for overcoming this discrepancy, not by devaluation of the transcendental value of the categories, but by revaluation of the transcendental value of judgment. This also allowed Cohen to approach the transcendental problem more radically, not simply restricting it to the question concerning the grounding of the principles, that is the transcendental grounding of the transcendental. As Jacob Gordin rightly remarks: "In the philosophical context every pure principle, every category, inasmuch as it is a specific method making knowledge possible, is taken into consideration by the transcendental method, since the following question arises with reference to every category: "in what way is it capable of grounding a possibility?." In other words . . . the justification of the transcendental method is to be found in the context of the method itself, inasmuch as it is a method of justification grounding possibility, i.e. the transcendental method is applied to the transcendental method itself."[14]

Before proceeding to a detailed treatment of the fundamental themes of Cohen's logic, which have only been mentioned so far, a look at the problem of the relationship between the transcendental and the dialectical methods, arising from this new formulation of the transcendental problem, might prove useful.

6. TRANSCENDENTAL AND DIALECTICAL METHODS

Cohen's new logical formulation of the philosophy of knowledge and radical approach to the transcendental method led him to complete it with the dialectical method. It was not a case of substituting the former method with the latter, nor of adding to it, that is having recourse to the dialectical method for presumed speculative areas the transcendental method cannot reach. It was a completion, in the sense that a coherent further investigation of the transcendental method must be able to discover and develop its dialectical essence.[15] As shown by Nicolai Hartmann, in a long essay published in 1912,[16] the dialectical method is nothing more than "the exact inverted image of the transcendental method, which is conditioned and founded by it, inasmuch as it is its presupposition."[17] The concept mediating between the two methods is that of 'hypothesis'.

The essential role of the Platonic element in Cohen's thought needs to be considered here. We have already seen that this role was to the fore in his earlier writings, to the extent of greatly influencing his last interpretation of Kant. In *Logik der reinen Erkenntnis* reference to Plato was essential for the new formulation of Cohen's philosophy. As will be recalled, Cohen had already stressed the continuity between διάνοια and νόησις the two stages of intelligible knowledge, in *Platons Ideenlehre und die Mathematik*. He saw them as two essential, complementary stages of pure thought, inasmuch as this thought consists of the search for a ground of concept in foundation itself, that is in idea as hypothesis. Here lies the anticipatory nature of Plato's dialectic as compared with Kant's transcendental method. Inasmuch as they are hypotheses, mathematical principles are also ideas in all respects, and so, straining the literal meaning of Plato's words,[18] Cohen had no doubts that they should also form part of the dialectical context. For Cohen the transcendental method is a stage of dialectic. This does not mean that the dialectical method cannot come to a halt at this point, since an a priori foundation stage of the principles themselves is still required, at which to consider, in the words of Plato, "assumptions not as absolute beginnings but literally as hypotheses, underpinnings, footings, and springboards so to speak, to enable it to rise to that which requires no assumption and is the starting point of all, and after attaining to that again taking hold of the first dependencies from it, so to proceed downward to the conclusion, making no use whatever of any object of sense but only of pure ideas moving on through ideas to ideas and ending with ideas."[19]

Plato thought he would find the first principle of the idea of good in ἀνυπόθετον, while, in *Logik der reinen Erkenntnis*, Cohen formulated the "principle of origin" (*LRE* 35), which enabled him to avoid all the ontological ambiguities linked to the concept of 'absolute' and provide an acceptable solution to the "problem of origin" (*LRE* 35), while remaining within the context of pure thought as "pure activity" (*Tätigkeit*) (*LRE* 29), as "ground" (*Grundlage*) which is resolved in "foundation" (*Grundlegung*): "*Hypothesis* is the bond: *foundation becomes ground*" (*LRE*

94; cf. *LRE* 116, 305, 428f., 528). The passage from the transcendental to the dialectical method is the response to the *critical* need for transcendental investigation of the transcendental itself. Thus, this investigation will no longer concern the relationship between principles and experience, but the interrelationship of the principles and their origin in thought. It will be a *dialectic*, which, starting out from the origin of ideas, should define the bond and division between them in continuity,[20] and end in the ideas themselves. *Logik der reinen Erkenntnis* is precisely the theory of pure thought, inasmuch as it is origin of itself and also of being, since, by means of the unity of unification and separation, it produces the object in knowledge.

Therefore, it can be concluded that, on the one hand, the very transcendental method, in its systematic needs, requires the passage to the dialectical method for the foundation of principles, while, on the other, the dialectical method is not merely an addition, but completion in respect of the transcendental method. As Hartmann points out,

> Pure dialectic would be a method for the σοφός already in possession of the knowledge of principles, but not for the φιλόσοφος who is striving for this very knowledge. Human knowledge struggles along the empirical road. And where it rises up to principles, it must seek support from the fact of completed experience and scrupulously stay in harmony with it. Therefore it must proceed transcendentally. It is only when behind it lies the route backwards to principles, that it can deduce dialectical relationships, starting off from the categories found in this way, as far as its conceptual means are sufficient for this. However, even in its utmost effort, it never reaches completeness. Rather, where the dialectical way of thinking becomes independent, the ground on which it stands soon gives way to uncontrollable speculation. Or else it accepts transcendental moments, without justifying them. Thus, the expectations of dialectical deduction become illusory. Where, on the other hand, dialectic is to become truly fruitful, it must cooperate very closely with the transcendental method. It must never allow itself to lose sight of orientation towards experience, its methodological dependency on which it cannot betray.[21]

Besides, origin, as the ground of pure thought, is not only the first judgment, previous to any other judgment, but also the principle of every judgment, which is immanent in the principles of pure knowledge, the ground of their validity:

> Origin is not only the necessary beginning of thought; it must act as the moving principle in every development. *All cases of pure knowledge must be variations of the principle of origin.* Otherwise, they would have no independent or pure value. The logic of origin, therefore, must be entirely realized as such. *The principle of origin must predominate in all cases of pure*

knowledge which are validated as principles. Thus, the logic of origin becomes logic of pure knowledge. (*LRE* 36)

7. THE LOGIC OF JUDGMENT

The true "place of source" (*Quellgebiet*) (*LRE* 585) in Cohen's logic of knowledge is judgment, not categories. The identification of thinking with judging, as the founding principle of logic, which had been announced by Kant but never adequately applied, was taken up by Cohen and given its true importance. It is, naturally, not a question of judgment in the meaning given to it in the psychological conception of representative knowledge, as unification of a given manifold. In *Logik der reinen Erkenntnis,* judgment means the unitary activity of thought, which produces the object. Cohen freed himself from the psychological distinction between form and matter (*Materie, Stoff*) of knowledge, and considered the object solely from the logical viewpoint, as content (*Inhalt*) of thought, and thus as a unity. This does not exclude, of course, the manifoldness of the content of knowledge. What is rejected is "given manifoldness," the conception of thought as an activity that must unify a manifold given from outside. Manifoldness, therefore, must also be produced by thought and in thought, and must partake of the unity of the latter (cf. *LRE* 60).

As we have seen, the logic of judgment is not only grounded in the principle that "grounds are *foundations*" (*LRE* 528), but also in the equally important principle that "*production itself is the product.*"[22] The object of knowledge, then, is nothing more than "content"; therefore, productive thought "does not depart from itself" (*LRE* 29). It does not produce a thing, an object that is independent of itself, but content which *is* thought: "*activity itself is content*" (*LRE* 60; cf. *LRE* 29).[23] Judgment is the productive process of thought inasmuch as it unifies a manifold which is not given from outside, but itself produced by judgment as unity.[24] Cohen also saw judgment as synthesis, though "*synthesis of unity*" (*LRE* 26), in his own sense: that is, synthesis must not be interpreted as composition (*Zusammensetzung*) (*LRE* 26) of a given manifold, but as unity of separation (*Sonderung*) and unification (*Vereinigung*) in judgment: "The synthesis of unity is just as much separation as unification" (*LRE* 61).

Judgment is, thus, presented as a dialectical process, that is, as "correlation" (*LRE* 60) of separation and unification. What did Cohen mean by correlation? This concept is fundamental for his whole philosophy, being the essential distinguishing feature between his critical philosophy and the philosophy of identity. In the present context, this term is used to avoid any distortion of the relationship between separation and unification in the sense of identity. Cohen argued that, in its most developed, Hegelian form, the latter restricts dialectic to a "reversal of opposites," eliminating the distinction between them. Cohen suggested that the relationship between separation and unification be understood as correlation, to be interpreted as "conservation" (*Erhaltung*), so as to avoid its being interpreted as an "arbitrary exchange," as continuous reciprocal happening, an interpretation in which "psychological interest" in logic is still present (cf. *LRE* 61):[25] "*There is no exchange, but conservation, at the same time, of separation and unification.* Unification is conserved in separation and separation in unification. . . . Therefore, it is to be expected *that unity be conserved in manifoldness and manifoldness in unity*" (*LRE* 62).

This concept of correlation between separation and unification as conservation even more clearly highlights the meaning of judgment as unity, that is, the ultimate meaning of judgment as task. In the ordinary sense, unity, as the conservation of unity and manifoldness, is simply a contradiction. This is because the product of thought is seen as present and completed, and its productive activity as past. If, however, one takes up the principle that production itself is the product, and that the activity itself is content, then the perspective shifts in the direction of the future. Unity as conservation becomes the no longer contradictory logical direction of judgment, where the dialectical activity of thought tales place:

> That is, in the direction of separation, we think of the *act*, which is fulfilled, and inasmuch as it is fulfilled. The same is true of unification. And, concerning content, the act is, therefore, considered to have reached fulfillment. Correspondingly, we think of the respective contents as concluded. Both activities, just like their contents, must not settle in a present, but incline towards the future, in relation to the future, starting from the present. Unification must not be thought as an event, whose fulfillment has been reached, but as a *task* and the ideal of a task, in the way that only logic can posit such a task, and formulate such an ideal. The task that is posited to thought in judgment can never be considered to have come to rest, to have been fulfilled. (*LRE* 64)

Thus, unity is conceived of as the fundamental horizon of judgment, and, therefore, distinct from unification, which is one of the two directions in which it takes place. Unity is, first of all, unity of judgment, that is, unity of thought (cf. *LRE* 66). Unity of thought founds *the unity of knowledge* and, in it, *the unity of the object* (*LRE* 67): "*the unity of judgment is the production of the unity of the object in the unity of knowledge*" (*LRE* 68).

Finally, it should be noted how this primacy of judgment over categories, this concept of Cohen's of pure knowledge as a system of judgments, is capable of overcoming many difficulties brought up against Kant's table of categories. First of all, the relationship between judgments and categories is no more inflexible than in Kant, since several categories can refer to the same judgment, and the same category can relate to different judgments (cf. *LRE* 50ff.). Second, the problem of adapting the table of categories to ever-changing scientific developments is overcome in this formulation of logic, where judgment is the unity and task of thought, while the table of categories and principles remains open and is free to evolve in accordance with the historical development of science, without, because of this, losing its fundamental link with the permanence of judgments (cf. *LRE* 585). Of course, it could be objected that, in this way, only the difficulties are shifted from categories to judgments. However, Cohen's answer to this objection is that, first, judgment is more ample than category, and, second, that his investigation is transcendental, for which the judgments formulated in his system are the guiding lines of the development of past and present science, in respect of which no future development will ever be able to present itself as a radical denial (cf. *LRE* 585ff.).

8. FROM ORIGIN TO CONCEPT

As has been seen, Cohen was not satisfied with *production* as the appropriate term for the pure activity of thought in knowledge, it only being useful as a "metaphorical expression." In the words of Holzhey: "The expression "produce" could still refer to a process of consciousness, whose product would then be seen as 'something placed outside' the production process, as a fulfilled product."[26] Certainly, this misinterpretation of thought as production is overcome by the principle that "production itself is the product," but it is still a question of adapting terminology to the correct meaning of pure thought (and in philosophical, just as in scientific thought, the use of precise terminology is not just a formal matter, but directly affects the formulation, and, consequently, the solution of a problem). Cohen chose the term origin (*Ursprung*):

> Therefore, if knowledge is the same as principle, it is conditioned by origin. And if thought is the thought of knowledge, then its beginning and ground are in the thought of origin. As long as producing has not been conceived as producing by origin, thought will not have been able to achieve clear methodical determination, even by means of producing, still being in metaphorical guise. Now the metaphorical expression can be put

aside once and for all. *Thinking is thought of origin.* Nothing can be given to origin. Principle is precisely and literally foundation. Ground must become origin. Accepting that thought must discover being in origin, then this being cannot have any other kind of ground than that which thought is able to give it. Pure thought only becomes true as thought of origin. (*LRE* 36)

Thus the first principle of pure knowledge is in origin and its termination in the concept of object (cf. *LRE* 397). It is not that Cohen's logic terminates with the judgment of concept (cf. *LRE* 310ff.), since it is followed by his treatment of the judgments of method (cf. *LRE* 404ff.). However, "*a certain conclusion*" (*LRE* 398) is reached with the judgment of concept, since, in it, the object as the unitary content of thought, to which pure knowledge inclines, is produced. Judgments of method are judgments of critique, that is, they do not have the function of grounds of the object in pure knowledge, but that of a check (*LRE* 403) on the results of pure knowledge in the face of the requirements of research.

Plato's influence is clearly to be seen emerging with this formulation. As will be recalled, Cohen saw the foundation of the Socratic concept in the Platonic Idea, the "giving account of the concept." Thus concept is the result of the dialectical process taking place in idea:

> The Socratic concept only asks, and the correctly understood meaning of concept goes no further. On the other hand, *idea is the self-consciousness of concept.* It is the logos of concept, since it gives *account* of concept. In connection with the verb "to give" logos actually means "account" (λόγον διδόναι). This juridical meaning now becomes the most profound foundation of logic. *Idea is the giving account of concept.* In the grounds or principles of pure knowledge reason posits its giving account in the mathematical science of nature. (*LRE* 15–6)

In Cohen's view it is this meaning of the centrality of idea that characterizes critical idealism (cf. *LRE* 6). It is in the area of idea to concept that Cohen's logic is operative.[27]

The unity of the object is the result on which all judgments, or "methods" (*LRE* 325) of mathematical science and the descriptive science of nature converge. The concept of the object is, therefore, a system, and as such is situated at the end of the process of pure knowledge.[28] However, this does not mean that the process reaches completion in concept; concept as a system is always open and in motion. This is the profound meaning of the Socratic concept, which, in Cohen's interpretation, does not consist of the answer to the question What is it? but of the question itself: concept is essentially a question, and thus a task:

This is the profound, eternal meaning, in which Socrates defined his concept as the question: What is it? (τί ἐστι). Concept is a question and remains one, nothing but a question. The answer it incorporates must be a new question, must provoke a new question. This is the intimate methodical relationship between question and answer: that every question must itself be an answer. Therefore, every answer can and must be a question. What is realized in the system of concept is a new kind of reciprocal conditioning or action: reciprocal action between question and answer. No solution can be definitive. Concept is not an absolute totality. (*LRE* 378)

Thus concept, as the unitary result of the various judgments of pure knowledge, has its foundation in them. However, this cannot be the end of the search for ground, since the judgments of pure knowledge, the very principles that make the object possible, require further foundation: pure thought, which founds concept, by the very transcendental founding principle, that is, that of origin, must also be able to found itself. Thought as thought of origin is able to carry out this foundation. Therefore, origin is not only a method, but also the principle of its foundation. In the words of Holzhey:

Cohen points out the unconditional validity of the originary knowledge of the logic of principles, steadfast in its self-foundation, by means of the formula, according to which the question "What is it?" incorporates its answer. Thought functions as *concept* in the question "What is it?" "What is 'what is it'?" or 'what is thought?' in this question can be expected to be accounted for. The answer, or giving account of concept is the (Platonic) Idea: "what it is" as foundation (hypothesis) or originary activity. Idea is the conceived concept, conceived as originary judgment. The interpreters of Cohen's logic of origin nearly always begin with the presupposition that giving account of concept removes the justification from any previous answer (from a "problematic concept"). They do not begin with the question as such. But the principle of origin does not consist in the method of methodical prescription of posing the question beyond any presupposition, thus legitimizing, for example, the initial concepts of a science, but in the foundation of this methodical-transcendental procedure.[29]

9. ORIGIN

Origin is the "moving principle" (*LRE* 36) on which Cohen constructed his logic of pure knowledge, which is thus logic of origin. Origin is the fundamental thought, in which Cohen's logical theory is grounded and develops: "I worked for decades on this logic, but I only decided to publish it when this fundamental thought had become powerfully determined and clear, and this can be seen in the motto that must be the touchstone for any systematic construction: δός μοι ποῦ στῶ" (*LRE* xi).

Cohen also saw origin as the distinguishing feature of the new logic in respect of that of romanticism, that is the logic of being: "In opposition to the direction followed by romantic philosophy, we support the logic of origin and the system of origin built up on it as the methodical continuation of the critical system" (*KTE* 797).

Origin is the "most fundamental foundation" of modern science, and therefore of true idealism, which is "scientific idealism" (cf. *LRE* 597).

The debate on the interpretation of this concept of Cohen is still open, both because it is the essential nucleus of his logic, and therefore of his entire system, and because his treatment of this point is not always characterized by precise terminology and exposition. I shall now attempt to present the meaning of origin in Cohen's logic briefly, analyzing it as a problem, a principle, and judgment.

a. Origin as a Problem

From its very beginnings (in the enquiries of Thales and Anaximander), philosophy has posited the problem of origin or ἀρχή. This problem was present as early as mythology, as is shown by the idea of chaos in Greek myths and the biblical myth of Creation. However, the true potential of the problem emerged when it entered science and the philosophy of science. Ancient science, particularly Democritus' atomism, and modern science, especially Leibniz's infinitesimal method, by positing infinity as the ground and principle of the finite, restored being to its origin in thought, by means of the methodical principle of infinity. Cohen returned to the results of his previous research on the infinitesimal and those of his interpretation of Leibniz, making them the nucleus of his new logical discourse. Thus, the results of Cohen's previous research on the tradition of critical idealism appeared, for the first time in a unitary, mature synthesis, in *Logik der reinen Erkenntnis*. Plato, Leibniz, and Kant were the sources of Cohen's new logical thought.

Cohen's reference to the history of philosophy and science as an introduction to the problem of origin was not merely conventional, but an essential stage in the transcendental method. The logic of pure knowledge, inasmuch as it is logic of science, cannot invent its problems. It must start from the fact of science, which can only be observed historically. The problem of origin is central to logic, since it is the fundamental problem of modern science (though having some precedents in ancient science).[30] For this reason, all logic not taking the problem of origin as its outset is not valid as logic of pure knowledge. Logic of pure knowledge is logic of origin. Thus Cohen was led by these historical observations to a highly critical judgment in respect of previous logical theories, including Kant's, and to awareness of having given "new ground" to logic (cf. *LRE* 37). Logic must be that of the mathematical science of nature:

> But has logic become generally aware of this new task? A decision on the question must take account of the principle of infinity. Has the *principle of the infinitesimal method* occupied its legitimate central position in logic? If the answer to this question is negative, then the answer to the previous one must also be negative. If this were the case, it would be established that logic is not fulfilling its true task, that over the last two hundred years it has never come to terms with the real problem presented to it by modern science. (*LRE* 34)

In Cohen's view, then, the principle of the infinitesimal method had not taken up its rightful, central position in logic. It had not become the "critical lever" (cf. *LRE* 35) even for Kant, though he had recognized its importance for the foundation of reality. For this reason, thought did not free itself entirely from sensibility in Kant:

> For logic this is the problem, this the question dealt with in the infinitesimal: integral preservation, unlimited, creative independence of pure thought. Therefore, the meaning of the new calculus for logic is not restricted to the fact that the triumph of pure thought is to be demonstrated on this typical example of infinitesimal calculus. The precise question and decisive answer for an indispensable, irreplaceable meaning of thought as production must be obtained from analysis of infinity. *It is the problem of origin* that set up the new calculus, at the same time, clarifying and specifying thought as production. (*LRE* 35)

b. Origin as a Principle

The solution to the problem of origin is incorporated in the principle of origin. We can identify two complementary meanings of origin as a principle: 1) the principle of origin as the supreme principle of pure knowledge, for which every content originates and is grounded in thought, and 2) origin as a principle, that is, pure thought as thought of origin (*LRE* 36), as the unconditional ground, not only of knowledge and being, but also of itself.

First, here are two of the most interesting formulations of the principle of origin: "*Only thought itself can produce what can count as being*" (*LRE* 81); "Therefore, this must become the *first* purpose of thought: *to situate* the origin of every content that it is able to produce *in thought itself* (*LRE* 82). It is in this principle that Cohen recognized his "Eleaticism" (*LRE* 588), in accordance with his interpretation of Parmenides' principle of the identity of being and thought, that is, as the grounding of being in thought. This principle dominates all the logic of knowledge, determining its direction at all levels. Knowledge must always restore its content to its grounding in productive thought, both in judgments as laws-of-thought, and in those of mathematics, the mathematical science of nature, and also in those of method. In this sense the principle of origin is not only realized in the judgment of origin, but also in those of reality, substance, and possibility, and in all the other judgments of pure knowledge. In Cohen's transcendental perspective, "the category of origin goes back to judgment, thus becoming the law-of-thought. However, its full strength is to be seen in the judgment of reality, where it is manifest as infinitesimal reality" (*LRE* 596). The a priori character of a formal principle cannot be separated from its transcendental meaning (cf. *LRE* 596). Therefore, the "formalism of origin showed its concreteness in the judgment of *reality*. Origin carried out its activity as infinitesimal origin and, as such, gave fulfillment to the new mathematics as mathematics of the mathematical science of nature" (*LRE* 587). If transcendental inquiry is necessarily an abstraction of the a priori formal principle from the context of its function in scientific knowledge, it is unable and does not desire to separate logical form from its incarnation (cf. *ERW* 65) in science, where this form exclusively acquires its full, concrete meaning.

Second, origin is also a principle in the strict sense of an unconditional condition of knowledge and being. If the method of purity requires that nothing be given to thought, that is, that thought itself, inasmuch as it is production, is able to found its content, the question about the foundation of thought itself is, however, still possible. In other words, if thought is the origin of being, what is the origin of thought? There was no answer to this question in the definition of thought as production, which, thus, can only be taken up as a metaphorical expression that is not decisive for identification of pure thought. The problem of the origin of thought can only be resolved if pure thought is seen as thought of origin. The principle, according to which ground is resolved in foundation, can only be fully clarified if foundation is defined as origin. As Holzhey explains:

> The question "What is thought?" is an expression of the reflection of thought, where "thought itself . . . is the purpose and object of its activity." "Thought is thought of origin," is the answer to the question, or the result of reflection. In this way thought counts as a *principle* (in the strict sense). When thought as "thought of origin," "thought" satisfies the requirements

addressed to the "principle"; it is determined in itself as unconditional ground. Its self-determination by means of a self-relationship is, therefore, not empty (or infinite in the bad sense), since it is determined as origin (of . . .). What is established in this way of thought also counts for thought asking the question about thought, for reflecting thought, which is also activity of origin. This is how Cohen's already quoted formula is to be interpreted, that thought of knowledge has its "outset and ground," therefore its origin, in the thought of origin . . . thought is "thought of origin" *as origin of origin* (i.e. origin of thought *as* origin). . . . The principle of origin can be applied to itself. It shows that it is "first," inasmuch as, as "foundation in the literal sense," it gives account of itself by virtue of being giving account."[31]

c. Origin as Judgment

If the principle of origin, as a "superior concept" (*ARG I:* 240) of all pure knowledge, founds the latter at every stage of its development, and, indeed, only acquires its "effectuality" (*LRE* 587) in the judgment of reality, it is first applied in the judgment of origin, which, as the first of the judgments of quality (*LRE* 118)[32] or judgments of the laws-of-thought (*LRE* 79), is the methodical outset (*KTE* 790) of the logic of pure knowledge, and the *actual origin* (*LRE* 104) of judgment, that is, of pure thought as thought of knowledge:

> Infinity is the fundamental logical instrument. It is in this judgment, before all others, that pure thought is posited in opposition to every representation, and, correspondingly, from the viewpoint of content, to everything *finite*. Everything depends on this opposition for the correct outset of pure knowledge. The finite in its multiformity is the general problem. However, the solution to this problem can only begin with the position of infinity, as origin of all pure thought and, correspondingly, of everything finite. If ever logical activity is to have and determine a methodical outset, then it must be defined in origin. *Methodical outset is origin.* Infinite judgment is the judgment of origin. (*KTE* 790)

Since pure thought is productive, not representative, its task is not only that of justifying the being of its content, but primarily that of founding the possibility of content in general. To make the determination of content in the judgments of mathematics and the mathematical science of nature possible, that is, in other words, to make these very judgments of pure knowledge possible—pure thought needs to found, by itself, the determinability of content, or content as a determinable. If, that is, we posit A as the initial content of thought, thought itself must give account of this A: "If A counts as a sign of the simplest content, then, first of all, one must ask: *whence this A?* One cannot begin to act with this A and only subsequently attempt to confirm its validity. Such a posteriori efforts cannot lead to any decisive result, but can be seen as suspect symptoms of the fact that at the outset legitimate progress was impossible. As soon as A appears, the legitimacy of its origin must be investigated" (*LRE* 82).

The Socratic concept, expressed in the question What is it?, does not only require foundation of the determination of the content of 'is,' but, first of all, the foundation of the determinability of a content, that is of 'what.' Therefore, the first degree of pure thought consists of the production of something as content, whose determinations of being can then be supplied by the judgments of mathematics and the mathematical science of nature, by objectifying it in concept. "Nothing can count as given for pure thought. It must also produce the given by itself. Even the 'what,' inasmuch as it is 'something,' cannot be the last word of conceptual language" (*ERW* 101). Thus, the content of the judgment of origin is not yet a determined *A* content, but simply an *x*, which does not only mean indeterminacy, but also the determinability of content. Therefore, the first judgment of logic is the question itself on being, which is not only, negatively, indicative of lack of content, but also of the inclination toward it, its determinability:

> "*What is it?* (τί ἐστι), asked Socrates, and in this question formulated concept. *What was being?* (τὸ τί ἦν εἶναι) asked *Aristotle*, making this question the crux of his metaphysical terminology. Thus the logical meaning of a *question*, inasmuch as it is the lever of origin, is shown in these famous examples. The lesser of a sentence the question is, the more important is its meaning as a type of judgment. It is the outset of knowledge. The corresponding affect is wonder. It is with wonder that Plato had philosophy begin. Thus, *question is the ground of judgment*, one could say, the fundamental foundation stone. (*LRE* 83-4)

The origin of 'something' cannot be posited in another something. It must, therefore, be found in a nonsomething, in a 'nothing' (*Nichts*). Here the idealist theme of the grounding of being in nonbeing, which Cohen had already highlighted in the thought of Democritus, Plato, and Leibniz, reappears. It is not a question of positing a 'nonthing' (*Unding*) (*LRE* 84) as the ground of being, but only one of showing a way, a method (the reason why Cohen uses the term judgment of origin), by means of which pure thought produces the deteminable itself, before its determinations:[33] therefore, not of *ex nihilo*, but *ab nihilo* production. The route to be followed for the production of this something is an indirect one (*Umweg*) (*LRE* 84), that crosses the nothing, in accordance with the principle of origin, for which being is grounded in nonbeing, in thought. This is the sense of the particle μή, which is different from οὐ and ἀ in Greek, especially in Democritus and Plato (cf. *LRE* 85ff.), from the Latin prefix *in-*, and the German one *un-*: not so much an absolute negation (*Nicht*), as a nothing (*Nichts*) (*LRE* 93; cf. *LRE* 104f.), which constitutes the true passage (*Übergang*) (*LRE* 91) to the something.

Therefore, judgment of origin is infinite or limitative. The importance of this judgment, often misinterpreted in philosophy,[34] was understood both by ancient (Democritus) and, especially, by modern (Leibniz) science, which has extensively built upon the principle of infinity as the origin of the finite.[35] The main reason for the misinterpretation of infinite judgment and for its fall from favor lies precisely in confusion between absolute and relative negation: the latter is only an "apparent nothing" (*LRE* 119), an "originary something" (*Ursprung-Etwas*) (*LRE* 105), a "stopping place" (*LRE* 84) on the road of something. One turns to infinite judgment "where it is a question of *leading the origin of the concept that constitutes the problem to a definition*, by way of infinite content. Thus, so called *nothing*, which, in fact, should not be seen as such, becomes the *operational instrument* for conducting the something in question into its origin, *every time*, only really producing and determining it in this way" (*LRE* 89).

The opponents of infinite judgment did not realize that it does not mean merely a negation, but, on the contrary, the indication of the direction of the problem, the origin of the determinability of content. On this point Cohen quotes Ockham: " '*Differentia est inter praedicatum infinitum et inter praedicatum privativum. Injustum non potest dici de quolibet, quod non est justum, quia non dicitur de asino, sed tantum de hominibus.*' Thus quodlibet is excluded, and attention to the conceptual problem involved, which constitutes the present requirement, presupposed" (*LRE* 90).

If this nothing is an operational instrument for the production of the something, a law of operations is also needed (*LRE* 91), and Cohen identified it with the law of continuity. Cohen argued that thinkers had discovered, if not formulated, this law long before Leibniz, even though the latter claimed to be its originator. Parmenides had already written of the συνέχεια of being (cf. *LRE* 90f.). Leibniz had then formulated this principle as the law of operations and applied it to various scientific contexts.[36] The law of continuity is "the law-of-thought of knowledge" (*LRE* 93), "protection against the given" (*LRE* 91), since:

> as a law-of-thought, continuity becomes, first of all, *independent of sensation*, for which only discretion exists, or only the *unity* of a bunch. Thought pro-

duces the unity and *connection of unities.* Thus thought, inasmuch as it is thought of unity, is *conditioned by connection.* And since thought is production of origin, origin is conditioned by connection. . . . If concept in general means the question: *What is it?*, and thus the *grounding of being in thought*, judgment, which produces concept, will be the question: *What is not?* But the "not" must correspond to μή. Thus the indirect route is justified as the direct route. And it is here that the profound strength of *connection* is demonstrated: that continuity crosses this nothing. It shows the way by saying: *there is a connection between the elements if they are thought and required only as elements to be produced and not as data.* Therefore, continuity is the law-of-thought of the connection that makes the production of the unity of *knowledge*, and through it the unity of the *object*, possible, leading it to continuous realization. (*LRE* 91–2)

Therefore, the law of continuity guarantees critical idealism, against both empiricism and speculative idealism, in which one would be trapped if the nothing from which being as an absolute, and not as a relative, that is, as a "launching pad from which the jump must be made thanks to continuity" (*LRE* 93) originates. It is on the basis of the law of continuity that relative nothing (*Nichts*) is wholly attached, without secondary meanings, to its entity (*Ichts*) (*LRE* 93).[37] Thanks to this law-of-thought, then, "*all the elements of thought, inasmuch they can count as elements of knowledge, are produced by drawing them from origin*" (*LRE* 92).

10. TRUTH

Among the many definitions provided by Cohen and others of the logic of pure knowledge, pride of place could legitimately be occupied by its definition as the *logic of truth.* The critical need to define pure knowledge as true knowledge and ground this truth in pure thought is an overwhelming constant. Truth does not appear in *Logik der reinen Erkenntnis* as one among many problems of logic, but as the complex, overall dimension, with reference to which logic takes place.[38] I shall now briefly deal with the most important aspects of truth highlighted by Cohen in *Logik der reinen Erkenntnis.*

In the first place, pure logic is the logic of truth, in Kant's terms, inasmuch as it is transcendental logic. However, Cohen, in contrast with Kant, does not confront transcendental logic, as the logic of truth, with formal logic. On the contrary, he entrusts the role of ground and guarantee of the truth-value of pure knowledge to the traditional principles of formal logic—identity, contradiction, and excluded middle—before which he places the new principle of origin. Therefore it is the the meaning of formal logic itself that is modified here. Cohen rejects the confrontation between formal and transcendental logic. He even denies that formal logic exists (cf. *LRE* 503). Formal logic is a "ghost" (*LRE* 13), generated by arbitrary separation of form and its content (cf. *LRE* 14). Kant's distinction between general and transcendental logic, on the basis of reference to a content given in intuition, evidently found no place in Cohen's new formulation, where pure thought produces its content; In Cohen's view, formal logic, which has the forms of thought as its object, can only refer to the content produced by and in them. Therefore, it is also transcendental logic, inasmuch as it is logic of knowledge.

Nevertheless, Cohen does preserve a distinction between the judgments of so-called formal logic and those of science and the critique of knowledge; a distinction between the laws-of-thought and the categories. The former are a presupposition for the latter, since determination of content is the task of science and its logical principles, while justification of the very possibility of a content of true knowledge is the task of the fundamental laws of thought. This prevents logic from being restricted to a simple scientific methodology and protects Cohen's logic from being accused of positivism.[39] This preliminary character of the laws-of-thought in respect of science determines another "*characteristic of formal logic*" (*LRE* 76), that is, its general nature, which is the source of its validity, not only for the science of nature, but also for the whole of pure knowledge, and thus, also for the moral sciences. Therefore, Cohen did not think that different logical principles needed to be formulated for nature and history, the two contexts of knowledge. At the same time, however, he did not positivistically restrict the principles of knowledge of history to those of knowledge of nature. In fact, he restored both to the principles of pure thought, that is, to philosophical fundamental logic. In this sense, it can be said that there is no primacy of the science of nature in Cohen, but one of logic, and therefore of philosophy, even though the science of nature constitutes the historical, theoretical model, starting from which philosophy elaborated its principles.

Second, the principle of origin is the ground of the logic of truth in Cohen's view. Cohen's already quoted statement should be recalled here: "Pure thought only becomes true as thought of origin" (*LRE* 36). In his logic Cohen reintroduced the re-elaborated principle of idealism itself, which he had already identified in his interpretation of Democritus and Plato: idea is the true being or the truth of being (cf. *LRE* 85f.). The principle of origin, in accordance with which being is grounded in thought, is the essential rule of true knowledge: no knowledge can be said to be true if it is unable to justify being by means of its origin in thought.

Third, truth is not only foundation, but also a statement. Cohen did not interpret statement in the sense of a sentence judgment, as a link between two contents (following Aristotle's scheme *S* is *P*). This conception belongs to representative thought, and implies that contents to be affirmatively linked are already given. Affirmative judgment precedes any manifoldness of contents. It is a judgment of the laws of thought, which must found the possibility of content as such. It is therefore a presupposition and condition of all subsequent judgments, which determine the relationships between contents: "It is not a question of linking here, but rather one of separating. And, as a consequence, a statement does not merely mean establishing, but, at the same time, *keeping stable*. A cannot disappear, even though, and because, agreements with other elements must be produced and made possible" (*LRE* 100).

A statement is to be understood as "*assurance (Affirmatio)*" (*LRE* 96) of the identity of content with itself: "Affirmative judgment only has to occupy itself with the *assurance* of A" (*LRE* 97). However affirmation of the identity of the content of judgment is, at the same time, "*affirmative judgment*" (*LRE* 97), since there is no true knowledge, if the judgments of knowledge do not posit stable, permanent contents. Therefore, the principle of identity is rightly placed next to that of origin, as a condition of the judgment itself, since, if the judgment of origin constitutes the origin of judgment (cf. *LRE* 104), inasmuch as it justifies the possibility of content, the judgment of identity "makes the judgment judgment" (*LRE* 95), inasmuch as it confers the stability that differentiates the judgment of knowledge from mere representation on the content of judgment.

Thus Cohen interprets identity as a principle of thought before it is one of being. With reference to Parmenides's statement of the identity of thought and being, he notes: "Making thought identical with being, he [Parmenides] especially characterized it by means of identity. It could not be identified with being, if this identity were not inherent in it. *The self of being is a reflection of the identity of thought.* This alone is able to offer its identity to being" (*LRE* 94).

The Platonic theory of ideas also posits the identity or unity of Idea in respect of the manifoldness and instability of representations:

In the *Platonic Idea* unity accompanies identity. There can only be one Idea, whatever problem it refers to. The problem indicated by the particle τις joined to the unity (μία τις) concerns this relationship. How many times it can be thought concerns the process of consciousness, in which this thought must take place. Its value, its content is not affected. A is A, and remains A, however many times it is thought, *or rather, however many times it is represented.* It is only thought as the *sole* identity. Its repetitions are psychic processes, its logical content persisting in identity. (*LRE* 95–6)

If the principle of continuity is the sure defense of pure thought from pressure of perception, the principle of identity "*separates . . . judgment from representation*" (*LRE* 95). Pure knowledge is true knowledge inasmuch as "*conservation* as stability in permanence" (*LRE* 94) of its contents is guaranteed: "Without the assurance of the permanence of pure thought there would be no guarantee for true being" (*LRE* 94).

Nevertheless, the principle of identity, as the "*law-of-thought of truth*" (*LRE* 115), cannot be separated from the principle of contradiction, as the "*law-of-thought of falsehood (Unwahrheit)*" (*LRE* 115). This is also not a case of a negative link between two contents, but one of the negation of the content itself. Negative judgment is the answer to the permanent possibility that the stability of stated content is threatened by a content that is not identical to the first. It is not a question of a *B* content and its possible relationship with *A*, but of an *A* content that is not identical with A: of a non-*A*, which is negated as content:

> The most important of the rights of judgment is that of rejecting and annihilating false judgment. It is in this annulment, or better annihilation, that the authentic, true "nothing" of "not" consists. . . . Being able to posit the *requirement of annihilation* in itself is the vital question of judgment. The "not" expressed by this requirement, is completely different from that "nothing," which is the source of something. It is the activity of judgment, it is judgment itself, that does not acknowledge this right and value in a content that insists on becoming content of judgment. The presumed *non-A* is decidedly not already a content. Rather it only claims to be one. Negation, however, denies it this value. *There is no non-A*, and there cannot be a non-A, which, in contrast with the nothing of origin, has a fulfilled content. All the doubts that non-A may, however, take on meanings that may be suited to the justification of its content, must come to an abrupt halt, since, in this way, doubt is cast on identity. No care or caution can be shown before this is definitely no longer a topic of discussion. *Assurance of identity against the danger of non-A is the sense of negation.* (*LRE* 106–7)[40]

Thus identity and contradiction, affirmation and negation, are two complementary acts of pure thought, which, together with origin, produce the content of thought in its permanence, that is, in its truth: "Identity is good (*das Gut*), it is value. Contradiction is protection, it is right" (*LRE* 108).

If the principle of origin founds a critical concept of 'truth,' inasmuch as it characterizes true knowledge as foundation, the principles of identity and contradiction develop another essential characteristic of the critical meaning of truth: truth as unity and stability and the exclusion of falsehood. A critical concept of truth, to qualify as such, must consider the real possibility, not only of error, but also of falsehood, and contain a criterion for recognizing and excluding it. Here also Cohen follows Plato's teaching (particularly in the *Sophist*), on which he had reflected previously.[41] Truth is under constant threat, not only from error as imperfection and deficiency, but also from falsehood, which is the negation of truth, nontruth in the guise of truth, with which critical thought can come to no agreement or be conciliatory, but must opt for rejection and annihilation (cf. *LRE* 115).[42]

Fourth, the first part of Cohen's *Logik der reinen Erkenntnis*, which deals with the laws-of-thought, only considers the judgments of origin, identity, and contradiction. However, other laws-of-thought are dealt with in the work as a whole.[43] In particular, the principle of the excluded middle, the third fundamental principle of traditional formal logic, appears as a law-of-thought in the judgment of concept, and the third aspect of truth is grounded in it. The truth of knowledge cannot be solely grounded in the truth of thought. It must also face the truth of the object produced in it. But truth as a relationship between knowledge and object, for pure knowledge, obviously cannot consist of adjustment to a given object: it is knowledge itself that must ground the truth of the object in itself.[44] As we have already seen, Cohen saw the object as the determined content of concept as a system. Therefore, it is in the system that the truth of knowldge as knowledge of the object must be guaranteed. For Cohen, disjunctive judgment is the place of concept as a system (cf. *LRE* 382ff.).[45] Its meaning is not only excluding, but also including, since, in the formula A is either B or non-B, the possible exclusion of a systematic relationship between A and B implies the statement of a systematic relationship between A and non-B (C or D or . . .). The principle guaranteeing this validity of the system is precisely that of the excluded middle.

Cohen would not restrict the meaning of the principle of the excluded middle to a simple pleonastic variation of the principle of contradiction. What is excluded is not a middle between two contradictory elements, as some traditional formulations would have it.[46] The third that is excluded is rather the possibility that concept as a system is an illusion (cf. *LRE* 394).[47] Therefore, the principle of the excluded middle is the "*law-of-thought of the system*" (*LRE* 395), and thus it is "*the law-of-thought of truth with reference to the meaning of the content of the concepts* which link up in it" (*LRE* 395), in contrast with the principle of identity, which is also, as we have seen, the law-of-thought of truth, but only with reference to the content of pure thought, which has not yet been enriched with the determinations of concept. Therefore, the critical meaning of the truth of knowledge reaches fulfillment, and the latter is guaranteed against skepticism:

Thus we can take this up as the *sense of the excluded middle*, we had predicted: that skepticism be excluded, according to which concept is only supposed to be a universal; according to which, wishing to ground the object in all its meanings in concept, and only acknowledge the ground of the object in this foundation is an illusion; according to which admitting the climax of the presuppositions of pure thought, the conclusion of pure knowledge, into concept is an illusion. Since the law now excludes this middle, i.e. the illusion, or rather skepticism of the illusion, it does include something else, i.e. the *system* in all its meanings. Just as it is true that concept is the system, it is also true that the system is concept. The system of concepts is the system of pure knowledge. And thus it becomes the *supreme* meaning of the system, which now emerges. *Concepts, pure presuppositions and pure knowledge constitute a system.* No system, like no concept, is fulfilled. New tasks arise from new solutions; but the new tasks must also grow within the previous solutions. This is a requirement of the system. (*LRE* 395)

The last lines of the passage quoted above underline the open nature of the system, and thus the meaning of truth as a task, opposed both to dogmatic, concluded, static truth, and to its skeptical rejection.

It is with this meaning of truth as a system that Cohen's logic concludes its analysis of critical truth: it is a logic of truth, in the real sense, since it places the grounds and guarantees of the truth of knowledge at the beginning and end of the latter:

We started out from the judgment of *origin* and placed a beginning in it, to the extent of completeness being unable to expect anything more drastic. And we rose up to the judgment of *concept*, to the category of the *system*, which led its supreme meaning to fulfillment in the idea of the system of pure knowledge, as a system of truth. System also means *end*. We do not acknowledge the supreme end of knowledge in the system of truth. (*LRE* 397)

However, Cohen was already aware, in *Logik der reinen Erkenntnis* that the full meaning of truth cannot emerge from logic alone, but only from the whole unity of the system, and particularly from the relationship between logic and ethics (cf. *LRE* 610).

6

Ethics

1. THE DEVELOPMENT OF COHEN'S INTERPRETATION OF KANT'S ETHICS

The best way of highlighting the critical meaning of Cohen's ethics is to begin with his interpretation of and departures from Kant's ethics, following the same procedure as in the previous chapter on logic. As has already been noted, in 1877, Cohen published *Kants Begründung der Ethik*, an interpretation of Kant's ethics, following his interpretation of Kant's theoretical philosophy (*Kants Theorie der Erfahrung*, in 1871), both of which, together with his 1889 book *Kants Begründung der Ästhetik*, make up his complete commentary on Kant's critical philosophy (to which should be added the later *Kommentar zu Immanuel Kants Kritik der reinen Vernunft*, published in 1907). In this early work, Cohen criticized several points of Kant's practical philosophy, going beyond its literal meaning, in an attempt to correct its weaknesses and fill in gaps. However, in the years that followed, Cohen's ethical thought, alongside his approach to Kant in the same area, underwent a substantial evolution, arriving at a systematic formulation in *Ethik des reinen Willens*, that is quite distant from that in the first edition of *Kants Begründung der Ethik*, even contradicting it in certain aspects. I do not propose to provide a detailed analysis of this evolution, mainly because this has already been scrupulously carried out by Eggert Winter,[1] to whose analysis brief reference will be made here.

103

104 THE CRITICAL PHILOSOPHY OF HERMANN COHEN

In the first edition of *Kants Begründung der Ethik*, Cohen had been particularly dissatisfied with Kant's failure to provide a deduction of moral law, which the latter considered impossible, owing to the different conditions of practical and theoretical reason. Cohen could hardly pass over such a failure, since, in his view, the transcendental method is the foremost point in favor of Kant's philosophy. Cohen was thus faced with an embarrassing problem. Though, in the first edition of *Kants Begründung der Ethik*, he had accepted Kant's denial of the possibility of the deduction of the practical a priori and substitution with its exposition (cf. *KBE* 179ff.) (actually, it is less of an acceptance than an intention to explain Kant's thought before judging it, in a book which is more of an interpretative commentary than a critical essay), he was already showing signs of dissatisfaction with this solution and looking for the possibility of founding the a priori principle of morality within the context of Kant's own philosophy.

Cohen's analysis of the meaning of an exposition of the practical a priori is an initial attempt in this direction. He rejects all the interpretations that explain its discovery either empirically or dogmatically-speculatively (cf. *KBE* 179ff.), trying to justify the position of a concept which is analytical in itself; that of 'pure will,' in the transcendental-methodical sense, as an 'abstraction' (*KBE* 186), needed for founding the possibility of morality: "Following the transcendental method, we start off from the *analytical* concept of pure will and develop its content concerning the construction of systematic connections of the knowledge regarding a need for the practical use of reason. *The formulation of moral law is to be deduced from the analytical concept of pure will*" (*KBE* 188).[2]

However, if Cohen's effort to justify Kant's practical a priori had stopped here, it would have been understood as a postulate position, an idea which Cohen did not accept. It should be recalled that one of the points on which he had criticized Kant is precisely that of the postulates (cf. *KBE* 344ff.). Actually, the effort to justify Kant's practical a priori went even further. The whole first part of *Kants Begründung der Ethik* (cf. *KBE* 23–133), which deals with the theory of ideas, is conceived with the objective of demonstrating that the need for a practical philosophy grounded in an a priori principle, and the foundation of such a principle, is already present in Kant's theoretical philosophy (cf. *KBE* 17). The interpretation provided here by Cohen of Kant's theory of ideas, therefore, does not only aim at completing the interpretation of the *Critique of Pure Reason* in the first edition of *Kants Theorie der Erfahrung* (which was definitely unsatisfactory concerning Kant's transcendental dialectic), as Cohen himself points out in the *Vorrede* to the second edition of the book (cf. *KTE* xv). Its purpose was also to show how the theory of ideas presented by Kant in the *Critique of Pure Reason* leads on to the *Critique of Practical Reason* and the foundation of the practical a priori, and thus reconstruct that unity of his philosophy, in which Kant himself believed, and of which Cohen was convinced (cf. *ERW* 227).

As well as scrupulously facing the problem of the thing-in-itself, in the sense of its resolution in idea, in his interpretation of Kant's theory of ideas, Cohen highlights the double meaning of Kant's critical philosophy, as the determination of the limits of knowledge, and as a continuous inclination toward the unconditioned. He does this by trying to show that ideas, whose general meaning can be unified in the idea of end, are an integral part of the new concept of 'experience,' founded by Kant, knowledge being posited as an infinite task. In particular, the idea of freedom, as seen by Kant in the transcendental dialectic, takes on a much more positive role in Cohen's interpretation than that found in Kant himself. As will be recalled, in the *Critique of Pure Reason*, Kant had limited himself to claiming that "causality through freedom is at least *not incompatible with* nature," without necessarily proving "the *possibility* of freedom."[3] In Cohen's view, however, it is experience that requires and founds the possibility of ethics, by means of the idea of freedom: "The teaching of experience shows that its very consequences lead to ethics; that the reality within its boundaries, its premises, and its grounds makes the concept of another kind of reality necessary, grounded in the same premises and rooted in the same methodological conditions" (*KBE* 16).[4]

The "intelligible contingency of experience" refers back to its grounding in the unconditioned of idea.[5]

There is no trace at all of this approach, which had already been put aside in *Biographisches Vorwort zu F.A. Langes, Geschichte des Materialismus etc.* (written in 1881, but published in 1882), in *Ethik des reinen Willens.* Cohen also systematically corrected the passages where this approach is most evident in the second edition (1910) of *Kants Begründung der Ethik.* However, he could not, and, as we shall see shortly, perhaps did not want to completely alter the main line of thought of his earlier interpretation.[6] Concerning the reasons for the changes in the original formulation of the foundation of the ethical a priori, Winter rightly points out that, though Cohen had accepted that the meaning of the concept of freedom, as "self-legislation," in its position as the ground of Kant's ethics, is "disparate" (*KBE*[1] 232) as compared with its meaning in the critique of theoretical knowledge, as mere independence from causal connection, he is actually not coherent with this view, when he argues for a grounding of Kant's ethics in the theory of knowledge, through the mediation of the concept of freedom.[7]

Cohen's awareness of this aspect, highlighted by Winter, is shown, then, both by his corrections to the second edition of *Kants Begründung der Ethik*, and by his insistence on the independence of ethics from logic, as far as content is concerned, in *Ethik des reinen Willens*. It should be added that he was also careful not to fall back on a Fichtian solution. We have already seen that Fichte played a very special role in the development of Cohen's thought. As regards ethics, we must agree with Gianna Gigliotti[8] that "the contrast with Fichte plays . . . a central role" right from the first edition of *Kants Begründung der Ethik*. Cohen's main objection against Fichte was that he had misinterpreted the meaning given by Kant to the primacy of practical reason, which consequently led to the abandonment of one of the fundamental principles of Kantian philosophy, that is, the distinction between logic and ethics. Actually, Cohen must have realized that grounding Kant's ethics in the theory of experience implied a return to Fichte's interpretation of the primacy of practical reason, inasmuch as idea, as an ethical unconditioned and intelligible, ended up by being the ground of the value of contingent experience. If the possibility of ethics is founded by the theory of experience, it is because it acknowledges intelligible freedom as the ground of the contingency of experience. If the theory of experience is thus the *ratio cognoscendi* of the principle of ethics, it becomes, however, the *ratio essendi* of experience.[9]

Therefore, from 1881 onward, Cohen changed the perspective of the problem of the relationship between logic and ethics, looking for a solution in the unity of method, rather than that of contents. Correspondingly, the solution of the problem of the transcendental deduction of ethics, which was still of concern to Cohen, was no longer sought in foundation as a limit of experience, but in the application of the method of purity, formulated in *Logik der reinen Erkenntnis*. As Winter clearly shows, the problem of identifying a science constituting the fact that gives rise to the transcendental method in ethics, along the same lines as what happens in logic, comes to the fore, for this reason, in the works following the first edition of *Kants Begründung der Ethik*. The search for this fact was long and difficult, and Cohen made various attempts,[10] before finally identifying the science of law as the analog of mathematics for logic, in *Ethik des reinen Willens*. His resulting definition of ethics was: "*The theory of the principles of the philosophy of law and the State*" (*ERW* vii).

So far I have provided, then, what amounts to a report on the essentials of Winter's scrupulous, insightful version of the evolution of Cohen's thought on these problems. Winter devotes careful attention to the end product of Cohen's difficult route toward a conception of ethics as the methodological foundation of the moral sciences, and as a transcendental reflection on law. This is undoubtedly the dominant feature of *Ethik des reinen Willens*, apart from being the most obvious one, and I do not believe that I have underestimated it. Nevertheless, Winter himself appears to me to have underestimated some other aspects and dimensions of Cohen's ethics,[11] as developed in its definitive form in *Ethik des reinen Willens*, which are of considerable interest and importance if a complete picture of his critical philosophy is to be obtained. Since Cohen's loyalty to and progress from Kant is also relevant to these other aspects, I shall now try to provide a succinct picture of Cohen's evaluation of Kant in *Ethik des reinen Willens*, so as to highlight the precision and complexity of critical philosophy in Cohen's ethics.

2. COHEN'S JUDGMENT ON KANT IN *ETHIK DES REINEN WILLENS*

First of all, it must be emphasized that, despite his numerous, substantial criticisms of Kant in *Ethik des reinen Willens*, Cohen's initial references to the former in the *Einleitung* to the book represent a clear, open acknowledgment of "Kant's eternal worth" (*ERW* 14) as regards ethics. This homage to Kant's merits is important for a full understanding of Cohen's general evaluation. Besides, it is entirely coherent with his dialectical relationship with Kant, previously mentioned. While remaining loyal to Kant, Cohen embarked on further investigations. Even the criticism and rejection of many aspects of Kant's ethics in *Ethik des reinen Willens* cannot be considered separately from recognition of the fundamental value of Kant's formulation. Cohen even refers explicitly to Kant himself as a justification for departures from the letter of Kantian philosophy. Awareness of this essential point is not only important for a correct, well balanced understanding of Cohen's interpretation of Kant, but also for avoiding the risk of missing certain fundamental features of Cohen's own ethics.

a. The Distinction between Being and What Ought to Be

Where does Kant's eternal worth lie? The answer is in the rigorous distinction between logic and ethics, being and what ought to be. "*Kant is in agreement with Plato*" (*ERW* 14) in making such a distinction. Without losing sight of the unity of philosophy, Kant clearly saw the need to separate what ought to be, the content of ethics, from being, the object of the science of nature. Thus he barred the way not only for eudemonism but also for *naturalism*, which Cohen saw as a more wide-ranging philosophical position, of which eudemonism is only one instance. What ought to be is not only independent of sensible being, but of being in general, as nature, which, however it is conceived, is the opposite of what ought to be (cf. *ERW* 12f.). Therefore naturalism, not only eudemonism, is "the mortal enemy of ethics" (*ERW* 12). Kant's distinction, with which Cohen was in complete agreement, then, involved grounds and not contingent content. In the *Vorrede* to the second edition of *Ethik des reinen Willens*, in reply to an objection by Friedrich Jodl,[12] Cohen writes: "I do not oppose the feeling of happiness, but only the idea of its absoluteness" (*ERW* xii). This is reiterated later in the book (cf. *ERW* 295f.) and contributes to the understanding of his conception of socialism and its relation to ethics.

By way of Kant's opposition to any naturalistic conception of ethics, going much further than this antagonism to eudemonism, critical ethics can be distinguished from logic as the ground of nature. All forms of pantheism, which, before identifying God with the world, do so with man (cf. *ERW* 16, can also be warded off as forms of naturalism.

As has already been noted,[13] for Cohen all forms of the philosophy of identity are limited to pantheism. Therefore, even Hegel's philosophy, which appears to belong to historicism, is no more than a form of naturalism (cf. *ERW* 44f.). Any philosophy that does away with the distinction between what ought to be and being, whether the latter is conceived as the sensible being, the mathematical being of physics, or historical being, is naturalistic, and no valid ethics can ever be built up on such a basis.

b. The Precedence of Being over What Ought to Be

In Cohen's view, Kant could claim the merit not only of having established a distinction between being and what ought to be, but also that of determining the precedence of the former over the latter, which is also an essential prerequisite for the critical foundation of ethics: "Kant's formula" is "*being and what ought to be, i.e. not: what ought to be and being* (*ERW* 23). Any philosophy wishing to invert this order (and, immediately afterwards Cohen mentions Fichte as the originator of this trend) distances itself from critical foundation, and inevitably falls back on metaphysical speculation.

There is absolutely no question here of reducing ethics to logic, as has already been shown, nor of attributing less value to ethics than logic. In fact, Cohen recognizes the crucial value of ethics and its privileged position in the system of philosophy: "*Ethics, inasmuch as it is a theory of man, takes its place at the very center of philosophy.* It is only in this center that philosophy achieves independence and specificity and immediate unity" (*ERW* 1).

Cohen only states that ethics cannot be the beginning and ground of philosophy, and that it must be presupposed in logic, though maintaining the following distinction: "This is the fundamental idea we cannot abandon: *ethics is presupposed in logic, but logic is not in itself ethics*" (*ERW* 38). At this point Cohen's view of Kant's primacy of practical reason needs clarification. It would be wrong to think that Cohen simply substituted the primacy of reason with that of logic. Admittedly, in *Kants Begründung der Ethik*, he had rejected the primacy of practical reason, in the sense of its being the grounding of the science of nature in ethics (a position he attributed to Fichte [cf. *KBE* 288ff.]) and only accepted it in the sense that the problem of man as end is the limit of theoretical reason: a problem that it cannot understand with its categories, but which it acknowledges as a limit for itself (cf. *KBE* 294).

Cohen's position did not change substantially in *Ethik des reinen Willens*. Despite an apparent contradiction between certain passages in this work, he in no way rejected his previous view. We have already seen how he places ethics at the center of philosophy, even recognizing that "only retracing our steps back from man do we come to nature again" (*ERW* 1). The passages that appear to be contradictory are really not so at all, if, on each occasion, what Cohen means by his formulation of the primacy of practical reason is precisely understood. The metaphysical sense is rejected (cf. *ERW* 88), while the sense described above is accepted by Cohen (cf. *ERW* 23). This double position, which, instead of being contradictory is actually complementary, on occasion seems unified, thus being absolutely clear, as is the case, for example, in *Religion und Sittlichkeit. Eine Betrachtung zur Grundlegung der Religionsphilosophie*, published in 1907, three years after the first edition, and in the same year as the second edition, of *Ethik des reinen Willens*:

> *In the history of culture, Protestantism means* the separation of religion and science. Logic, in the sense of the logic of the mathematical science of nature, being placed before ethics is the philosophical expression of this *fundamental idea of the Reformation, in which Kant is linked to Luther.* This is not neglect of ethics; on the contrary, it is only thus that ethics gains its privileged position as the *primacy* of practical reason. It is only after logic has prepared the terrain of scientific experience that ethics can avoid assembling its building of moral ideas in the form of a castle in the air, and, instead, build up the historical world of men solidly and surely on nature, beyond it and, nevertheless, within it.[14]

Cohen's criticisms of Kant could now be securely grafted onto this fundamental acknowledgment of the validity of the latter's formulation. Where Cohen identified ambiguities, weak points, gaps, and even errors in Kant's ethics, he decided to maintain the sense and "avoid the formulation" of Kant's thought (*ERW* 177). As will be seen, Kant's formulation often needed correction, so as to remain faithful to those very principles which Kant himself had neglected.

c. The Being of What Ought to Be

Until the being of what ought to be is clearly defined, Kant's distinction between being and what ought to be remains ambiguous. What ought to be cannot be contrasted with being in the sense that the reality and value of being does not belong to it, but only in the sense that the being of what ought to be is in contrast with the being of nature. This formulation cannot be clearly identified in Kant.

One of Kant's merits was undoubtedly that of having distinguished the meaning of idea, not only from representation, with which it had been identified by modern gnoseology, but also from the principles of the knowledge of nature (thus going further than Plato, whom Kant criticized for not having made this distinction). It is well known that, theoretically, idea only has a regulative use in Kant's view. Thus the problem of the thing-in-itself was basically overcome for him, since the principles of knowledge only refer to the phenomena of experience and the thing-in-itself means nothing other than "what the regulative idea must operate" (*ERW* 26). The relationship between idea and the thing-in-itself must also be clarified in ethics, by entirely resolving the thing-in-itself in ethics, by recognizing and justifying a genuine being of what ought to be. However, Kant did not carry out this operation satisfactorily. Cohen's dissatisfaction over the failure to deduce the practical a priori transcendentally can be clearly seen. Thus Kant is criticized by Cohen, in the name of the transcendental method, which lies at the heart of the former's teaching:

> Here Kant neglected the application of the transcendental method . . . he did not deduce ethics with reference to the science of law, as he had done for logic with reference to the science of nature. There can be no doubt that the consequence of this would inevitably be an irreparable error in the concept of the transcendental method. If it is true for logic, why should the same not be true for ethics? Admittedly, here it is not a case of science in the sense of the science of nature, but it is still a question of knowledge, not only of faith. Otherwise ethics would really be resolved again in religion, and theology would have to become ethical-theology. It would therefore need to be grounded in an independent branch of ethics. As a matter of fact, it is here that the profound difficulties with Kant's system lie. (*ERW* 227–28)

d. Right and Law

What are the reasons for this fundamental missing element in Kant? It has been seen that the transcendental method cannot be applied, if it does not start off from the fact of science. This is also fundamental to Kant's teaching: *"This reference to the fact of science is valid for us as the everlasting component of Kant's system"* (*ERW*65). But it was Kant himself who did not follow this principle: "He [Kant] rather indicated the analogous fact of a science as a desideratum, but only made use of the analog of a fact" (*ERW*227; cf. *ERW*67). Kant distinguished morality from right, conceiving ethics as the foundation of the former, excluding the latter. In this way he removed the scientific fact, which alone could be the valid point of reference for transcendental investigation, from ethics (cf. *ERW* 227) The reason for Kant's failure to recognize the science of law as an analog of mathematics, in the fields of ethics and logic, is a double one. On the one hand, *"A precise concept of the moral sciences as a methodical analog of the sciences of nature is missing from this whole system"* (*ERW* 228). On the other hand, in Cohen's view, Kant was influenced by a mistaken conception of legality, linked to his concept of (especially Jewish) religion, whose origins can be traced back to St. Paul's contrast between freedom and law. This biased view of law opened the way for a paradox in Kant's ethics, since, while on one hand it is centered on the concept of law, on the other it is this very concept that is the distinguishing feature behind the ejection of right, as the field of legality, from ethics, as the foundation of morality (cf. *ERW*267f.).

e. Freedom and autonomy

This ambiguity in Kant's concept of law is also significant for another serious defect in Kant's ethics, as regards the concepts of 'freedom' and 'autonomy' and the determination of the ethical subject. This insufficiency is also linked to Kant's lack of clarity over the relationship between the thing-in-itself and idea. Here also Cohen, in accordance with his characteristic approach to Kant, acknowledged that while the latter had clarified all the fundamental elements for the correct formulation of the problem, he had not then applied his own principles entirely coherently.

Thus Cohen recognized that Kant had renewed Platonic ethics, again putting forward the need for universality, in contrast to egoism, as the content of ethics. Kant established this universal value of ethics by means of the concept of 'humanity' (*Menschheit*); a universal value only intuited by Plato, but introduced to Western culture by the Jewish tradition, especially by the prophets. Kant not only took up this concept in the generic sense of utopian cosmopolitanism, but also endowed it with historical and political content. He "explained it, restricted it, and speci- fied it universally with reference to the unambiguous example of eco- nomic concepts" (*ERW* 146), attributing to it the concretely political meaning of "*social humanity*, which introduced the concept of man to every people, and thus to humanity, to political truth and, in this way, to ethical determination" (*ERW* 147). In the formulation of the categorical imperative requiring the respect of the humanity in oneself and in other persons (a formulation that Cohen always considered crucial), the rela- tionship between the concept of humanity and the conception of the ethical subject as ultimate end, that is, as the concrete task of moral, juridical and political action, and thus the importance of reference to Kant for a correct conception of socialism clearly emerges (cf. *ERW* 320).[15]

Cohen also acknowledged that Kant intended to go beyond the metaphysical conception of an intelligible being as the principle of free action. In *Ethik des reinen Willens* he returned to the interpretation of Kantian freedom as the noumenon of freedom rather than as the free- dom of the noumenon, a theme already foregrounded in *Kants Begründung der Ethik* (cf. *KBE* 125, 257). Kant did not intend his "intelligi- ble character" to be interpreted as a thing-in-itself, as it sometimes was (Cohen refers particularly to Schopenhauer [cf. *ERW* 318]), but rather as an idea "that has no existence, but only a being, inasmuch as it promotes an *end*" (*ERW* 318). However, here too, Kant was not entirely coherent with his principles and intentions in the formulation of his ethics (cf. *ERW* 315). He had resolved the meaning of freedom in autonomy but had not clearly recognized that autonomy, the genuine principle of criti- cal ethics, must *substitute* the ancient concept of freedom, which is inevitably linked to speculative metaphysics. In Kant the problem of the *origin of action*, that is, the metaphysical problem of freedom, still coexists with the problem of the *origin of law*, that is, with the genuine ethical problem of autonomy: "Concerning autonomy . . . it is a question of the *origin of law*. Law alone makes action what it is, not the person, nor the ego. Therefore, even interest in the problem has changed. It is no longer connected with the impenetrable obscurity of the free beginning of action, but moves in the direction of the fundamental question of every genuine science, the question of law" (*ERW* 319).[16]

I have already shown how in other areas, despite the turning point reached between the first edition of *Kants Begründung der Ethik* and *Ethik des reinen Willens*, there is some continuity between the first and second phases of Cohen's ethical thought. However, in the case under discus- sion here, there is a clear break between the two works. While, in his commentary on Kant, as we have already seen, Cohen highlights the continuity between the theoretical and the practical concepts of freedom (though not entirely convincingly, as Winter rightly points out), in *Ethik des reinen Willens* he identifies a radical contrast between the two concepts. This contrast is substantial, since its neglect would inevitably lead to falling back on an ontological conception of the thing-in-itself, however refined one wishes to make it appear.

This completely alters the terms of the discussion of Kant. If Kant was unable to deduce the concept of freedom, as the origin of action, so as not to fall back on an ontological, speculative foundation, Cohen can now provide a deduction of autonomy, as the origin of law. Thus freedom, even in its meaning as autonomy, in Cohen loses its role as the ultimate principle of ethics and is transferred from the level of fundamental principles to the subsequent one of application, albeit in its first, highest degree.

f. Self-Consciousness

Confusion of the ethical problem of autonomy with the theoretical one of freedom still keeps Kant in an ambiguous position as regards the ancient ontology of the thing-in-itself. The "intelligible character" is conceived by Kant as an idea, but is still not entirely devoid of metaphysical meaning. It "as *homo noumenon* . . . is always thought, if not exactly as a person, at least as a law which, as such, exists. . . . In Kant . . . autonomy, substantially, only means the freedom of reason in respect of sensibility. The self resides in reason. Reason represents the thing-in-itself of intelligible character, realizing and making law and legislation possible. *The self is not resolved in the task*" (*ERW* 341–42).

This is why Kant, who had rightly gone beyond Descartes's concept of 'self-consciousness,' which was still too metaphysical and psychological, by formulating the principle of the 'unity of apperception,' could only then apply this principle to mathematical knowledge of nature, excluding not only the descriptive science of nature from grounding in it, but also ethics. The latter is not knowledge of the object, except instrumentally, as a function of the constitution of the subject itself. Therefore the unity of consciousness is in effect self-consciousness, in ethics. However, this position can only be maintained, without falling back on metaphysical dogmatism, if the self of self-consciousness is understood, not as a dogmatic principle of moral law, but as an ultimate end: "Action is no longer simply the manifestation of the self. It is conditioned by legislation, which is that of the self, so much so that the self is also conditioned by legislation. Therefore, *self-legislation is not legislation leading out of the self, but leading to the self*" (*ERW* 339).[17]

g. Ethical Formalism and the Problem of the Concrete Individual

Finally, the problem of formalism must be included in this general survey of Cohen's criticisms of Kant in *Ethik des reinen Willens*. This problem is particularly important for highlighting another of the critical themes present in the book. Cohen showed great sensitivity to the accusations of formalism made against Kantian philosophy. This is understandable, when one thinks of the meaning of the transcendental a priori highlighted by Cohen. Its applicability to experience and concrete reality is just as crucial as its pure origin. In *Kants Begründung der Ethik* Cohen shows how the theme of duty, in the *Critique of Practical Reason* concerns the problem of the application of moral law and not its discussion as a principle (cf. *KBE* 307ff.).[18] In *Ethik des reinen Willens*, as will be seen, the problem of the application of the principles of ethics to concrete reality is one of Cohen's main concerns.

Cohen's position concerning the problem of Kantian formalism, then, is the characteristic one with which we are already acquainted with. On the one hand, accusations of formalism are exaggerated and attributable to a superficial, erroneous interpretation of Kant's thought. On the other hand, there are elements justifying these criticisms: the distinction between morality and legality and the form and content of law (cf. *ERW* 269, 347). Kant's merit was that he considered moral law to be purely formal, as far as its origin is concerned, that is, independent of all material content. This is how he endowed it with a universal character. However, the distinction between juridical legality and moral law prevented him from additionally attributing the character of necessity to law, that is, a value, not only for *all* cases, without exception, but for *each* case (cf. *ERW* 274ff.). It is Cohen's view that, in critical philosophy, a priori principles must effectively refer to the concrete individual, and that, in ethics, this can be realized, once Kant's mistaken distinction between morality and legality has been overcome (cf. *ERW* 348).

The three fundamental aspects of the judgment of Kant to be found in *Ethik des reinen Willens* analyzed here—the distinction between being and what ought to be, the transcendental deduction of the practical a priori, and the problem of its application to the concrete individual—also provide three points of reference for interpreting Cohen's ethics in all the complexity of its critical meaning. I shall now attempt to provide an outline of the problems and arguments interwoven into *Ethik des reinen Willens*, which make it so difficult to read and interpret.

3. THE PROBLEMS OF COHEN'S ETHICS FROM THE POINT OF VIEW
OF CRITICAL PHILOSOPHY

Three fundamental themes, then, can be identified in Cohen's
judgment of Kant. These themes also constitute the three branches of
Cohen's ethics.

a. The Transcendental Deduction of the Ethical A Priori

In *Ethik des reinen Willens,* Cohen also applied the transcendental
method to ethics. As we saw in the previous chapter, he interpreted this
method, with great originality, as the "method of purity," thus justifying
the two statements to be found in this work: on the one hand, logic is the
"presupposition" (*ERW* 38) of ethics, in the sense that ethics can and must
take up the method of purity only from logic, and proceed with it in a
critically grounded fashion; on the other hand, as a consequence of the
choice of this method, ethics is the "positive logic of the moral sciences"
(*ERW* vii), in the sense that it contains the fundamental methodological
principles of the latter.

As regards logic, it is well known that Natorp accused Cohen of
confusing its two constituent features—"general logic" and "theoretics,"—which identified as the methodology of science.[19] As we have
already seen, however, Cohen differentiated both the autonomy of philosophy from science and its methodological foundation of science function, but he deliberately did not separate these two aspects, being
convinced that the speculative, dialectical character of philosophy and
its methodological, transcendental character are inseparable. Similarly,
on the one hand, ethics is the dialectical deduction of the fundamental
principles and, on the other, it is the transcendental foundation of the
moral sciences, through the mediation of law. Thus it takes the place of
the ambiguous concept of 'natural law' as the grounding of the science
of law and, through it, of the moral sciences (cf. *ERW* 70f.).

This is how Cohen intuited an obvious structural parallel between
logic and ethics: as there the fundamental principles of thought in general, through the mediation of the principles of mathematics, established the validity of the science of nature, so *by analogy* here the
fundamental principles of will, action, and self-consciousness, through
the principles of law, established the validity of the moral sciences.
Furthermore, in ethics, as in logic, the fundamental principles are
deduced dialectically, that is, purely, though deriving from a transcendental reflection on law and being applicable to moral and historical
reality, through law, as their sole legitimate function (cf. *ERW* 65f.).

This is certainly the dominant and most obvious feature of *Ethik des reinen Willens*, tempting some commentators[20] to interpret Cohen's ethics solely as a methodological foundation of the moral sciences. However, it is not the only feature, and making it absolute would prevent his ethics from being understood from a correct, balanced viewpoint, and would deprive it of other, equally interesting, productive features.

b. The Distinction and Relationship between Being and What Ought to Be

This theme, though being one of the least developed in *Ethik des reinen Willens*, if not in statements of principle, at least in their development, occupies a position of crucial importance in Cohen's critical idealism and ethics. It can also be found in this work, especially in the considerations on history, in the analysis and development of the themes of the ideal and idea of God. The affirmation of the being of what ought to be adds a double meaning to the critical character of Cohen's ethics. On the one hand, the stable reality of ethical value with respect to the contingency of the historical existent is a reliable criterion for interpretation of and judgment on history; on the other hand, the certainty of good justifies a progressive conception of history, which differentiates critical philosophy from skepticism, quietism, and utopianism. History can and must be effectively interpreted through the idea of progress, despite the continuous inadequacy of contingent historical phenomena, with respect to idea; and, on the other hand, the idea of progress must not be a simple, falsely optimistic illusion, but a rule of concrete historical action, grounded in certainty of reason.

Cohen's historical optimism, which is one of the most important aspects of his socialism,[21] is not only the result of a contingent illusion, grounded in the hope that had grown in him and others in a brief, happy period in German politics after the victory in the 1870 war.[22] Neither did this hope disappear under changed circumstances, which Cohen did recognize as very serious.[23] His optimism is not even a senseless, blind utopianism, believing for the sake of illusion, or under the illusion of believing. It is the courage of reason, acting effectively as a rule of concrete action with the purpose of political, economic, and social change (cf. *ERW* 558f.). Cohen's ethical and political thought, which has also been defined as "a philosophy of progress,"[24] is grounded in his critical idealism and *thus* takes on the guise of optimism, where he sees himself as the heir of Leibniz and Kant (cf. *ERW* 296) and of the Jewish prophetic tradition.[25]

c. The Applicability of General Principles to the Concrete Individual

The problem of the application of the ethical a priori to concrete reality is a central feature throughout Cohen's book. From the first part, in which he deduces the fundamental principles of ethics, and thus does not yet really face the problem of application, the ground is nevertheless prepared for its subsequent discussion in the particular stress put on the concept of 'action.' The correlation between origin and continuity I analyzed in the chapter on logic, here, is taken up for the interpretation of the relationship between pure will and action: pure will is pointless if it is not the origin of action; its meaning is entirely resolved in action:

> The difference in the examination of will, as it must be carried out by ethics, in respect of psychology, lies in the consideration of the concept of *action*. It is neither possible nor legitimate for ethics that a will be given that is not realized in action. Inasmuch as the grounds of the rise of will need to be investigated and its development followed, one should not stop at this. End must also be the subject of just as much attention. Without the result of will, no will can be admitted. So called *intention and disposition* (*Gesinnung*) are beyond human understanding. To whatever extent an impulse can be innate and hereditary, it cannot be considered, however, as the epicenter and source of will, in the sense required by ethics. All this psychology belongs to the *metaphysics of the thing-in-itself,* which offers the enigmas of the world as enigmas, in order to make them appear resolvable in enigmatic words. Ethics does not separate the outset of will from its end. *Therefore will and action go together in its view.* This is already the first sign of the meaning of continuity for the ethics of will. (*ERW* 103–4; cf. *ERW* 130, 186ff.)

In this way the ground has already been prepared for an ethics that, in contrast with all formalist ethics of intention, is constituted on the central concept of action. Starting from the chapter on autonomy, Cohen develops the principles that make possible and regulate the ever-more-specific and -concrete application of the pure concepts of reality. Obviously, since the moral sphere has nothing to do with given objects, the application of principles to reality can only take on the form of the *task of realizing* them. But here the difference between ethics and logic in Cohen is much less obvious than in Kant, since the object is also not taken as given in logic, but as a task. A radical difference remains, inasmuch as, while the application of principles in logic has the purpose of realizing the object in concept, in ethics its essential purpose is the realization of the subject.

A parallel with logic then is also easily identified in this case. It is more interesting to note, as has already been mentioned, that, having deduced moral law by means of the method of purity from the pure concepts of will, action. and self, Cohen no longer posits autonomy as the supreme principle of ethics, like Kant, but places it in the role of principle of application, albeit at the highest degree. Similar to what happens in logic, the first part of ethics remains in the realm of abstraction, of the deduction of the pure possibility of a content. In the case of ethics the fundamental pure concepts are used to found the very concept of 'man.' However, 'freedom as autonomy,' is a concept that presupposes a moral subject and, inasmuch as it is autonomy, establishes the possibility for its action in the real world. For this reason, Cohen develops the meaning of autonomy in the concrete operational terms of the realization of moral action, through the four features of self-legislation (*Selbstgestzgebung*), self-determination (*Selbstbestimmung*), self-responsibility (*Selbstverantwortung*) and self-preservation (*Selbsterhaltung*) (cf. *ERW* 324ff.).

Cohen also attributes a role to the idea of God, with reference to the application of principles, as a guarantee of the possibility of conciliation between the realm of nature and that of ends, that is, of the possibility for the realization of moral action in the world.[26]

The last part of *Ethik des reinen Willens*, finally, deals with virtue, considered as the last degree in the solution of the problem of the realization of moral action (cf. *ERW* 472f.). This function comes out particularly clearly in the treatment of the last two virtues, which complement each other: justice (*Gerechtigkeit*) and humanitarianism (*Humanität*).[27] In *Ethik des reinen Willens*, virtue takes on the role that, in Cohen's view, duty had in Kant's ethics. In *Kants Begründung der Ethik* Cohen had challenged all the interpretations of Kantian ethics as the ethics of duty, showing how duty has no role in the foundation of morality, but only in its application (cf. *KBE* 19, 309ff.). In *Ethik des reinen Willens*, he chooses to replace the concept of duty with that of virtue (cf. *ERW* 467ff.).

The problem of the concrete individual, of the application of ethical principles to existing reality, is present throughout *Ethik des reinen Willens*. The fact that Wilhelm Herrmann's criticisms of the inability of Cohen's ethics to understand the concrete individual[28] are explicitly dealt with by Cohen in the second edition of *Ethik des reinen Willens* (cf. *ERW* xiii, 350f., 502) cannot, therefore, be attributed to chance, personal friendship, or intellectual affinity. Though attempting to defend himself from Herrmann's criticisms, Cohen was affected by them, since they concern a problem of which he was fully aware. As confirmation of this, it is enough to point out that he revised his position concerning these criticisms in subsequent years. It was their partial acceptance and a return to the problem of the concretely existing individual that make up one of the essential elements in Cohen's attention to religion during the last stage of his intellectual career.[29]

In conclusion, it appears that these three themes in Cohen's critical ethics can be summed up in the threefold meaning of the relationship between being and what ought to be, in which the following are to be found: a) the affirmation of the being of what ought to be, inasmuch as it is founded by means of the method of purity and is valid as a method of the moral sciences (cf. *ERW* 24); b) the contrast between what ought to be and being, inasmuch as it is separate from the being of nature (however it is understood), its criterion of judgment and rule of transformation (cf. *ERW* 13); and c) the proposition of the task of realizing what ought to be in being, in the sense that it must find concrete, operational application in existing reality, understanding and transforming it (cf. *ERW* 82).

The considerable problems encountered in reading *Ethik des reinen Willens*,—which is undoubtedly one of the most demanding of Cohen's works, all of which are complex and difficult for readers,[30]—are certainly due to all the reasons highlighted by many interpreters: unfamiliar terminology, complex style, unsystematic discourse development, repeated infiltrations of psychological themes; and contingent political, religious, juridical, and social controversies.[31] There appears to be an additional, more radical, difficulty, consisting in the simultaneous presence of the three branches discussed above, which, though being distinct, are interwoven in a complex network that is not always well amalgamated and harmonious, though stimulating for this very reason. Each of these branches, as we have seen, bears one or more specific features, which contribute to the enrichment of Cohen's critical philosophy with new meanings.

4. THE CRITICAL FORMULATION OF THE PROBLEM OF MAN

Right from the outset of *Ethik des reinen Willens*, Cohen had formulated the problem of ethics clearly: "*The object of ethics is man*" (*ERW* 2). This determination of the object of ethics, as a presupposition of the whole treatment prior to any discussion of this direction provoked objections from Eggert Winter, who notes that "Cohen's philosophy on the whole lacks . . . the hermeneutic-phenomenological dimension of the evaluation of the meaning of philosophical-scientific problems as problems of man's everyday life. Cohen constantly presupposes the problematic meaning and horizon of the moral question regarding the foundation of ethics."[32]

I am unable to agree with Winter's objection, and discussing it seems a good departure point for shedding light on the characteristics of the formulation of the problem of man in Cohen's critical philosophy. Winter is undoubtedly right when he draws attention to the lack of a "hermeneutic-phenomenological" analysis of "man's everyday life" in Cohen's ethics, but this lack is not a real gap in his analysis, neither does it deprive his ethics of the preliminary determination of its object, in such a way as to cause its grounding in an arbitrary presupposition of the problem and of the direction of its solution. Cohen did not carry out a hermeneutic-phenomenological analysis of man, since he did not believe it to be a task of critical philosophy (as it would simply be an empirical deduction of the concept of man). He did believe that philosophy should presuppose it and take it as a starting point to provide a universal, necessary (i.e., a priori and transcendental) foundation of its contents. This analysis is missing from Cohen's ethics, because he believed that it was presupposed by philosophy and not one of its tasks.

This conviction of Cohen is not explicitly theorized in *Ethik des reinen Willens*, but in a piece he wrote in memory of *Leopold Schmidt*, in 1896, there are some extremely explicit pages dealing with this subject.[33] The following points emerge from the basic formulation in *Ethik des reinen Willens*: a) ethics takes up its problem from experience; b) it founds it critically, determining its concepts by means of the method of purity, independently of all experience; c) by means of these philosophically determined concepts it enables science to actually understand experience with well grounded certainty.

Repeated recourse to the historical reconstruction of the meaning of the concepts to be determined, which, as we have already seen, is a constant feature of Cohen's style, has the purpose of foregrounding the meaning and environment of these concepts in common culture and mentality. However, Cohen frequently observed that the content of ethics is not unlike that which culture, and especially religion, had accumulated throughout the ages.[34] However, critical philosophy, though starting out from these contents, has the specific task of abstracting itself from their common, empirical meaning to provide an a priori foundation for them, in accordance with the method of purity, the sole valid philosophical method, which ethics takes up from logic: in this sense philosophy can and must be the "the logic of the moral sciences" (*ERW* vii) and, as such, a "critique of practical reason" (*ERW* 228).

Winter also writes:

> But when ethics must determine the criterion of exactness itself, and the science of law must only supply the conceptual material for it, then this again presupposes (and this is a point worth emphasizing) the capacity for

investigating the material, i.e. the concepts of jurisprudence, under a
determined aspect, under an already familiar idea. The ethical problem,
therefore, must be capable of formulation in advance as a question, so as
to obtain for juridical concepts more than that which they can supply for
the juridical problem.[35]

Actually, Cohen did formulate the problem as a question; it has a
fundamental role in the systematic construction of critical ethics. He
simply did not believe that the question on man could be philosophically
formulated by hermeneutic-phenomenological means, then searching
for the solution and answer in law. Following the transcendental
method, perfected in *Logik der reinen Erkenntnis* as the method of purity,
the question rises from reflection on the fact of science, transcendental
in respect of it, but not separable from it, in accordance with the meaning of idea as hypothesis, as origin.

If Winter brought out the parallels of Cohen's ethics, as a method
of the moral sciences, with his logic, as a method of the sciences of
nature, he does not seem to have attributed enough importance to the
parallels between Cohen's ethics and logic as the philosophical foundation of the possibility of their respective contents.

Just as the originary problem of the possibility of the object in general, of the something, presented itself, in logic, even before the problem of the determination of the objects of the science of nature in their
relationships and laws, so the problem of the foundation of the possibility of the ethical subject in general, that is, the concept of man presents
itself in ethics, even before the determination of the laws that regulate
human reality and understand it by means of the moral sciences. This
foundation is pure, both in logic and in ethics, but it is not for this reason that it has no relationship with science, in view of which it is sought.
It is rather the result of transcendental reflection upon it. Just as Cohen
amply demonstrated in logic, the concept is essentially and above all a
question, but in the sense of hypothesis: that is, a question that already
contains the indication of the direction to be followed in the search for a
solution.[36] Ethics thus has man, above all, as its object, inasmuch as it
must determine concept of the former. The meaning of 'man' remains
multiple and ambiguous until its concept is determined by philosophy,
in ethics: "*Inasmuch as it is a theory of man, ethics is the theory of the concept of
man*" (*ERW* 3). The whole first part of *Ethik des reinen Willens* covers the
formulation and foundation of the concept of man, as a hypothesis of
the moral sciences. The ambiguity of the word man, basically, in Cohen's
view, is to be found in the possibility of attributing a meaning of individuality, plurality or universality to it. The difference between the first two
meanings was soon overcome by Cohen, with the consideration that

man as an individual does not contain the unity of the concept. He is still an individual among a plurality:

> The first [the ambiguity of the word *man*], logically, lies not so much in the contrast between unity and plurality, as in the apparent contrast between singularity and plurality. This contrast has no consistency in thought. It only derives from the appearance of popular consciousness. The individual is in himself single in plurality. He is in no way an independent unit, however much common appearances would have us believe the contrary. (*ERW*4)

Thus the true ethical problem remains the determination of the concept of man as plurality and universality. Admittedly, plurality is, a conceptual unity, but it is always defined as the sum of its members. The unity of the concept is only fully realized in universality, not as a sum nor as a final totality going beyond, and removing the meaning of the particular, but rather as "infinite unification" (*ERW*5; cf. *ERW*4f.).[37] The superior unity of the universal concept of man is the reason it is posited as the ground of ethics: "*Therefore without universality, indeed without beginning with universality, the concept of man can be neither fulfilled nor developed nor formed.* Universality does not only comprise happy fulfillment, it is also the correct outset" (*ERW*7).

This does not mean that critical ethics, positing the universal concept of man as its ground, should eliminate or not consider the particular concept, but the foundation of the concept of man must be posited in its universal meaning, since, only in correlation with it, can man as an individual and as plurality take on a nonempirical, but authentically ethical meaning, in the critical sense. By means of the fundamental concepts of 'pure will' and 'action' or rather 'unity of action' (cf. *ERW*184), Cohen was able to completely determine the universal concept of man a priori, as unity of moral consciousness, as "self-consciousness,"[38] characterizing it on the basis of the juridical person, a term in private law, which is fully developed in State law. Cohen did not claim to have solved the ethical problem in this way, but simply to have founded the universal concept of man, purely, in the concept of juridical person, on the basis of which the ethical approach to contents can be developed, that is, on moral persons and the relationships between them. The universal concept of juridical person is thus, in Cohen's view, still abstract, but, owing to its pure character, allows the construction of critical ethics, not grounded in an empirical, naturalistic concept of man (cf. *ERW*78).

Thus the juridical person is still a concept without content, as it were, a "fiction" (*ERW*78), similar to the something constituting the initial formulation of the object, the result of the first part of logic.

However, this fiction is to be understood in the sense of a hypothesis, of idea, of the formulation of concept as a well-grounded question, which, as such, can guide subsequent research:

> *This unified, representative, ideal will is the unity of will and the unity of the person, the concept of the juridical person.* Now, however, the great idealist enlightenment, which guides the science of law to ethics in this concept of the juridical person, is weakened by the fact that this fundamental concept is usually described as *fiction.* Thus the meaning of *hypothesis* is misrepresented. It must be acknowledged by fiction and inasmuch as this is so . . . the greatest damage consists of the fact that, in this way, further credit is given to the opinion that only the physical person can be a juridical subject, so that association (*Genossenschaft*) could only be thought as the fiction of a person. On the contrary, the concept of juridical person creates a new kind of will in association, and a new kind of self-consciousness and, in conformity with it, a new kind of juridical subject. *Therefore this concept must not be designated as a fiction; it must be endowed with the fundamental value of hypothesis.* It is the hypothesis of ethical self-consciousness, of the ethical subject, that which is realized in the juridical person of association. (*ERW* 231–32)

The correlation between community and state is grounded in that between universal and particular and plays an important role in Cohen's ethics and the link between his philosophical conception and political thought. Cohen rejected the concept of 'community' (*Gemeinschaft*) for the determination of the universal concept of man. For Cohen, community is a naturalistic, specific concept. Only 'society' (*Gesellschaft*) is the concept suitable for determining the universal meaning of man, in its true degrees: 'association,' 'state' and 'humanity' (cf. *ERW* 237ff.). The universal concept neither eliminates nor denies the particular one, but is in correlation with it, with the following two basic characteristics: a) the primacy of the universal over the particular, in that the particular only takes on an ethical rather than a naturalistic ground and meaning in the universal; b) the critical function of the particular as regards the universal, since only in the ability of the universal to understand, satisfy and reconcile the demands of the manifold particular coexisting in it, is its actual validity as a universal, that is, as "infinite unification" verified. Likewise, correlation exists between state and community:

> The particular community deserves to be drastically contested only when it claims to completely represent society, when it substitutes universality, when it does not take the need for universality as its guiding concept and corrective. Otherwise it must not be fought against. On the contrary, one cannot doubt that moral self-consciousness should also be realized with

> reference to and within the respective communities, as long as they, as we have already noted, have their guarantee in the common center of universality. Then there will no longer be a contradiction between community and universality, then the community is subject to universality. Unconditional submission must be required; no exceptions to universality can be snatched. The community becomes immoral as soon as it loses the guarantee of universality. (*ERW* 486)

This correlation between universality and manifold particularity, between state and relative communities, between the affects linked with 'honor' (*Ehre*) and 'love' (*Liebe*), two aspects of the concept of man, is the ground of the explicitly critical structure of the theory of virtues, which takes up the final part of *Ethik des reinen Willens*.

Cohen makes a distinction between first- and second-degree virtues. First-degree virtues are those peculiar to man in his universal value, whose driving force is the universal affect of honor: of man as humanity of the state. They are the virtues of truthfulness (*Wahrhaftigkeit*), valor (*Tapferkeit*) and justice (*Gerechtigkeit*). The second-degree virtues are those of man as a member of a particular community, and their driving force is the particular affect of love. They are also three in number: modesty (*Bescheidenheit*), loyalty (*Treue*) and humanitarianism (*Humanität*). The three second-degree virtues are respectively correlated to the three first-degree ones. Though being subordinate to them, they act as critical checks and mediators for their concrete realization. Thus there is a conflict between the first- and second-degree virtues, though this conflict is not a contradiction, but rather a critical correlation (cf. *ERW* 487f.). The conflict is not transformed into a contradiction, but constitutes a critical correlation, if, that is, on the one hand, the second-degree virtue is subordinated to the first degree one (cf. *ERW* 528f.), and, on the other hand, the universal meaning of the first-degree virtues is subjected to a critical check by and realized through the mediation of the second-degree virtues (cf. *ERW* 625).

The influence both of the Platonic and of the Jewish traditions, by way of and also beyond Kant, is clearly amalgamated into an original synthesis by Cohen in his formulation. It is obvious that the first-degree virtues are very similar to the virtues discussed by Plato in the *Republic*. From the outset of *Ethik des reinen Willens* (cf. *ERW* 6f.) Cohen acknowledged Plato to be his precursor and model for his formulation of the ethical problem, inasmuch as the latter had been the first to associate the problem and concept of man with the universal one of the state. However, there is also clear influence from the biblical conception of the complementary nature of justice and mercy, a conception developed by the post-biblical Jewish tradition.

5. THE CONTRIBUTION OF ETHICS TO THE CRITICAL CONCEPTION OF TRUTH

The theme of truth is of fundamental importance in all aspects of Cohen's critical philosophy. As a conclusion to *Die Nächstenliebe im Talmud*,[39] a work dating from 1888, Cohen wrote: "The same thing is essential for both science and life: reverent awe of truth." In the previous chapter, I analyzed the various aspects of the problem of truth in Cohen's logic. My purpose now is to bring out the new contributions of ethics to this problem. Bearing in mind the three fundamental themes in *Ethik des reinen Willens* identified above, it is now also possible to understand the critical meaning of the problem of truth, as Cohen approached it in his ethics.

In Cohen's view, the problem of truth is crucial for the foundation of ethics, so much so that the first chapter of the book deals with it. He formulates the "fundamental law (*Grundgesetz*) of truth" in this chapter: "*Truth means the connection and agreement between theoretical and ethical problems*. This law must precede the whole construction of ethics. For this reason we name it the *principle of truth*" (*ERW* 89).

Now the various meanings of this connection between theoretical and ethical problems need to be analyzed.

The first aspect is the dependency of ethics on logic, or, in other words, the presupposition of logic by ethics, and this is the main concern of the chapter in *Ethik des reinen Willens* to which I refer. This aspect of truth should be linked to the above-mentioned theme of the being of what ought to be. Ethical truth cannot be considered different from logical truth and separated from it, since only the foundation of ethics as knowledge on the basis of the principles of logic endows the former with solidity and certainty protecting it from empiricism and relativism. We must not think of an ethical foundation of truth relegating understanding and its principles to the area of mere comprehension of phenomena as pure appearance. Such a route, already followed by Fichte (cf. *ERW* 23), had been rediscovered, in new aspects, by the philosophy of Cohen's own time, especially by Schopenhauer. Cohen severely condemned this new form of metaphysics, which he even termed "diabolical" (cf. *ERW* 20), and emphasized how the rejection of the logical foundation of philosophy inevitably leads to an essentially aesthetic, skeptical philosophy, hiding under the appearance of the primacy of ethics (cf. *ERW* 19f.).

Thus, truth as the connection between logic and ethics, first of all, means correlation between the two areas of knowledge, where ethics finds its sure grounding as the science of logic. Neither logic nor ethics possesses the truth in itself; it only lies in the connection between the two. However, the order of precedence must be kept: logic presupposed by ethics and being by what ought to be, and not vice versa (cf. *ERW* 89f.). What does this link (*ERW* 89) between logic and ethics, where truth lies, consist of? Certainly not of its contents, since "the extension of logic is limited . . . it does not go as far as man in universal history, inasmuch as the content of concepts is concerned (*ERW* 85). What it does consist of is method. With reference to Lessing's famous image,[40] Cohen rejected the distinction between truth and the search for truth: the sole truth for man is the search for truth, therefore, it is *method.*

However, Cohen was careful to specify that there is no question of transferring the method of logic to ethics, but that the method is common to both, discovered by logic as the foundation of the science of nature (which justifies the priority of logic with respect to ethics). The method can only be acknowledged as common from the point of view of ethics, since ethics alone exhaustively poses the problem of truth, as a connection between being and what ought to be:

> It is not simply a question of transferring the productive method of logic to ethics, so as to see whether it will also be productive in this case. Ethics goes beyond the sphere of logic, as it presupposes and requires the unity of the method for the two interests of reason. This presupposition is the enactment of the fundamental law of truth. What takes place here is not a transfer, but rather a retroactive move. The principle of truth sheds new light over the fundamental method of logic: the fact that it, in turn, requires ethics. (*ERW* 90)

Refusal to restrict the problem of truth to a transfer of the method of logic to ethics, the recognition both of the new horizons opened up by ethics for this problem and of the influence of the ethical problem of truth on logic itself (to the extent that Steven S. Schwarzschild, as we have seen, uses one of Cohen's own terms when he writes of the "retroactive" move of ethics with respect to logic),[41] and, acknowledgment that the whole problem of truth can only be placed in ethics (as is shown by the position of the discussion of the principle of truth at the outset of ethics and not logic) are themes to which reference is frequently made in the first chapter of *Ethik des reinen Willens* (cf. *ERW* 84, 86, 87, 90, 106, 107f.). Nevertheless, they are not adequately discussed there, since, as I have already pointed out, it is the question of methodology, and thus the theme of the presupposition of logic in respect of ethics that predominates. However, the careful reader will realize that the analysis and discussion of the problem of truth cannot be limited to the first chapter of the book. Discussion of the aspects only briefly mentioned in Cohen's first chapter must be looked for elsewhere; the concept of truth in Cohen's ethics cannot be restricted to the question of methodology. These other aspects, highlighted above, apart from the theme of the being of what ought to be, to which the formulation of the fundamental law of truth as method responds, the theme of the distinction between being and what ought to be and that of the realization of the latter will be our guides in the search for further developments of the problem of truth.[42]

First, the theme of the being of what ought to be is inseparable from that of the distinction between being and what ought to be, in critical philosophy (cf. *ERW* 395 f.). From the critical viewpoint, what ought to be cannot be taken as being entirely detached from the being of nature, having no relationship with it, and thus being unrealizable (cf. *ERW* 390f.). As Cohen had already stated in "*Das Grundgesetz der Wahrheit*," the first chapter of *Ethik des reinen Willens*, the connection between logic and ethics must be understood as identity, as a restriction of ethics to logic, of what ought to be to being:

> *Identity is correct for logic, but becomes a trap for ethics.* It is incorrect and dangerous to say: *voluntas et intellectus unum et idem sunt.* This is a mistake, not because it is not recognized by psychology, but because it contradicts the possibility of ethics. If this were the case, then the theory of will would actually be identical to mathematics and logic, and thus there would be no ethics at all. The power that affection can acquire for and in itself cannot be the justification for any ethics. (*ERW* 459–60; cf. *ERW* 462)[43]

The correlation between logic and ethics, being and what ought to be, then, must be a unity, but one that has the three stages of unit, distinction, and unification. Truth consists of this correlation, and, thus, cannot be understood from the logical viewpoint, even though it is its methodological presupposition, but solely from the ethical viewpoint, because only here does the problem of what ought to be, the ideal, and its relationship with being appear. In one of his last works, *Vom ewigen Frieden*, Cohen writes:

> *Truth*, as we know it, as the fundamental idea of *critical idealism*, consists of the *distinction of idea* as the infinite *task* for every moral end of the human race, as of each individual, in the distinction of this *ethical* meaning of *idea* from any *real existence* of nature and from any *historical experience*. Both are necessary: the distinction, but, at the same time, *the maintenance of both elements* in their logically equal value, so that real existence affirms its value in the face of idea, and idea only establishes its specific meaning in warning and guidance, with which it takes charge of real existence. This truth of idealism, which, at the same time, pays homage to real existence, guaran-

tees our personal truthfulness in all our thoughts, investigations and actions.[44]

These lines briefly summarize what Cohen had already discussed in *Ethik des reinen Willens*, especially in chapter 9, "*Die Idee Gottes.*"

Logic can posit the grounds of the certainty of knowledge, but not those of truth, since the mathematical science of nature is restricted to the world of experience; and yet it perceives its own limit and the need for overcoming it. However, only recognition of the ideal by reason can satisfy this need (cf. *ERW* 441f.). The ideal must be able to realize itself in a process of transformation of the real, which has never been carried out, is infinite and still authentic. The idea of God guarantees this possibility and is the idea of the connection between nature and spirit, not of identity, but of the harmonization between the two realms (cf. *ERW* 462f.).

God guarantees complete harmony between being and what ought to be, but is and can be so for reason, only as idea. This does not mean, as we shall see, that this idea is not effective in reality, but that harmony can never be considered to be fulfilled and immanent in the world, but always an infinite task and that this task really affects reality, because it is grounded in truth, as a guarantee of its fulfillment. The idea of God is truth:

> Truth only requires of nature that the grounds of the logic of knowledge remain unchanged, and that, in conformity with them, nature continue to exist. Truth requires this of logic, but also, and above all, of ethics. Logic and nature could pass if they were self sufficient, but they have a relationship with ethics. The problem of truth now appears and becomes the fundamental law. This fundamental law is represented by the idea of God. *God means that nature endures with the same certainty through which morality is eternal.* The ideal in itself cannot supply this certainty, just as nature in itself cannot supply it. What is needed is the method by which concepts, or rather these components of the system, enter into a mutual relationship. (*ERW* 446)

This is why Cohen rationally supported the transcendence of God: not only is reason incapable of difficulty in recognizing this transcendence, but it requires it, for the principle of truth. The difference between nature and morality, which is absolutely essential for critical thought, should not be understood either as radical diversity, denying any relationship between the two areas, or as an unreconcilable contradiction, contrasting them in a watertight fashion. The difference "requires its harmony and finds it in the idea of God" (*ERW* 466). God's transcendence is thus the necessary ground for the mutual immanence of nature and morality: "God is undoubtedly transcendent, both in respect of nature and morality. *But this transcendence does not mean anything more than the fact that, thanks to it, nature is not transcendent in respect of morality, nor morality in respect of nature*" (*ERW* 466).

Therefore, the introduction of the idea of God makes significant additions to the meaning of truth presented in the first chapter of *Ethik des renen Willens*. It goes beyond the unilateral nature of the meaning of the relationship between being and what ought to be set out there and completes the critical meaning of truth. It also highlights the shift of focus of critical philosophy caused by ethics in respect of logic: from origin to task, from idea as hypothesis to idea as ideal. It is not a change in Cohen's critical conception, but a further exposition: idea as task does not substitute idea as hypothesis (which keeps all its validity) but completes its meaning. In Cohen's critical system, as in every system, principle coincides with end. What differentiates his system from all systems of totality is that the principle, as origin, is infinite, nonbeing, just as the end as ideal is equally infinite, what ought to be. It is between the two that the actual, unrealized progress of science, morality, and natural, historical reality develops.

Cohen expressed this completion of the meaning of truth by means of the idea of God, suggesting that, even if this idea is dealt with at the end of the treatment of the fundamental principles of ethics (in *Ethik des reinen Willens*, only the part concerning the virtues, which is limited to the problem of the actual application of the principles of reality, was to follow) it is, nevertheless, implicit in the fundamental law of truth, formulated at the beginning of the book. The full meaning of the connection between logic and ethics is to be found in the idea of God:

> God is now a fundamental concept in ethics; there is no longer any need to be shocked even by its apparently being an appendix to ethics. The order of succession of principles is unimportant. It could already be seen from the outset that it stood in the background: in the problem of pure will and the fundamental law of truth. It is only formulated after the conclusion of the fundamental concepts, since it is precisely this that is important for its meaning: that ethics, whose construction it has concluded, is its presupposition. Thus it is exactly linked to the whole method of ethics. (*ERW* 455)

Therefore, the contributions of ethics to the system of Cohen's critical philosophy are essential, so much so that only at this stage does his critical idealism take on a clear, definitive profile. Besides the foundation of knowledge in the critical method of hypothesis (which has already been clarified in logic and is also valid for ethics), the critical horizon of the ideal, as a complement to it, is now defined in ethics, in its three meanings: "*These three stages are contained in the ethical ideal: completeness, fulfillment, the incompleteness of fulfillment*" (*ERW* 424; cf. *ERW* 439ff.).

The connection of these two cornerstones (idea as origin and idea as ideal) of Cohen's system, which is a truly open, critical system, since it does not enclose knowledge and reality in the immanent circle of totality, but extends them between an infinite origin and equally infinite task, at last endows with adequate meaning that definition of idealism, which I highlighted in the first edition of *Kants Theorie der Erfahrung*: "To resolve the diversity between things into distinctions between ideas: this is the secret of idealism"(*KTE*[1] 270), and expressed the intention of investigating further in its critical meaning.

7

Aesthetics, Psychology, and Critical System

1. The Aesthetics of Pure Feeling

The principle of truth, which I treated in its manifold aspects and meanings in the previous chapter, already endows Cohen's logic and ethics with a systematic character. However, he did not believe that these two branches were sufficient for critical philosophy. His system was planned, like that of Kant, to include logic, ethics, and aesthetics, to which he intended to add a fourth, psychological branch. Though this was his original plan, the last part was never written. We must now turn to the third part, *Ästhetik des reinen Gefühls*, published in two volumes, in 1912, and also to his remarks on the fourth, psychological part, which can be found in his published works, highlighting those features that are of interest for the analysis of Cohen's critical philosophy. After completing the survey of the whole system, certain considerations will be possible on the characteristics of the "critical system" built up by Cohen (*ARG I*: 4 *passim*).

a. Aesthetics and System

Throughout *Ästhetik des reinen Gefühls*, and especially in the first chapter, Cohen emphasizes the systematic character of aesthetics. Actually, this character has at least two, closely connected, though distinct, fundamental meanings. However, Cohen does not insist on the dis-

131

tinction between them, tending to move from one to the other, according to the specific context. In one sense, for Cohen, the systematic character of aesthetics means the role of the discipline as the unitary foundation of the arts in the unity of art, while in another, it means the specific, indispensable role of aesthetics in the system of philosophy. As we shall see, the first aspect is linked to the second and, to be more precise, follows it. Nevertheless, each one has its own problems.[1] Given my general topic, it is certainly more appropriate here to consider aesthetics as a part of the system of critical philosophy. Still, some comment, however brief, needs to be made on the problem of the unitary ground of the arts.

Especially in the first chapter of *Ästhetik des reinen Gefühls*, Cohen argues not only against the opinion that art does not need a ground beyond itself, but also, particularly, against the claim in support of the traditional kind of art history or the more recent "science of art" (with reference to this second trend, Cohen mentions writers such as Semper, Wölfflin, Schmarsow, Fiedler, and, especially, Hildebrand)[2] as the unitary foundation of art. He challenges these claims with several arguments, which space does not allow me to elaborate on here (cf. *ARG I:* 45ff., 56ff.), and concludes that only one philosophical aesthetics can justify the pure, unitary principle that founds the possibility of art, and thus the unity of the arts. But the investigation of the pure ground of art brings aesthetics, by right, into the system of critical philosophy and sets it up as an essential part of it. For this reason, as I mentioned above, only consideration of aesthetics as part of the system of philosophy can justify the claim of aesthetics to be the systematic foundation of the unity of the arts.

b. Aesthetics and the Method of Purity

From the methodological stance, Cohen's aesthetics has some notable differences, which have rightly puzzled his interpreters, as compared with the other parts of his system. The main methodological novelty is the lack of reference to a science, as a fact acting as a starting point for critical investigation. In his previous works, Cohen had frequently insisted that an essential condition for transcendental investigation is the opportunity of referring to a science, from which to start off the investigation of its pure foundation. He had remained faithful to this principle, both in his logic and in his ethics (at least as far as his stated intentions are concerned), developing his investigation, in the first case, with reference to the sciences of nature, through the mediation of mathematics, and in the second, with reference to the moral sciences, through the mediation of the science of law. For aesthetics, however, he not only rejected the idea of referring to the "science of art," in the form in which it had been formulated by his contemporaries, but did not even pose the problem of reference to other possible conceptions of it. This refusal to refer to the fact of a science, as I have already noted, seems to obstruct the possibility of a critical investigation of art, from Cohen's methodological perspective, and the consequent placement of aesthetics in the system of critical philosophy.[3]

Apart from this, it appears to me that the abnormality, so to speak, of the aesthetic branch of the system extends further than the lack of reference to a specific science, and that this lack is linked to an even more drastic question: the very identification of a work of art is problematic in Cohen's aesthetics. Admittedly, he does theorize aesthetic objectification, without which it would not even be possible to posit the purity of the aesthetic principle, since the concept of 'purity' cannot be distinguished from that of 'production' and thus from that of 'objectification.' Cohen also acknowledges the traditional objective (*Objekte*) points of reference of the aesthetic experience of nature and works of art, but the identification of a true object (*Gegenstand*) of art is more of a problem for him, to the extent that he first tried out the route of the investigation of the object (cf. *ARG I*: 72ff.), only to break off soon, owing to the difficulties he encountered which could only be overcome after working through a wide-ranging theory of the foundation of the subject. Even then the determination of the object is constituted by its resolution in the specific process of aesthetic objectification as the realization of the subject itself (cf. *ARG I*: 191ff.).

In this Cohen remained faithful to Kant. He acknowledged the latter's supreme merit in this area of philosophy for having clearly formulated the principle of the limitation of aesthetic objectivity: "The limitation of objectivity, as the only possible value meaning of aesthetic consciousness, had already come about, to all intents and purposes, with the words that are the cornerstone of the foundation of Kant's aesthetics: '*No objective principle of taste is possible*'" (*ARG I*: 85–6).

Therefore, on what basis could Cohen, despite these serious limits regarding aesthetics in respect of method and object, believe that he could and should see it as an integral part of the system of philosophy? First, he starts off from a fact, even in the area of aesthetics. As we have seen, this fact is not a science, but an important aspect of culture, in the "heart of culture" (*ARG I*: 222), art, which constitutes a central problem for philosophy (cf. *ARG I*: 5). Owing to its systematic character, critical philosophy cannot reject the rational foundation of art, thus abandoning this area of culture to the indeterminacy of mystery and the irra-

tional, since, thus, it would give up its essential task of rational foundation of the unity of culture:

> No miracle or mysticism can survive criticism. Legality must eliminate all
> miracles. *Culture is unitary*, because a unitary law can and must be discov-
> ered in it, on the basis of a unitary method; this is the task of systematic
> philosophy: to make culture unitary in its methodical unitary legality. If art
> is an exception to systematic legality, then it should leave the concept of
> unitary culture, since the latter is grounded in legality, which is unitary
> from the methodical point of view. (*ARG I:* 18–9)

Inevitably, we notice the arbitrary division of culture into the three
branches of the science of nature, morality, and art. Actually, other no-
less-important cultural areas could be considered.[4] It is easy, however, to
identify the historical reasons for this perspective of Cohen, not only in
the model of Kant's system, but in Cohen's exclusive reference (and this
is also the case with most of his contemporaries) to European culture,
which was identified as the sole cultural model available. Further proof
of Cohen's exclusively European view of culture is the fact, already noted
by other interpreters,[5] that he only considered European art and its
sources (Greek and Hebrew art), while there is absolutely no reference
to non-European art.

After recognizing art as a fact of central importance in culture and
thus as an essential requirement for critical philosophy, which aspires to
being a system, that is, as the unitary foundation of culture, another serious question remains to be resolved: If and how can philosophy provide
the rational, pure foundation of art, since the factual datum of a science
to which to refer is missing? Cohen justifies the legitimacy of the inclu-
sion of aesthetics in a system of critical philosophy by means of the concept of 'legality' (*Gesetzlichkeit*), which he carefully distinguishes from
that of 'law' (*Gesetz*): "It is legality, not law that makes the artist a genius.
It is from legality that law springs, from which law comes out in that relativity from which even the work of art of the highest value cannot be
entirely freed. The law of the work of art can preserve its historical weaknesses, but systematic legality is revealed in the authentic genius" (*ARG I:*
71).

Referring to Kant's concept of 'genius,' Cohen interprets it as
"legality" and thus as a method of pure, rational production, analogous
to that of logic and ethics:

> Art is the art of genius. With these words Kant had opened the ethics of
> Classical art. With these words he had founded the method of an
> autonomous aesthetics ... there is a new, specific legality next to logic and

ethics. The genius is not only a magic word of fantasy, not only a miraculous word of mysticism, or of a sovereign instinct, for which there is no other legality; the art of the genius makes the genius of art the legislator of art. (*ARG I:* 14)

The genius, then, in the sense of legality, is the method of production of the aesthetic object.[6] By means of this identification of the concept of legality with that of production and therefore that of foundation,[7] Cohen was able to justify the legitimacy of placing aesthetics in the system of critical, rational philosophy and its consideration in the area of the method of purity (cf. *ARG I:* 74f.). These arguments do not entirely remove doubts, caused by failure to refer to a science, about the application of the transcendental method to art. In *Ästhetik des reinen Gefühls*, Cohen is able to demonstrate convincingly the idealist character of art as pure production, but actually the transcendental character of his aesthetic investigation is less clear, at least in the usual sense of the word *transcendental*, to which Cohen adhered. Cohen was aware of this, and proof is to be found in his recognition of the fact that the method of hypothesis already "becomes . . . weaker" (*ARG I:* 76) in ethics, since, as we have seen, for ethics, the science of law is merely an "analog" of mathematics for logic. This recognition, in the context in which it appears, implicitly suggests that an at least similar, if not greater, weakening of the critical method appears in aesthetics. Confirmation of this is provided by the fact that, being unable to start off from an aesthetic experience determined as a science, Cohen was forced to carry out the deduction of pure feeling from the subject, on the basis of arguments in which psychological considerations, which had already challenged ethics at certain moments (from the viewpoint of the method of purity), are preponderant. To a great extent, Cohen reworked psychological theories on feeling from his youthful works, when he was still influenced by the theories of Lazarus and Steinthal,[8] which he had also included in *Kants Begründung der Ästhetik*.[9]

c. Aesthetics and Critical System

However, if Cohen's aesthetics shows these defects and incoherences in respect of the method of purity—the methodological aspect of the principle of truth—it does represent an interesting stage in the critical system, with reference to the other aspects of the principle, highlighted in the previous chapter: the relationship of being with what ought to be and that between the universal and the individual. We shall need to evaluate the actual contribution of aesthetics to critical philosophy regarding these aspects. Thus, in this interpretation of Cohen's critical philosophy, the principle of truth ascends to the role of supreme principle of the system, including aesthetics. There is no need for surprise, if it is not mentioned even once in *Ästhetik des reinen Gefühls*, since the very concept of system, on which, as we shall see, Cohen placed great emphasis, is nothing more than an extension of the principle of truth.

The branches of being and what ought to be, of thought and will, of nature and man appear to complete the area of consciousness and its object (cf. *ARG I:* 92). Nature and man are the two objects of knowledge, and there are no others. As such they must constitute the preconditions (*Vorbedingungen*) of the aesthetic object. Nature and man are not, however, only preconditions, that is, preliminary conditions of the aesthetic object; they are also its conditions:

> The work of art is not only linked to these two types of object, *but it is also conditioned by them from the methodical viewpoint.* The work of art must be, absolutely, *first of all* an object of nature, and as such an object of the knowledge of nature. It is the work of art that must be, *besides,* close to the first condition and closely connected with it, an object of morality, and must be producible as a *pure* object of moral knowledge. *These two conditions are indestructible, fundamental conditions of the work of art and artistic creation. . . . Preconditions are, rather, permanent conditions,* almost an integral part of the work of art. They are only preconditions in the methodical sense, i.e. for aesthetic fulfillment, but they are present, and cannot be evaluated, in every step and degree on the route followed by the work of art, right up to the last stage, when fulfillment is reached. They are only preconditions, however, and how can this great enigma be solved? All the difficulties with the aesthetic problem are present in this question. (*ARG I:* 80)

The problem only finds an answer in the identification of a new branch of consciousness, able to produce a *new* object from logic and ethics: this is pure feeling.

d. Pure Feeling and Its Content

Through a phenomenological analysis, upon which space does not allow me to elaborate,[10] Cohen establishes aesthetic consciousness as pure feeling, as "the behavior of consciousness within itself, remaining within itself, withdrawing for private activity, resting and establishing itself in this activity, self-satisfaction with this behavior, without going out, or moving in the direction of the outside, so as to reach an object as content of knowledge or will, beyond the specificity of the activity grounded in self" (*ARG I:* 97).

Therefore, feeling, in this meaning, accompanies every productive act of consciousness: both of the theoretical kind, of the unity of consciousness (Cohen identifies a "feeling of perception" [cf. *ARG I*: 149ff.] and a "feeling of thought"),[11] and the practical kind, of self-consciousness (Cohen identifies a corresponding "feeling of will" (cf. *ARG I*: 163ff.]). All these feelings are relative; that is, they are only an "*annex to a degree of content* of consciousness" (*ARG I*: 144). The presence of feeling in all the activities of consciousness is grounded in the fact that every process of consciousness, inasmuch as it is production and therefore movement, does not originate from a passive stage, like perception, but from a more originary active one: (the condition of) feeling (*Fühlen*), "*the disposition* of consciousness as such, both that directed towards *content* and that directed *inwards*" (*ARG I*: 136).[12]

The foundation of aesthetic experience as productive activity, and thus of aesthetics as a part of the critical system, in Cohen's view, is possible, if it can be demonstrated that feeling does not merely accompany the productive process of consciousness, in the theoretical and practical areas, that is, it does not only have a relative value as an annex of the production of the object of knowledge, but can also play its own independent productive role, through which, incorporating the meaning of the relative feelings, it overcomes them, nevertheless, in the independence of pure feeling, which is able to produce a new object independently, starting off from the objects of science and morality. For Cohen, this pure feeling is "love" (cf. *ARG I*: 174ff.). The "universal meaning" of love, which endows this feeling with the character of purity, is seen by Cohen as the Platonic *eros* (cf. *KBA* 9f.; *ARG I*: 174). The pure feeling of love provides proof of its purity, since it shows its capacity to produce a new content, by means of conferring a new figure (*Gestalt*) on nature and man, inasmuch as consciousness, through pure feeling, contemplates these two objects in their achieved unity, rather than in the distinction between them. The object of love is the 'nature of man,' and therefore, also, 'man in nature.' Man and nature, that is, are realized in unification and fulfillment (*Vollendung*)[13] in the new figure, produced by aesthetic feeling. Man and nature are united in aesthetic objectification, both in the sense of the unity between body and soul (the nature of man),[14] and in that of his natural environment (man in nature). So, even when a work of art only represents the natural environment, and when aesthetic experience has nature as its object, man is still present as the center transmitting his meaning in nature (cf. *ARG I*: 215ff.): "We have always used the formula: *the nature of man and man in nature*. There is very substantial content in this *double formula*. Man's nature is firstly his body, which becomes a *figure* when the soul within it is first penetrated by art.

But surrounding nature also belongs to man's nature. His organism belongs to this general nature. It is to the latter link that the second part of the formula (man in nature) refers" (*ARG I*: 213–14).

Man, who, following the principle of truth, moves in the direction of the realization, the fulfillment of self, as will and action, in nature (fulfillment that remains an infinite task in ethics), achieves this fulfillment in the figure in art:

> How does art realize this unity? It is here that plastic art is so instructive: it produces this unity in the *figure* of man. This figure is not only his body, as it is not merely his soul. *It is the unity of body and soul.* . . . If the soul of the figure is to become the content of production, *then the subject must become immanent in the object.* Pure feeling does not exhaust its concept in the content of the object: this only happens in the production of the subject. The soul builds up the body and the plastic figure is the building. The soul, both during rest and movement, flashes in each of its muscles. This soul of the figure is, however, above all the soul of feeling. The artist's soul takes on vitality in the soul of the figure. *It is also not complete at first,* only needing to shine out from the work of art. Instead it produces itself, only reveals itself in the figure, in its production. (*ARG I:* 191–92)

This is how pure feeling actually produces a new object, which does not only consist of the sum of man and nature, but is the fulfillment of their unification in a *new* figure (cf. *ARG I*: 191).

One could take the last lines of Goethe's *Faust*, as a motto for Cohen's aesthetics:

> What fails ineluctably,
> The undeclarable,
> Here it was seen,
> Here it was action[15]

Pure feeling realizes the infinite task of self-consciousness in the figure, and thus in the individual:[16]

> *Only aesthetic consciousness aims at a self, which is not posited as a content, the solution only in the task, but makes the individual its task, par excellence.* In this way this task can only require a solution in which *one remains in the individual.* Systematic aesthetics has its *outset* with the concept of the individual: *art is the art of the genius.* And what is valid for artistic creation must also be roughly valid, once and for all, for aesthetic experience. So here an ego, other than that of will, is at stake. . . . The fundamental relationship of links with plurality and universality is now overturned. Aesthetic feeling is love for man, for man's nature, for the man of and in nature. This nature of man is not only the norm, not only typical, and even less a reproduction

of moral humanity, of which he could never again be the original. In the end, what is this man of aesthetic feeling, of the aesthetic work of art? *Here the sought for ego becomes an actual event.* Here the first real production of self takes place, not as self-consciousness, but as *self-feeling.* (*ARG I:* 198–99)

The object of aesthetic feeling is therefore none other than the subject itself: man as an individual. This does not mean that pure feeling is resolved in an egoistical, narcissistic love of self, since self has now been enriched and made universal by the productive activity of pure feeling, which collects the content of nature and humanity and unifies them. It has become the ideal of the nature of man and of man in nature (cf. *ARG I:* 199, 209f.). The self of feeling, as the realization of the ideal in the individual, does not contradict man as the infinite task of ethics. Rather a new correlation between idea and realization, universal and individual, infinite task and fulfillment is placed there: "*Even if this self* [the self of feeling] *is not given as concluded.* It is not distinguished at all from moral self-consciousness in the character of infinite task. The difference lies solely in the fact that, in pure feeling, even every universality, not to mention every self, must always, inexorably, immerse itself in the pure individual" (*ARG I:* 200; cf. *ARG I:* 212f.).

e. The Idea of the Beautiful

These themes are further developed by Cohen in the discussion of the idea of the beautiful. He attempts to respond to the need for determination of the set of principles that, when deduced from a supreme principle, make aesthetic objectification possible. However, he immediately found himself facing the difficulty I have already mentioned of the absence of an aesthetic object comparable to the logical and ethical objects (cf. *ARG I:* 238). This specific case of aesthetics appears to make it impossible to identify a principle of objectification, and indeed makes objectification itself in the field of art and, consequently, the application of the method of purity in aesthetics problematic:

> Scientific knowledge confers value and a specific imprint on foundation in the categories, which are the foundation stones of being. Moral ideas expect an analogous determination of being in the institutions of law and the State. . . . But what is the situation regarding the idea of the beautiful? It appears only to refer to the concrete reality of the work of art, thus only appearing to take on existence in the single phenomenon. What more can it mean inasmuch as it is *foundation,* if the foundation must mean the ground of an authentic being? (*ARG I:* 245–46)

The problem can only be overcome if we consider the particular type of objectification realized in art. It is defined as "reflexive objectification" by Cohen (*ARG I*: 246), or "objective subjectification" (*ARG I*: 254), or "subjective objectification" (*ARG II:* 419). In art, that is, the work produced is only the objective point of reference, while the true content is the subject itself, the self of feeling. Thus, in art, a new type of correlation is realized between subject and object, which consists of "objectification in the self," in the "*first, authentic self founded in itself,* as the self of self-feeling" (*ARG I*: 238). The "*mediating* idea" (*ARG I*: 246) of this reflexive objectification is the idea of the beautiful. This conception allows any meaning of the idea of the beautiful to be excluded, not only as a given inherent in things themselves, but also as an objective law of artistic taste: the beautiful is the mediating principle of aesthetic objectification, but, owing to the characteristic correlation between subject and object current in art, it cannot be considered an objective principle like logical and ethical ones. Therefore, the idea of the beautiful is, even more than the logical and ethical principles, an infinite task, and only as such is foundation. Task is an inherent characteristic of any logical and ethical idea, but, while the logical and ethical principles, though having this character of infinite task, make the actual foundation of an object possible (concept in logic, the state in ethics), even though this object is never a conclusive, exhaustive realization of the infinite task, in aesthetics the situation is overturned. The idea of the beautiful is production, only inasmuch as it is a task, and yet any objectification of the feeling of self in the work of art is an actual, concluded realization of idea as task, even though this does not prevent further inclination toward the infinite task. One could say that, while the opening for an infinite task is always immanent in ethics, in aesthetics the principle of production is nothing more than a task, and any product, that is, any work of art, is the immanent solution of such a task: "*What is the meaning of the idea of the beautiful as foundation? . . . The idea of the beautiful means the task of the beautiful. . . .* Foundation is only a task, to which the solution is immanent" (*ARG I*: 247–48; cf. *ARG II:* 419).

f. The Sublime and Humor

The particular aesthetic correlation between task and fulfillment led Cohen to the articulation of the idea of the beautiful in the subordinate concepts (*Unterbegriffe*) of 'the sublime' and 'humor.'

Refusal to consider the sublime a coordinate, rather than a subordinate, aesthetic category, in respect of the beautiful, is one of the points where Cohen's distance from Kant's aesthetic theory is most striking.

This distance first appeared in *Kants Begründung der Ästhetik,* the work commenting on Kant published in 1889. It takes its place in a series of objections to Kant listed and justified by Cohen in *Ästhetik des reinen Gefühls* (cf. *ARG I*: 100ff.), but which are already mostly to be found in *Kants Begründung der Ästhetik* (cf. *KBA* 232ff., 238, 251ff., 268ff., 276ff.). Owing to lack of space, I cannot analyze Cohen's objections to Kant in detail. I shall limit myself to highlighting the common denominator of most of them. In Kant's *Critique of Judgment,* in Cohen's view, there is no satisfactory solution of the relationship of the beautiful with knowledge and morality. On the one hand, Kant provided an intellectualistic interpretation of the beautiful, inasmuch as he only placed it in a relationship with the faculty of representations, and underestimated its relationship with morality, to the extent of needing to place the sublime, as an artistic moment bearing ethical values, next to it, externally and in unresolved coordination. However, at the same time, the indispensable need to posit a relationship between the beautiful and moral value is resolved by Kant by, paradoxically, overturning the essentially intellectualistic interpretation of the beautiful as a symbol of morality: a confusion between aesthetic and ethical ideals threatening the autonomy of aesthetics in respect of ethics.

For these reasons Cohen could not accept the Kantian foundation of the traditional distinction between beautiful and sublime and worked out the system of aesthetic judgments anew, insisting, on the one hand, on the idea of the beautiful as the sole "superior principle" of aesthetic foundation (cf. *ARG I*: 250; *II:* 417f.), and, on the other, considering the sublime and humor two complementary "subordinate concepts," two integrating, inseparable (though distinguishable) stages of the beautiful (cf. *ARG* I: 347f.). For the deduction of the sublime and humor, in their distinction and complementarity, Cohen referred to the considerations already made on the specific relationship of art with knowledge and morality. It will be recalled that he acknowledged knowledge and morality to be not only the preconditions but also the permanent conditions of aesthetic production. Admittedly, nature and man, the latter in his universal ethical meaning, do not constitute the aesthetic object. This would invalidate the independence and originality of aesthetic production. However, logic and ethics condition aesthetics, not only inasmuch as their object constitutes the material of the contents of art, but also methodically (cf. *ARG I*: 252ff.).

Cohen was especially careful about details here, so as not to be misunderstood. When positing a relationship between the sublime and humor with knowledge and morality respectively, he was conscious of risking criticism for having reduced aesthetic content to the mere sum of the contents of logic and ethics, a position that he wished to avoid. For this reason, he was careful to explain that the preponderance of knowledge in the sublime and that of morality in humor does not imply the exclusion of the other feature from each of the two subordinate genres of the beautiful, since, otherwise, they could certainly not be considered subordinate concepts of the beautiful. In fact, both preconditions jointly converge in the latter. Second, Cohen explains that the preponderance of one or the other method must be solely as an impulse (*Ausschlag*) in one or the other branch, knowledge or morality, in the context of a dynamic relationship between these two preconditions. The beautiful is thus conceived, not as an immobile state of consciousness, but actually as a dynamic game of all the faculties, in accordance with Kant's conception, to which Kant himself did not always adhere satisfactorily:

> The advantage of our conception of *methods* as conditions also appears again here. If conditions consisted only of materials, it would be more difficult, or even only metaphorical, to understand that the new method is grounded in the continuous effect of the first two contents. But these contents are themselves methods, which, as such, still continue to be efficacious, but, in their efficacy, they must constitute a *contrasting movement*; and this contrasting movement is now oscillating from one side to the other. From one side to the other, never exclusively in one direction. The relationship remains, but, as a relationship, it can only consist of a movement, a contrasting movement. From one side to the other, this must not be taken literally, which means vaguely. It is not at all necessary, not at all possible that an *exchange in the impulse* should take place. Rather, this impulse can repeat itself, grow stronger and thus take on the appearance of permanence. This must remain appearance, since the relationship always requires an inclination in the other direction, and thus the constant cooperation of the other condition. But one of the two directions may prevail, may become decisive. (*ARG I:* 257)

Several interpreters[17] have emphasized the drastic difference between *Ästhetik des reinen Gefühls* and *Kants Begründung der Ästhetik*, with reference to the theoretical or ethical valence attributed by Cohen to the sublime or humor. While, in *Kants Begründung der Ästhetik*, Cohen linked the sublime with the moral impulse, and humor with the theoretical one (cf. *KBA* 280f.), in *Ästhetik des reinen Gefühls*, he inverted this relationship. Here I should like to give, if not an exhaustive account of the reasons for this change in his position, at least a brief explanation which seems relevant to the meaning of Cohen's critical philosophy.

One of the main (if not the only) reasons for this change is the clear intent to oppose an aesthetics of the sublime and detach the meaning of idealist aesthetics from it. This intention is a coherent consequence of Cohen's conception of a contrast between critical and absolute idealism. As briefly mentioned above, Cohen had already noted the risk of art being subject to morality in Kant's aesthetics, and especially in the entry of ethical meaning into art through the category of the sublime and the conception of the beautiful as a symbol of morality. What is more, this morality is actually resolved in religion and mysticism, being deprived of its character of knowledge. For Cohen, there was already a risk that the aesthetics of the beautiful is reduced and distorted in the aesthetics of the sublime, understood as religious, mystical symbolism: "Some attention could be dedicated to the fact that in *Kant* all the true theory of beauty in art, the art of the ideal, the art of the genius, is only discussed *after* the analytic of the sublime. Thus it could appear that the sublime, rather than the beautiful is the true fundamental creative concept, so that the sublime would become the superior concept" (*ARG I*: 251). Romanticism developed the trend, unilaterally (cf. *ARG I*: 9ff.), and this deviation "is still present in our own time" (*ARG I*: 11).

The "appearance" (cf. *ARG I*: 257) of a preponderance of morality in the sublime leads to a serious error in idealist aesthetics. In such a way,

> nature must be beautiful in itself, but only beautiful inasmuch as it is sublime. For, otherwise, how could it be beautiful? It is this that led to the consequence that only morality makes nature beautiful, i.e. sublime. These coordinate concepts coincide in nature. However, they do not only coincide in this way, but become identical. If nothing remains for beauty, with reference to nature, beyond that which lies in its sublimity, this should also count for beauty in general, therefore also for beauty in art. Thus, however, an absurd situation would arise. Art would only be the art of the sublime, since nature can only be the object of feeling in the guise of sublime nature. Again the result is the elimination of the specificity of art. The source of the sublime in nature only lies in morality. If, however, art is only really sublime, then its specificity only lies in morality. (*ARG I*: 339)

This reduction of art to morality, is, in Cohen's view, even more serious, since, in such a context, morality itself is distorted by "religious symbolism" (*ARG I*: 256) and is resolved in mysticism (cf. *ARG I*: 255). It is interesting to note how this criticism of symbolism prepared Cohen for recognition of the just requirements of impressionism and its meaning in an authentic idealist conception of art and art criticism (cf. *ARG I*: 110, 337ff.; *ARG II*: 326).[18] Thus, Cohen recognized a preponderance of the theoretical direction in the sublime, though this does not imply the absence of a moral element (cf. *ARG I*: 258). This does not mean (and this seems to me to be one of the most interesting elements in relation to the critical character of Cohen's philosophy) that Cohen rejected the characteristic, traditional interpretation of the sublime as an opening and inclination toward infinity, but rather that he recognized the prevalence of the theoretical, rather than ethical, direction in this inclination.

An essential critical formulation, which was already present in Cohen's logic and ethics, emerges, transformed in its new meaning in the aesthetic context, from his interpretation of the sublime and humor. We have already seen, in the first two parts of the system, that nature, and thus science, cannot be considered as the area of the finite, and man, thus history and morality, as the area of infinity, in Cohen's critical perspective. There is always a correlation between finite and infinity, existence and idea or task, both in knowledge and in morality. Contrary to other possible philosophical conceptions, Cohen's critical philosophy sees science as knowledge of the finite, inclining, by its very nature, toward the infinite task of the universal, while morality, grounded in pure ethics, is knowledge of the universal, of the infinite task, and action continually aiming at the realization of this task in the finite. The theoretical trend toward the widening of the finite into infinity, and the practical one of the realization of infinity in the finite are two indistinguishable features, in their distinction and complementarity, in their irreconcilable difference, but also in the ideal of their unification, for critical philosophy. All this had already clearly emerged as one of the essential contents of the principle of truth. The reflection of this critical correlation reappears, in the new aesthetic context of completed unification, though in an ideal reality, in the correlation between sublime and humor as subordinate concepts of the beautiful.

Therefore, the sublime is characterized by an inclination to infinity, the task, which is not an overcoming, but rather elevation of the finite to infinity:

> The finite is not happy to remain finite, but has the courage to overcome the distance from infinity. The limitations of the finite are eliminated, there is an aspiration to elevation (*Erhebung*) to infinity. Infinity must not remain something alien, external. It may well be that it must be and remain something transcendent. This is unimportant, as long as it must not be something external or heterogeneous. But is what happens in this aesthetic sublimity (*Erhabenheit*) arrogant, or a presumption (*Überhebung*)? This cannot be right, since presumption is contrary to moral law, but the latter is the indispensable premise, concerning matter and method, of aesthetic purity. The sublime thrust towards infinity is not at all presumptuous, otherwise, sublimity would be presumption, as well as elevation. (*ARG I:* 266–67)

Owing to the fundamental characteristic of aesthetic experience, and thus of the beautiful, that is the correlation between task and the solution realized in it, 'fiction' (not in the negative sense of illusion, but in the positive one of hypothesis) of the infinite process, proper to the sublime, must be integrated by the fiction of the conclusion (*Abschluss*) of this process. The infinite task and realization must be integrated in a correlation where one term does not exclude the other, but both coexist continually and dynamically (and dialectically, though in the sense of an ever-open dialectic that does not need to be overcome, since it bears all its wealth and productivity [cf. *ARG I*: 271f.] in the dynamic correlation itself). The aspect of "conclusion" is that represented by humor. If the sublime represents, within the beautiful, the stage of inclination towards infinity, "tireless work" (*ARG I*: 267), humor is the stage of realization of infinity in the finite, of the recognition of the immanent, infinite value in finite reality and thus of peace: "the other route, as we have mapped it out, must proceed towards the end of infinite work, carried out under the sign of conclusion, towards the end of the struggle in victory and peace" (*ARG I*: 275). Cohen contrasts an idealist aesthetics where titanic struggle and victorious peace are dynamically balanced with the Titanism of the aesthetics of the sublime: "There is not only moral blame in the titanic attribute, which is normally given to the sublime; there is also a precise aesthetic verdict in it. The Titans were cast down from Olympus, but the genius must not only stretch out towards the heavens, but conquer them in the work of art" (*ARG I*: 274).

The realization of the infinite task in the finite, of idea in existing reality, had already emerged as a fundamental direction for ethics, but it was precisely there that this trend, as a direction for action, had revealed itself as an infinite task. How can art reach the realization that ethics, in its own area, has shown to be unreachable? Precisely because art does not pursue it through will and action, but through pure feeling, that is, love. Aesthetic experience is essentially love of man's nature. Therefore, it is principally inspired, in the direction of humor, by love of man in the limits of his concreteness and finiteness, and thus by an ethical impulse. However, at the same time, it cannot be restricted to ethics, since it is not an infinite effort for realization through action, but calm, smiling contemplation[19] of the infinite value of man in his integral, concrete reality through love. Thus Cohen was able to bring the uncomfortable theme of the ugly into the aesthetics of the beautiful. This theme had not been "completely ignored by ancient art, but neglected in its full meaning" (*ARG I*: 58).

As a parallel to what has already been said about the sublime — that, though not being an inclination of the finite towards the infinite, it, however, never goes beyond the finite, but is rather its elevation—similar considerations must be dedicated to humor and its relationship with the ugly. The ugly represents the lowest level of the finite, "man's animal nature" (*ARG I*: 281). Consideration of the ugly by aesthetic consciousness through humor is certainly not complacent satisfaction for the ugly. This would be vulgarity, with which humor cannot be confused; it is actually its opposite. The consideration of the ugly by humor is, instead, ability to love beauty even in the low, animal condition of man. The ugly is also beautified (*verschönen*) through love:

> This is the indispensable task of art, not to superficially cover over or disguise man's links, in his whole culture, with the animal world. This link is represented, threateningly, for any truthfulness of art, by the ugly. This task belongs to the beautiful.
>
> Is the ugly a problem of the beautiful? Humor supplies and establishes the answer. The ugly does not remain ugly; it becomes a stage of the beautiful, it is a stage of the beautiful. The beautiful is not, in itself, an object of art. It is only an idea, only the general need and trust, the methodical task of pure feeling. This task is, firstly, resolved through the sublime, but, in an equally necessary way, by humor. For man's nature shows itself thoroughly and convincingly in the ugly. Love would not be true if it did not also wish to embrace the ugly. Love embraces it, transforms it, makes it one of the stages of the beautiful. Love understands the ugly, filling it with its own power. Thus satire becomes eros. *Love ennobles the animal, turning it into man.*" (*ARG I:* 288–89)

Through humor, love, the pure feeling, fully reveals its universality, inasmuch as it is love of the individual, or rather love of humanity in the individual. It is "humanitarianism":[20] "Man's love of nature thus receives its most profound foundation in this *respect for man's dignity in all men.* This dignity of man must be the undoubted, unmistakable mark of every work of art" (*ARG I:* 233). Therefore, in humor, and not in the sublime, ethics is preponderant, since "in the sublime, the body, above all as a figure, always seems to remain the most important feature, where the soul lies, into which the soul is poured. . . . But the body is still the ground of the unity of body and soul: here the soul becomes the consequence. On the other hand, in the art of humor, the main task seems to reside in the fact *that a figure coming from the soul is given to this unity in the body*" (*ARG I:* 295).

For this reason, Cohen, though insisting on the complementarity of sublime and humor, without which there can be no idea of the beautiful, contrasts the primacy of humor, if not exactly an aesthetics of humor, with the aesthetics of the sublime, which is not entirely coherent with his conception of aesthetics in the area of critical idealism, in opposition to absolute idealism:

> Just as there is no fixed state of consciousness that corresponds to the sublime and humor, so there is not even a single sublime work of art, nor an isolated work of humor. Both concepts, being only stages of the beautiful, are also only stages of the work of art, impulses in the oscillation of creation and experience, but not stabilized directions. Here, we are only considering the advantage of this conception for the concept of the aesthetic self. Therefore, it is once again necessary to specify that this result should be attributed more to humor than the sublime. Since humor is preponderant for morality; thus it swings more in the direction of the objectification of the self as self, while the sublime, the direction towards knowledge being preponderant, must objectify the ego in concept. Will, however, leads to *self-consciousness*, and this is closer to self-feeling than the consciousness of the ego proper to concept. Thus humor plays a more obvious role in the clarification of pure feeling as the unity of consciousness, inasmuch as it is thought in abstraction from any conceptual content. (*ARG II:* 421)

We shall conclude this brief analysis of Cohen's aesthetics by summarizing its important achievements for a conception of art in the area of idealist, but, above all, critical philosophy: a) the rational foundation of art in accordance with the method of purity (though this is the weakest aspect); b) the role of aesthetics in respect of the critical problem of the relationship between nature and morality, and between idea and reality; c) the role of aesthetics in respect of the critical problem of the foundation and understanding of the concrete individual; and d) opposition to any kind of aesthetics of the sublime, and its contrast with the primacy of humor.

2. Psychology

Aesthetics seems to have completed the system of philosophy. It provides a philosophical foundation for art, the third fundamental branch of culture. Besides, the possibility of the unification of the logical and ethical objects, the realization of the ideal of humanity, is justified in aesthetics. Therefore, the task formulated in the principle of truth appears to have been definitively achieved. Last, aesthetics demonstrates how, in art, the unification of man and nature is realized in the individual, consciousness thus achieving the complete reality of the self.

Nevertheless, Cohen did not believe his philosophical system had been completed yet. As has already been mentioned, he planned a treatment of psychology, as the fourth and last part of his critical system. Actually, this psychology was never written, though forming part of the overall plan for the system right from the outset, as references to it throughout the previous parts confirm. Even though he never actually wrote his psychological treatise, Cohen did work out some parts of it, going beyond a mere plan. Evidence for this is provided by the classes he held at Marburg University on psychology as the encyclopedia of philosophy, in the winter semesters of 1905 through 1906 and 1908 through 1909 and in the summer semester of 1916. Unfortunately, there exists no documentation of these classes (though we know of unpublished material used for reference by Cohen in a letter written by Natorp on May 17, 1918),[21] which can help us to reconstruct the development of Cohen's systematic psychology.[22]

Nevertheless, the references to psychology in the three published parts of the system and in *Einleitung mit kritischem Nachtrag zu F. A. Langes Geschichte des Materialismus etc.* do provide a relatively clear picture of Cohen's psychological project. Here I shall briefly look into its characteristic traits, exclusively from the viewpoint of the present work, that is, the critical character of Cohen's philosophy. Therefore I shall not deal with the manifold, important, and interesting problems raised by the project, except that of its place in the system of critical philosophy. Neither shall I look into the relationship between Cohen's conception of psychology and other internal developments of the Marburg school (it is sufficient to recall Natorp's psychology and Cassirer's philosophy of culture), or that with the numerous contemporary and subsequent attempts by thinkers outside the Marburg circle to work out a philosophy of culture.[23] In order to foreground the relationship between Cohen's psychological project and his critical philosophy, it may prove useful to start off with a criticism of this psychology. Willy Moog writes:

Is not the unity of logic alone sufficient? Is not a different kind of consideration in principle introduced through this psychology? If it has "the subject, the unity of human culture, as its sole content," then an empirical viewpoint seems to have been introduced, and this cannot be well reconciled with the pure, logical one. If, on the other hand, the task and concept of psychology are to be taken ideally and logically, then must not logic, in principle, be able to contain and determine this unity? Does not the new need for such an explicit grouping in unity simply depend on inadequacy in the conceptual exposition, while this is already ideally prescribed immanently in the logical union of knowledge, and only means its concretization and, in no way, a new systematic foundation, and so we must do without it from the point of view of rigorously systematic foundation?[24]

So Moog does not accept the placing of psychology in the critical system, since, either it would not have a founding role, like the other parts of the system, or it would be identified with logic. I cannot agree with this objection, and it seems to me that discussion of it could be a good occasion for a precise definition of the position of Cohen's critical psychology within his system.

Moog points out that if psychology is not to be identified with logic and restricted to it, it cannot play the same role as the other parts of the system. This seems an acceptable view, but it is precisely this specificity that justifies its placement in the system, and, at the same time, develops the meaning of critical philosophy by adding a new feature. Among the various, mostly similar formulas used by Cohen to define the problem of psychology, the simplest is "unity of consciousness" (*ARG II:* 426). It is essential here to refer to the explanation and discussion of the concept, or rather category, of "consciousness," developed by Cohen in *Logik der reinen Erkenntnis* (cf. *LRE* 420ff.).

First, it must be emphasized that, in Cohen's view, the "place" of the category of consciousness is the judgment of possibility (cf. *LRE* 420), the first of the judgments of method, which are also deliberately termed judgments of critique (*LRE* 403). What distinguishes judgments of critique from other judgments? Precisely the fact that they do not have a founding role, but one of verification with respect to the method and results of the research, one of solution of controversy over jurisdiction; and, above all, one of unifying overview, though respecting distinctions, of the various judgments, with reference to knowledge, which is the object of logic; of the various branches of the spirit, in the wider cultural context (cf. *LRE* 402f.).

Thus the category of consciousness is considered by Cohen in close relationship with the *critical* judgment of possibility. For reasons of space, I cannot discuss here his analysis of the historical development of the concept of 'possibility' (cf. *LRE* 404ff.). However, it is, necessary to pause over certain stages and problems, which he saw as decisive in this development.

In Cohen's view, all ancient, and medieval and some modern thought, from Aristotle onward, has struggled over two extreme meanings of the concept of the possible: on the one hand, a negative meaning, for which, what is thinkable is possible, but, since what does not go against the principle of noncontradiction is thinkable, that is, what is not unthinkable is simply thinkable, the result is the reduction of the possible to what is not unthinkable; on the other hand, the possible is understood in the sense of strength and developed by theological speculation as absolute strength, that is, as the "*originary source of all positiveness*... the originary ground of the thinkable, and, as such, of what it is" (*LRE* 408).

A decisive turning point in the history of the concept of possibility is represented, in Cohen's view, by Leibniz's distinction between the terms *possible* and *compossible*, in which the compossible takes on the meaning of "*connexion avec le reste de l'univers.*"[25] The concept of the possible is thus enriched by the meaning of connection of one element with all the others and thus that of a mutual, harmonious, and systematic relationship between all the elements. However, Leibniz, according to Cohen, restricted the application of the new concept of possibility to the area of logic. Actually Cohen emphasizes the fact that, in order to show the new meaning of possibility, Leibniz used an example from aesthetics, that is, whether the story of *Astrée* is possible or not.[26] But this approach to aesthetics, however interesting it may be, is still limited to the use of an example that is not taken further. However, the field of ethics is also linked in Leibniz to the theological ground, and the possibility of moral action is still grounded in God. This is where the influence of medieval theology on Leibniz can be seen.

The great novelty deriving from Leibniz's thought was taken up by Kant, who distinguished analytical from synthetic judgments, on the basis of the double meaning of the concept of possibility: as pure possibility and connection with possible experience. However, this new meaning of the concept of possibility remains restricted and reduced to the area of knowledge and has no application in ethics or aesthetics.

This reduction of the area of application of the concept of the possible to logic left room for a revival of ontology in romanticism. Cohen provides the example of Hegel, in whom the dialectical process is nothing other than a "*self-disclosure of the concept*" (*LRE* 416). Concept, the *logos*, thus takes on the role of an absolute principle and so does not differ, except for its name, from the absolute being of ontology. Actually, this ontological development, which in Hegel reaches its climax, has its roots in Fichte, who used a terminology which brings us right back to the problem of psychology: for Fichte self-consciousness is the absolute principle from which everything is deduced. This principle of self-consciousness, originating with Descartes, had already been criticized by Kant, who had preferred to use the term *unity of consciousness* for the supreme, unitary principle of knowledge, so as to avoid confusion and false interpretations in the substantialist, or absolute, and thus ontological, sense. Kant's unity of consciousness is none other than the unity of principle, not the unity of self-consciousness. Kant's unity of consciousness, however, only concerns the theoretical area and is totally unconnected with ethics and aesthetics.

Fichte's interpretation of Kant's philosophy as the "method of self-consciousness" (*LRE* 419) opened the way for a revival of ontology, for which consciousness had become the new absolute principle, that is, the substitute of substance in the new ontology. For this reason, Cohen had always seen the philosophical psychology and ontological metaphysics in romanticism as two aspects of a single formulation of thought, and this already emerges in his arguments against Kant's physiological-metaphysical interpretation.

Now that these presuppositions have been clarified, it is easier to present the intention and fundamental formulation of Cohen's psychological project and its entry into the critical system. Once he had ascertained that empirical, experimental psychology cannot be an autonomous science, nor constitute the ground of philosophy, since it must base itself on the founding principles of the philosophical system,[27] and had turned his attention to the possibility of philosophical psychology, Cohen planned a critical psychology, which would return to the results emerging from the history of critical thought, basically in Leibniz and Kant, though going beyond them in his widening of the functions of the concept of consciousness, beyond the theoretical area, with reference to the general context of culture. In this new formulation of the critical conception of psychology Cohen continually confronted the romantic conception, polemically, so as to bring out the contrast between the two formulations: a contrast which is none other than a reflection of the more general antithesis between critical and absolute idealism (cf. *E* 40f.).

The two polemical cornerstones of Cohen's psychology are, therefore, on the one hand, psychophysiology and, more generally, empirical, experimental psychology, but only inasmuch as the latter aims at being a founding discipline; on the other hand, within the philosophical conception of psychology, romantic psychology and its coda in contemporary thought, inasmuch as it is metaphysical and ontological, with which he contrasts his own critical psychology.[28]

Concerning the latter contrast, consciousness does not take on the meaning of the absolute principle from which to deduce all knowledge and reality, in Cohen's philosophy, but rather that of a principle of critical verification, unification and connection between the different directions of the spirit. So psychology can only be the last part of the system, rather than the first, and its role can in no way be confused with that of logic, as Moog hypothesizes:

> It is usual to speak of a relationship between psychology and philosophy. However, the concept of philosophy remains undetermined from the methodical viewpoint and, by way of this nondetermination, it becomes

surreptitiously possible to determine and realize philosophy through psychology. If, on the contrary, only systematic philosophy is mentioned from the outset, it is being claimed that its beginning can only lie in logic, and thus any determination of a relationship of psychology with philosophy must start with the determination of its relationship with logic, that it can only spring from this source. (*E* 53)

The system is grounded, first of all, in the fundamental principles of the method of purity, formulated in logic; these principles are valid for all the parts of the system, including psychology, since it also uses a transcendental method. It certainly does not set out from the fact of a science, but from culture, which is still a fact,[29] to return to the unitary principle of its unity and possibility. Second, the system consists of specific principles of the various directions of the spirit, that is, of the knowledge of nature, man, and ethical action, and, finally, of artistic creation. However, the system would not be complete and critical in an all-embracing meaning of critical philosophy if it were not concluded by that moment of verification, coordination and unification of the various directions of the spirit, in their distinction, but also in their mutual connections and influences, which constitute psychology. The result of this concluding part of the system must be the justification of the convergence of all the different directions of the spirit in a unitary spiritual reality, which is the unity of culture. In this sense psychology does not have the specific problem of the establishment of a direction of the spirit, beside the others, but is rather the "*hodegetic encyclopedia of the system of philosophy*" (*ARG II:* 432). It can therefore only be placed at the end of the system.

In Cohen's project, then, psychology was to be the concluding part of the system, its "head" (*ARG II:* 427), its "climax" (*ARG II:* 426). Cohen defines it as the "teaching of the *unity of the consciousness of culture*" (*E* 43).[30] Actually, each part of the system aims to found the unity of consciousness, but only in a specific area, in a specific direction: as the unity of thought, will, and feeling. Aesthetic consciousness, which includes and unifies knowledge and morality, as conditions and materials, in itself, transforms these contents into a new direction, which must be placed next to the others and cannot be either originary unity or final synthesis:[31]

The three preceding systematic disciplines build, each for itself, a unity of consciousness, and aesthetics, particularly, contains moral and logical unity. And yet it is also nothing more than a *degree on the way to unity*, not in itself already *the* unity of consciousness. The unity of consciousness, as a *problem of psychology*, presupposes those three unities. It contains them, but with its own material builds a new unity, the living unity of consciousness, and only this is the authentic, true one, of which the preceding ones are only the initial features. (*ARG II:* 426)[32]

Only psychology, inasmuch as it is the concluding part of the system, can present the unity of consciousness as the systematic unification of its various directions. But the systematic unity of consciousness can only be determined in relation to the unity of culture. Critical philosophy rejects any abstraction of the subject from its relationship with the object, which would still be a dogmatic, metaphysical attitude: "The spirit of man . . . is not absolute, since it is produced in its productions" (*E* 44). The unity of consciousness can be determined on the basis of the hypothesis of the unity of culture. Cohen, developing the definition of psychology quoted above, writes that it is "*the psychology of the unity of consciousness of unitary culture*" (*ARG II:* 429). This definitively clarifies, on the one hand, the placing of psychology at the end of the system, since it can only define the unity of consciousness by the unification of the various directions of culture, and on the other hand, Cohen's conception of psychology, not as a theory of the subject contrasted with the other parts of the system, which supposedly refer to the object (as is the case in Natorp),[33] but as an "encyclopedia of the system of philosophy."

Further investigation of the definition of psychology appears in *Einleitung mit kritischem Nachtrag zu F. A. Langes Geschichte des Materialismus etc.*, where it is called "*the teaching of man in the unity of his cultural consciousness, as of the development of this unity and the genetic connection of all its features and their embryos*" (*E* 11). Actually, the idea of the unity of humanity is the condition for the possibility of the idea of the unity of culture: "The unity of humanity is the hypothesis of the unity of culture; the unity of culture is the hypothesis of the unity of systematic consciousness" (*ARG II:* 429). Only in culture in its entirety, in the unity of its various features, does man realize the universal value of humanity in himself: "*The great task of psychology is to represent this macrocosm of humanity in the microcosm of the man of culture*" (*ERW* 637).

3. THE CRITICAL SYSTEM

Thus system, truth, and humanity emerge in all their essential connectedness in the critical system, which should be completed by psychology. The system is the widening of the principle of truth, as the latter is the principle of the unification of logic and ethics. The system is the task of unification of all the different directions in which the productivity of the human spirit develops in the ideal unity of culture (cf. *LRE* 610).

Psychology, then, was intended to conclude Cohen's philosophical system. As we have seen, the characteristics of his critical system are confirmed in the plans for this last part.

The apparent paradox in this formula is justified by the fundamental difference in Cohen's philosophical standpoint in respect of the concept of system in romantic idealism. Cohen's is first not a dogmatic system, since it is not grounded in an absolute originary unity. The unity at the base of the system is purely methodological, while the unity of the systematic principle is resolved in the unity of task, that is, in the unity of culture. This basic characteristic makes a system based on "a *weak* concept of the unity of reason,"[34] but also an open system, which is not subject to the serious criticisms from contemporary philosophy of any conception of the truth as a totality.

Admittedly, if working through the system clarified and resolved many problems, it does not appear to have dealt with others with the same thoroughness. Cohen himself was aware of this and, as we shall see, in the years to follow, posited again some problems already elaborated in the system, in a new light. Two points in particular seem to me to be important for the present investigation of Cohen's critical philosophy and the possible relationship between it and his philosophy of religion, with which I shall deal in the next chapters. On the one hand, it is legitimate to ask oneself if the three branches developed in the system—science, morality, and art—do actually cover the whole area of culture that is the object of philosophy. Stimulated by external criticism, he was to return to this, reflecting, in particular, on the relationship between religion and system. On the other hand, the question needs to be asked whether the system was successful, both in its single parts and as a whole, in achieving its purpose of understanding the individual concretely existing in a relationship with the idea of humanity. This purpose, as we have seen, is always present in Cohen's critical philosophy. Nevertheless, doubts can be raised about the ability of the system to achieve it.

I have already identified at least three fundamental factors in Cohen's critical philosophy, which are all present in the principle of truth, and thus also in that of the system, of which it is an enlargement: a) the method of purity; b) the unification of the directions of the spirit; c) the relationship between the idea of humanity and man as an individual, that is, the ability of critical reason to understand the concretely existing individual. Cohen himself did not appear to have been entirely satisfied with his system, concerning the last two points, and would return to them in later years, deliberately turning to the problem of religion.

Franz Rosenzweig notes a "fundamental experimental characteristic" in Cohen's approach to philosophy, which can be seen in the fact that

> he always thinks only when he thinks. His thought is always a task, whose results are never announced. The only architectural element in his works is their biographical succession. Thus the contradiction already pointed out between his treatment of religion in ethics and his most profound wisdom regarding it is evidently grounded in the circumstance that he was thinking of positing further contents in aesthetics. Thus this work had to be written, this intellectual experiment done, before the thinker could be convinced that now something had been left out.[35]

Rosenzweig then explains Cohen's advancement beyond the experiment of aesthetics and the system to the field of religion as being due to a subjective, rather than objective, need on his part to develop coherently problems that had already been opened up in his systematic philosophy, and not yet completely worked out: "Cohen the man still has some hidden treasures in him, which have not yet been uncovered by the spade digging up the treasures of the system."[36] This viewpoint justifies the interpretation of Cohen's late works on the philosophy of religion as a turning point from critical to existential philosophy, from the starting point of subjective, personal needs. One of the objectives of the rest of the present study will, on the contrary, be to show that, in this religious philosophy, Cohen further investigated problems that were already present in his system, and that, therefore, his new results are not a turning point, but a coherent further investigation of critical philosophy.

8

The Philosophy of Religion
and the System of Philosophy

1. CONTINUITY AND TURNING POINT: THE PHILOSOPHY OF RELIGION AND THE SYSTEM IN THE PERSPECTIVE OF CRITICAL PHILOSOPHY

One of the most interesting problems in the interpretation of Cohen, on which opinions differ, often considerably, and which is still open, is that of whether there was continuity or a break between his last works on the philosophy of religion and his system. Either standpoint involves the identification and analysis of the themes and concepts determining one or the other thesis. It is a well-known fact that issues of this kind, which have frequently been raised with regard to many philosophers, never have an exclusively historical meaning, but always imply theoretical intentions, upon which the overall evaluation of a philosopher's thought depends. Cohen himself had posited such a turning point between pre-critical thought and Kant's critical thought. Indeed, the category "turning point" was used throughout the historiographical reflections both of Cohen and of the whole Marburg school. The intention was always theoretical as well as historical. My task in this part of the book—to study the relationship between the philosophy of religion and critical philosophy in Cohen—requires me to look into this important issue, starting off from the most critical standpoints regarding it. I shall pass over the view (expressed by Joseph Klein)[1] that Cohen's religious thought merely fulfilled a personal need, conditioned by his own biography and the situation of Jews in German society, and examine the views of those in favor of the turning-point thesis, such as Franz Rosenzweig and Siegfried Ucko, and of those in favor of continuity with Cohen's previous thought, such as Heinz Graupe and Alexander Altmann.[2]

For Rosenzweig it was Cohen's new concept of 'correlation between God and man,'[3] and for Ucko it was the ontological meaning of his later theological studies[4] that marked the abandonment of the idealism and rationalism which had been basic to his philosophical system. However Graupe[5] argued against Ucko that Cohen's concept of God did not go beyond the methodological meaning of the whole of his idealism. Altmann,[6] against Rosenzweig, showed the methodical, formal character of the concept of correlation.

Thus, the positions taken up by the various interpreters on the relationship between philosophy and religion in Cohen are very different and, on occasion, diametrically opposed to each other. In the attempt to understand and evaluate this open problem once again, one cannot fail to acknowledge one undeniable feature: Cohen's conviction that it was legitimate to place his later religious thought within the system. On February 5, 1918, two months before he died, he wrote to Franz Rosenzweig's mother, Adele: "It is a good thing for us that, in this confusion, we still have a sure line of thought, whose advantage consists of the fact that our philosophy of culture entirely agrees with our religion."[7]

One of Cohen's fundamental studies of religious philosophy, dedicated to the Marburg school in 1915, was entrusted to his pupils with the following significant title: *Der Begriff der Religion im System der Philosophie*, and with the explicit intention of showing them the direction the system of the philosophy of religion was to take (cf. *BR*v).

Many further quotations could be made of passages bearing witness to Cohen's conviction concerning continuity throughout his thought. Furthermore, one could show not only that he announced the fact, but also that he theorized it. For the moment, it is enough to be aware of his conviction. This, of course, does not avoid the issue of whether the situation actually corresponded to Cohen's description. This is the real problem, and to test it, we must return to the examination of the fundamental aspects and concepts of Cohen's philosophy of religion. The hypothesis that will act as the ground of my enquiry is that if, instead of positing Cohen's idealism or ontology or panmethodism as the crucial issue, that of the viewpoint of his critical philosophy is faced, subordinating the other aspects to it and interpreting them in its light, a more convincing reinterpretation will be possible both of the aspects of continuity and those of contrast in Cohen's thought in respect of his system.

2. The Religion of Reason and Religious Experience

˅   Before embarking on this investigation, it should be noted that the above hypothesis excludes both the restriction of Cohen's religious thought to a mere expression of his personal experience of faith and the idea of a turning point in his later thought being simply determined by this personal experience. Whether or not one can recognize change or continuity (at this stage the question should remain open), Cohen's religious thought must be considered philosophical reflection, upon which personal experience may well have had some influence, but not a determining role, nor one of substitution. As Julius Guttmann rightly points out: "He is a Jew both in the originativeness of his feelings and in the awareness of philosophical knowledge. The strength of faith of Jewish messianism lives in him, and takes on a philosophical form in his system"[8]

I do not intend to deny Cohen's profound religious convictions, which remained with him all his life: from his youth, when, despite a tendency to overcome religion in ethics, he never rejected, or abandoned a profound feeling for his own religion,[9] up to the more intense religious convictions exhibited during the last years of his life, in the Jewish community in Berlin. What cannot be accepted is the idea that this "sentimental" dimension, to use Cohen's own term, was the driving force behind his religious thought, even if there is widespread evidence in his works of his personal participation in the object and contents of his religious research, which is, however, inspired by purely philosophical requirements and problems. Opting for philosophical speculation, and not the free expression of personal religious experience, was a definite choice on Cohen's part, indeed, as he himself wrote in a letter dated March 27, 1907 to Leo Munk, a "destiny": "Now I sincerely hope you will be in a fine state of mind on our wonderful holy day. My destiny is of a special kind. If there are men who make the sacrifice of the intellect, I make that of feeling. You know how attached I am, deep in my heart and in the most intimate feelings of my spirit, to the inner life of our religion, but even here my destiny is an abstraction, and only the pure can understand and tolerate me."[10]

3. Rational Religion and Constructive Method

It must also be pointed out, at this preliminary stage, that Cohen's religious thought, even during the last period, is not posited simply as a philosophy, but as a philosophy of the rationalist kind.

I shall not enlarge on whether the term *constructive* is a suitable adjective to describe the method of Cohen's religious philosophy,[11] or whether to see him as the "founder of a religion."[12] My view is that the issue is mainly one of terminology, since, from the methodical point of view, he did not abandon his choice of the transcendental method. This method could also be defined as constructive or founding, as long as the precise limits of such definitions are not forgotten. As has already been pointed out, there are three indispensable stages in the transcendental method: 1) a fact as a departure point; 2) the identification of the rational conditions of the fact; 3) the determination of the fact on the basis of those a priori conditions. If one of these stages is missing, there is no transcendental method. In Cohen's view the only correct method for investigation of religion is also the transcendental one:

> It must be pointed out, ever more clearly and precisely that *philosophy is a homogeneous factor with religion,* if true cultural maturity is ever to be the dominant factor in philosophy. The question cannot have a different development than that of the other fundamental cultural phenomena. We start off from its being factive and then pose the question concerning its right. *Physics* and *mathematics,* as well as *law* and the *State* and, lastly, the cultural fact of *art* have had to subject themselves to this transcendental investigation. How could religion be dealt with as a fact that can escape the question on the ground of the right to its existence and stability? (*BR* 8)[13]

Therefore, the definition of the method of Cohen's religious philosophy as constructive or founding cannot legitimately mean that he suggested that a new religion be invented and then built it up from the beginning by means of rational deduction. Even if there is a constructive or founding stage in the method, it can never be separated from Cohen's reflective philosophical horizons. Critical philosophy is above all, and always, *reflection* and only within this fundamental horizon can the various stages of the method be correctly evaluated. Since the definitions under discussion are at least ambiguous on this point, it appears best to put them aside.

Finally, some important considerations must be made on the rational nature of Cohen's religious philosophy. It is not enough, as is the case with Ucko, to acknowledge that the rational-transcendental method is incompatible with the descriptive-phenomenological one, and, therefore, criticism of the former based on the presuppositions of the latter are illegitimate.[14] It is also not enough to claim rights and legitimacy at least equal to those of the descriptive-phenomenological method for the rational-transcendental one, as Graupe does.[15] More needs to be done; the specific demands on religion of rational philosophy must be clearly stated and supported as important, indispensable, everlasting, and productive. This is what Emile Bréhier does, in an admirably clear and convincing fashion, in his excellent article *Le concept de religion d'après Hermann Cohen*.[16] Bréhier understood and defended Cohen's demand for rationality in the religious sphere, observing that failure in this respect would remove religion from culture, and thus from the area of human interst, reducing it to dogma and superstition.[17] This identification of the critical problem as the horizon within which Cohen's philosophy of religion is situated allows Bréhier to highlight its continuity with and belonging to the system, understood as philosophy of culture. He is also able to show the importance of a position such as that of Cohen for the purpose of facing up to and resisting the contemporary trend in the direction of relativism and subjectivism, in the general religious and cultural areas. This trend easily and almost inevitably, as can be seen in our own time, ends in skepticism and atheism, to the nourishment of which it may also contribute:

> Cohen's great task is to show the unity of consciousness in the different forms of culture. He does not want our intellectual city to be what Nietzsche calls this "multicolored cow." Systematic philosophy combats impressionism, a characteristic fault in the modern spirit, which, through "insufficient" understanding accepts all that lives and moves with total intellectual indifference. This fault is clearly visible, it must be added, in recent conceptions of religion, whose source is merely the claim to a unique experience, isolated and remote from the rest of the spirit. The solution to the religious problem cannot be based on such illusions, however brilliant. Religion only appears, then, as a bizzare phenomenon, grounded in passing, unstable states of consciousness; the only way to resolve the issue is to see whether religion has or does not have a necessary place in culture.[18]

4. The Peculiarity of Religion as Regards Ethics

Two basic characteristics of critical philosophy emerged in the previous chapters: its connection with the system and that between system and truth. Critical philosophy, system, and truth are the co-ordinates of a unitary, inseparable point of reference. Therefore, the issue of the relationship between religion and critical philosophy will need to find an answer in the relationship with the system and the principle of truth.

It is well known that the thesis of the reduction of religion to ethics[19] was abandoned by Cohen in his later writings, where, though not attributing independence (*Selbständigkeit*) to religion, he did accept its peculiarity (or specificity) (*Eigenart*) in respect of ethics, and more generally, in respect of the system. Cohen's change of view was undoubtedly substantially influenced by criticisms by Wilhelm Herrmann, who argued that Cohen had neglected the main characteristic of religion—its relationship with the individual—with his concrete, existential reality.[20] Cohen himself stated that he accepted Herrmann's criticisms and wished to make some partial corrections to his previous position after reading them (cf. *BR* 41ff., 56f.).[21] It is interesting to ask the question of whether Cohen's acceptance of Herrmann's objections on this point really agrees with the intentions of his interlocutor and does not actually have another aim that is more coherent with the former's general approach, that of critical philosophy. This issue can be a useful testing ground for the basic question of whether Cohen's change of view on this question is really a turning point or only a further investigation in the context of his previous philosophy.

Herrmann's objections are centered on the individual, in the concreteness and inscrutability of his or her existential experience and personal relationship with God, as the only true subject of religion. It is in this principle that Herrmann's thesis on the irreducibility of religion to ethics and to philosophy in general is grounded. If Cohen had really accepted this position and adapted his philosophy of religion to it, one could accept Rosenzweig's position that the former had abandoned idealism and rationalism to follow the route of dialogic, existential thought. But this is not the sense in which he returned to and accepted Herrmann's considerations. He agreed to entrust the theme of man as an individual to religion, which ethics cannot understand, and puts aside, or actually rejects the theme of existential existence as the source of religion, which reason cannot understand. In Cohen's view, the peculiarity of religion, instead of separating the latter from the system of philosophy, ensures it will have a secure position within it. Herrmann's objections are therefore for Cohen only an occasion to have a fresh look at problems in his religious philosophy such as that of real existence, of the realization of moral action and the individual, for whom the same system required further development and investigation.

It is significant that the determination of the peculiarity of religion in respect of ethics and the system in general was presented by Cohen in a work entitled *Der Begriff der Religion im System der Philosophie*. He clearly intended to define this peculiarity *within* the system rather than outside it. If the former were unable to fit into the system, then it would not be rationally understood at all by philosophy, and therefore religious philosophy would be impossible, since real philosophy is critical, that is, systematic: "If there is to be a philosophy of religion, this problem is only acceptable in the precise sense that *religion be placed within the system of phi-*

losophy; there is only one type of philosophy and that is systematic" (*BR* 16).

5. THE PECULIARITY OF RELIGION AS REGARDS THE SYSTEM

Thus Cohen denied religion independence in the system, that is, a specific "direction" of consciousness corresponding to it, preferring to write about peculiarity of religion as regards the system. This peculiarity consists of a "modification" (*BR* 44) of the ethical problem, an "enrichment" (*BR* 51), "expansion" (*BR* 58), and "completion" (*RV* 14, 18; Eng. trans. 13, 16) of ethics. Must the relationship between religion and philosophy be restricted to ethics then? Is the place of religion in the system only that of an appendix to ethics, however irreducible to it? If this had been the case, Cohen would not have distanced himself excessively from his previous view, from the reduction of religion to ethics. Certainly religion would no longer be resolvable in ethics, but it would still be an exclusively complementary area to it.

However, the situation is different. Above all in *Der Begriff der Religion im System der Philosophie*, Cohen develops the theme of the relationship of the philosophy with all the other areas of the system and clearly formulates the problem of the peculiarity of religion in this sense: "How is this peculiarity realized? To be more precise, the question is: *in what relationship with the pure types of consciousness is it realized?*" (*BR* 107).

In *Religion der Vernunft* this point is not foregrounded,[22] but here too it is obvious that the placing of religion in the system does not only imply a relationship with ethics, but also with the other parts of the system. How can coherence be found between the peculiarity of religion as regards ethics and the relationship of religion with the other areas of the system? My intention here is to demonstrate that the contribution of religion covers the whole system precisely through ethics, and this is because the germs are already present, not only of its "expansion" into religion, but also of expansion of the whole system, of a modification of its basic problems and of their solutions through religion. In short, Cohen's philosophy of religion is not a forgotten chapter of the system, nor a new approach to it, but the coherent development of a series of still-open problems in the various areas of philosophy and particularly apparent in ethics.

6. THE CENTRALITY OF ETHICS IN THE SYSTEM

Cohen states that ethics is "the center of philosophy" (*ERW* 1) and returns to this in *Der Begriff der Religion im System der Philosophie*, where he highlights the "systematic centrality of ethics" (*BR* 11). If these statements are to be taken seriously, what definite meaning must be attributed to them?

The meaning of the centrality of ethics is undoubtedly connected to the centrality of the problem of man, the specific object of ethics, for philosophy. The fundamental nature of the problem of man for the whole of philosophy makes ethics the meeting point for all the problems of the system. It is here that they emerge in their full significance, and their ultimate meaning, or at least the outline for its clarification, connected to all the elements of the system, is transmitted in all directions. That is, ethics, has a decisive influence, not only forward on aesthetics and psychology, the subsequent parts of the system, but also backward, on logic, owing to the problems it posits and the requirements emerging in it. Here I shall not analyze the influence of ethics on aesthetics and psychology, which should have already partially emerged in the previous chapter, so as to look into the meaning and significance of the "retroaction" (*ERW* 90) of ethics on logic. If this retroaction can actually be demonstrated and its meaning brought out, and if the continuity between the problems of ethics connected to it and certain central themes of Cohen's religious philosophy shown, a determined sense will finally be given to the "systematic ubiquity" of religion in Cohen, mentioned by Rosenzweig, and also to the relationship of religion to the system, through the mediation of its relationship with ethics, and, particularly, to the connection of Cohen's religious philosophy to his logic. In this context, the problem of his ontological turning point, supported by Ucko and denied by Graupe and Altmann, can also be faced.

7. TRUTH, GOD, AND BEING IN COHEN'S ETHICS

In chapter 6 I demonstrated that a solely methodological value cannot be attributed to the principle of truth formulated in *Ethik des reinen Willens*. The identification of truth with the idea of God, apart from endowing the former with the value of the principle of the unity of method in logic and ethics, also makes it the guarantee of the possible harmony between nature and morality, of the possible realization of the moral action of the existing world. This is the basic function of the idea of God in Cohen's ethics, enabling him to state that his ethics "more definitely than any previous one, adopts the idea of God into the content of ethical teachings" (*RV* 23; Eng. trans. 20). Ucko rightly points out that "nature is not conceived in the scientific sense, as a connection of validity among concepts; the issue concerns, rather, *really existing nature, really existing man* and his future,"[23] in this development of the principle of truth. It is indeed clear that by developing the principle of truth in the idea of transcendent God, Cohen moved from the level of methodological unity between logic and ethics to that of harmony between nature and morality (cf. *ERW* 466). It cannot be denied, therefore, that, with his affirmation of the transcendence of God, Cohen placed the problem of a unitary ground of being and what ought to be, and not simply of knowledge of them, in ethics. Though the problem is placed here, it is not exhaustively dealt with and resolved through the idea of God and his transcendence. Satisfactory development of this problem can only be found in the theme of the uniqueness of God, as Cohen works it through in the philosophy of religion.[24]

8. THE IDEA OF GOD AS A REGULATIVE IDEA AND AS A CONSTITUTIVE PRINCIPLE

The idea of God does not appear in Cohen's logic. It is present in his ethics, though not as a principle of foundation, but only "at the conclusion," as a regulative idea of the eternity of nature as an area of the realization of moral action: "The logic of the knowledge of nature does not need it [the concept of God]. Ethics was able to be built up without a single reference to it. It is only at the conclusion that dissatisfaction becomes evident" (*ERW* 439).[25]

Here Kant immediately springs to mind. As is well known *Religion innerhalb den Grenzen der blossen Vernunft* opens with the following words: "So far as morality is based upon the conception of man as a free agent who, just because he is free, binds himself through his reason to unconditioned laws, it stands in need neither of the idea of another Being over him, for him to apprehend his duty, nor of an incentive other than the law itself, for him to do his duty," continuing, a few lines below: "But although, for its own sake morality needs no representation of an end which must precede the determining of the will, it is quite possible that it is necessarily related to such an end, taken not as the ground but as the [sum of] inevitable consequences of maxims adopted as conformable to that end." This end is "the idea of a highest good in the world for whose possibility we must postulate a higher, moral, most holy, and omnipotent Being which alone can unite the two elements of this highest good."[26]

Actually, Cohen never accepted Kant's conception of the idea of God as an ethical postulate, but only because his postulate was linked to the subjective end of the highest good, and thus of happiness, which for Cohen must not be part of the ethical end. He did, however, always accept the function of the idea of God as the ground of the objective unity between nature and moral action, that is, of the everlasting character of nature for the realization of moral action.[27] While logic and ethics are constituted in accordance with the method of scientific reason, without the need to posit the idea of God as the principle of their foundation, the philosophy of religion (especially its systematic presentation in *Religion der Vernunft*) begins with the idea of God and grounds it in the possibility and legitimacy of all the other concepts.[28]

God and man are the object of religion, whose content is thus the same as that of ethics (cf. *BR* 19). And yet, as we have seen, religion does have one peculiar characteristic in respect of ethics. The first fundamental meaning of this characteristic consists in positing God as the first, originary principle for the foundation of nature and man.

In an article entitled *Mahnung des Alters an die Jugend*, published at the end of 1917, four months before his death, Cohen encouraged Jewish youth not to reduce Judaism to ethics. He recalls *Die kulturgeschichtliche Bedeutung des Sabbath*,[29] a lecture he had delivered long before, in 1869, in which he emphasized the ethical meaning of the Jewish Sabbath, and he reaffirms the universal, eternal value of the moral, social, and political message of the Jewish prophets. However, with reference to a subsequent lecture given in 1870 on "the effect of monotheism on the education of humanity," he adds:

> I now interpret the progression from the first to the second of my themes in the sense that I believed that I understood that all the references to ethical politics were still not enough to ensure religion, Judaism as a religion: that establishing the very *idea of God* as the center of gravity of Judaism was indispensable. The strength of Judaism lies in its pure monotheism. *All religious ethics is only the consequence of the principle of the unique God.* We are moving away from the focal point of the issue, if we direct our predominant interest towards consequent propositions. We abandon the task and possibility of entering the most intimate innerness of religion, if we quickly pass over the concept of God, and only pause to consider moral teaching, which is only the consequence of the monotheistic principle.[30]

Here two interconnected themes outside pure ethics clearly emerge: the uniqueness of God as the principle and ground of morality and the realization of morality in history and politics. We do not know to what extent and how the themes were developed in the 1870 lecture mentioned by Cohen, since it was never published and no trace is left of it. However, he was probably consistent with his basic approach at that time and highlighted the second theme at the expense of the first. In this case, the result would be that the continuity in Cohen's position, claimed in the passage quoted above, was not quite so rigorous and was heightened by the a posteriori perspective of memory. What is certain, however, is that these two themes are the nucleus of the meaning of the correlation between God and man, the object of Cohen's late philosophy of religion, and that taking up the idea of God as the principle of the foundation of morality and history is one of the essential meanings of the specificity of religion in respect of ethics.

However, this shift in perspective had profound repercussions, not only on ethics, but also on logic. Logic and ethics, or rather ethics, and logic starting from it, could only see the idea of God, in connection with the principle of truth, in a regulative fashion, since they complied with the fundamental critical principle of the distinction between theoretical and practical reason, between being and what ought to be. But if critical philosophy restricted itself to this definition, it would be incomplete and would not really be critical philosophy at all, which must consider the distinction and unity of being and what ought to be. The principle of truth, which is not a principle of ethics, but one of logic and ethics in their interconnection, though being posited in the context of the emergence of the ethical problem, is certainly a purely methodological principle: *"Truth means the connection and agreement between theoretical and ethical problems"* (*ERW* 89). Nevertheless, the methodological needs of truth shift it back to a further ground, and thus to a meaning of truth that is not merely methodological, and that also emerges in the area of pure ethics, though not being open to penetration by it:

> Does not the positive sense of *purity* lie in the productivity of application? It is only of this that the logical legitimacy of pure will consists for ethics: that this purity is applied in the subject of will and action, as it occurs in nature and history. The latter two are then the inevitable presuppositions of purity. The method of purity comes not only from the principle of truth, which places ideal and nature in correlation, but also from the natural presupposition that comes before all others. Natural will is not pure will. Natural man is not pure man. The empirical ego is not the pure ego. But if there were no natural man with a natural will and self-consciousness, the method of purity could not begin; it would have no sense at all. (*ERW* 436–37)

The identification of truth with the idea of God (or with the associated concept of the 'transcendence of God') means the answer to this problem, or rather the indication of an answer that is still methodological to a problem which is, however, no longer only a problem of unity of method.

Cohen's later philosophy of religion returned to this problem, *no longer from the viewpoint of scientific idealism*, like ethics, *but, nonetheless, from that of critical idealism.* Since the unity of being and what ought to be is a limit problem in critical philosophy, the only illegitimate approach is the metaphysical one, which aims at glimpsing something beyond the limit (or border). Otherwise, critical philosophy legitimizes, or rather requires, not only an approach on this side of the limit, but also an investigation *on* the limit; this is the content of religion, and critical philosophy can and must approach it by its own rational means and methods. The double critical principle of the distinction and unity of being and what ought to be involves the legitimization of a double recourse to reason. The latter is not only theoretical reason in the science of nature, and practical reason, in the moral sciences, but is placed in this practical reason before the limit problem of the unity of being and what ought to be and the ground of this unity. Critical reflection *on* this limit problem certainly leads reason beyond its scientific use, but not beyond the limit: *an investigation on the limit beyond science but not beyond reason is therefore legitimate, from the critical viewpoint.* Referring to the difference between natural causality and divine creation, Cohen writes:

> Abundant problems tower up before us at this point. Out of the misty sea of myth, questions emerge; chaos arises. There also arises an opposition to all metaphysics with its claim to the exclusive ownership of the specific share reason has in religion. Causality may remain the special field of science, but there may be another kind of causality that originates on the border of science. And because it originated on the border we are positively permitted to step *beyond* the knowledge of nature and natural science in order to discover and fulfill, with its aid, the world of the spirit, the human world of morality. Thus there originate new meanings for the uniqueness of being in God and for God: new meanings for God, because for the world of becoming, for which the unique being is the foundation. (*RV* 70; Eng. trans. 61)[31]

If logic and ethics only glimpse the truth and God on the horizon, since they only remain faithful to the methodological principle of the distinction between being and what ought to be, the philosophy of religion starts off from the fact of religion and, thus, from its viewpoint, that is that of the unity of being and what ought to be. Since it will not give up the critical-transcendental method of foundation, it begins with the origin of being and what ought to be in their unity, from the idea of the one and unique God.[32] In religion, man faces the problem of the limit. He can try to answer it through mystical immersion in the absolute, beyond the limit, or remain on the limit, attempting to embrace correlation between the reality on this side of the limit and its transcendental sense, or rather its transmission to the limit with his spiritual gaze. Certainly, however, critical philosophy can only reflect on this form of religion; reason can only accept and interpret the latter route and must reject the other one because it is illusory.

For Cohen, philosophical reason, in his reflection on religion, must start off from the Jewish religion, not for sectarian reasons, but because he saw the originary fact, the source (not the sole development) of the religion of reason in the sources of Judaism (cf. *RV* 39f.; Eng. trans. 34).

Cohen's philosophy of religion is the philosophy of the limit, as Graupe notes.[33] However, *the philosophy of the limit is that of religion.* If critical reason desires to face the problem of the limit, a task it cannot fail to undertake, it must reflect on the fact of religion.

This initial aspect of the specificity of religion in the system can be summarized as follows. Ethics had already brought up the problem of unity, with the basic methodological principle of distinction between being in nature and moral what ought to be. The problem is not only that of the unity of the scientific method between logic and ethics, but also that of the guarantee of the possibility of the realization of moral action. However, ethics, could postulate this unity, in a regulative sense, in the idea of God and his transcendence, but could not overcome the methodological perspective of the difference between nature and man (as a moral being). Religion alone, in the cultural field, is placed in the perspective of the above-mentioned unity, since it starts the idea of God as an explanation of nature and man and their unity in history. Therefore, critical philosophy must investigate religion so as to face up to that perspective, that limit problem, which ethics poses and for which it requires an answer, though being unable to offer it itself.

9

The Uniqueness of God
and Correlation

1. THE UNIQUENESS OF GOD

If Cohen preferred the concept of the 'unique' God to that of
'one' God for the God of monotheism,[1] it is not simply for reasons of terminology, but concerns the fundamental meaning of religion. The unity
of God indicates the opposition of monotheism to polytheism: only one
God and not many gods. However, this opposition is insufficient to completely cover the essential meaning of monotheism: the affirmation of
the radical difference of God from nature.

The unity of God is not a concept peculiar to religious monotheism; it is also shared by Greek philosophy. In Eleatic philosophy, and in
Xenophanes particularly, God had already been conceived as One, and
identified with the unity of the cosmos. It was through the concept of
'unity,' then, that Xenophanes had identified being, cosmos, and God.
The concept of the unity of God had subsequently led Greek philosophy
to pantheism.[2] But "pantheism is not religion" (RV 47; Eng. trans. 40).[3]
The opposition of true religion, i.e. monotheism, to pantheism cannot
be seen in the same way as its opposition to polytheism. It is in the latter
that the difference between religion and myth resides. This is why the
concept of the unity of God is sufficient. But though necessary, this distinction is not a negative delimitation of monotheism. It does not yet
include "the positive element for the new God" (RV 43; Eng. trans. 37).

171

However, opposition to pantheism brings out, not only the peculiarity of Jewish monotheism in respect of Greek philosophy, but also that of religion in general. For this reason, Cohen, especially in his late works on religion, was emphatically opposed to pantheism and tended to reduce to it all those religious and philosophical concepts different from the religion of reason (such as ontological proof of the existence of God, mysticism, Hegel's philosophy of identity, etc.).

The central idea of monotheism concerns the problem of being, and the definition of the idea of God basically means an exact conception of being. This is an essential feature linking the philosophy of religion to logic.

If the conception of one God differentiates monotheism from polytheism, though only characterizing it negatively, and therefore unsatisfactorily, to the extent that it is also common to pantheism, the conception of the unique God expresses, negatively and positively, the essential character of monotheism, that is, of the only true (rational) religion.

The uniqueness of God means, first of all, his incomparability, not only with other gods, but with any other being in nature (cf. *RV* 51; Eng. trans. 44). Second, it means the distinction between God's being and existence (*Dasein*) of the world. The concept of one God does not imply such a distinction, as Xenophanes' pantheism shows. However, the uniqueness of God posits a drastic difference between God and every entity (cf. *RV* 51f; Eng. trans. 44). Third, the meaning of uniqueness implies that it "is also distinguished from *simplicity*" (*RV* 52; Eng. trans. 44). Uniqueness has the lack of composition in common with simplicity, but it means more. It means that God not only is not composed in himself but does not even participate in any composition with the existing. Since pantheism is also a mixture (*Mischung*) of God's being and existing nature, in this meaning the uniqueness of God also differentiates monotheism from any form of pantheism, including medieval ontologism, which promoted a logical and ontological implication between being and existence in God (cf. *RV* 51f.; Eng. trans. 44f.). Besides, the uniqueness of God also means his superiority in respect of the limits of space and time, to which nature is subject, that is, his "permanence" (in "analogy" with the concept of substance, but solely in the Kantian logical sense) and his "unchangeableness" (cf. *RV* 52f., 69; Eng. trans. 45, 60).

All these meanings converge in the identification of God with being. If the one God means that there is only one God, the unique God means that only God is, that the true being can only be attributed to God (cf. *BR* 46; *RV* 69; Eng. trans. 59f.).[4] This is the essence of God's revelation to Moses in the burning bush: "*The uniqueness of God* from the outset does not mean *the absence of division* in him, and not even his *incomparability* with another being, but his absolute *identity* with being, *so that no other being continues to count before it*" (*BR* 26).

2. CREATION

The uniqueness of God means that God alone is. This evidently brings with it the negation of being, not only of the gods, but of the world. If God alone is, then the world is nothing. This, however, does not mean the negation of all meaning of the world, but only its incomparability with God in being and the nonexistence *in itself* of the world (cf. *RV* 52; Eng. trans. 44f.).

The uniqueness of God is not the antithesis of pantheism (everything in God instead of God in everything), but the alternative to, and confutation of, pantheism, in the affirmation of the distinction and correlation between God's true being and the existence of the world (cf. *RV* 68 f.; Eng. trans. 59f.). So as to clarify the relationship between God and the world, removing any ontological ambiguity, Cohen turned to the analogy with Kant's logical-transcendental category of substance, which he had fully analyzed both in Kant's writings and in *Logik der reinen Erkenntnis*. The problem of being, in logic and the science of nature, is only faced in relation to that of becoming: substance is exclusively conceived as permanence, the presupposition of the causality of becoming. Similarly, the rational definition of God as the unique being must be considered an immanent condition of its relationship with the existence of the world (cf. *RV* 69f.; Eng. trans. 60).

The fact that Cohen only posits an analogy between the logical concept of 'substance' and the idea of God must keep us from interpreting it as an identification of the idea of the unique God with the concept of substance, as a reduction of religion to logic. The analogy is only valid inasmuch as it avoids any ontological interpretation of God's being and creation. However, there is a further meaning in the idea of the unique God, for which the analogy with substance is useless and even misleading. This depends on the different perspectives of religion and the science of nature, to which we referred above. Cohen was aware of the partiality of this phase, and we, as faithful interpreters, must follow him in the subsequent stages of his presentation: "Only gradually can all these meanings of the uniqueness of being be developed. To begin with, we remain at the abstraction of being in its relation to the abstraction of becoming" (*RV* 70; Eng. trans. 61).

Taking these reservations into account, the analogy with the concept of substance is certainly important for clarifying the fact that, in

Cohen's view, the teaching of creation, the relationship between God and the world, does not satisfy the ontological problem of the beginning of the world, but rather the rational-ontological one of its ground. God is the creator of the world means that God's being, the true being, is the permanent ground of the becoming of the world: this is an intrinsic meaning of God's being. It is not ontological but transcendental (a term we can use provisionally, although its purely methodological sense is insufficient). For this reason, the uniqueness of God not only does not exclude the being of the world, it implies it. The uniqueness of God means both his difference from the world and his founding relationship with it: "Creation is God's primary attribute; it is not only the consequence of the uniqueness of God's being; creation is simply identical with it. If the unique God were not creator, being and becoming would be the same; nature itself would be God. This, however, would mean: God is not. For nature is the becoming that needs being as its foundation" (*RV* 77; Eng. trans. 67).

The analogy with substance precludes the interpretation of creation as the emanation of the world from God, or creation of matter from nothing or, in general, as a reply to the mythical question on the beginning and ontological origin of the world (cf. *RV* 74f., 76; Eng. trans. 64f., 66). Creation is the response to the problem of the relationship between God's being and the becoming of the world. This relationship is a correlation, a mutual relationship in the distinction between God's being as ground and the becoming of the world as grounded.

In *Der Begriff der Religion im System der Philosophie* (cf. *BR* 48ff.), Cohen associates the religious concept of 'creation' with the logical one of 'conservation,' returning, once again, to the analogy with substance. It is useful to recall that, in *Logik der reinen Erkenntnis* (cf. *LRE* 233ff.), precisely in the context of the analysis of substance, he deals with certain concepts to which he then refers in his religious philosophy, especially those of conservation, correlation and the relationship between substance and origin. When coming across these concepts in Cohen's philosophy of religion, one needs to retrace his steps to the logical meaning in which they were initially formulated.

a. Conservation

Cohen writes about substance: "*The category of substance acts as a category of conservation in its correlation with movement*" (*LRE* 234). With reference to Cartesian coordinates, he showed how, in this logical sense, substance has no meaning except with reference to movement, just as movement cannot be defined except with reference to the conservation of substance.

b. Correlation

Cohen defined the mutual relationship between conservation and movement as correlation: a different kind of relationship from immanence. Cohen had provisionally used the expression *immanence of conservation in movement* (*LRE* 234). However, he immediately pointed out that it was not a question of immanence, but correlation, of a mutual logical relationship unifying the two terms, though keeping them distinct.[5]

c. Substance and Origin

Through the consideration that movement is production for pure thought, Cohen linked the physical-logical category of substance to the general logical one of origin: "*movement must become production.* . . . Thus we must also clarify . . . *unification with the category of origin* in substance. (*LRE* 237).

These very brief remarks on the logical meaning of the above concepts now allow us to evaluate the validity and limits of Cohen's analogy between them and the religious concepts of the unique God and creation. The analogy between his concept of creation and that of conservation, in the sense of a shift from the mythical problem of the beginning to the critical one of foundation is immediately obvious. Furthermore, it should also be noted that the logical concept of conservation has a dynamic, rather than static, meaning. If movement is production, substance, *inasmuch as it is conservation*, is continuous, ever-new production, renewal. In this sense, when Cohen, in accordance with the rabbinical tradition, interprets creation as renewal (cf. *RV* 78ff.; Eng. trans. 68ff.), he can do so without leaving his previous logical theory, but is actually in harmony with it, through the concept of conservation (cf. *BR* 47f.). The analogy between God's being and the logical concept of origin is appropriate, since the correlation between God and the world, as a founding relationship between being and becoming, legitimately recalls the logical principle of origin, according to which all production must have its ground in origin (cf. *LRE* 53).

The analogy is valid up to this point but also meets its limit here. This limit is the already-mentioned difference in perspective between the science of nature and logic, on the one hand, and religion and philosophy of religion, on the other. When the concepts of conservation and renewal are applied to correlation, as correlation between God and the world, they find themselves on a teleological horizon that is outside the area of logic, as Cohen himself explicitly acknowledged (cf. *BR* 48).

The logical concept of correlation, applied to religion, is also insufficient, owing to the impossibility of involving the teleological perspective in the being-becoming (or else substance-movement) relationship. The God-world correlation, owing to the specific religious perspective in which it is foregrounded, has no independent meaning, but only one in relation to the correlation between God and man, since the world is not an object in itself for religion, but only inasmuch as it is the world of man, actually, only with the problem of man as its starting point.[6]

Last, the concept of origin, applied to the idea of the unique God, can only be an analogy within the limits mentioned. In religion the idea of God involves a meaning that goes well beyond the logical method of origin.

3. GOD AS ORIGIN AND THE TEACHING OF GOD'S NEGATIVE ATTRIBUTES

In *Religion der Vernunft*, Cohen relates the idea of God to the logical principle of origin, through historical reference to the teaching of Maimonides on the negative attributes of God.[7] In Cohen's view Maimonides gave a new, specific meaning to the teaching of the negative attributes, as compared with the Arab and Jewish philosophers before him, since he highlighted the fact that what is denied in them is not their positive content, since, in that case, the content would have to be acknowledged as more originary than God himself (cf. *RV* 71; Eng. trans. 61f.). The content that is denied already has a privative meaning, and the denial thus consists of a negation of a privation. The negative attribute of God is the negation of a privation and, as such, affirms "a new and genuine positivity" (*RV* 73; Eng. trans. 63). To say that "God is not inert" means more than saying that God is active: it means that he is the "*originative principle of activity*" (*RV* 73; Eng. trans. 64). To deny God existence (*Dasein*) means that "God is *the origin* of existence" (*BR* 47). Thus Cohen, through Maimonides's teaching of the negative attributes of God, connects the idea of the unique God and creation to the logical principle of origin. Now we must also identify the validity and limits of this reference.

Admittedly, Cohen had already emphasized the difference between infinite and privative judgments in *Logik der reinen Erkenntnis* (cf. *LRE* 90) and had clearly stated that origin is only thought as negation, inasmuch as it is the productive ground of being. It is not "an absolute nothing, but only a relative nothing, oriented towards a specific route of discovery" (*LRE* 105). Up to this point, the comparison of the creative relationship between God's being and existence (*Dasein*), the becoming (*Werden*) of the world, and the logical concept of origin, and precisely the privative character of the being of the world, with the logical concept of origin is fitting and clarifying. Logic did and could not recognize privation in movement, becoming, and existence, because the conception of the existence and becoming of the world as a condition of the missing, defective, incomplete being, lies outside logical consideration. The privative character of becoming is the object of "ontological" consideration, which, though it cannot be considered a metaphysical affirmation of speculative reason, cannot refer to the area of critical-theoretical reason either. It does refer to the area of practical reason, since this evaluation only emerges from the position of the teleological-practical problem: for whom, for what, for what end is the being of the world? Only from the practical viewpoint, where the existence and becoming of the world are considered under the realization of good, of man's moral action, are they discovered to be unsatisfactory and defective, and only by starting from this perspective can the logical relationship between origin and being of the world be reinterpreted, widening it and enriching it with a new meaning of truth, in which, however, the concept of origin also takes on a positive sense, which logic cannot identify alone, in the limit of its jurisdiction.

4. THE IDEA OF GOD AND PLATO'S ἀνυπόθετον

In my attempt to clarify the intricate problem of the relationship between religion and logic, I shall take up the suggestion for a possibly effective route made by Cohen himself:

> Platonic idealism, on the strength of the productivity of his method of hypothesis, leads the strategic route of thought to fulfillment, in the light of *history*. Once we have accepted that *ethics* must also depend on logic, therefore on this hypothesis-idea logic, then the following question will arise (and we shall not oppose it or even avoid it): *what is the relationship between moral ideas and the methodical value of idea as hypothesis?* Finally, accepting that religion is linked to ethics: *what is the situation regarding the relationship of the idea of God with Plato's fundamental value of idea as hypothesis?* (*BR* 31)

Therefore, we must, return to Cohen's interpretation of the idea of good in Plato. Cohen was always highly aware of the importance of this theory, though he often found himself in the embarrassing position of having to give an exhaustive, satisfactory interpretation of it. His embarrassment was mainly due to his identification of two, equally important, but not easily reconcilable, problems.

On the one hand, he pointed out the importance of Plato's view of good as idea, and, therefore, of his view of ethics as rational knowledge, which is, methodologically, equal to logic, and, at the same time, of the distinction between the mathematical knowledge of nature and ethics, expressed by Plato in the differentiation of the idea of good from mathematical ideas. Plato can thus be seen as a precursor of Kant in the formulation of the fundamental critical principle of the distinction between theoretical and practical reason. In Cohen's view, one of Plato's fundamental contributions to critical philosophy was his consideration of good as an idea, and his consequent subjection of the area of morality to the critical method of hypothesis, together with his distinction of the idea of good from other ideas, placing it "beyond being" and making it "eminent in the meaning of value."[8]

On the other hand, the Platonic idea of good also means Plato's answer to the problem of an ultimate foundation, of a prime term to which to have recourse in the method of idea as hypothesis. It constitutes the ground, which does not need foundation itself, of the whole process of pure foundation through hypothesis, not only of knowledge, but also of being. It is owing to its having this meaning that Plato calls the idea of good "ἀνυπόθετον," and it is considered the "sufficient" hypothesis (ἱκανὸν) and not simply "trustworthy" (τὸ ἀσφαλές τῆς ὑποθέσεως), like the other ideas.[9] It is in this meaning of the idea of good that Cohen sees not only all the importance of the problem, but also the difficulty of its solution.

Both in his earlier and in his later writings, although in a very different way, Cohen acknowledged the legitimacy of the problem of an ultimate foundation of knowledge and being, which coincides with the ultimate end, without which knowledge of nature would not be satisfactorily legitimized, and its very being would not have sufficient justification and a completed meaning for reason.[10] But he also saw the trap, into which post-Platonic philosophy had fallen of considering the Platonic ἀνυπόθετον, inasmuch as it is unconditioned, as the absolute, of hypostatizing it in the absolute being, in the transcendent God of speculative metaphysics. Cohen not only rejected such an interpretation of Plato, but also refused to take this step, which would have led him beyond rational, critical philosophy, into the area of speculative metaphysics.

For this reason, he often treated this aspect of Platonic philosophy with caution, attempting to project the same reservations and diffidence onto Plato himself. Starting with Glaucon's reaction to the well-known metaphor of the sun, used by Socrates in the *Republic* (508-509c):

"Ἄπολλον, ἔφη, δαιμονίας ὑπερβολῆς," Cohen credits Plato himself with being aware of having used hyperbole to overcome, to go beyond (*Übertreffen*) hypothesis.[11] Cohen's conviction grew ever stronger that Plato's ἀνυπόθετον was a paradox (cf. *ERW* 429) peculiar to Platonic irony (cf. *KBE* 175, 176; *ERW* 429), and not recognition of an ontological absolute, or at least that, if a hypothesis transcending being were actually to be recognized in the idea of good, this could only be interpreted as Plato's "way of expressing the religious affect" (*ERW* 88). In *Ethik des reinen Willens*, the problem of the transcendence of the idea of good is resolved drastically, and the interpretation of Plato's theory falls into line with Cohen's systematic requirements. The transcendence of good is rejected and denied and good given identical consideration to that of other ideas; thus ethics is entirely restored to the area of rational knowledge and that of the critical-scientific method (cf. *ERW* 88, 418, 425, 429, 431, 469).

However, in this way, the problem of ἀνυπόθετον, of the ultimate, unfounded ground remains unresolved. In *Ethik des reinen Willens*, Cohen denies that this ground is the idea of good. He also refuses to posit this ultimate ground metaphysically, but the problem remains, and, as we have seen, is legitimate and inevitable for Cohen himself. Besides, it is precisely in *Ethik des reinen Willens*, where Cohen forcefully argues for the immanence between logic and ethics, that he is obliged to face this problem. Actually, as long as the immanence between logic and ethics is understood in a purely methodological sense, the principle of truth, as unity of method, is sufficient, but when, in *Ethik des reinen Willens*, Cohen has to posit the problem of of the realization of moral action in the world, when the immanence between ethics and logic means the a priori possibility of harmony between the being of nature and what ought to be of good action, then Cohen himself must have recourse to the idea of a transcendent ground, to the idea of God: "The advantage of God's transcendence is that the transcendence between nature and morality is eliminated; that morality can look back on nature, and that this is not done in vain. Likewise, the advantage is that nature is no longer a desert, owing to its being abandoned by morality, and that I am not forced to seek refuge in aesthetics, or even less in some psychological feeling, so as to establish a link between nature and morality" (*ERW* 466).

God's transcendence is only acknowledged in this transcendental meaning, so as to avoid any metaphysical deviation, and yet it is reproposed as a problem, or rather as a necessary idea for critical reason.

Briefly summarizing Cohen's route through this subject up to *Ethik des reinen Willens* (putting aside the position to be found in his early writings), one can say that in *Einleitung mit kritischem Nachtrag zu F.A. Langes Geschichte des Materialismus etc.* he was already fully aware of the problem, without, however, being able to solve it:

> Must good be only foundation. And yet Helios gives not only vision, and therefore recognizability, to the being of nature, but also existence and growth. Should there or could there not be such a kind God for good, but is it only permissible and possible to think and conceive him merely as a foundation of pure thought? You can question priests and wise men and their answer only appears to be mockery of the questioner. But here it is the wise man himself who asks the questions, so his answer will also be more than just mockery, it will take a different direction from that taken by this mockery. . . . Thus thought is trapped in the worst alternative. Either the idea of good is idea: then it cannot expect a higher, different value from that of foundation, or it must mean a higher value and thus one that is different from that which belongs to the ideas of nature. Thus it gives up the fundamental logical value of idea. By coining a term that presents and requires antithesis in respect of hypothesis, Plato teaches the perspicacious thinker near to him, centuries after him, that he has not resolved the alternative in either sense; otherwise he would have also to have put aside the name idea for the idea of good. (*E* 32–3)

In *Ethik des reinen Willens*, Cohen had resolved the alternative in the sense of the denial of the transcendence of good and of the consideration of the latter only as idea, thus returning ethics to the area of critical, scientific knowledge. However, in this work the problem of the ultimate transcendent ground, now distinct from the idea of good, is reproposed by Cohen, through the idea of God. In his writings over the following years, he highlighted the fact that the origin of the concept of 'transcendence' does not lie in the Jewish religious tradition, but in that of Greek philosophy, in which, however, transcendence was only attributed to the idea of good, to indicate the difference of moral what ought to be in respect of the being of nature.[12]

In *Charakteristik der Ethik Maimunis*,[13] a work published in 1908, following *Ethik des reinen Willens*, but earlier than his last writings on the philosophy of religion, Cohen finally provides a clear, open account of his interpretation of the twofold meaning of Plato's idea of good, though also explicitly formulating the shift he intends to operate in respect of this meaning, from the Platonic idea of good to the monotheistic idea of God:

> *If good is also acceptable as an idea, how can it, only as an idea, become knowledge?* This is the difficult question in Plato's teaching of ideas. This is the ques-

tion that tests scientific idealism . . . the idea of good is an idea just like the idea of equal, as mathematical ideas (τὰ μαθηματικὰ) are in ideas in general. There is no plus or minus here. But one can attempt a transformation with the hypothesis. Thus he [Plato] makes it a being of *non-foundation* (ἀνυπόθετον).[14]

In this transformation of the hypothesis of good into ἀνυπόθετον, however, one should not look for recognition of the metaphysical absolute, of the "substance of dogmatism," but rather "birth of that slandered idealism," which pursues the need for foundation up to the ultimate limit:

Yes good cannot want to be any more than idea, and, therefore hypothesis. But certainly the *content* of morality distinguishes the idea of good from everything that exists in heaven and on earth. And, therefore, thanks to this distinction in the value of content, the privilege of terminology must also be granted to hypothesis. Thus, the idea of good can be defined as the *adequate* hypothesis (ἱκανὸν) and, whereas the predicate of *trustworthiness* belongs to idea in general (τὸ ἀσφαλὲς τῆς ὑποθέσεως) it can be the hypothesis by which the account of reason simply reaches its end and *purpose.* . . . I cannot desire to search for a ground beyond and outside morality, in which it had its root. Good is the ground of the world. Thence hypothesis, more accurately and more precisely considered, does not receive its end, as much as its *origin; non-foundation becomes the origin of foundation.* In this great example the meaning of infinite judgment as the judgment of origin is shown. Thus in Plato, the terminology of hypothesis links the ethical problem and ethical certainty to that of exemplary knowledge, to the problem of mathematical knowledge. Both these points are important: good is idea as that which is mathematics is idea. But the second point is to be added to the first: the method of idea, in a backward direction, becomes different from that of the other ideas. It is only modified in a backward direction, by going forward, on the other hand, it remains the same. There is no other method than that contained in the idea of good, as idea, for all these questions of morality. Only regressive justification of hypothesis here produces the surprising difference, the *difference between ethics and mathematics*; or, inasmuch as the latter is based on the logic of the theory of ideas, *between ethics and logic. Idea links ethics and logic; the idea of good distinguishes ethics from logic.*[15]

In the fourth section of the same work, devoted to the interpretation of Maimonides's theory of the negative attributes of God, continuity, but also the shift in the meaning of ἀνυπόθετον as origin from the Platonic idea of good to the idea of God are explicit.[16] Thus Cohen finds the moral meaning of the idea of God and its function as origin united in Maimonides's philosophy.[17]

The work concludes with the renewed statement of the importance of Maimonides' contribution to rationalist philosophy, in his rejection of the metaphysical, Aristotelian conception of being, and in his connection between teleology and ethics. In this concluding judgment there is a reference, which is of interest for our investigation, to the antimetaphysical consequences that this position also implies for the creation:

> This is the clear ultimate sense of the teaching of the attributes: that God is not a God of metaphysics, of the substance of the world, but is rather the God of ethics, i.e. the God of man. God is the model and ideal for the human race and for the human self. Only inasmuch as he is this ideal of human morality does he take on a relation with the world and human beings. The *creation of the world*, then, as a metaphysical problem, in Maimonides' ethics is of secondary importance.[18]

Already in this work, then, ἀνυπόθετον is recognized as a problem historically claimed by metaphysics, but is actually a "birth of that slandered idealism."[19] The same conviction is present in *Der Begriff der Religion im System der Philosophie.* In this work, Cohen highlights the fact that the Platonic idea of good places philosophy "at the very door of metaphysics, which is situated at the crossroads where the science of nature and the moral sciences separate, where logic terminates and ethics will begin" (*BR* 35). It is up to philosophy, naturally, to go through this door, stay, and take up a route that is more coherent with its unavoidable rational and critical character. But this option between metaphysics and critical philosophy only regards the solutions to the problem, not the problem itself. The latter is real and inevitable for philosophy, which runs into it when passing from the logical to the ethical area:

> *Does not the reality of morality seek and require a higher guarantee* than the one that idea as hypothesis can provide? Does good stand on the same *level of validity*, of need to know and right to validity, where mathematical ideas are situated, inasmuch as they constitute the ground of nature? Can I also believe here that I shall find total peace in the ultimate conclusion of this wisdom: that greater *certainty* would only be *illusion*, that the *ultimate guarantee of truth* also consists here in the value of idea as foundation? And if it were true that another kind of certainty is simply not possible, at least the *question* should not be a necessary *problem*, so that, with reference to this question, a methodical formulation can be found of the *difference of the problems* between morality and the nature of existing reality? The question

has a methodical meaning and thus also productivity, even if its positive solution should not occur in every sense. (*BR* 36)

The two meanings present in Plato's theory of good are not reconcilable and thus did not allow him to find a satisfactory solution to the problem, which remained open. In the space left vacant by Plato, in the problem of ἀνυπόθετον, metaphysics intervenes, interpreting the 'beyond being' referring to good ontologically, thus overcoming the limits of philosophy toward religion, or taking over religion: the idea of good is thus identified with the idea of God (cf. *BR* 36ff.).

As can be seen in *Der Begriff der Religion im system der Philosophie*, everything is ready for the new formulation of the problem of Platonic ἀνυπόθετον and for its solution in the sense of critical idealism: a) recognition of the legitimacy, rather the unavoidability, of the problem; b) recognition of the fact that it is placed on line and in continuity with the critical problem of foundation; c) indication of its essential relationship with ethics, by which it is posited though not being able to find a solution, inasmuch as it is a limit problem of ethics and, retroactively, of logic; d) awareness that it overcomes the merely methodological significance of the logical problem of foundation, though being unable to find its solution beyond rational and critical philosophy, in metaphysical ontology.

In Cohen's view, the religion of reason, owing to its peculiarity, involving the particular perspective in which it is situated, can take over this problem from ethics and give it a solution with the idea of the unique God and his correlation with man and the world. This solution is not that of the metaphysics of ontology, which posits God as the absolute being, the ground of the end of human action and thus of history. This critical formulation of the problem has its most profound, complete development of the meaning of the uniqueness of God and his correlation with man and the world in the investigation of man and his ultimate end. This does not mean that it must also posit God as hypothesis and origin, since it is idea, at the beginning of its investigation. God as the origin of the world and man is thus an incomplete idea for critical philosophy, since it only finds its complete justification beyond itself, in the teleological meaning of messianism. The important thing, in the as yet abstract and partial phase of the investigation of God as origin, is, on the one hand, not to fall into the metaphysical ontology of God and, on the other, to be aware that in the concept of origin applied to God there is a positive meaning, which is not yet explicit though present, that overcomes the purely methodological significance of the logical nonbeing of infinite judgment. The meaning of the absolute being of the unique God, already posited in the concepts of creation and revelation as the originary ground of man and his world, will be fully developed in the concepts of redemption and messianism.

5. REVELATION

The theme of revelation is also present in the context of the idea of God as origin. Cohen sees this as a specific stage of creation. We have seen that the uniqueness of God implies creation, that the essential meaning of God's unique being lies in correlation with the becoming of the world, not inasmuch as it is its cause, but as its precondition, its ground and origin. The correlation between God and man must be considered part of this correlation between being and becoming, and, at the same time, as distinct from the foundation of becoming as simple existence. Man is not merely material existence; he is also reason. Reason is the specific difference of man from other creatures. So God, as the unique ground of reality, must also be considered the origin of reason, the creator "of man in reason" (RV 99; Eng. trans. 85). Since reason is not only theoretical, but, "in an eminent way" (RV 101; Eng. trans. 87), moral reason, God's creation of man in reason takes on the form of revelation.[20] In one way, then, revelation is a special case of creation, that is, of the correlation between God's being and the creature's becoming (cf. RV 82f.; Eng. trans. 71f.).

The consideration of the homogeneous relationship between creation and revelation, even the consideration of revelation as a special case of creation, allows the application of certain fundamental characteristics, identified in the God-world correlation, to the God-man correlation: first, the distinction of the correlation relationship from that of identity, like that of causality from that of mediation. God is not identical to man, as he is not identical to the world: the unique God is transcendent. Again, owing to transcendence, God is not the cause of human reason, as he is not the cause of the existence of the world. He is rather ground, precondition, origin of man and the world. Last, the correlation between God and man is not mediation, but unification of two different terms: not conciliation, but correlation. As with the relationship between God and the world, Cohen excludes any mediation that refers to a teaching of emanation, he also excludes any hypostatization of reason, or of the spirit, as an intermediate degree between God and man (cf. RV 103f.; Eng. trans. 89). For this reason, in his examination of biblical sources, he prefers the second account of the creation of man (Gen. 2, 7ff.) rather than the first (Gen. 1, 26ff.). Apart from the positive traits Cohen highlights in the second account, the reason for his choice also resides in his rejection of the concepts of 'image' and 'likeness' of man in respect of God, that appear in the first account, which he considers to be still mythical in respect of correlation (cf. *RV* 99ff; Eng. trans. 85ff.).

However, in another case, the specificity of the creation of man as compared with creation in general needs emphasizing. It is precisely this specificity and difference that justifies the function of revelation:

> Creation is the logical consequence of God's unique being, which would have no meaning if it were not the presupposition of becoming. In all becoming, however, man is the focal point, not, to be sure, insofar as he is a living creature, but insofar as the tree of knowledge blooms for him. . . . Thus the question of creation, in the case of man, now concerns the relation of man to God. The serpent calls it identity; our philosophical language calls it correlation (*Korrelation*), which is the term for all concepts of reciprocal relation. A reciprocal relation exists between man and God. God's being is the foundation for the being of creation, or rather for the existence of creation. But in the case of man's existence, creation does not suffer; if it did, God's being would be the presupposition only of man as a living creature. In the case of man, God's being must be the presupposition for knowledge. And knowledge is concerned not only with the knowledge of nature, but is also concerned with "the knowledge of good and evil." The essence of man is dependent on the knowledge of morality. Reason is not only theoretical, but also practical, ethical. The creation of man must mean the creation of his reason. (*RV* 100f.; Eng. trans. 86)

Thus man's spirit, his reason (which, as we have seen, is "in an eminent way" moral reason) is distinguished from the sensible existence of man and the world, and is the specific term of the correlation between God and man: that is, not of a different correlation from that of God-world, for the reasons explained above, but rather of the single correlation with completed meaning that it only takes up, inasmuch as it manifests itself as a God-spirit and man-spirit correlation:

> Creation and revelation take effect only through reason. Both of these concepts turn out to be expressions of the correlation, and therefore both of them are based on the concept of reason that is achieved in the creation of the man of reason and also in the revelation of God to man. Already the creation as the creation of reason does not leave man in passivity, for this would be in contradiction to the concept of correlation. And revelation even more so cannot make man passive. For this would contradict the concept not only of correlation but even more so of reason, which revelation has to reveal. (*RV* 103; Eng. trans. 88)

If, as we have seen, in one sense, revelation can be considered a special case of creation, in another, the creation of the world only finds the fullness of its sense in revelation, in the correlation of God and the man of theoretical, but especially practical, reason. That is, it is not only foundation of the becoming existence *of* the world, but also foundation of this becoming *for* the knowledge and *for* man's action.

This development of the meaning of correlation also implies an enrichment of the idea of God; the uniqueness of God is now identified with his spirituality. God is the unique being: this means that he, as the origin of "moral reason" and of man's "moral becoming" (cf. *RV* 83; Eng. trans. 71 f.) is spirit: "*God is unique. This now means: God is spirit*" (*RV* 103; Eng. trans. 89; cf. *RV* 95; Eng. trans. 82).

It is only at this stage that correlation begins to take on its meaning as reciprocity. Man is not passive in revelation. God is he who gives the spirit of knowledge to man in revelation, and man, through this gift, knows God. The two correlated terms are certainly not equal in status and originativeness, but definitely in terms of reciprocity: "Reciprocity enters man's knowledge of God in accordance with correlation" (*RV* 103; Eng. trans. 88).

Finally, it is still necessary to emphasize the fact that human reason is "in an eminent way" practical and moral reason. For this reason Cohen, intervening in an ancient, uninterrupted rabbinical dispute, also common to Jewish philosophy, on the definition of revelation, does not only give secondary importance to the historical fact of the event on Mt. Sinai, preferring the content of revelation (cf. *RV* 90f.; Eng. trans. 78), showing that his approach is greatly influenced by Kant, he also emphasizes the exclusively moral character (underestimating the cultural character and noting the absence of theoretical content) of revealed law, in the spirit of the announcement of the prophet Micah (6, 8): "It has been told thee, O man, what is good" (cf. *BR* 32, 42; *RV* 39; Eng. trans. 33). Man's knowledge of God is therefore not knowledge of his essence, as pantheism and mysticism hold, but knowledge of his actions (*Handlungen*) and his law (cf. *RV* 123, 126; Eng. trans. 106, 109).

Nevertheless, if moral reason were limited to knowledge, religion would still be intellectualism: the spirit as the correlative term between God and man is not only knowledge, but also, and above all, action. But, in order to pass on to this practical dimension, the God-man correlation must be considered in the teleological area of morality: God must be conceived no longer in relation to the logical problem of origin, but in relation to the ethical problem of the end (or purpose) of becoming, and man's reason must be considered as action and no longer as knowledge:

> The correlation elevates and guides me beyond causality to the new interest, which opens the question of purpose. The purpose of man is now in question. And the new question arises: is the purpose of man contained in

God's purpose, as correlation requires it to be, and does God's spirit and his correlation with man's spirit make it possible to accomplish the necessary unification of these purposes? Hence purpose becomes the new guiding concept of knowledge and at the same time a new concept of correlation moves from the realm of theoretical knowledge into the realm of the ethical. (*RV* 108; Eng. trans. 93)

6. HOLY SPIRIT

In his consideration of spirit as morality and action, rather than understanding and knowledge, Cohen has recourse to a new concept, which thus becomes crucial: the concept of 'holiness.' Spirit, as the constitutive concept in the God-man correlation, is only fulfilled in meaning in the specification of holiness. 'Holy spirit,' or, in Cohen's translation from Hebrew, "the spirit of sanctity or of holiness" (*RV* 121; Eng. trans. 104), is the concept through which the God-man correlation reaches its full meaning (cf. *RV* 116; Eng. trans. 100). Holiness is the attribute in which God's thirteen "characteristic qualities," mentioned in the Talmud and defined as "attributes of action" by Maimonides, are collected. These thirteen attributes of action, can be reduced, in Cohen's view, to two basic ones: love and justice (cf. *RV* 109; Eng. trans. 94). Holiness is the idea of unification of these two principles in God as in man (cf. *RV* 114; Eng. trans. 98).

The conception of God moves from the ontological-causal level to the moral-teleological one. The question about God is no longer dominated by the being-causality relationship, but by that of action-end. Nevertheless, how can one use the word *end* when referring to God, the unique being, radically different from any becoming? This can be done only by considering God in correlation with the becoming of human will. The God-man correlation here takes on its essential function; not only man, but also God can be exclusively included in the correlation:

> What does purpose mean in the case of God? This question already implies the problem of correlation. . . . Action in the case of God is related to the possibility of action in becoming, namely, in man. And this possibility is related not to causality but comes under the viewpoint of purpose. Hence the attributes of action are not so much characteristics of God, but rather conceptually determined models for the action of man. The unity of the concepts of love and justice in the concept of action, and consequently in purpose, elevates characteristics to norms (*sh^e losh 'esreh middoth*). (RV 110; Eng. trans. 94f.)

Holy spirit is a key concept in *Religion der Vernunft*. It is only hinted at in *Der Begriff der Religion im System der Philosophie* and only refers to man as an individual (cf. *BR* 104f.). *Religion der Vernunft* develops it fully.[21] This concept has not always been sufficiently highlighted in its importance for Cohen's religious philosophy by his interpreters.[22] Here I shall attempt to demonstrate how crucial it is, even for the most controversial problems of interpretation, such as the concept of correlation and the peculiarity of religion in respect of ethics.

7. HOLY SPIRIT AND THE IDEA OF GOOD

Returning to the evolution of Cohen's reflection on the idea of Platonic good, we notice how the arrival point of this reflection finally and definitely emerges in the concept of holy spirit. Through this concept one can return to the two implicit meanings in the idea of good: the primacy of good over being and the transcendence of good, separating them, though, and transforming the sense of the latter in the direction already indicated in the transcendence of God.

a. The Primacy of Good

If we do not allow ourselves to be distracted by the substitution of the term good by that of holiness, it can easily be seen that Cohen attributes the merit of ensuring the critical distinction between theoretical and practical reason, being and what ought to be, to his theory of the holy spirit. It is this same merit that, in the history of idealism, is to be attributed to Plato's idea of good and Kant's theory of the primacy of practical reason.

Returning to the expression used by Plato to indicate the ulterior nature of good in respect of being (ἐπέκεινα τῆς οὐσίας) Cohen states, "The question of the purpose of being transcends being proper and relates itself to correlation" (*RV* 110; Eng. trans. 95). The question concerning end (or purpose) thus finds its answer in the concept of holy spirit. In the God-man correlation, the human spirit is defined in its moral and teleological meaning by the character of holiness, and, in this way, is distinguished from theoretical reason, in agreement with the critical principle formulated by Kant through the affirmation of the primacy of practical reason, the fundamental guarantee of critical philosophy against pantheism in all its forms:

> For the holy spirit limits that area of the spirit that connects God and man to holiness. And through this limitation and its exclusiveness, holiness

becomes morality. The ethics of critical idealism has clarified this determination, because, to begin with, it laid down the distinction between the certainty of scientific knowledge and that of ethics. . . . By ignoring or disputing this basic critical insight, *pantheism* puts itself into the irreconcilable opposition not only to ethics but in general to scientific philosophy, which cannot begin at all if it does not start with this distinction. The tension between pantheism and religion is also based upon this deficiency. Pantheism simply uses the holy spirit for all kinds of knowledge; Judaism, on the contrary, limits its meaning to morality. Judaism in its biblical sources does not philosophize, but the basic logic of monotheism carries through its consequences beyond biblical limits. Through the "statutes and ordinances" the holy spirit actually becomes morality; in the same way the holy spirit in later history always more and more definitely stamps itself onto moral spirit, onto moral reason. And the priority given to it over any other qualities of the spirit makes it possible to recognize in it the nucleus of the thought that Kant expressed by the "Primacy of the Practical reason." The holy spirit does not remain "the God of the spirits of all flesh." In this phrase the lack of differentiation of the theoretical and moral spirit is inherent. The holy spirit determines the spirit through holiness. (*RV* 123; Eng. trans. 106)

b. The Transcendence of Good

As we have seen, Cohen parted company with Plato on this aspect, refusing to think of good as merely transcendent, and consequently rejecting the inevitable process of its ontological hypostatization as absolute, which actually took place in the history of philosophy. And yet the problem of transcendence was still there, and Cohen, starting with *Ethik des reinen Willens*, was inclined to transfer it to the idea of God. However, rejecting its transcendence does not resolve all the problems of good. Cohen certainly could not accept Aristotle's alternative (and that of his school) of considering good as simply immanent, and thus resolving it in manifold empirical "goods." Actually, there is no real alternative between the metaphysical hypostatization of good, identified with God, and the reduction of ethics to sensualist eudemonism, but rather complementarity, as can be shown, in Cohen's view, in Aristotle's thought and the philosophical tradition to which it gave birth.[23]

For Cohen, then, being neither absolute transcendence of good nor total immanence, good is rather the mean term of the correlation between God and man. Religion has neither God nor man as its peculiar content, but rather the God-man correlation, which takes place through the attribute common to man and God—good: "*Religion, monotheism to be precise, arises with this concept. This concept seems to put both God and* man in the shade, as if both only rose up and were legitimate thanks to the concept of good" (*BR* 33).

In *Der Begriff der Religion im System der Philosophie*, then, the idea of good is seen as the content of the correlation between God and man. The same terminology can also be found in *Religion der Vernunft*.[24] However, there, Cohen preferred the concept of holiness for dealing with the problem. He certainly saw strong ties between the two terms. He noted that the Bible uses both "goodness" and "holiness" to unify God's "moral qualities" (cf. *RV* 111; Eng. trans. 95). In my view, among the many factors contributing to Cohen's preference for holiness rather than goodness in his analysis of the God-man correlation, his intention to keep goodness for the correlation of God with man in the more specific area of the problem of the individual sinner and redemption was paramount (cf. *RV* 243ff., 249; Eng. trans. 208ff., 213). Through the concept of holiness, Cohen resolved and overcame the Platonic problem of the transcendence of good in an original way. Holiness is not God, but God is holy and grants his spirit of holiness to man, placing it in man as his essence. This is the full meaning of of God's creation of man in revelation: "The creation of the spirit, as the holy one, is now understood as a continuously new creation. And since the creation itself is only a kind of correlation, becomes a necessary consequence of the creation of the holiness of the spirit. The holy spirit in man must therefore be active in the same way in the continuous new creation as the holy spirit in God, which also is dependent on the correlation" (*RV* 121; Eng. trans. 104).

The new formulation of the problem of transcendence involves an important difference, in Cohen's position here, in respect of classical idealism, understood in the form of Platonic idealism. It is this difference that Cohen presents as the novelty in Jewish monotheism in respect of scientific idealism. In an interesting passage in his essay *Der heilige Geist*, his intention was to affirm the substantial agreement between scientific idealism and Jewish monotheism. However, he actually brought out the essential difference between the two conceptions: that between the Greek conception of mediation, which, owing to an unsatisfactory concept of transcendence, tends to lose its true nature in unification, and the monotheistic one, which is precisely grounded in the unsurmountable otherness between God and man:

> Through the holy spirit, Jewish monotheism is connected to *scientific idealism* as a natural link of simplicity and certainty. The interest, in the service of which the holy spirit offers itself as a *mediator*, not a *unifier*, is that of the specifically and absolutely scientific world, which cannot ascertain the difference between God and man and thus, in the last analysis, cannot even understand those who profess the uniqueness of God. The *Greek* spirit,

which is the type of the scientific sense of the world, looks for mediation, as they call it, between God and man. *Philo*, with his *Logos*, was a victim of this Greek magic.[25]

So the moral problem of God's transcendence is that over which Greek idealism failed, in Plato's idea of good, its most daring enterprise. However, Jewish monotheism, made one of its most original contributions to idealism: correlation between God and man, the holy spirit:

> This humility of recognizing the limits of human knowledge, which at the same time is the greatest human pride, is surmised by the Greek mind in the *Idea of the Good*. But the latter, in the Greek mind, becomes a God, and thus there is no correlative link to the holy spirit of man. Because there is no unification, one has to look for a mediation. And it was the misfortune of monotheism that the Jew Philo, and his *Logos*, followed Plato, whom he thought he was only understanding logically, when at this point he should have maintained the independence of monotheism. (*RV* 124; Eng. trans. 107)

All the differences between scientific idealism (which originated in Platonic idealism) and Jewish monotheism, apart from the former's preference for investigation of nature, and the latter's for the problem of morality (cf. *RV* 54 passim; Eng. trans. 47), are consequences of the basic difference consisting of the absence of the idea of humanity in scientific idealism (cf. *RV* 26, 295; Eng. trans. 22f., 253) and, in general, that of universalism in the conception of love (cf. *RV* 167; Eng. trans. 144) and knowledge (cf. *RV* 299, 407; Eng. trans. 256f., 349f.), the lack of optimistic hope in the realization of good, which inspires messianic idealism (cf. *RV* 24, 339ff., 505f.; Eng. trans. 21, 291ff., 437f.).[26]

This problem of the transcendence of good, which Platonic idealism had failed to resolve, for Cohen, was undoubtedly a difficulty for the whole of scientific idealism. We find it again, for example, in his criticism of Kant's idea of the supreme good (cf. *KBE* 344ff.) and in the attempt to overcome it by means of the idea of the transcendence of God in *Ethik des reinen Willens*, as we have already seen. The answer to this problem, which Cohen found in Jewish monotheism, is certainly a new solution, but it answers a problem which had been developing in his thought since the period of his reflections on Kant, an intrinsic problem in critical idealism.

Cohen's overcoming these limitations of scientific idealism through reference to Jewish monotheism is certainly not to be considered, either in his intentions or results, as an exit from idealism, but, on the contrary, as an enrichment of idealism, an expansion beyond systematic scientific knowledge, into religious messianic idealism, which, without rejecting rationality, pushes it to its limits. Thus it is no longer a "religion within the limits of simple reason," as the Kantian version proclaimed its intention to be, but a "religion of reason," a religion as reflection of the rationality on and at its limit. This is why the religion of reason cannot be part of the system of philosophy, though it is linked to it and completes the perspective of critical philosophy, of which the system is also an expression.

8. HOLINESS AND CORRELATION

The God-man correlation, which is the keystone of Cohen's philosophy of religion, reaches its full meaning in the concept of the holy spirit. Undoubtedly, this completeness still has to emerge and be transmitted through the various stages of anthropology and philosophy of history, which Cohen dealt with in *Religion der Vernunft*, but the mature meaning of correlation is already reached in the concept of holy spirit: "The spirit is nothing else but the connecting link of the correlation, and holiness even more is nothing else but the medium that accomplishes the correlation: how could the holy spirit be anything other than that function which signifies the correlation?" (*RV* 121; Eng. trans. 105).

The gradual determination and enrichment of concepts which characterizes *Religion der Vernunft* clearly emerges in the development of the concept of correlation in its first chapters. This concept is frequently present from the outset, taking on a crucial role, but its meaning is not given a clear definition before the chapter on the holy spirit. As we have already seen, Cohen speaks of the correlation between God and the world, with reference to the creation. The meaning of correlation is still severely limited, being reduced to the logical-functional relationship between substance and function.[27] The reciprocity between the unique God the Creator and nature is reduced to the mere logical interdependence between the two concepts of 'being' and 'becoming.'

With the introduction of the God-man relationship in revelation, in the creation of rational man, correlation is more accurately defined by means of the concept of 'spirit.' Spirit is common to God and man, and reciprocity comes about through it. God is man's creator inasmuch as he grants him his own spirit, but, on the other hand, man is, as it were, God's "discoverer," since it is through man's spirit, that is, his reason, that God's being becomes "actual," in his knowledge of revealed law: "It is as if God's being were actual in man's knowledge only, so tremendous is the effect of the correlation. Man is no longer merely God's creature, but his reason, by virtue of his knowledge and also for the sake of it, makes him at least subjectively, as it were, the discoverer of God" (*RV* 103; Eng. trans. 88).

Here reciprocity is no longer merely logical interdependence, but a true reciprocal relationship. However, this relationship is still mostly indefinite and thus ambiguous. For this reason, in the passage quoted, Cohen is forced to treat it vaguely, using cautious expressions such as *it is as if, at least subjectively, as it were, the discoverer of God*. The difference between man and God has still not been clearly determined, and thus this is also true of correlation, which is unification, but not identification, of different terms. The reciprocity of correlation, which is manifest in man's knowledge of God thus remains vague, since it could easily be mistaken for the mystical identification of man with God in knowledge, and, consequently, in Cohen's view, for the pantheistic identity between man and God.

With the further specification of the concept of spirit as spirit of holiness, these gaps are filled and the concept of correlation determined satisfactorily. Holiness does not take the place of spirit in building up correlation, but actually completes and determines it, just as the concept of spirit is also needed for the correct determination of that of holiness: "Holiness determines and actualizes the spirit as moral spirit. And in the same way the spirit determines and actualizes holiness as the action of moral reason" (*RV* 130; Eng. trans. 112).

Cohen refers to several passages from the Bible in the development of the meaning of the God-man correlation through the holy spirit: "Ye shall be holy; for I the Eternal your God am holy" (Lev. 19, 2) etc.; "I will be hallowed among the children of Israel" (Lev. 22, 32); "Sanctify yourselves...and be ye holy" (Lev. 11, 44); "I am the Eternal who sanctify you" (Exodus 31, 13; Lev. 20, 8; 21, 8). We shall now follow Cohen's suggested itinerary to analyze the articulation of the correlation between God and man through the holy spirit.

a. "Ye shall be holy; for I the Eternal your God am holy."

Holiness therefore is the concept that unifies God and man: it belongs to them both. Not only in the spirit, but also in the holy spirit are God and man in correlation, in reason as action and not as speculation. However, unification in holiness maintains the difference between God and man; both have been holy in the same way. In correlation God has primacy: he *is* holy. God's absolute being is identical to his holiness: "God's holiness is identical with God's uniqueness" (*RV* 468; Eng. trans. 403). Origin and absolute end are identical in the idea of God.

God's holiness, inasmuch as it *is* holiness, establishes man's holiness: God grants man the spirit of his holiness. Man's holiness, then, is grounded in that of God; it is granted to him when fulfilled. Holiness, for man, is not a being, but a what ought to be, a task for moral becoming, of which his spirit consists (cf. *RV* 111; Eng. trans. 96). Man's holiness is identical to his morality. This thesis, however, should not be confused with resolution of religion in ethics (an earlier position favored by Cohen, as we have already seen). The identity of holiness and morality in man should be interpreted in the sense of grounding of morality in religion. This is the novel trait in Cohen's religious philosophy in respect of his ethics. Ethics must be able to found moral action on pure reason, without having recourse to external postulates. This principle was rigorously observed by Cohen in his ethics and is not rejected in his religious philosophy. But, in his view, religion goes further than ethics. It has a peculiarity in respect of ethics, since it considers man's morality in a different perspective, which is not contrary to reason, but at the limit of reason.

Religion considers man's morality in correlation with God's holiness. In accordance with the fundamental principle of religion: "In monotheism every characteristic of man proceeds from God" (*RV* 116; Eng. trans. 100; cf. *BR* 32). In the light of this correlation, man's morality *is already* holiness, inasmuch as the task, what ought to be, is already participation in being. What we could call this "constitutive holiness" of man is crucial for understanding aspects of human moral reality that escape ethics (such as love for fellow man, sin, and redemption), as well shall see later. But this is only acceptable to reason in the peculiar perspective of religion and allows expansion and addition to the understanding of moral man, in this perspective, beyond the borders of ethics. Correlation between God's holiness, which only has meaning for man's morality, and this morality, which already partakes of God's holiness, is the very core of Cohen's religious philosophy. Nevertheless, it remains to be further analyzed and determined.

b. "I will be hallowed among the children of Israel."

Thus, correlation, inasmuch as it is the unification of two terms, which do remain separate, however, can be actually constituted as reciprocal action, without the danger of mystical-pantheistic identification: "God has to remain God, and man, man, if the holy spirit is to be common to them" (*RV* 122; Eng. trans. 105). Despite this—actually, for this very reason—the holy spirit is not a mediating entity between God and man, but a correlation, a reciprocal action "if it is truly to mean the sanctification of man through the spirit of God, and again the sanctification of God through the spirit of man" (*RV* 122; Eng. trans. 105).

For man, God's holiness is nothing other than the sanctification of God through his own moral action. God's holiness is not an ontological hypostasis, but an absolute and moral truth. The road of theoretical, metaphysical, or mystical knowledge is illusory. Only moral action is the authentic road to knowledge of God, since it is the road of the realization of his holiness. In accordance with correlation, the fundamental principle of religion, the idea of God is only meaningful with reference to man. Therefore, God's holiness is also correlated with man and thus depends on man's moral action: "God is not determined as holy through the secrets of his being. In general he does not become the holy God through knowledge; but only sanctification, the action that man has to carry out, produces his holiness" (*RV* 128; Eng. trans. 110).

c. "Sanctify yourselves . . . and be ye holy."

How can man carry out the sanctification of God? Through sanctification of himself, through moral effort, through action constantly directed to the infinite task of holiness: "The holy spirit comes alive in man inasmuch as he sanctifies himself. In this self-sanctification he carries out the sanctification of God" (*RV* 128; Eng. trans. 110).

d. "I am the Eternal who sanctify you."

In correlation, not even man's action is understandable, if it is not "linked to God" (*RV* 129; Eng. trans. 111). Man's self-sanctification is grounded in his possibility by participation in God's holiness, which is both for "archetype" (*RV* 128; Eng. trans. 110) man and for "infinite task" (*RV* 129; Eng. trans. 111). This is why self-sanctification is a real task for man, not only despite its being infinite, but precisely because it is infinite. God's idealness grounds that of man in correlation (cf. *RV* 128f.; Eng. trans. 110f.).

The God-man correlation, as unification in diversity, thus takes on its full meaning as infinite dialectic of the action between God and man, in the concept of the holy spirit. God is Holy, the archetype of holiness for man, he who grants holiness to man. However, this creative holiness of God does not drain human morality, but stimulates it in the direction of its infinite task and guarantees the value of moral effort, since the eternal incompleteness of this effort, far from meaning unproductive and inconclusive, bears witness to its actual value of sanctification and holiness.

9. HOLY SPIRIT AND THE PECULIARITY OF RELIGION

The holy spirit, or God-man correlation, represents the true peculiarity of religion in respect of ethics. In his last years, Cohen changed his attitude considerably toward the relationship between ethics and religion.

In all his previous work, including *Ethik des reinen Willens*, he had connected preference for the ethical content of religion in respect of the theoretical-mystical and practical-cultural contents with the consequent conviction that religion should be overcome by the pure ethics of reason. He always actively defended Judaism, even against the historical danger of conversion to Christianity and assimilation. However, this struggle was carried on by Cohen in the name of loyalty to his own spiritual, cultural, and religious identity. This loyalty was basically historical, and, as far as its contents are concerned, mostly meant the profession of Jewish monotheism, which was made to coincide with the essence of the ethical idealism of the Western philosophical tradition. The religion-ethics relationship is also formulated in this way in *Ethik des reinen Willens*:

> Loyalty must also operate with *religion*. It has an important role in the continuation of culture. *Ethics absolutely cannot recognize the independence of religion. . . . It can . . . recognize religion only as a state of nature, whose cultural maturity is part of ethics.* But this maturity of culture can only be considered to have begun, from the methodical point of view. The situation and general way of the world is opposed to it and is in contradiction with it. Even the activation of theoretical culture, as truthfulness demands, is not realized. *Therefore one cannot practically be without a substitute for religion.* So there is no option but to use religion as a cultural tool and make it evermore useful for the clear end: *that it lead to its own elimination.* (*ERW* 586)

The constancy of this position in Cohen's thought adds great interest to the novelty of his recognition, in his last years, of a peculiarity of religion in respect of ethics, for which the essentially moral content of the former does not imply its overcoming in the latter, but rather a permanent validity of religion itself, beside ethics and complementary to it. It would be misleading to interpret this change in Cohen's thought as his abandoning critical idealism and conversion to existential-religious thought. Actually, as we have seen, Cohen's own pure ethics had given rise to problems, to which it was unable to reply satisfactorily. This is especially true of the problem of the unification of being and what ought to be, the concrete realization of moral action, and the problem of understanding man as an individual and of his relationship with the ideal of humanity.

Critical idealism, in the context of its scientific method, discovers its borders (*Schranken*) and manages to transform them into the positive sense of limits (*Grenzen*), *within which* reason can carry on its reflection with a rigorous, well-founded method, only if, at the same time, it refers to reflection *on* its limit. The God-man and God-world correlation, the object of religion, is the limit that critical reason not only cannot remove, but must in some way make the object of its reflection, if it wants its investigation *within* the limits of reason not to be deprived of the ultimate horizon, without which it remains suspended and impotent with respect to its own scientific problems. Therefore, the God-man correlation is also the object of philosophical reason which finds common ground with religion in its critical character.

Many of Cohen's interpreters have identified the peculiarity he attributed to religion in respect of ethics in the themes of man as an individual, of guilt and redemption; this opinion is on occasion supported by Cohen himself, particularly in *Der Begriff der Religion im System der Philosophie*. Already in the *Vorrede* to this book, he states that he is attempting "to ground the systematic concept of religion in that of the individual" (*BR* v). In the whole work, the theme of the redeemed individual sinner is highlighted as the fundamental novelty of religion in respect of ethics. Even if, in *Der Begriff der Religion im System der Philosophie*, the question of this peculiarity of religion is not reduced to the theme of man as an individual (see, for example, the more complex treatment of the problem in *BR* 42ff.), the subject is greatly emphasized in the work.

I do not intend to deny, or even reduce, the importance Cohen attributes, in his religious philosophy, to the theme of man as an individual, nor do I intend to deny that this important novelty regarding religion is also highlighted in all its value in *Religion der Vernunft*; in the latter work Cohen writes:

> With regard to religion the autonomy of ethics consists in the laying down of first principles for its own concepts. These first principles, however, separate themselves into a system, and have no effect beyond it. Thus, we have recognized humanity and the individual as the limits of ethics, at which point religion establishes its own foundation. In the concept of the individual, the ethical concept of man is incorporated into religion. (*RV* 37; Eng. trans. 32; cf. *RV* 193, 208, 437; Eng. trans. 166, 178, 376).

In his posthumous work, more clearly than in *Der Begriff der Religion im System der Philosophie*, Cohen contextualized the novelty of the theme of the individual and the other themes peculiar to religion in respect of ethics in the fundamental characteristic of religion, that is, in the new perspective of man's correlation with God, in which the themes of pure philosophy (the nature of logic, man in ethics, love of man in aesthetics) are placed. Thus their meaning is seen in a new light and is expanded and enriched. The shift in attention from the theme of the individual to that of the correlation and understanding of the first in the context of the second is not without importance for the correct interpretation of Cohen's late philosophy. It should be recalled that Rosenzweig's opinion that Cohen's religious philosophy in this last stage was an abandonment of idealism and conversion to the existential philosophy of relation is grounded on radical emphasis and identification in Cohen's arguments of the theme of the individual and on understanding of Cohen's concept of of correlation in connection with the latter theme.

The opposite seems to me to be more correct and faithful to Cohen: the situating of the theme of the individual in the context of the critical concept of correlation and its new developments in Cohen's late religious philosophy. As we have seen, the God-man correlation, in the general meaning contained in the concept of holy spirit, must be considered not as Cohen's flight from critical philosophy, but as a last, necessary extension of critical reflection in the direction of the limit, so as to be able to outline the necessary horizon for all the areas of systematic investigation in this new perspective. Therefore, it can be clearly stated that the holy spirit, as a general definition of correlation, is a key theme in Cohen's religious philosophy. It guarantees its critical character and thus its fundamental continuity with Cohen's previous thought. If this hypothesis is a valid one, the holy spirit, as the essential content of the God-man correlation, will also have to show itself as the ground of the expansion of understanding of man in respect of ethics in *Religion der Vernunft.*

10

Man in Correlation with God

1. Jewish Monotheism and Scientific Idealism

We have already referred to Cohen's idea of the complementarity between Jewish monotheism and scientific idealism. It is neither a question of overcoming it nor even less of antithesis, but rather one of expansion and enrichment. The peculiarity of monotheism, interpreted as religion of reason, by way of the concept of 'correlation,' in respect of ethics, implies this expansion of critical idealism beyond scientific idealism.

The ethics of pure will follows the critical-idealist method of purity, that of foundation of being in idea. It also follows the scientific principle of the consideration of the object in its universal meaning, as a concept, and not in its particular material conditions. However, the critical-transcendental character of the ethics of pure will, as we have seen, brings with it the need to posit the problem of the realization of moral action, and thus of the concept of 'man,' in nature and history. Thus ethics posits a problem which it is not able to resolve, since refusal to consider the material conditions of morality, which is intrinsic to scientific idealism, necessarily makes the consideration of man as a universal concept prevail. In *Ethik des reinen Willens*, Cohen had distinguished the three meanings of man: individual, plurality, and universality, but, precisely because of the empirical implications of the first two meanings, he only discussed the theory of man and his moral action with reference to man as universality and state, not considering the individual, except as a "bearer of humanity," and limiting the analysis of man as plurality (in

199

the theory of relative communities) to the relationship with universality (state). Therefore, in the ethics of pure will, the theory of morality is developed scientifically, and thus man is only understood as a universal concept, and the individual is also only considered as a "symbol of humanity" (cf. *RV* 15f.; Eng. trans. 13).

Furthermore, the ethics of pure will, inasmuch as it is critical ethics, raises the problem of man's concrete reality and moral realization, but, inasmuch as it is scientific ethics, it cannot resolve it, owing to its methodical inability to consider the empirical conditions of morality. Thus, it posits the realization of morality in the world as a regulative ideal and introduces the idea of God as a postulate of unification in general between the being of nature and moral what ought to be, without being able to actually penetrate the historical process of this unification, nor the material conditions of man as a moral being:

> As man in ethics is merely an example of humanity, so God is only the guarantor of humanity. Humanity is the subject of universal morality. According to ethics, the individual man is able to fulfill the demands of morality only in the image of humanity and, therefore, only within ethics' own competence, namely, in *the autonomous law of its reason.* The latter is not responsible for anything that happens beyond its borders and basically, therefore, is not interested in the outward success or failure of moral duty. Yet here, too, religion objects to this fiction of indifference. It must not be a matter of indifference whether my morality and all men's morality remains dutiful striving only, sufficient in itself; rather, I have to take an interest in the question of whether the *ideal* has life and actuality. Even though this identity can only be achieved in the approximation to the ideal, the inexorable goal of approximation is the permeating of actuality with the ideal. However, this proper goal of ethics has to recede in face of the scientific rigor of ethics, because of which it has to maintain the separation of actuality from the ideal, and generally between idea and actuality. This rigor brings about the illusion that ethics deals only with law and rule, but never with human actuality.
>
> Religion opposes this kind of "rotten reasoning," and thereby establishes its own worth. The God of whom religion teaches means nothing else but the repeal of this prejudice of ethical rigor. (*RV* 23f.; Eng. trans. 20f.)

In Cohen's view, Jewish monotheism allows these difficulties of ethics to be overcome and a solution to the problem of concrete man and the realization of moral action to be found, though *still remaining in the area of idealism.* However, this contribution of Jewish monotheism to ethics can only be partially integrated into the scientific theory of ethics.

Cohen recalls that he had done this, as far as possible, in *Ethik des reinen Willens*:

> We have depicted the messianic God as the God of ethics, but in the inter-
> est of historical clarification we must add that in our *Ethics of Pure Will* this
> messianic God appears only as the God of ethics. Just as scientific ethics
> must use all its literary sources correctly, so have we transplanted this God
> from the religion of monotheism into ethics. And yet this God, derived
> from religion, is an ethical God merely in virtue of the connection that
> exists between monotheism and morality; he is not yet God of religion
> proper. The apex of monotheism is Messianism, but its center of gravity
> lies in the relation between God and the individual. (*RV* 25; Eng. trans.
> 21f.)

In its new specific idealist meaning, monotheism must preserve its religious physiognomy, which does not distinguish it from ethics either in its content (man and his moral action) or in its method (the method of purity), but only in its overcoming the scientific condition, that of consideration of the object solely as a universal concept. God-man corre-lation, the center of religious reflection, allows understanding of empiri-cal, material conditions of man and his moral action, not simply considering them in their empirical character, but raising them up to an ideal by means of the correlation of idea with God.

Wilhelm Herrmann[1] had objected that Cohen had wished to resolve religion in ethics, neglecting the peculiar characteristic of religion itself, its reference to the concrete reality of man as an individual. He accused Cohen of wishing to justify religion with the scientific method of ethics, instead of examining its own specific language, which cannot be reduced to science. In Herrmann's view, Cohen considered man, the *Selbst*, only as a task, completely neglecting the existential experience that he has of himself as an individual in his own empirical historical sit-uation. But this immediate experience that man has of himself, in Herrmann's view, is precisely the object of religion. Neglecting it, as Cohen does, means, not only draining religion of its content and reduc-ing it to ethics, but also not taking the sense of history seriously.

Cohen's reply to Herrmann, as mentioned earlier, was actually only a partial acceptance of his arguments. Cohen recognized in his last works that he had neglected man as a concrete, historical individual and accepted the consideration of religion as an area of comprehension of the existential experience of man, and therefore the peculiarity of reli-gion in respect of ethics (cf. *BR* 55ff.). However he rejected Herrmann's approach, which identifies the place of religion in an individual experi-ence of man, which cannot be translated in philosophical terms nor

understood rationally, in a "hidden life of the individual,"[2] whose knowledge essentially consists of his or her experience in life. Cohen rejects a
phenomenological-existentialist conception of religion, so as to try to
understand man's concrete historical existential dimension, the object
of religion, in the context of an idealist, and therefore rationalist, interpretation, which philosophy cannot be without. The religion of reason
represents this attempt, and correlation constitutes the method by
means of which man's historical experience with reference to an idea
can be understood and the sense of concrete man and his history in relation to the idea of God be idealistically founded.

Thus the God-man correlation is not, as Rosenzweig argues, the
theme that determined Cohen's abandonment of idealism and his conversion to a philosophy of experience, but, on the contrary, it is the
method, by means of which Cohen also tried to understand again man's
empirical, contingent aspect and the historical, existential conditions of
morality, in the context of a critical, idealist interpretation. For this reason Cohen can state, in the *Einleitung* to *Religion der Vernunft*, that the
concept of a religion of reason, not only does not imply reduction of religion to ethics, but not even the recognition of the incapacity of ethics to
master the entire content of the concept of man (*RV* 14; Eng. trans. 12)
and thus the need to fill this gap through religion. Religion does expand
and enrich the ethical concept of man (and it is of this that his specificity
consists), but this contribution and this specificity of religion cannot be
considered external, or autonomous in respect of ethics, since the religion of reason remains in the area of the critical-idealist method of philosophy and is only differentiated from ethics in the abandonment of
conditionings forced on the latter by its scientific character. The specificity (or peculiarity) of religion is thus formed in the area of ethics, and
more generally that of critical philosophy: or, rather, religion further
investigates the understanding of man "for ethics" (*BR* 77), in a different
way.

2. SUFFERING

To leave the "abstraction" (*RV* 131; Eng. trans. 113) of man considered as holy spirit and a being of reason and to understand him in his
relationship with "historical experience" (*RV* 131; Eng. trans. 113), the
problem of evil must be faced, in its twofold aspect of suffering and guilt.
The religion of reason, through the concept of correlation, is able to
understand the concrete historical aspect of evil in a critical-idealist
interpretative frame.

These two aspects of evil must be initially differentiated and kept independent, if one does not wish to abandon the rational method and admit a metaphysical-mystical interpretation of evil as universal suffering, a product of universal guilt, or a mythological-tragic interpretation of suffering as the fatal consequence of the individual's, the hero's, guilt. But suffering is a moral, not a metaphysical or mythological, problem only in the figure of the suffering of an innocent. In such a case, it is an unavoidable problem for a theory of morality, and ethics is unable to resolve it following its principles. Only religion can supply the necessary concepts for satisfactory understanding of the problem of suffering:

> There is a historical model for the necessity of supplementing ethics by religion, this is offered by *Stoicism* in its relation to the *suffering* of man. Stoicism proclaims suffering as indifferent (ἀδιάφορον) and therefore excludes it from morality. This conclusion drawn from the dualism of Stoicism, which with regard to all questions wavers between spirituality and materialism, is doubly in error. In the first place, suffering is in no way an indifferent element for the I. Perhaps because of its moral demands, the self-consciousness should not be indifferent to one's own physical suffering. Secondly, the observer should not let himself be indifferent to the other man's suffering. There arises the question of whether it is not precisely through the observation of the other man's suffering that the other *is changed from the He to the Thou*. The affirmative answer to this question brings to light the specific power of religion, without detriment to its participation in the method of ethics. (*RV* 19; Eng. trans. 16f.)

A correct methodological approach to the moral problem of evil will thus be to consider guilt as an attribute of the individual and suffering as a social phenomenon (cf. *RV* 160; Eng. trans. 138). Thus, for Cohen, suffering becomes the fact, the starting point for critical reflection of religion to further investigate the concept of man as plurality, which ethics cannot satisfactorily found. The figure in which suffering is the object of moral and religious reflection is not above all death, which, inasmuch as it is suffering, is a metaphysical problem (cf. *RV* 155; Eng. trans. 134), but rather social suffering. The latter is where I discover man as fellowman, as the Other and as "my" Other: You, the *Mitmensch*.

3. FELLOWMAN AS *MITMENSCH*

It is clear that simply taking note of and accepting diversity among men makes any moral consideration of society and history impossible. Only the principle of equality among men is a moral principle. The mere ethical affirmation of this equality, in the name of universal participation in humanity, or, in religious terms, of common descent from God, is not sufficient for exhaustive understanding of men's relationships with one another. The reduction of plurality to universality, of diversity among men to the equality of humanity, overshadows otherness, thus impoverishing the relationship. Ethics, precisely because of its need to found the concept of man solely with reference to the universal meaning of humanity, cannot understand the other man as "You," but only as 'He,' not as a *Mitmensch*, but only as a *Nebenmensch*[3] and, being unable to reach the full meaning of the interpersonal relationship, turns out to be unsatisfactory for such a task (cf. *RV* 17f.; Eng. trans. 14f.). Only religion can face this task, since it can begin with the historical fact of suffering, and interpret it by means of the principle of correlation. Only correlation, the unification of otherness kept as such, can found the concept of '*Mitmensch.*' Religion discovers the other man as *Mitmensch* in suffering. Cohen emphasizes the discovery of *Mitmensch* in man's experience as the Other, as someone different.[4] In national diversity (the foreigner) and in economic discrimination (the poor man) man is met as the Other, whom Jewish monotheism teaches should be regarded as equal to oneself.

The suffering of the Other, of the foreigner or poor man, however, as has already been pointed out, will not take up its full significance as a moral problem until it has been assimilated by the problem of the suffering of the just man. We shall look into this important development of the theme of suffering, in which Cohen, through the Talmudic theme of Noachic law and Maimonides's concept of the "pious among the peoples of the world" (cf. *RV* 135ff.; Eng. trans. 116ff.), shows the recognition, in Jewish tradition, of the possible justice for the foreigner and recognizes in the poor man the just and pious type, connecting this meaning to the the messianic function of suffering. I again observe here that Cohen underlines prophetic teaching showing the poor man as the archetype of man, seeing in poverty, in social suffering, not only an individual evil, but also a cultural situation involving human consciousness in general:

> *Only social suffering is spiritual suffering.* All the complexity of consciousness, including knowledge, is affected by it and brought to take part in it. This is the profound meaning of social suffering: that the entire consciousness of culture is implicated in it. *Stoic apathy* is therefore entirely inadmissible; it excludes ethics and at the same time includes the renunciation of culture. I cannot be indifferent to poverty, because it is the sign of the distress of culture, and because it calls into question true morality. Poverty cannot be compared to physical suffering, because the latter is individual and subjective, whereas social suffering is not only the suffering of the majority but also the qualitative evidence of the low level of the culture.

This situation brings about a new tragic motive of its own. However, in tragedy only the hero, only the individual suffers; in social suffering the entire culture assumes a tragic role. And culture here is not an abstraction, but the most vivid actuality, the majority of the human race in every people and in every epoch. Thus the poor man typifies man in general. Thus the next man becomes fellowman. For even if I had no heart in my body, my education alone would have brought me to the insight that the great majority of men cannot be isolated from me, and that I myself am nothing if I do not make myself a part of them. In these unavoidable connections between myself and the majority, a relationship arises that means more than merely coordination or even subordination, but which produces a community. And this community produces the fellowman. (*RV* 158; Eng. trans. 136f.)

4. CORRELATION AS LOVE

Thus man's suffering cannot be considered a mere contingent phenomenon, nor simple physical pain; it has a cultural and spiritual meaning, owing to which it is precisely an unavoidable problem for morality. However, suffering remains, in Cohen's view, the simple datum of a historical, empirical fact, which moral reason must face, not the concept through which it works out its answer. Man discovers *Mitmensch, in* suffering, not *through* suffering. The religious principle of correlation provides an answer and solution to the drama and problem of suffering. Correlation is not therefore reduced to the experience of suffering, but rather supplies an answer to it, raising it from the level of experience to that of ideality. This explanation is necessary so as to be able to reject, once again, the interpretation of Cohen's principle of correlation as a transitory stage from critical idealist philosophy to a philosophy of the immediate experience of the interpersonal relationship, and to confirm, on the contrary, a methodical function for the ideal, critical understanding of historical and existential reality.

The true key concept for the foundation of the *Mitmensch* in the religion of reason is 'love,' in its articulation: man's love of man, God's love of man, man's love of God. If Cohen preferred this succession to the more predictable scansion of the three stages of love, following the double movement, falling from God to man, and rising from man to God, the reason is to be sought in his intention of clearly defining the moral character of religious love, against any mystical conception, seeing that the above-mentioned cyclical movement is a schema that is traditionally used in mystical thought. This does not mean, however, that, for Cohen, man's love of man is originary in respect of love of God, as Heinrich Scholz and Trude Weiss-Rosmarin maintain.[5] Scholz in particular draws his opinion from a passage in *Der Begriff der Religion im System der Philosophie*, where Cohen states: "The originative factor in religious consciousness is not love of God, but love for suffering man. Love of God enters only under manifold interpretations when God is recognized as the protector of those who suffer. Thus *religion and mysticism* are differentiated in the function of God for suffering man; therefore, even the infiniteness claimed for consciousness does not make religion accessible to feeling" (*BR* 89–90).

In this passage, Cohen's obvious concern is to radically differentiate rational, and thus critical and moral, reason from mysticism. Nevertheless, in *Religion der Vernunft*, the meaning of the methodical opportunity to begin from love as a relationship between man and man, to reach love between man and God is more accurately reconciled with the general meaning of correlation. Here Cohen explains that man's love of man is the "objective foundation" (*RV* 168; Eng. trans. 145) from which only man "has to understand" (*RV* 169; Eng. trans. 145) God's love of man. The priority of man's love of man is therefore solely a priority for knowledge, not for value. More correctly, Leo Strauss explains: "It is in the light of 'the social love' of our fellowmen that we must understand the love that proceeds from God and the love that is directed towards him."[6] In man's love of man, God's love of man is revealed (cf. *RV* 183; Eng. trans. 158) and man's love of God is manifest (cf. *RV* 154 f.; Eng. trans. 133), but this does not contradict the fundamental movement of correlation, for which God is the origin of correlation (cf. *RV* 174; Eng. trans. 150): he "gives rise in us" to love of our fellowman and "sets up" pity for men, for us (cf; *RV* 183; Eng. trans. 158). God is the "goal" of man's love (cf. *RV* 190; Eng. trans. 164). God's love of man is the archetype (*Urbild*) for man's moral task to love his fellowman, and, inasmuch as it is a task, love of fellowman is an infinite movement toward God as the supreme end. The characteristic movement of correlation is conserved thus: "The love for man has therefore to be the beginning, because although God created man, man must create the fellowman for himself. And religion must assist in this creation. Thus God must become the creator a second time when, through the share of reason in religion, he teaches man himself to create man as fellowman" (*RV* 170; Eng. trans. 147).

5. LOVE FOR *MITMENSCH:* COMPASSION

The other man, as my Other, You, *Mitmensch* is therefore discovered in suffering (*Leiden*). It is in his suffering that I establish a relationship with him, not only as another man (*Nebenmensch*), but as my Other

(*Mitmensch*). This relationship, which, in Cohen's view, is a true correlation between man and man, within that between God and man (cf. *RV* 133, 153f., 169, 264, 405; Eng. trans. 114, 132f., 146, 226f, 348) is love in the religious sense.

In *Ethik des reinen Willens*, Cohen had refused to recognize a function for love as a factor of pure will. He had only accepted a function for it as an impulse to moral action, in particular of the second-degree virtues, in a subordinate position to honor, to the affect accompanying the first degree virtues (cf. *ERW* 216ff., 481ff.). In *Religion der Vernunft*, however, he considers love as a true factor of pure will, as the originary strength of pure will and, paradoxically, carries out this operation through the idealization of a feeling that philosophical tradition has generally considered in its passive and reactive meaning: compassion (*Mitleid*).

Cohen observes that rejection of compassion as a moral factor in the history of philosophy (he explicitly refers to stoicism [cf. *RV* 160f.; Eng. trans. 138f.], in Spinoza [cf. *RV* 162; Eng. trans. 140] and also in his own ethics [cf. *RV* 164; Eng. trans. 141f.],[7] rises from its interpretation as passion and reaction. However, it is possible to understand compassion differently, as correlation between man and man. In this sense it is not man's reaction to the suffering of his *alter ego*, but the ground of the action that transforms the other man into a You (cf. *RV* 164; Eng. trans. 141). Religious love, compassion, thus leaves edifying vagueness and is determined in a meaning in contrast with the mystical one, that is, as man's moral action toward the other suffering man, as an effective act to eliminate his suffering. In this active correlation, man takes as his own the suffering of the Other, not in Schopenhauer's sense of the elimination of otherness, but by taking up the task of actually eliminating his suffering. He thus transforms the other man into *Mitmensch*, into his own You, and at the same time becomes You for the other:

> For the distinction between pessimism and optimism is only concerned with the practical reform of earthly existence. Optimism is in no way "the wicked way of thinking," as Schopenhauer defames it, but its wisdom has a practical significance that always has been confirmed by theodicy, namely, to better the existence in the world in accordance with moral rule and thus to lessen human suffering. If, however, pessimism objects that all these endeavors are futile, are love's labor lost, then although this objection is in contradiction to the still recognizable progress of world history, the thesis of pessimism is not thereby refuted; for this thesis arises out of a metaphysics that claims to be independent of experience. The metaphysical meaning of suffering makes suffering the only reality in human existence proper, and the practical consequence of this metaphysics of pessimism is therefore the realization and verification of this principle in the negation, in the repeal of existence. However, if this wisdom is consid-

ered to be metaphysics, in no case can it be considered ethics; for the latter is throughout the affirmation, development, and elevation of human existence. If ethics now sees existence afflicted with suffering then compassion becomes for it only a signpost for the question: How can suffering be overcome? Subjectively, suffering is pain; does compassion abide on one level with pain, or does it contain in itself a means of dissolving it? Is it perhaps the wound itself, which brings with it its own healing?

This is the turning point at which religion, as it were, emerges from ethics. The observation of another man's suffering is not an inert affect to which I surrender myself, particularly not when I observe it not as a natural or empirical phenomenon, but when I make of it a question mark for my whole orientation in the moral world. (*RV* 20f.; Eng. trans. 18)

The idealist meaning of religious correlation, but also its peculiarity in respect of scientific idealism, is therefore evident in man's love of man. The religious principle of love for fellowman is not resolved in the experience of the suffering of others, nor in the affective relationship with it, but is raised up to the idealization of compassion as the originary strength of moral action, and the constitutive principle of the interpersonal relationship between men. Suffering is the simple given, compassion is the ideal principle of the realization of pure morality with reference to the concrete reality of suffering man: "If the meaning of physical suffering, of physical ill in the human world, has always been a question for theodicy, then one could perhaps state this meaning in a paradox: the suffering, the *passion* (*Leiden*) is the sake of *compassion* (*Mitleid*). Man is so much in need of the affect of compassion that suffering itself is explained through it" (*RV* 19; Eng. trans. 17).

6. God's Love for Man: Mercy

Man's love of man leads to the discovery and understanding of God's love of man. God "must of necessity love poor men, because man has the duty of loving his poor *Mitmensch*" (*BR* 80). As has already been pointed out, this does not mean that man's love of man is the origin of God's love of man. Rather, man seeks and finds a ground for his love for his fellowman in God's love. The ultimate ground of the moral imperative of love for fellowman is certainly, at least in part, equality among men: "Love thy neighbor as thyself" (Lev. 19, 18). Biblical religion posits the ground of equality and unity among men in the unique God the creator, and, in this sense, ethics can accept this principle and make it its own.[8] The unity of men as God's creatures is also foregrounded in *Religion der Vernunft* (cf. *RV* 138, 144 f.; Eng. trans. 119 f., 124 f.).

Nevertheless, religious correlation implies a further, peculiar meaning of the foundation of the love of fellowman in the relationship with God: man must love the other man (the foreigner and poor man), because God loves him. God's fatherhood of men only takes on a specific, detailed meaning inasmuch as God is revealed in it, not merely as the creator, but also as the defender of the poor: "When I love God, I do not love *the universe pantheistically*, not the *animals*, the *trees*, and *plants*, as creatures together with me, but I love God only as the *father of men*, and the term *God the father* has this higher meaning, this social fullness; he is not so much the creator as the author, but rather *protection and help of the poor*" (*BR* 81; cf. *RV* 171; Eng. trans. 147).

This new meaning of God's relationship with men is the concrete expression of God's creative act, inasmuch as it is, as we have seen, a conservation and continual renewal of the creature, since divine creation is identical to divine providence (cf. *RV* 173 f.; Eng. trans. 149 f.).

Once the complete idealization of the religious affect had been fulfilled in the analysis of compassion, Cohen had no reservations about using biblical language and pointing to the affect of pity as the expression of God's love of man. Obviously, man is not a *Mitmensch* for God, but pity, correlative with compassion, is God's affect for man (cf. *RV* 174; Eng. trans. 150). All the laws and institutions that God granted to Israel, for the protection of the foreigner and the poor man, are the fruit of God's pity. They have their compendium in the institution of the Sabbath: "*The embodiment of this love is to be recognized in the Sabbath*" (*RV* 182; Eng. trans. 157).[9] In the Sabbath. God ensures equality in human dignity and the joy of the community for suffering man, and in particular for those who suffer most, the poor, laborers, slaves (cf. *RV* 183; Eng. trans. 158).

Naturally, God's pity only manifests itself through man's compassion. For this reason, God's institution of the Sabbath is a commandment for man. It is the complete manifestation of divine love inasmuch as it is also the essence and fundamental commandment for human morality. However, this is perfectly coherent with the critical-idealist meaning of the God-man correlation. God's pity means no more for us than the origin and ground of human compassion:

> We asked, what meaning does the love of God have? The answer is now found to be the pity for the poor, which God awoke in us through his commandments. This has become for us the intelligible explanation of the meaning of God's love. The Sabbath has removed that deplorable appearance of bondage and of inequality from men. As God originated in us compassion for men in presence of despicable poverty, so in this social insight he has revealed to us his love for men. (RV 183; Eng. trans. 158)

7. MAN'S LOVE FOR GOD: YEARNING

Correlation between God and man in love implies man's love of God as the third stage. Here also, Cohen has recourse to the analogy of a feeling: yearning (*Sehnsucht*).[10] The psalms, in particular, show man's yearning for God. In contrast with nonreligious lyrical poetry, however, they do not sing of the object of this yearning, but only of man's inclination:

> Yearning penetrates body and soul, and its expression knows no limitations. But the psalm describes and sings only of anguished yearning and of the flight of the soul. God, however, remains outside of this description.whereas lyrical poetry usually describes the beloved person, for whom one yearns and to whom one is attracted, the psalm describes only the heart which feels the yearning, and appeals to God not so much in his beauty, but rather exclusively in his goodness, thus only as the archetype of moral action. (RV 188f.; Eng. trans. 162f.)

God, even as the object of love, is an idea, not a person. For this reason, love of God is resolved in an inclination towards the realization of the idea in moral action. If mystical love of God, owing to its aesthetic and erotic implications, is "the unchaste desire for union with God" (*RV* 190; Eng. trans. 164), religious love is "striving for God's nearness" (*RV* 190; Eng. trans. 164).

The biblical concept of 'God's nearness,' an alternative, in Cohen's view, to 'unification with God,' drastically excludes not only the personalization of God, and therefore any confusion of religious love of God with aesthetic and erotic love but also any representation of God in an image (*Bild*), and also the representation of God as a model (*Vorbild*). The aspiration to God's nearness also means that the idea of God is not an object for imitation (*Nachahmung*) for man, but only for aspiration (*Nacheiferung*): the idea of God, as origin and unity as the term of reference of the infinite task of action, maintains its transcendence even in correlation with man:

> God is compassionate; this attribute the rabbis explain thus: as he is compassionate, so are you to be compassionate. The attribute has only the meaning of a model. But the model makes only emulation possible, and not imitation; it is only an archetype. This whole trend of thought carries into effect the idea: "Be thou holy for I am holy, the Eternal your God." As holy, God is not so much the model that never can be reached, but rather the archetype and, therefore, the idea which, in the case of action, has the meaning of the ideal. This idealistic meaning is the clear, exact sense of the *love for God.* (*RV* 188; Eng. trans. 162)

Therefore, in this context too, love is not so much a feeling as the sense of moral action. It is the infinite sense of love for man, which stretches out in love of God. Yearning for God's nearness concretely means drawing near, or to use Cohen's favorite term, man's infinite *self nearing* to God. This is why this love of man for God does not contradict the "ethical principle of moral autonomy":

> Love is considered as the impulse to action because it makes man himself the original source of action. If love arouses action, then no extraneous and foreign object is its motive force. The love for morality is the love for God. This thesis means for religion what the following thesis means for ethics: action does not result from an extraneous and foreign matter, nor from an extraneous command. It is the result of the will, to which autonomy belongs. Love has to exclude every extraneous and foreign motivation. This foreign is the distant, from which nearness liberates; not, to be sure, nearness in itself, but the drawing near, and indeed the self-nearing. This is the love to which the philosophy of monotheism has raised the notion of the near God and the nearness of God. (*RV* 190f.; Eng. trans. 164)

Thus the idea of God, as the archetype of man's love for man, as origin and ideal, repeats and realizes the fundamental structure of the God-man correlation, presented in the concept of holy spirit, in the concreteness of the social situation: "This love, which is the self-nearing to God is therefore the only right love for God, because in it the holy God is loved, who makes us holy, who demands our holiness, which can become actual only in the self-nearing to God's holiness" (*RV* 190; Eng. trans. 164).

8. THE INDIVIDUAL IN ETHICS AND RELIGION

The problem of suffering is present not only in others, but also in us. My suffering is a fact before which reason cannot but search for a sense: "Furthermore, even one's own suffering need not now be accepted with plain indifference. To have compassion with one's own suffering does not have to be simply inert and fruitless sentimentality. Corporeality belongs, as matters stand, to the soul of the individual and the soul is neglected when the affliction of the body is neglected. Humanity requires consideration for one's own suffering" (*RV* 22; Eng. trans. 19)

Before directly facing up to this problem, the religion of reason must clarify the concept of 'man as an individual,' since, only with reference to it, can the problem of my suffering be resolved. Man discovers he is an individual in the isolation and loneliness of guilt (*Schuld*) and sin (*Sünde*) (cf. *BR* 62). The problem of guilt is also posed in ethics, as a problem in which the individual is alone with himself. But for this very reason, ethics cannot find a satisfactory solution to the problem, since the scientific problem of pure ethics has no option other than that of resolving the individual in humanity:

> The guilt and the merit of man remains hidden from man. This is not the fault of aesthetics, but of science, which in turn receives its limits from logic. For ethics, man is, in the last analysis—one can see it clearly now— only a point to which it relates its problems, as for science also he is only a particular case of its general laws. In relation to the laws, however, only the particular man originates, and indeed as nothing other than a case. The case that comes under a law is, however, not the individual, who addresses himself as I. The case addresses only the law. The individual, however, thinks himself isolated and therefore absolute. And in this isolation he is at his wits' end, as long as he cannot absolve himself from the consciousness of his guilt and, according to his subjective membership in the realm of moral creatures, may not absolve himself. If at this point the correlation to God did not come into force, he would be absolutely lost to the moral world, lost to his consciousness of it. (*RV* 195f.; Eng. trans. 168)

It is precisely the overcoming of the isolated singularity of the individual and his or her understanding in the universal of humanity that constitutes "the highest triumph of ethics" (*RV* 208f.; Eng. trans. 178), but also its limit. Here ethics cannot consider the concrete, historical conditions of human existence. It does not even consider man as an individual, except to deny him as such, by resolving him in humanity. The overcoming of the problem of man's weakness and guilt in the ideal perfection of the law, of the state, and humanity also implies, for ethics, the overcoming of man's individuality, which incorporates weakness. The defect of ethics certainly does not consist of the idealist inclination to overcoming the individual's guilt in his or her participation in humanity. Cohen is a long way from denying this idealist formulation which his ethics had conceived for the theory of morality: "The individual does not complain about his own dissolution, but about the fact of continuing to be an individual, of remaining so and missing ascent to humanity. The individual gives account of the individual's complaint concerning his remaining, not his disappearing" (*BR* 55).

The defect of ethics consists of directly and solely positing in humanity not only the task but also the ground of the meaning of the individual, of being forced to eliminate the individual to eliminate his or her guilt. This limit of ethics, as we have already seen, derives from its scientific, not its idealist, character:

If we . . . reflect that the transition to universality needs *equipment, which the individual in his sinfulness still lacks,* then he must not simply disappear, but must be preserved precisely for this *preparation* for universality. *This is precisely what is missing from the antinomy between individual and universality, when it is led to a solution only by means of political universality.* What is missing then is *the rest of the individual* which, as yeast for universality, for its development and realization, must always be preserved in it. Thus directing the individual to his *self transformation in universality* demonstrates that it is only a superficial quietening, at the moment of knowledge of his sinfulness; therefore the following important perspective is opened up here: *the concept of man is absolutely not determined under all points of view by ethics eliminating the individual in the universality of the State and of the alliance between States of humanity.* This transition reveals itself to be a jump, an interruption in moral *continuity.* Ethics can only make this transition the final agreement; it also needs a pause at the station of sin. (*BR* 55–6)

It is precisely the idealist and critical character of ethics—its understanding of man as idea and of morality as a task and the need for understanding man's concrete reality and ensuring the possibility of realization of the moral task—that make the problem of the individual and guilt unavoidable for it. However, it is the scientific method of pure ethics that prevents it from finding a satisfactory solution to this problem and refers it, beyond itself, to religion:

If man is not permitted to lay aside the consciousness of his guilt then it is ethics itself which refers man to religion, to the correlation with God. Ethics can only set up the first principles which determine the possibility of this correlation. To prescribe the boundary of the applicability of the correlation is in contradiction to the insight of ethics into its own limitations. . . . We repeat: if we claim that religion is concerned with man's guilt, and if we impart to religion the origin of the I as individual, we do not dissolve its connection with ethics, but, on the contrary, make the connection effective, so that ethics itself must demand the transition to religion, just as it will also have to demand that transition for the concept of God. (*RV* 195f.; Eng. trans. 168)[11]

Actually, the passage from ethics to religion, is not so much a transition (*Übergang*), a passage to something else, but an "enlargement of the problem" and a "solution" to it, by means of the abandonment of the scientific method, and the taking up of the peculiar, higher perspective of religion, which is not in contradiction with scientific ethics, but rather, as we have already seen, constitutes its complement (cf. *BR* 58). It is of this that the "the triumph of religion" consists (*RV* 210, Eng. trans. 180), being complementary and noncontradictory in respect of that of ethics: when understanding the individual as a rational, that is, moral being, *inasmuch as he or she is an individual,* and not only a participant in humanity, and therefore bringing the individual's specific wealth into the process of the realization of humanity.

How can the God-man correlation,which constitutes the content and method of religion, reach the solution of the problem of the individual and the individual's guilt, in the face of which ethics is aware of being impotent? In the meanings of correlation considered up to this point, man presented himself, first as a "rational being," then as "*Mitmensch*," but never as an "absolute individual,"[12] and the problem of guilt had still not been posited. Actually, guilt was decisively put on one side and separated from the problem of suffering in the analysis of the relationship of man with the other man. Cohen acknowledged that the religion of reason, both in the theme of the holy spirit and in that of *Mitmensch*, had still not faced the problem of man as an individual (cf. *RV* 192 f.; Eng. trans. 165f.), except in the answer to the question, "whether this concept of an absolute individual is legitimate . . . the peculiar character of religion is actualized more clearly and precisely than in the concept of the fellowman" (*RV* 193; Eng. trans. 165f.).

Man as an absolute individual in correlation with God is a new meaning of correlation, through which religion not only enlarges previous meanings, but completes and founds them. In correlation between God and man as a rational being, human morality is explained as moral action in correlation with God's holiness, and this moral action is analyzed in its motivations and social contents in the relationship between man and *Mitmensch.* However, moral action does not explain itself: just as in ethics there is a foundation of moral action in the a priori condition of pure will, in religion a foundation of the historical concreteness of moral action must also be sought in a concrete historical concept (even if it is ideal rather than empirical): the correlation between the unique God and man as an absolute individual realizes this fundamental task of religion (*RV* 193; Eng. trans. 166).

9. THE INDIVIDUAL AND SIN

As man in social plurality, *Mitmensch,* discovers himself in the suffering of the Other, so man as an individual discovers himself in sin: the experience of suffering places man before his fellowman, the experience of sin places him before himself.

However, as we saw above, the simple experience of the suffering of the Other in itself is only the occasion for the determination of *Mitmensch.* Only through the ideal production of the relationship of compassion can one proceed from the simple experience of suffering to the religious-moral relationship of love of one's fellowman and then to the concept of man as *Mitmensch*. However, for this to happen, man's suffering must be methodically restricted in its meaning to the suffering of the poor man and considered only in this sense. Something analogous happens with sin. The human experience of sin is not sufficient in itself to found the concept of man as an individual. Only methodical determination of its meaning and use of it as a "transitional concept" (*RV* 216; Eng. trans. 185) allows the concept of man as an individual 'I' to be reached through other concepts.

It is again appropriate to highlight the "specific delimitation" (*BR* 56) within which Cohen accepts Herrmann's requirements. Certainly, religion demonstrates, with particular emphasis, its peculiarity in respect of ethics, in the capacity to understand man as an individual *starting from* experience of sin, and, in this, religion completes ethics. However, Cohen refuses to found either the meaning of religion on the individual experience of sin or the meaning of the individual on the religious experience of sin. Religion, in Cohen's view, is an activity of reason, like philosophy, from which it distinguishes itself with the abandonment of the scientific method in favor of the method of correlation, but not with that of idealism in favor of an empiricist—existential approach. One could say, schematically, that, while for Herrmann, and the phenomenology of religion in general, the individual, sin, and religion are complementary aspects of a single immediate, relative experience, for Cohen sin is certainly a given of experience, which, however, must be rationally worked through by religion, so as to lead from the discovery of the contingent, empirical individual to the determination of the ideal concept of the individual I. Only the determination of this concept legitimizes religion as a rational discipline within ethics, though having its own peculiarity. As we have seen, religion has the task of filling the space left by ethics in its jump from the individual to humanity. This transition can only come about among ideas (cf. *BR* 57). How then can human experience of sin be a fruitful means for the discovery of the individual as I, that is, not only as an empirical individual, but as "the true individual" (*RV* 210; Eng. trans. 180)?

The sin of others must be eliminated, since it not only does not open me up to the understanding of the Other as an individual, but also prevents me from considering him and loving him as a man: "the possibility of love, as pity, arose out of the refusal to ask any question about the guilt of man, out of the refusal to be at all interested in this question. In metaphysics, also, guilt appeared as a residue of myth. In any case, the question of human guilt had to be recognized as an obstacle to the vivification of social love" (*RV* 193; Eng. trans. 166).

Thus sin, for my experience and reflection, can be only my sin: "Now I shall not fall again into the unhappy thought that the Thou suffers for his sins; a thought by which my compassion would be rendered incurably insensitive; now I am penetrated by the thought that I do not know the badness of any man so profoundly and clearly as my own" (*RV* 25f.; Eng. trans. 22).

However, it is possible also to consider my sin only as social sin, and in this sense it cannot lead me to the discovery of my individuality. Referring to Jewish sources, Cohen considers this point a distinguishing feature between social prophetism and Ezekiel.[13] The prophets had fought against the mythological conception of evil as a hereditary destiny of man and had contrasted it with the conception of evil as social injustice and, as a consequence, human and social responsibility for evil with the ideal of justice. This prophetical attitude has its most radical expression in the fight against sacrifices (cf. *RV* 198ff.; Eng. trans. 170ff.) and in the preaching of justice: "And the holy God is sanctified through justice" (Is. 5, 16b). However, this conception of the social prophets does not take up the problem of sin in its most radical aspect, or in the sense of man in his individuality:

> And yet the question of the guilt of man is not settled when one attains the insight that man is not merely the grandchild of his ancestors. What is he positively, as a creature in his own right? And how can he sin out of, and by, himself? Nor can this question be resolved by recognizing sin as a product of social plurality. For the latter, as already mentioned, remains an abstraction for sin, as well as for positive morality, if the individual does not elevate himself to the moral model and incorporate the abstract plurality into himself, and give it soul and spirit. (*RV* 211; Eng. trans. 181)

The problem of the individual and that of sin are closely linked and cannot be resolved separately. The social prophets did not reach this solution, because they reduced religion to social morality. Ezekiel opened up the possibility of a twofold solution, going further into the peculiar meaning of religion beyond morality; not against it, but as its ground: "Ezekiel is distinguished from the social prophets in that he establishes sin as the sin of the individual and in that he discovers in sin the individual. This distinction has as a further consequence that he does not consider sin merely as a social sin, therefore as mainly committed between man and man, but, more than his predecessors, attributes to sin the meaning of a sin against *God*" (*RV* 214; Eng. trans. 183).[14]

Consideration of social sin, then, does not take into sufficient account the individual responsibility for sin. It cannot reply to the question: "How can man sin by himself spontaneously?" (*RV* 211; Eng. trans.

181). Recognition of social sin definitively refutes the superficially optimistic conception of man's innocence (cf. *RV* 213; Eng. trans. 182), but
precisely for this reason makes the question on the origin of sin unavoidable: "Where does sin come from?" (*RV* 215; Eng. trans. 184).

Cohen rejects any conception of sin as radical corruption of human
nature, including the interpretation of the biblical narration of Adam's
first fall as original sin, transmitted hereditarily to every man. He remembers having rejected this interpretation of "radical evil" in Kant (*BR*
59).[15] Referring to Kant's theory of radical evil, Cohen considered man's
sinfulness (*Sündhaftigkeit*) not as a bad instinct but rather as a weakness
(*Schwäche*) in all men (but not for this an essential part of his nature),
because of which he occasionally strays from the realization of his moral
task, as an inclination of the human heart to perversion of principles. In
Der Begriff der Religion im System der Philosophie (cf. *BR* 54), Cohen contrasts
Genesis 8, 21b: "The imagination of man's heart is evil from his youth"
with *Genesis* 4, 7, according to which sin lies at man's door, not in his
home. In *Religion der Vernunft* (cf. *RV* 212; Eng. trans. 181f.), Cohen, with
a new interpretation of Genesis 8, 21b, explains that the Hebrew word
yetzer does not mean "instinct" of the heart (which would be a
pleonasm), but "operation" (*Gebild*) of the heart. In Cohen's view, then,
a mistaken interpretation of the word *yetzer*, in *Genesis* 8, 21, gave rise to
the teaching of original sin (*Erbsünde*, literally: "hereditary sin").

The fundamental meaning of the God-man correlation, the holy
spirit, does not allow man to be considered radically bad: "Rather good is
radical in man, though it is contorted into what is bad" (*BR* 59). The
guarantee of radical good in man, founded on correlation with God,
allows the establishment of a triple presupposition for the consideration
of sin:

1. Man has a natural disposition to good not evil:

   > This idea, which would solve our question by attributing the origin of evil
   > to the predisposition to evil of the human heart, of the human will, cannot
   > be supported by the passages in Genesis. Rather, man has the holy spirit in
   > his heart. To it is issued the call, that is, the calling to holiness. The natural
   > predisposition to evil would be in contradiction to the fundamental com-
   > mandment of holiness. More fundamentally, it would be a contradiction
   > to God's holiness. "God, the holy One, is sanctified through righteous-
   > ness" [Isa. 5:16]. The holy God could not have put evil into the human
   > heart. (*RV* 213, Eng. trans. 182)

2. Sin, which must be taken into serious consideration in its reality,
   cannot suffocate man's fundamental disposition for good: "The

holy spirit is fully as much the spirit of man as the spirit of God. The holy spirit of man is the bulwark against the predominance of sin, it is the protection against the illusion that sin could efface the concept of man. The concept of man consists in his spirit, and this spirit is holy. Therefore sin cannot destroy the spirit of man, the concept of man" (RV119; Eng. trans. 102f.).

3. The consciousness that man has of his own sinfulness is not evidence of his radical evil, but, on the contrary, of his fundamental goodness: "Thus consciousness of man's sinfulness does not have the same meaning as the wickedness of his being. Consciousness of sin is rather a witness against his wickedness and in favor of the watchfulness of good" (BR59).

We must now ask ourselves further questions on man's consciousness of sin, so as to resolve the twofold problem of sin and the individual. The question on the origin of sin, if it is understood in the sense of the search for a cause, is a theoretical problem, and its answer remains in the area of myth. Religion, which operates in the area of practical reason, can only ask that question in the sense of the individual's explanation of the consciousness of the purpose of his sin and can supply a satisfactory reply precisely because it overcomes the conception of sin as a solipsistic experience of the individual within his own consciousness (*Gewissen*) and arrives at consideration of "sin before God":

> We have recognized the question of the origin of evil as one that has its own origin in myth. Alleged metaphysics also maintains its interest in it. Ethics, on the contrary, teaches us that the ground of freedom, consequently the ground of the good and that of evil, must be inscrutable. The kind of ground that myth seeks is always only causality. The latter, however, rules only over the realm of knowledge of nature. The realm of freedom, however, is the realm of ethical knowledge, and it is governed by the principle of purpose instead of causality.
>
> Consequently, if the question about the wherefrom of sin cannot refer to the ground and origin of sin, then its connection with God cannot mean that the ground can be imputed to God, for we have disposed of the problem of ground as cause. What meaning, then, does this question still have? The answer to this question should be mediated by another question: what meaning has sin against God as opposed to sin against man? And how can the former be protected against the suspicion of being merely an illusion or a superfluous fiction? (RV 215; Eng. trans. 184)

The limit of pure ethics in the face of man as an individual is revealed in the need to consider the possibility of guilt so as to maintain the principle of moral responsibility but abandon guilty man to the unsurmountable isolation of his own consciousness, in the face of which ethical understanding must come to a halt, as though facing a closed door. If the judge, as the representative of the law, must pass judgment on the transgressor who is guilty (cf. *ERW* 374f.), but can accuse him only of the *dolus, culpa,* accusation (*Zurechnung*) (cf. *ERW* 366f.); if the guilty man himself, from the ethical point of view, can only consider his guilt in the perspective of self-accusation (*Selbstzurechnung*), of self-responsibility; if for ethics "*the question of guilt is excluded and drastically rejected in every sense*" (*ERW* 366), then the guilty individual, removed from men's courts of justice, seems to be irreparably left alone before the court of justice of his or her own consciousness. However, the court of consciousness has nothing to say to the guilty individual, except for repeating his or her sin, lonliness in sin and the impossibility of redemption. In sin, man "loses . . . his human dignity" (*BR* 54–5). Before the court of justice of his own consciousness, therefore, the individual sinner finds himself permanently and irreparably facing himself not as a man, but as a sinner. Religion alone allows the individual sinner to examine his or her own guilt in the face of another requirement, which is not consciousness, but God, God's court of justice.

The meaning of the phrase *sin before God* lies in the possibility for man to recognize himself, in the experience of sin, as an individual (and thus not only as a member of society and humanity) though not isolated in the "labyrinth of consciousness" (*BR* 65), but in correlation with God. Sin before God thus shows its methodical productivity, since it opens up to the individual sinner the way to possible redemption and return to his human dignity. It shows him that this dignity is not lost, even in sin, since God is its origin and guarantor through revelation, through the continual renewal of man's holiness. Sin before God is thus a point of transition toward the realization of the authentic individual I, that is, of the redeemed individual:

> The I sinning before God should open the path to this new problem of the religious I. If, however, the sinful I is to be only a transitional point for the begetting of the new I, not yet begotten by ethics, then it cannot remain the sinning I. *Liberation* from sin has to become the goal, and only through the attainment of this goal will the new I be begotten. Thus the sin is brought up before God, not in order that the individual should remain in it but in order that he be liberated from it, which liberation is necessary for the transformation of the individual into the I. (RV 218; Eng. trans. 186f.)

10. PENITENCE, LIBERATION AND REDEMPTION

Knowledge of his or her own sin before God prepares the individual for reconciliation (*Versöhnung*), the way of penitence and redemption, which constitutes the most profound and fundamental, and most specifically religious, meaning of the God-man correlation, the meaning of the correlation between the unique God and unique man, between God and the absolute individual (*BR* 61f.). For his reflection on the theme of reconciliation, Cohen begins, not only with Jewish sources, but also Jewish institutions. As we have seen, he had referred to the Sabbath. Here reference is made to Yom Kippur, another of the great Jewish feasts, the Day of Atonement (or reconciliation) (*Versöhnungstag*).[16]

Knowledge of his own sin before God allows the individual to be reconciled with himself, his own consciousness, and also with God. These reconciliations are correlative; through reconciliation with God the redeemer, the individual sinner is able to overcome his or her own inner division and achieve the realization of his or her individual I. This move toward reconciliation of the individual I places the individual in full correlation with God: "The sin before God leads us to the redemption by God. The redemption by God leads us to the reconciliation of man with himself. And only the latter leads us in the last instance to the reconciliation of the I with God. It is only the reconciliation with God which brings the individual to his maturity as the I" (*RV* 221; Eng. trans. 189).

Thus it is not in knowledge of his or her own sin that the individual is realized as I, but in liberation and redemption from it. However, religion is never mere knowledge of sin, and in this it is drastically different from pessimism,[17] not contrasting it with optimistic overcoming, which removes the gravity of sin, but with critical idealism, which starts off from the recognition of sin, from the individual's sinfulness, to reveal its ideal meaning in the realization of the individual I, freed and redeemed from sin, as an infinite task:

> Thus *the new concept of man* does not arise from knowledge of *faults in themselves, inasmuch as they are connected with the concept of man*; it arises through the *continuation* of thought from fault to its overcoming, from poverty to help, from sinfulness to redemption and *reconciliation. The new concept of man*, which knowledge of moral fault and sin has provoked, *comes about in these positive moments. Thus this new concept of man arises as a homogeneous integration of the concept of man in ethics: an integration as continuation.* (*BR* 57–8)

From the religious point of view, "*guilt cannot be an offense*," it cannot be a hindrance to the liberation from sin. There is a liberation from sin"

(*RV* 226; Eng. trans. 193f.).[18] This is possible if the individual knows his or her own sin before God. Ezekiel reveals that God's behavior in the face of sin is not pleasure in condemnation, but desire for the conversion of the sinner: "God's being has also changed correspondingly. Punishment is not the infallible sign of his dominion; he is pleased with the return of the sinner from his behavior and, consequently, is not pleased with his death, but rather with his life" (*RV* 225; Eng. trans. 193).[19]

Religion then rejects the mythical correspondence between sin and conversion, both at the level of the individual and at that of *Mitmensch*, substituting it with that between sin and conversion (cf. *RV* 225; Eng. trans. 193). Not only does religion not consider man's evil from the metaphysical-practical consideration of its origin, but, consequently, in considering it from the practical-teleological point of view always and only considers it a correlate of conversion and redemption. The religion of reason reveals the way of conversion, the critical-idealist way of the transition from the individual sinner to the ididividual freed from sin:

> Thus the new man is born, in this way the individual becomes the I. Sin cannot prescribe one's way of life. A turning away from the way of sin is possible. Man can become a new man. *This possibility of self-transformation makes the individual an I.* Through his own sin, man first becomes an individual. Through the possibility of turning away from sin, however, the sinful individual becomes the free I. And only with this newborn man can the correlation between God and man become true. (RV 225; Eng. trans. 193)

The phenomenology of the various stages of conversion clearly brings out the critical-idealist character of religion. Knowledge of his sin causes repentance (*Reue*) in the individual. However, repentance is only an affect and, as such, is still not a stage in the positive process of conversion, but only a negative precondition for it (cf. *RV* 237; Eng. trans. 203). It is only in genuine abandonment of the way of sin to turn actively to the way shown by God that authentic conversion lies. This happens at the moment of repentance (*Busse*) that of confession (*Bekenntnis*) of one's own sin, of moral action (*Handlung*) or, to use another of Cohen's expressions, of moral labor (*sittliche Arbeit*), and punishment (*Strafe*).

a. Penance and Confession of Sin

Knowledge of one's own sin is not sufficient: man who knows he is the cause of evil, which is in him, must also confess his own complete responsibility:

> If the individual must have the knowledge of himself as the originator of his guilt, he also must acknowledge and confess himself to be such. In this acknowledgment and confession the I comes to light. *The confusion of sin is the penance, which the sinner must take upon himself.* This confession with all the agony and distress, with all the overwhelming remorse which borders on despair, is the beginning of the execution of the punishment the sinner must impose upon himself, if God is to liberate him. This self-punishment is the first step on the road of the return which is open to him. (*RV* 227f.; Eng. trans. 195)

As has already been noted, religion does not contradict ethics, but completes it. For this reason religious man cannot avoid the full responsibility of his will and actions. The peculiarity of man's religious attitude before God does not consist of avoiding knowledge of his complete responsibility in guilt, but of the possibility of achieving redemption from this knowledge, without letting himself be caught up in the labyrinth of consciousness. This possibility begins with the full acceptance of his responsibility, with confession of sin.

However, in order that confession of sin, and thus conversion, does not remain a mere inner act of consciousness, in order that it really take place before God, an institutional area is required. This area is the service of God, community worship. Thus the community that had been rejected by Cohen in ethics, as a naturalistic concept, in favor of society, is brought back into religion as a necessary area for the individual's ideal relationship with God.

In the historical circumstances of his time, Ezekiel abandoned the radical struggle of the social prophets against sacrifices and saw in them the area for conversion and remission of sins. But, naturally, sacrifice no longer had a pagan meaning for Ezekiel, having been denounced by the social prophets. It took on a symbolic value being the community institution, which makes possible correlation between the individual who confesses his sin and God the redeemer: "Then history unveils the great question: whether perhaps the difference between Ezekiel's and the other prophets' relation to the sacrifice has its ultimate ground in the new relation of Ezekiel to the new concept of man and consequently to the new concept of God" (*RV* 207; Eng. trans. 177).

The institution of the Day of Atonement thus became the most significant symbol of the God-individual correlation, just as the institution of the Sabbath is for the God-*Mitmensch* correlation. Referring to certain texts of the foundation of the expiatory sacrifice (Lev. 5, 18; Numbers 15, 26), in which it is made clear that expiation is only valid for unconscious sin (*shegagah*), Cohen interprets the passage in the broad sense that all the sins of man are *shegagah*: "And the fundamental condition for sacrifice, which makes it permissible, is this basic ethical idea: the sin of man, that is to say, the sin in which man is and remains man, is *shegagah*. This is the condition under which he is not considered an animal or a monster, for which latter possibilities pathological explanations have to be consulted" (*RV* 233f.; Eng. trans. 200).

By confessing his sin before God in the community, the individual receives the revelation that his sin is not considered deliberate by God, and for this reason can be redeemed. How can God's goodness forgive sins without contradicting his justice? Only because he considers each of man's sins as *shegagah*. This is the limit of man's sin, and it is only revealed through confession of sin before God:

> To err, to go astray is man's lot, but therefore *shegagah* is the limit of man's fault. Whenever this limit is overstepped, only God knows what happens to man. Human wisdom is at a loss in the presence of the possibility of *evil* in man. The Day of Atonement maintains the fiction of the unshakable moral preservation of everything human: all man's sin is *shegagah*. Therefore, God can forgive without relinquishing his justice. Therefore he can make man innocent. Guilt should not be a "stumbling block." Guilt can in no way establish the evil character of man. Rather it is the gateway to his perfection, to that higher elevation where his innocence can be recovered. Such a point of view is found in the Talmud (Menahoth 48a). (*RV* 260; Eng. trans. 223)

Being unaware of sin before God seems to contradict taking on full responsibility for it in confession. But it is not a contradiction, rather the dialectic of correlation, as long as it is correctly situated *between* the individual and God, and not in the individual's consciousness. Man cannot consider his sin as unconscious. He must confess his responsibility. It is God who responds to this confession with the liberating revelation of the unawareness of sin, and so redeems it. This is why the community is necessary, as an area in which the individual's confession and God's redemption enter into correlation: "The not knowing explains the erring. But man is not permitted to give himself this explanation, this security of man against his own mistake, for then he would impair his self-knowledge. This justification can be granted to him by a public institution only. The mediation for this purpose is taken over by the sacrifice" (*RV* 234; Eng. trans. 200).

The community and expiatory sacrifice are, however, only a symbolic mediation, which does not corrode the immediate nature of the God-individual correlation. God alone is the redeemer. The priest does not have the power to redeem sins, neither is he a mediator of divine redemption. His expiation is only a symbol (cf. *RV* 234f.; Eng. trans.

201). So the expiatory victim is also a symbol that does not substitute man's necessary penitence (cf. *RV* 236; Eng. trans. 202). Confession of sin before God in the community does not eliminate the need for man's moral labor, as the essential moment of repentance, but makes it possible and requires it, since, only in correlation with redemption does repentance have any sense, only the certainty of redemption excludes the uselessness of repentance: *"Without pardon penitence would have no sense, and without penitence God could not become the God of the individual"* (*BR* 65).

b. Penitence and Moral Action

Liberation from sin is a task belonging entirely to man. It is an essential moment in his penitence and conversion. The autonomy of moral action, the fundamental principle of ethics, is not denied, but is confirmed in religion. God does not intervene in the human action of self-sanctification; he is solely the goal of man's infinite task, and, as such, is the redeemer. Redemption is not within man's capabilities, just as the work of liberation is not one of God's tasks. They are two correlative terms. God guarantees the success of redemption, whose realization is entirely entrusted to man's moral action (cf. *BR* 63).

The meaning of concrete man emerges, then, in individuality, beyond universality and plurality, but it is not for this reason that man as an individual represents the rejection of his ideal meaning. It is the infinite task of self-sanctification that preserves the ideal, critical meaning of the individual from abstraction, but also from empiricism: the term *absolute individual* certainly refers to the individual who is not resolved in the abstract universality of humanity, but also the individual who is not reduced to contingent empiricism:

> The new heart and the new spirit are and remain *tasks*. The I, too, can be considered as nothing other than a task. . . . The I, therefore, can mean nothing higher and certainly nothing other than one step, a *step* in the ascent to the goal, which is infinite. Does the I thereby perhaps become a mere abstraction? On the contrary, it thereby first becomes a true reality. It remains an abstraction, on the contrary, both within the social plurality and as an isolated subject. If, however, it is lifted up in the moment of its ascent, it achieves true moral life. Repentance provides man with this new life, which, to be sure, can last only in the bliss of a moment. But this moment can and should repeat itself unceasingly: It should never grow old, and it must and can constantly rejuvenate and renew itself. This constancy, which is demanded by the task of this ascent, liberates the I from the suspicion of being a mere abstraction, and it is only from the continuity of these moments of ascent that the I acquires the capacity to subsist

and endure. All other alleged phenomena of subjectivity are nothing but the ghosts of materialization. The subject as I is determined by the moment and by the continuity of moments. (*RV* 238f.; Eng. trans. 204)

Thus the concept of 'free will,' that religion takes from the abstraction of pure ethics, for which it is solely the will of good, and transfers to the level of concrete historical morality, as ability to choose between good and evil, is not reduced to the indifferent, empirical factuality of free judgment. For religion, the individual's freedom to choose between good and evil only takes on meaning in the light of the choice of good. The reality of sin only has religious sense as a transitional stage toward conversion and redemption. Only the redeemed individual fully realizes the meaning of the individual I. The individual sinner is a transitional stage toward the redeemed individual: "*Sin is a ferment of morality* and the *stage* of the individual's sin is thus a permanent part of the conceptual chain of moral man" (*BR* 65).

From the phenomenological viewpoint, man the sinner, man who is conscious of his sin, and man who is converted and obtains redemption are three separate stages in religious experience. From Cohen's critical point of view, however, they are inextricably linked. Man's sin is always considered from the standpoint of awareness of one's own sin, and this is a critical stage "checking" the infinite task character of morality (cf. *BR* 59f.). The individual's stage of critical self-consciousness, of knowledge of his own sin, is thus already a stage of conversion and redemption. However, consciousness of one's own sin is not abstract theoretical learning, but practical knowledge. Thus it is resolved in moral action, in the moral labor of conversion and self-sanctification, which is rewarded and guaranteed in its result by the redeeming grace of God. In this way, as confirmation of the connection between religion and ethics, the individual is not defined in contrast with the universality of humanity, since, inasmuch as he recognizes himself as a sinner, he faces the task of moral action, and works to overcome his sin, that is, to realize humanity in himself and others;

Thus the sinner-redemption relationship, which defines the individual, actually constitutes the concrete condition of morality and history in their mutual relationship. However, to face the theme of history it is still necessary to shed light on another point, which I have left waiting up to now: suffering and its meaning for the individual.

c. Penance and Suffering

The individual is redeemed before God, but is guilty before himself. As we have seen, the consciousness of redemption does not eliminate that of responsibility for sin. Religion does not contradict or in any way restrict the fundamental ethical principle of moral autonomy. It is man's moral autonomy, as can be seen in *Ethik des reinen Willens* (cf. *ERW* 375ff.) that demands guilt be punished. It is not through God's needs, then, that penitence must include the punishment stage. God, in the mystery of his goodness, could even not demand punishment.

Suffering is man's punishment. Life itself as suffering is the punishment for sin, fulfillment of penitence, and self-sanctification. Suffering, as we have seen, cannot be linked to sin in judgment on the other man. It must be freely desired by the individual for himself, as a stage of self-sanctification (cf. *RV* 264; Eng. trans. 226). The empirical fact of suffering is thus also endowed with an ideal meaning in "readiness (*Bereitwilligkeit*) to accept suffering" (*RV* 264; Eng. trans. 226), that is, in "acknowledgment of suffering as the just punishment" (*RV* 265; Eng. trans. 227).

Cohen does not intend, here, to re-establish the causal sin-suffering relationship, which he had denied for *Mitmensch*. Since suffering, like punishment, takes on sense in the individual's autonomous acceptance, confessing his sin, it should not be thought of in relation to sin, but penitence and conversion. Suffering is a moment of self-sanctification:

> The confession of sin, despite it all, would be merely a formality if the declaration of my willingness to suffer did not confirm it. *Suffering is related not so much to sin as to its forgiveness*, and its redemption, insofar as the latter is dependent on self-sanctification. Self-sanctification culminates in the insight into the necessity of suffering and in the voluntary self-sacrifice of submission to the suffering of punishment. (*RV* 265; Eng. trans. 227)

Besides, suffering is never an end, but only a means. There is no mysticism of pain. Man suffers for his own redemption, but the latter does not reside in suffering itself; rather, redemption is the final result in which the individual is freed from sin and suffering: "Suffering is the precondition for redemption. The latter, however, is the liberation from all the dross of empirical humanity and the ascent to the ideal moment in which man becomes a self . . . suffering is only a prelude, even if it lasts thousands of years" (*RV* 274; Eng. trans. 235; cf. *RV* 268f.; Eng. trans. 230).

Though being a means rather than an end, however, suffering has eminent meaning in Cohen's critical-idealist conception, since the value of suffering represents critical opposition to eudemonism: "For 'man doth not live by bread only' (Deut. 8:3). Bread stands here for earthly happiness in general. This saying wards off the idea of eudemonism. The value of human life lies not in happiness but rather in suffering" (*RV* 307; Eng. trans. 263).

During penitence and self-sanctification, the stage of readiness to accept suffering is the moment of the critical conception of morality as an infinite process of approaching holiness, not happiness.[20] For this reason, penitence and conversion, without, this readiness, would be incomplete and ambiguous.

Last, in Cohen's view, the suffering accepted by man as a punishment is not only his suffering as an individual, but, above all, suffering for man, for his own human condition and for that of other men (cf. *RV* 263; Eng. trans. 225). This is how Cohen begins his formulation of the basic traits of "absolute theodicy of suffering (*BR* 132), which will be further developed in the analysis of messianism as a profound sense of history. The meaning of suffering as punishment, which is not eliminated in the individual's consciousness, is overshadowed by the clear delineation of the relationship between suffering and redemption:

> Thus the *correlation between man and God as theodicy* is also clarified. Suffering is not the cause of *pessimism*. It does not contradict God who grants grace, whose operations it *prepares*, without being the determining cause. Man takes upon himself suffering as punishment. This is how punishment fades. *As suffering it transfigures both God and man.* Man suffers punishment for his guilt inasmuch as his suffering represents the *preliminary stage of his redemption. Suffering belongs to the preparatory study for the labor of penitence,* but already touches the *limit,* which the idea of man constitutes under divine glory. Thus man and God are linked in this *correlation,* which shows itself as *theodicy* at the same time. Suffering is no longer a question mark against God's being, and not even against that of man. Neither is it only a pedagogical means, because trees do not grow in the heavens; to deny the opinion that the sweetness of joy can be better tasted in contrast with suffering. Suffering as punishment belongs to the ethical concept of man and, on this ethical ground, the palm of redemption rises up, for the *peculiarity of religion.* (*BR* 69–70)

Suffering is not only suffering *of* but also *for* man, in the individual's consciousness. As soon as it leaves the individual's limited circle, as we have seen, it takes on the meaning of compassion for the other and, in the perspective of universal history, the meaning of vicarious suffering for humanity. But these more extended, profound meanings are grounded in the suffering of the individual for his own redemption. The individual who Cohen identified as the protagonist of history, is not only the man of moral action, but also the one of suffering. Man's active, autonomous presence in history is not only realized through action, but also through suffering. The latter makes just as significant a contribution as the former to the messianic task of realization of the kingdom of God: "the suffering Christ" and "Faust at work" are man's two complementary aspects in history (cf. *BR* 132f.).

According to Cohen, all these aspects of the meaning of suffering are collected together in the Book of Job: Job's friends mistake in wanting to posit a causal relationship between sin and suffering, the meaning of Job's suffering for others; the relationship between Job's suffering and its justification; and the antieudemonist meaning of Job's suffering (cf. *RV* 265f.; Eng. trans. 227f.). Thus Job, is a man who suffers though innocent: "Job, the hero of suffering, represents *man's ideal*" (*BR* 126) and is a prelude to the messianic figure of the servant of YHWH.

11. The God-Individual Correlation and Reflections on the Limit

The concept of 'sin before God,' then, as we have seen, is the crucial point of transition for the establishment of man as an individual. Only in correlation with God can the individual be reconciled with himself, just as, only in correlation with God, can man authentically realize the relationship of love with his fellowman in compassion. On the level of individuality, as on that of plurality, man's correlation with man (with the other man or with himself) is only possible as an inner stage in man's correlation with God. But if correlation with God establishes the meaning of man, the concept of God also acquires additional meaning and becomes more profound for the purpose of correlation with man. The discovery and identification of man as an individual implies a new concept of God and correlation: "This is the most important content of the correlation of God and man" (*RV* 249; Eng. trans. 213). As we shall see better further on, God's goodness, the attribute of God, which is revealed in the forgiveness of sins, "as the fundamental concept of the moral world, reaches beyond the individual and beyond the forgiveness of sin and becomes the precondition for the further development of the Kingdom of God" (*RV* 251; Eng. trans 215).

Returning to Ezekiel's terms, Cohen defines the individual, in correlation with God as "the son of man" (*ben 'Adam*) (cf. *RV* 246; Eng. trans. 211). As the son of man, the individual acknowledges, despite the efficient operation of self-sanctification, his own condition as a sinner and his own unsurmountable inadequacy: "Everything which belongs to man, both outside of himself and within, cannot give him the certainty that the preparations for his rebirth, which are his own, will be successful. Therefore only God can help him. God's goodness is his only refuge.

Therefore he puts his confidence in it. Thus arises *trust* in God" (*RV*247; Eng. trans. 211).

The conception of the individual as the son of man is essential for a critical knowledge of morality, which, though fully acknowledging the autonomy and effectiveness of man's moral action, still must also recognize its inadequacy in the face of the infinite task. This critical attitude shows itself, on the one hand, in humility, that is, the awareness of "dissatisfaction with oneself," and thus in "striving beyond oneself" (*RV*249; Eng. trans. 213), and, on the other, in desire for the nearness to God, that is, in "the desire for nothing else but God. For nothing else concerns the soul more than God's forgiveness of its sin" (*RV* 247; Eng. trans. 212). However, desire for God would not have adequate justification, if it could not be grounded in faith; that is, in the sure conviction (in accordance with the authentic sense of the Hebrew term (*'emunah*) for God's forgiveness of sins: "Biblical faith allows no tinge of doubt to arise. The faith is fundamentally rooted in the firm trust in God as the Good One: who, beyond doubt, in his goodness, forgives the sins of man" (*RV*247; Eng. trans. 211).

Forgiveness of sins, the guarantee of God's redemption, is thus an essential stage in correlation, though entirely conserving man's autonomy in the work of conversion: "The solution is infinite, for it is only a moment in the infinite task; but the solution as this moment signifies infinite success, the infinite result. God can assign no task that would be a labor of Sisyphus. Self-sanctification must arrive at its infinite conclusion in the *forgiveness* of sin by God" (*RV*241f.; Eng. trans. 207).

Thus redemption must not be thought as an eschatological event, just as creation and revelation must not be conceived as protological ones. It is more a question of a continuous process, of an open sin-redemption, or rather self-sanctification-redemption dialectic, of the "unity of the infinite task with the infinite solution" (*RV*241; Eng. trans. 206): "Redemption is to be thought of only for one moment's duration. Only for one moment, which may be followed by moments of sin. No matter! They also will again be relieved by the moment of redemption" (*RV*269; Eng. trans. 230f.).

The divine attribute in which God's redeeming power is made manifest is 'God's goodness.' Careful attention should be paid to this concept, since it is not only in the relationship between God the Good and the son of man that the God-man correlation reaches its most important content, but man's critical thought pushes reason beyond its limits.

The God-individual correlation occurs in the context of the general meaning of correlation: holiness. As we have seen, penitence, man's process of conversion, is none other than the process of self-sanctification activated by the individual. Thus God as the origin and goal of the individual's self-sanctification is the holy God. God's holiness is the ground and end of self-sanctification: God's holiness is the origin of the individual's self-sanctification, inasmuch as God "giving the command-ment" (*RV* 240; Eng. trans. 205) is its end, inasmuch as God's holiness is the "archetype" (*RV* 251; Eng. trans. 215) for the individual's moral action.

The novelty of the formulation of the religion of reason, in respect of the ethics of pure will, is already evident in these elements: man's humanity as the ideal of will and moral action is no longer the ultimate ground, but itself is grounded in holiness, that is, in correlation with God. Nevertheless, up to this point the God-individual correlation only confirms the meaning of the God-man correlation in general. However, in the emergence of God's goodness, correlation acquires additional meaning, which does not contradict that of holiness, but certainly goes well beyond it, in the profundity of the sense of God's relationship with man.

As we have seen, a possible objection—that correlation with God's holiness might limit man's autonomy in the process of self-liberation from sin—is overcome by Cohen with a simple explanation. On the one hand, the ground of human action in divine law should not be under-stood as heteronomy, since: "This command of God is in the heart of man and has been elucidated in the spirit of man's holiness" (*RV* 236; Eng. trans. 202). On the other hand, God is only the guarantor of redemption, of man the sinner's purpose, regarding its result, and this does not imply at all the intervention and collaboration of divine grace in the human effort toward self-sanctification: "In no way can God help in this human labor. How could God form a *community* with man? Just as redemption cannot be God's *gracious gift*, so it cannot be the product of his *cooperation* in moral labor, since God's being resides above it. No *pan-theism* and no lowering of the contrast between God and man can be attempted here" (*BR* 63).

Nevertheless, another objection, in contrast with the first, can be raised against correlation: man's penitence–God's forgiveness:

> Is not the entire element of forgiveness through God external to the idea of self-sanctification? And should not forgiveness be replaced by self-sanc-tification insofar as the latter contains in itself the infinite solution, even though it ever remains an infinite task, so that self-sanctification would be identical to forgiveness? Ezekiel says "yes": "Cast away from you all your transgression . . . and make you a new heart and a new spirit" [Ezek. 18:31]. Does he not thereby identify the task with forgiveness and does he

not thereby eliminate redemption through God? (*RV* 242; Eng. trans. 207).

Do not rejection of a still eudemonist conception of God's forgiveness as a reward[21] and the autonomy of moral action imply total immanence of the forgiveness of sins in respect of penitence, thus making the idea of God the redeemer superfluous? Cohen's answer is unusual and, at first sight, surprising: acknowledgment of redemption as the work of God is necessary, not so much to found man's moral labor, but especially to protect the concept of God:

> Regardless of whether we would be able to achieve the solution of the task by our own independent work, and to succeed in liberating ourselves from sin, it is necessary for the notion of the correlation with God, for the concept of God himself, that he and only he be the redeemer; it is necessary that he only accomplish this redemption by pardoning, by forgiving the sin. In the spirit of the theodicy one could say: sin is explainable through God's forgiveness of it. God's being could not be conceived as understandable in his perfection, if the forgiveness of sin were not his proper achievement. (*RV* 242f.; Eng. trans. 207f.)

At first sight, this answer may seem very weak, if not useless. If acknowledgment of God's redemption exists only to maintain sense for the concept of God, is not the objection, for which it would be simpler, more rational and coherent to abolish the hypothesis of God and reduce man's redemption to a process of self-redemption, confirmed? Actually Cohen's answer goes deeper. As we have seen, the idea of God is necessary, as origin and end, to found the process of man's self-realization, which occurs through the stages of confession of sin before God, and in penitence: man's sin and self-sanctification have no sense before the idea of God. God is the sense, the holiness, without which sin—abandonment of holiness, penitence, that is, return to holiness—would have no meaning, and actually would not even exist. Nevertheless, and the novelty lies here, *in the case of God, of the supreme idea, the two fundamental meanings of idea, as origin and end, are insufficient to manifest its sense: the fulfillment of the idea of God lies in attribution to it of active meaning in correlation with man, and this is the content of the divine attribute of "goodness."*
Up to this point, Cohen's idealism moves forward to the limits of the mystery of God in history! It is not a question of abandoning idealism, nor of giving up reason, but rather of an extreme, but coherent, development of the critical requirement to stimulate reason to think the limit. Not only is idea limit, but there is also a limit of idea. This consists of its being more than the origin, and more than the end of the infinite

process of improvement of reality, in its also being the principle responsible for success, of fulfillment of this process. Redemption is that "more" (*RV* 240; Eng. trans. 205) that the idea of God produces in respect of the normal meaning of ground and end, for the human task of self-sanctification. The emergence of the divine attribute of goodness does not only represent a deeper meaning of God-man correlation, but also progress in rational, critical idealism up to its limit, where critical reason must recognize not only a normative principle, but also an active principle in history.

It is also possible to have a correct, balanced view of God's personality in this perspective. As is well known, many criticisms have been made of Cohen's conception of God as idea and not as a person. Martin Buber, among others, can act as a kind of spokesman for Cohen's critics. Cohen rejected the objection that God cannot be the object of love as idea, but only as a person: "*How is it possible to love an idea?* To which one should retort: how is it possible to love anything but an idea? Does one not love, even in the case of sensual love, only the idealized person, only the idea of the person?" (*RV*185; Eng. trans. 160). Buber replied that idealization of a loved person always presupposes a relationship of experience with the real person,[22] adding: "Let us suppose that ideas be loved: but only people love."[23] This argument of Buber seems decisive, and actually is, if the idea of God criticized here only has the meaning of a philosophical hypothesis: the "God of philosophers and the wise," whom Pascal had already contrasted with the "God of Abraham, Isaac and Jacob." Buber is wrong on this point. Cohen's God, in his late works on the philosophy of religion, is the God of faith, the God of Judaism, not merely a necessary hypothesis for a philosophical system. The very reflection on the attribute of God's goodness has shown us how the idea of God is understood here as being beyond the meaning of hypothesis and end, in a sense in which critical idealism is certainly taken to its extreme limit, since it finds itself reflecting on the limit but is not abandoned for this, nor shows itself to be impotent. The inadequacy of the critical-idealist view of God as idea, though being evident in the very fact of having to strain the general meaning of idea, is not, however, a total failure. Even in his inadequacy, Cohen has something important to say about God.

Even Buber's personalist-existential alternative view of God as a person does not escape inadequacy. Buber, also, in order to speak of God, must strain his concepts and reach the limit of his arguments, by formulating the concept of 'absolute person,'[24] which he himself acknowledges to be a paradoxical expression, used for overcoming the inadequacy of the concept of 'person' with reference to God.[25]

From this brief analysis certain interesting conclusions can be drawn:

1. Cohen's critical-idealist philosophy proves inadequate to understand God through the concept of 'idea,' but this inadequacy is common to *any* human reflection on God, including Buber's personalist-existential one, and his concept of person. The reason for this inadequacy does not lie in the concepts used, either that of idea or that of person, but in the object itself. God whom no concept can understand and whom philosophy, especially critical philosophy, inasmuch as it is critical, cannot even attempt to approach, in its ultimate need to be thought of the limit, and not only thought inside the limit.

2. The drastic difference between Buber and Cohen does not lie in the conception of God as idea or person: the latter is only the consequence of the choice of conceptual instruments and a different method for practicing philosophy, in the choice between critical idealism and existential personalism. Both routes experience the inadequacy of their concepts concerning the limit problem of philosophy and human thought in general: the problem of God and that of evil, which is in correlation with that of God.

3. Cohen's idea of God, even in its above-mentioned inadequacy, actually manages to express some important contents of authentic religious faith, concerning God, and especially man, and, as we shall see, history. The critical idealist viewpoint thus shows its inadequacy, but not impotency, and is no more inadequate than others in repect of the contents of faith. Actually, though trying a hurried evaluation of the positive and negative aspects of the approach to faith through critical reason, one should note that at least Cohen's reflections on God, more than those of others, for example, more than Buber's, stays far away from any kind of anthropomorphism, being rigorously faithful to the biblical commandment forbidding images, and the theological tradition of God's attributes. Besides, inasmuch as it never abandons the discipline of reason, it always proceeds by means of clear, determined concepts, never by means of vague analogies and poetical metaphors, and, in is in continuity with other areas of philosophical discourse, without claims to drastic differentiation or lunges into ineffable mystery.

11

Messianism and History

1. MESSIANISM AND UNIVERSAL HISTORY

Cohen saw Jewish messianism as the source of inspiration of the idea of universal history: "Messianism must be considered as a creation of ideas brought about by the prophetic concept of history. *The concept of history is a creation of the prophetic idea.* If one bears this in mind, then the religious one-sidedness of monotheism grows wider and turns into its opposite" (*RV* 305; Eng. trans. 261).

The prophets of Israel, in their messianic announcement, went beyond the narrow limits of present reality and the borders of the national political physiognomy of their people had began the idealist perspective of history as "the future of mankind under the guidance of God" (*RV* 292; Eng. trans. 250). The idea of mankind and the future dimension are among the essential contents of the messianic conception of history, and this deserves brief treatment here.

a. The History of Mankind

History, understood in its ideal meaning, is universal, that is, the history of mankind and not of individuals (single persons or peoples). The idea of mankind is a result of religious thought: "It is indeed the highest triumph of religion that only it has produced the idea of mankind" (*RV* 278; Eng. trans. 238).

Greek philosophy, of which Plato, in Cohen's view, was the climax and the mirror, did not and could not produce the idea of mankind. It was produced by the religious elaboration of the idea of good, which is brought from transcendence, where it had been confined by Plato, as we have seen, into history, becoming its ultimate purpose (cf. *BR* 32f.). This idea passed from Jewish monotheism to philosophical thought and exercised powerful influence on it. In Kant the two fundamental meanings contained in this idea (i.e., mankind as a synonym of the rationality constituting every man and cosmopolitic universalism as the ideal of the unity of all men—cf. *RV* 281f.; Eng. trans. 241) clearly emerge. Both meanings of the idea of mankind, in Cohen's view, originate in and bear permanent witness to the Jewish religious tradition and reach fulfillment and unitary realization in messianism, as the historical final stage of man in correlation with the God of monotheism. Man as a being of reason, as we have seen, is a moral man, as he is formed in correlation with God in the spirit of holiness. The fight of the prophets against the priests of Israel reiterates this fundamental principle of universalism: the holy spirit is the spirit of every man, for his correlation with God and cannot be reduced to the exclusive charisma of a single individual (cf. *RV* 300; Eng. trans. 257).

The cosmopolitic meaning of the idea of mankind has Israel as its living symbol, a people without a state: "This explains the duality of Israel's political fate. That the state declined, while the people were preserved, is a providential symbol of Messianism; it is the sign of the truth of monotheism. No state, but yet a people. But this people is less for the sake of its own nation than as a symbol of mankind. A unique symbol for the unique idea, the individual peoples have to strive to the unique unity of mankind" (*RV* 295; Eng. trans. 253).

For this meaning too of the idea of mankind, the ground is in monotheism, in the correlation of mankind, unified with God, "Lord of the whole earth" (cf. *RV* 284; Eng. trans. 243).[1] The Messiah, interpreted as a universal, not an individual, human, not a divine figure, unifies in himself the two fundamental meanings of the idea of mankind and thus constitutes the idea that is the inspiration of universal history (cf. *RV* 297f.; Eng. trans. 255). Monotheism, from which messianism is inseparable, of which it is the "straightforward consequence" (*RV* 297; Eng. trans. 255), the "apex" (*RV* 24; Eng. trans. 21), the "purest fruit" (*RV* 341; Eng. trans. 293), is the origin and ground of universal history, because only in messianism does mankind appear as the result of the correlation of human morality with divine holiness:

> Thus monotheism is the immediate cause of Messianism as well as of the concept of *world history*, as the history of one mankind. Without the unique God, the idea of one mankind could not arise. And without the idea of mankind, history would remain a problem of knowledge of the past of

peoples, on the basis of the past of one's own people. National history, however, is in general not yet history. It cannot even be a methodological foundation, because it cannot be the point of departure for scientific orientation. Mankind must just become first the object of *human love* in order to become the point of orientation for the problem of history. (RV 306f.; Eng. trans. 262f.)

b. History and Future

"The prophets are the idealists of history. Their vision begot the concept of history, as the being of the *future*" (*RV* 305; Eng. trans. 261f.). Universal history is the history of the future, since mankind which is its object is an idea:

> The Greeks never had this thought of a history that has the future as its content. Their history is directed to their origins; it is the history that narrates the past of its nation. Other nations constitute a historical problem only for their travel descriptions. A history of mankind is, within this horizon, impossible. Mankind did not live in any past and did not become alive in the present; only the future can bring about its bright and beautiful form. This form is an idea, not a shadowy image of the beyond. (*RV* 291f.; Eng. trans. 249f.)

Any mythical attempt to think of the past, primeval time, as an ideal condition of innocence and happiness, as a myth of the Golden Age, is not in the direction of ideal universal history (cf. *RV* 290ff.; Eng. trans. 248ff.). The Scriptures, though incorporating the myth of earthly paradise in Genesis, do not leave space for the utopia of man's primeval innocence. Disobedience of divine commandments annuls this innocence from the beginning, and the first murder makes this break with utopia definite. The messianic age is thus projected forward toward the future, not backward toward the past. It is not the utopian image of man's primeval natural innocence, but the ideal term of a cultural process toward the elimination of war and the fulfillment of mankind. Like the mythical conception of the past, the eschatological conception of the future is also utopian. Cohen attributes this to Christianity (cf. *RV* 360; Eng. trans. 309f.). Here too attention is transferred from the present to a "world beyond," which in the case of eschatology, is future, but an ahistorical, transcendent future which cannot have ideal meaning for the transformation and historical-political progress of mankind (cf. *RV* 336ff.; Eng. trans. 290ff.).

Both myth and eschatology, in the apparent radical overcoming of empirical reality existing in a past or future ideal "world beyond" retain their links with the present from which they wish to escape. Their utopia simply has the form of a heightened image of present reality, not that of authentic novelty, while the messianic future is the true idea of the supersensible, that is, of novelty in respect of the real conditions of the present (cf. *RV* 291; Eng. trans. 249).

The prophetic interpretation of the people of Israel as a symbol of mankind not only must be drained of any empirical identification with the national reality of the present of biblical Israel, thus becoming the "remnant of Israel," but must be enriched by ideal meaning through projection into the future. Only thus can the people of Israel actually operate in history as the bearer of the idea of mankind: "This "remnant of Israel," however, is the Israel of the future and not the historical Israel of the past or the present. It is the ideal Israel, which indeed, as every-thing ideal in the life of men and peoples, must be deeply rooted in the actual. But these depths are from the outset of ideal significance" (*RV* 303; Eng. trans. 260).

But this idealness of the future, its radical novelty and contrast with the present, does not involve a reality defect, actually "the future becomes the actuality of history" (*RV* 294; Eng. trans. 252). The ideal-ness of the future is contrasted with the sensible reality of the present, but, for this very reason is ideal reality, true historical reality (cf. *RV* 338ff.; Eng. trans. 290ff.). Therefore, the messianic future is posited crit-ically as ideal in respect of the present historical-political situation, as "being of the future" (*RV* 291; Eng. trans. 249), truer, and thus more real, than the being of the present, since sensibility is the "instrument for knowing the actual present" (*RV* 341; Eng. trans. 292), but idea is the instrument for future reality. Universal messianic history, as we have seen, is an idealization of empirical man in the idea of mankind. Thus it is also an idealization of empirical reality in the ideal future.

2. MESSIANISM AND THE PECULIARITY OF RELIGION

The idea of mankind and dimension of the future are thus without doubt two important contents of the messianic conception of history, but they do not seem decisive features of the peculiarity of religion in respect of ethics. Cohen himself observed that ethics had been able to take over the fundamental themes of religion—monotheism and mes-sianism—and elaborate them autonomously through its scientific method (cf. *RV* 25, 277f.; Eng. trans. 21f., 237f.). Certainly, ethics found these themes in religion, in the sources of Judaism, but this would only impose recognition of the historical anteriority of religion in respect of ethics, which Cohen had never denied (cf. *ERW* 53f.), but not its pecu-liarity concerning method and results.

The peculiarity of ethics in respect of the theme of man as an individual is particularly to the fore, given the explicit inability of ethics to face this theme. Concerning mankind, the central idea of ethics, it seems that religion has "nothing to add to ethics" as Cohen states in *Religion der Vernunft*, and that it must simply be its source, its area of experience, the fact from which the former takes some of its fundamental contents, to work them through autonomously (cf. *RV* 277f.; Eng. trans. 237f.), since it cannot be denied that ethics "takes from religion the concept of mankind" (*RV* 278; Eng. trans. 238). However, if the contributions of religion were limited to this, then the "the supreme triumph of religion," the fact that "only it has produced the idea of mankind" (*RV* 278; Eng. trans. 238), would prove to be solely a case of historical primacy, with little theoretical interest. In the same part of *Religion der Vernunft* Cohen himself is puzzled:

> But the independence of ethics is ratified and maintained in the two concepts: mankind and the God of mankind.
> At this point the question arises: does perhaps religion, with the character peculiar to it, have a share in these two concepts and their correlation? If it were not so, if religion had nothing to contribute to mankind and to the God of mankind, then certainly the value of religion would be greatly diminished, and all the peculiarity which religion could show with regard to the two meanings of man, and correspondingly also of God, could not make up for the deficiency which religion would exhibit with regard to mankind and its God. (*RV* 277; Eng. trans. 237)

Cohen's question here is a stimulus to investigate further all the new implications of religion in respect of ethics, concerning the theme of mankind. The historical primacy of religion and its function as material of experience for the ethical elaboration of the idea of mankind is only the beginning, the initial result of this investigation, but not yet the essential, peculiar contribution of religion. Just restricting ourselves to Cohen's main works, it is sufficient to recall how in *Ethik des reinen Willens* the idea of mankind is explicitly taken from Jewish messianism (cf. *ERW* 214). The idea of the future is foregrounded in *Logik der reinen Erkenntnis* (cf. *LRE* 156ff.), and in *Ethik des reinen Willens* it is revived in specific reaction to its logical meaning, on the one hand (cf. *ERW* 106) and to its messianic meaning on the other (cf. *ERW* 405ff.). In general, the ethical-historical interpretation of messianism appears frequently in all of Cohen's works.[2] Thus ethics takes the monotheistic idea of God and the messianic idea of mankind from the sources of religion, but, then, works through the problem of history autonomously,[3] in the context of its scientific method, formulating it and developing it by means of certain fundamental conceptual tools: law and the state. However, in the Jewish sources, on which ethics draws, there is something more than that which is taken. There are elements peculiar to the religion of reason (cf. *RV* 25; Eng. trans. 21).

We have already seen how, for Cohen, the peculiarity of religion is linked to a methodical peculiarity of Jewish monotheism, which characterizes the thought of the prophets of Israel concerning that of the Greek philosophers. Monotheism is considered by Cohen to be an unscientific critical idealism. The lack of a scientific character in religious thought is not, however, a defect, but rather a characteristic feature, an aspect of that peculiarity of religion which places it in its essential function in respect of ethics and the system in general. This specific position of religion takes on a concrete, historical form in the "cultural peculiarity of Israel" (*RV* 298; Eng. trans. 255), in the "religious one-sidedness of monotheism" (*RV* 305; Eng. trans. 261).

As we have seen, the limit of ethics can be indicated in its inability to consider the individual, except by absorbing him in the universal meaning of mankind. The individual is only seen by ethics as a symbol of mankind, and the mediating concepts of the law of the state, which partake of the interpretation of the relationship between individual and mankind, are actually, concepts of the universal, in which the individual is absorbed and resolved (cf. *RV* 15f.; Eng. trans. 13). Full, authentic understanding of man, however, cannot be restricted to considering the ideal of the identification of the individual with mankind: it must also consider "*inclination to universality*" (*BR* 55) by man. It must take into consideration the fact that "transition to universality needs equipment" (*BR* 55). This dimension of the problem, in the face of which ethics proves inadequate, is the specific object of religion.

From another point of view, the problem left open by ethics is that of the realization of the ideal. In ethics, mankind is the synonym of autonomy of moral reason, and God is the ideal guarantor of mankind. But only in religion is the problem of the actual realization of morality considered crucial :

> It must not be a matter of indifference whether my morality and all men's morality remains dutiful striving only, sufficient in itself; rather, I have to take an interest in the question of whether the *ideal* has life and actuality. Even though this identity can only be achieved in the approximation to the ideal, the inexorable goal of the approximation is the permeation of actuality with the ideal. However, this proper goal of ethics has to recede in face of the scientific rigor of ethics, because of which it has to maintain the separation of actuality from the ideal, and generally between idea and

actuality. This rigor brings about the illusion that ethics deals only with law and rule, but never with human actuality. (*RV* 24; Eng. trans. 20f.)

As we have already seen, ethics is not uninterested in the problem of realization of the ideal: overcoming the Kantian distinction between morality and legality and the methodical use of the concepts of state and law bear witness to this central concern of ethics. It goes as far as posing the question of the relationship between the universal and the particular in the theory of the relationship between state and community, between virtues of the first and second degrees, between the affect of honor and that of love. Nevertheless, ethics remains necessarily stationary at the viewpoint of the universal and can only consider the problem of realization from there. This problem is only the object of ethics to the extent that being an infinite task for concrete existence is part of the meaning of the ideal, but not because the actual process of the existing toward the ideal is itself a problem: "The problem of God is exhausted for it in God as the guarantor of morality on earth. The shortcomings in the actualization of morals on earth do not in principle concern ethics at all, since the infinite goal provides the remedy. The question of the time of actualization concerns ethics as little as the degrees of actualization in particular periods of time or in particular representations of mankind" (*RV* 277; Eng. trans. 237).

Last the problem can be posed from a different viewpoint. Ethics has the idea of good and its reality as its central object. But the question on the realization of good cannot be faced adequately except in relation to the dynamic reality of evil. Ethics, owing to its own scientific method, is unable to consider the relationship between good and evil, except as a conceptual contrast. Only religion can face this problem in the concrete terms of a historical process; this peculiarity of religion is made manifest in messianism:

> Plato once says in passing, although in the *Theatetus*, that evil can never cease, for it has to remain in opposition to the good. This idea separates Judaism from paganism, even from the paganism in Platonism. If the prophet, in opposition to Parsiism, makes God also the creator of evil, *this evil is rather the ill*, which men usually identify with evil. The prophet, however, intends to teach that God can be the creator only of perfection, which is expressed and signified by *peace*. Hence, it is understandable that monotheism reaches its summit in Messianism. *Messianism*, however, means the dominion of the good on earth. One daily encounters the opinion that the Messiah could come only when injustice ceases. However, this is exactly the meaning of the Messiah: that injustice will cease. (*RV* 24; Eng. trans. 21)

The problem of the individual-mankind relationship, that of realization of the ideal, and that of the triumph of good over evil, are nothing but three different aspects of the single problem of history. Ethics turns out to be inadequate in the face of the problem of history. It is not that this problem is alien. Ethics is actually able to posit it in adequate, well-grounded terms. Ethics grounds the horizon and task of history in the ideal of mankind and God as the guarantor of that ideal. What it cannot interpret adequately is the concrete contribution of man as an individual and *Mitmensch* to mankind, the concrete process of realization of this ideal and the actual possibility of realizing the triumph of good over evil. The peculiarity of religion, therefore, inasmuch as it is capable of meeting these difficulties, is again revealed as an authentic novelty in respect of ethics, but at the same time, as a further contribution to demands already formulated in ethics, which had inaugurated them. With respect to the problem of history, once again, the novelty of religion is the result of its specific method of correlation. However, continuity with ethics is constituted by their common root in reason, by critical idealism.

3. MESSIANISM AND SUFFERING

The theme of suffering, as we have seen, pervades Cohen's religious anthropology. It is the dimension in which man is discovered as *Mitmensch* and causes compassion as a moral response. Compassion has its roots and ground in the suffering of the individual as an essential means of moral liberation from sin and of self-sanctification. Nevertheless, a further meaning of suffering for others emerged as an anticipation from the examination of the theme of suffering at these two levels of anthropology, that of the individual and that of *Mitmensch*, suffering for mankind as the climax of messianism. This supreme meaning is part of the messianic concept of 'vicarious suffering.' By means of this concept, man, as an individual and as plurality, is placed in relation with mankind. The ideal of mankind is concretely realized by the individual's free will toward his *Mitmensch*. History takes on the form of the triumph of good over evil owing to man's moral action.

The function of suffering is the radically new characteristic of the messianic conception of history. All other conceptions are the history of the powerful, of heroes. Even divinities intervening in history, according to the mythical conception, are powerful, the allies of victorious heroes. History concerns these alliances and their rule over peoples. This is not the case with the Scriptures. In them the powerful and conquerors are accused of their injustices; the poor and suffering are presented as models of man who pleases God, and God himself appears as the God of the suffering, the defender of the poor. The mythical idea of the end of the world and of the last judgment, in the Scriptures, become the "Day of the Lord":

> The myth celebrates power in gods as well as in heroes. Religion cannot be the worship of power. In the myth, only the heroes are "loved by God" (θεοφιλεῖς). The new concept of God, however, demands justice and love for all men. This fundamental thought changes the meaning of the *Last Judgment* into the "Day of the Lord." Woe to God's own people, its princes and mighty ones, its priests and its false prophets! Thus admonishes the prophet. Agreement, even the agreement of the nation with God, cannot be assumed and celebrated in an ecstatic feast, as men have hitherto imagined. Power does not join power; rather, in true religion the Lord of morality demands submission to his commandment. The earnestness of the moral commandment frightens complacent joy and self-assurance away from the "Day of the Lord." This Day is ominous with punishment and grief. (*RV* 288; Eng. trans. 246f.)

In the biblical tradition, the Messiah, who must prepare the "Day of the Lord," is idealized. The figure of the "son of David," the restorer of the kingdom of Israel, can no longer correspond to the idea of the poor man as a model of perfect man, nor to the idealization of the people of Israel in the "remnant of Israel," the symbol of mankind. Thus, his place is taken by the figure of the "servant of JHWH," the suffering Messiah representing the whole of Israel, or rather all men, who, by accepting suffering freely for the salvation of mankind realize the messianic task historically (cf. *BR* 77f.; *RV* 304f.; Eng. trans. 260f.).

Let us now analyze briefly this supreme concept of messianism: vicarious suffering. Religious idealization, which transfigures the poor man's social suffering from a sign of injustice to a sign of devotion, goes a step further in messianism and raises suffering to a historical means of salvation of mankind. The suffering servant of JHWH, and in him all men who suffer, bears upon himself the suffering of the other man and that of all mankind.

It is not a question of substitution in guilt, which would violate the principle of moral autonomy,[4] but only in suffering. Freeing suffering from the meaning of punishment of guilt so as to place it on the road toward redemption—an operation which, as we have seen, Cohen carried out, for two different aspects, in the analysis of man as plurality and individual—now allows the overcoming of the problem that vicarious suffering poses to the idea of God's justice, considering this suffering as an effect of God's love, which is not in conflict with his justice:

Suffering is not punishment. The suffering of men, which is to be considered mainly as the social suffering of the poor, is in God's hands. And God, as the God of justice, is at the same time the God of love. Justice and love are reciprocal concepts of God's being. The suffering of the poor is based on the justice of God that is united with love. Justice is love, hence it is in no way exclusively punitive justice. Thus justice, counterpointed by love, becomes the principle of theodicy. Justice becomes the lever for vicarious suffering which is separated from punishment. (RV 502; Eng. trans. 433; cf. RV 308; Eng. trans. 263f.)

Messianic man is thus the poor man who had already been identified with the pious man. However, vicarious suffering implies a further, conscious intention in the pious man: humility (*Demut*), freely taking upon himself suffering *for* mankind:

Why is *humility* the most sure sign of piety? Ascetic disdain of earthly things is not its true meaning, but rather opposition to the acceptance of superficial human reality as displayed in power, in splendor, in success, in dominion, in autocracy, in imperialism; as an opposition to all these signs of human arrogance, to vain pride and to presumption, humility constitutes the counterpart of the ideal man. At this point the distinction between— and the progress from—the notion of the *pious to that of the humble* must be delineated. The pious man represents the isolated I; the humble man bears the whole of mankind in his heart. Therefore he can become the representative of suffering, because he can fulfill his moral existence only in suffering. He knows the guilt of men; how could the poor man not know it since he suffers from the injustice of the world's economy? Although he cannot unburden men from their guilt, he suffers under the weight of a consciousness of guilt that includes his fellowmen. (*RV* 309f.; Eng. trans. 265)

Humility is the virtue that includes modesty (*Bescheidenheit*), though being more fundamental than the latter. Modesty is a virtue of man in his relations with other men, while humility is the messianic meaning of the correlation of man with God (cf. *RV* 496; Eng. trans. 427f.). Thus, in the context of correlation, one can also speak of God's humility (cf. *RV* 311, 494; Eng. trans. 266, 462). Further on we shall return to the meaning of humility. Now it is worth looking further into vicarious (or representative) suffering.

What is the exact universal historical value of the messianic function of suffering? Since, as we have seen,[5] for Cohen suffering is never an end, but only a means, the question can be legitimately posed on its end. That is, on the one hand, what is its product, and on the other, what is the ultimate point at which it is overcome? First, recognition of the messianic function of suffering has a negative meaning, in that humble, voluntary suffering bears witness to rejection of eudemonism. The suffering servant bears witness to the fact that the value of man and life does not lie in happiness and power but in suffering for good, that only the latter is the true sign of love and divine blessing:

> The Messiah, who is the representative of suffering, brings with his dark shadow the most shining light upon the history of mankind. Poverty is the moral defect of previous history. But the poor have become the pious. And the pious are the forerunners of the Messiah. The representative of suffering brings into the world this teaching, and with it the foundation of the ethical concept of history: that every eudemonistic appearance is nothing but an illusion; and that the genuine value of life for the entire history of peoples lies in moral ideas and is therefore represented among men only by those who are accredited as carriers of these ideas. (*RV* 309; Eng. trans. 264f.)

The people of Israel, who, in its history of continuous suffering, was and is the prominent figure of the servant of JHWH (cf. *RV* 311ff.; Eng. trans. 266ff.), bore and continue to bear witness among the peoples, with its loyalty to monotheism. Faith in the unique God is the radical refutation of idolatry, inasmuch as it is loyalty to the moral ideal, a sure affirmation of the value of good, against any eudemonist illusion.

However, taking on the burden of suffering does not only have the negative meaning of loyalty to idea. The suffering of the just man is not a sign of condemnation for the unjust, but of their way to salvation, exclusively through vicarious suffering. Israel can convert other men to monotheism, and, in general, the just man can convert sinners to the authentic value of life. Cohen, commenting on Isaiah 53, 4ff., writes:

> The problem of *evil* which traverses the whole of biblical literature, is here transferred from the individual to the historical image of the peoples. All the peoples are slaves to idol worship and they glitter and blossom in history. Only Israel suffers from the persecutions of the idol worshippers, and Israel has the calling not only to maintain the true worship of God but also to spread it among the peoples. Such a contradiction in historical imagery between past and future history does not permit any other solution but the following: *in suffering for the peoples Israel acquires the right to convert them.* This historical suffering of Israel gives it its historical dignity, its tragic mission, which represents its share in the divine education of mankind. What other solution is there for the discrepancy between Israel's historical mission and its historical fate? There is no other solution but the one which the following consideration offers: to suffer for the dissemination of monotheism, as the Jews do, is not a sorrowful fate; the suffering is, rather, its tragic

calling, for it proves the heartfelt desire for the conversion of the other peoples, which the faithful people feels. (*RV*330; Eng. trans. 283f.)

But the mission of the suffering servant is "tragic" only inasmuch as he cannot find a "justification" among the other peoples of history (cf. *RV*331; Eng. trans. 284f.), though not inasmuch as he finds no justification in God. Thus we reach the second aspect of the question regarding end. The Greek sense of tragedy is substantially alien to biblical messianism: "It does not have to be the case, and certainly it shall be different in the future, that there should be only tragic representatives of morality. This is a conception of dramatic poetry, to which ethics in no way has to consent" (*RV*309; Eng. trans. 265).

Suffering is in no way tragic, not only inasmuch as messianic suffering does not have sense in itself, as we have seen, nor that it is deprived of sense, but that it is a historical means; it is a mission, not a destiny. The messianic meaning of suffering is not tragic, also, and above all, because it does not cast doubts on divine justice, inasmuch as it is blessing and not punishment and is the prelude to historical redemption, of which it is not the price, but only the means of love, in such a way as to make this redemption universal. God's justice "is to be revealed truly only in the future. At that time suffering will not only cease, but its result will have been achieved: all the peoples will worship the unique God" (*RV*330 f.; Eng. trans. 284).

Myth links suffering to sin and punishment, and thus to past and lost innocence, while religion connects suffering to forgiveness and redemption, thus to a sure future holiness. The guarantor of this ultimate result is God himself, the good, redeeming God of monotheism. He does not only ensure this final goal of suffering, he is the granter of it, so that man may follow the path toward redemption. But God is the redeemer; man frees himself from the burden of sin, but only God can remove sin. At the end of the historical-messianic path mankind will be taken into a kingdom of God where the social sin of injustice and the historical one of war will be annulled in messianic peace and justice:

However, the unique God is the forgiving God for each human individual, and therefore also for all men. The liberation of men from the burden of sin is therefore provided for in the very concept of this God. It is not possible for the matter to remain at the fact that men always sin and that God always merely forgives. If, instead, the concept of God and the proper meaning of his love and goodness is to forgive man for his sin, then this concept must include this meaning: he will bring about the complete disappearance of sin from the human race. And if this consequence did not explicitly become part of Messianism, it is still evident that the cessation of political and historical sin committed in wars and the cessation of the social injustice of pauperism clearly governs the hopes of the messianic prophet. (*RV* 342; Eng. trans. 293f.)

We shall return to all these themes, but first of all it is interesting to note how the possibility of defining and founding the historical process, more adequately than the ethics of pure will had done, is the result of the messianic correlation we have described so far, and thus, in the last analysis, of the specific religious conception of correlation between God and man.

4. PRECEDENTS FOR THE CONCEPT OF EVOLUTION IN COHEN'S PHILOSOPHY

We must go back as far as *Logik der reinen Erkenntnis* in order to trace the precedents for the theme of historical evolution in Cohen's thought. What is interesting about this work, concerning the subject in question, is not so much the discussion of the concept of 'evolution' (cf. *LRE* 530f.), which is only dealt with in its biological meaning, as the analysis of the concept of 'movement' (*Bewegung*) as a correlate of 'conservation' (*Erhaltung*) (cf. *LRE* 234).

We have already examined Cohen's analogy between God the Creator and substance, highlighting their meaning and establishing the fundamental differences. Cohen's logical context is that of substance as conservation in correlation with movement. According to *Logik der reinen Erkenntnis*, "the future contains and shows the character of time" (*LRE* 154), while the present is "a *moment of space*) (*LRE* 228). Movement, then, is "the relationship between time and space" (*LRE* 229), a relationship that is realized with the "*resolution of space and time*" (*LRE* 231), or with the resolution of "juxtaposition" (*Beisammen*), that is, of the present in the future and with the transformation of space in a "*background*," "in the *field of projection*, in the scene for *changes*" (*LRE* 231), that is, in conservation as a correlate of movement.[6] Despite the fundamental differences of logical argument as compared with religious discourse, which I have already pointed out as regards the analogy between God the Creator and substance, and which, also here, do not allow anything other than simple analogous reference, it is clear that, for Cohen, there is a relation between these logical developments of the concepts of 'future' and movement, and the subsequent developments of the same concept of future and that of evolution in the philosophy of religion.

In *Ethik des reinen Willens*, the concept of evolution is considered in order to deny sociology a founding function among the moral sciences.

It would incorporate this concept into its method from the biological sciences arbitrarily and illegitimately, since, in the study of man and his social and spiritual reality, there is no possibility to presuppose as already given a complete organism, with reference to which the formative process of the parts are to be interpreted as evolution (cf. *ERW* 40ff.). Cohen thus considers mere social understanding of man as naturalism, and this conviction can be found again in *Religion der Vernunft*: "The Darwinian theory cannot be the teleology of the human race because the ethical sense of mankind requires its own teleology" (*RV* 307; Eng. trans. 263). This is also one of the interpretive features that justifies Cohen's accusations of naturalism against romantic idealism and, especially, Hegel's philosophy of identity (cf. *ERW* 44f.).

With this criticism of the concept of evolution, Cohen did not intend to entirely reject the concept itself, concerning the area of the moral sciences, but only to reinterpret it in an adequate ethical meaning (cf. *ERW* 43). His arguments thus go beyond the simple rejection of the biological concept of evolution for the moral sciences and formulate a more adequate meaning of this concept, for which the process is not determined with reference to an already complete organism, but to an ideal, what ought to be, which is the ultimate end of an infinite task. This infinity of the task is, in Cohen's view, the ethical meaning of eternity: "Eternity, released from time and referring to pure will, only means the *eternity of the progress of moral labor* (*ERW* 410). In this ethical idealization of history, where emphasis is given to the orientation of reality toward the ideal more than to the actual presence of the ideal meaning of the evolution of the real process, concrete historical reality is resolved in the infinite process of realization (cf. *ERW* 416f.). This formulation of the problem encouraged Cohen to reject immortality as a specifically religious concept, not suitable for ethics. It is actually securely linked to the concept of the individual soul, to man as an individual, well outside the ethical conception of historical evolution (cf. *ERW* 412ff.).

A last remark on the consequences of the formulation concerning the problem of evil. It was the great importance that he attached to the ideal horizon of historical evolution and his insignificant attention to the concrete reality of the ongoing process that led Cohen, in my opinion, to a decisively unsatisfactory theodicy, in which the triumph of good is confused with the nonexistence of evil. However, this was the coherent result of a scientific ethics, of discourse on the principles, in which the methodical distinction between what ought to be and being does not allow an exhaustive examination of their reciprocal influence, except in the sense of final conciliation in the ideal:

If we, through the optimism of moral idealism, put our trust in the idea of God, the problem of *theodicy* is solved. The very concept of God contains theodicy. All the defects and ills of nature enter the economy of the divine plan of truth. But also evil, which we must recognize in human action, or rather that which he who acts must recognize in his action, can only be an expression of moral judgment on themselves. It cannot venture beyond the interiority of consciousness. But in the judgment that moral thought must give to history, its events, its heroes and martyrs, evil cannot ever become anywhere the sole determining principle. However distorted and shadowy are the ways of *law* and the administrations of *States*, trust in eternal progress and the success of good can never falter. (*ERW* 451–52)

5. IMMORTALITY AND HISTORICAL EVOLUTION

After remarking on some of the precedents in Cohen's elaboration of the concept of evolution, let us now examine their further investigation in *Religion der Vernunft*, by means of the analysis of the idea of immortality.[7] In this work the messianic evolution of history becomes the place of the immortality of the soul. The individual soul, understood by myth as a vital principle, is considered by religion as a spiritual principle, as the spirit of holiness, correlative with divine holiness, by which it is created in revelation. Death can only constitute the end of the empirical individual, not the end of the infinite task of nearness to God, which is man's spirit as an individual. Faith in the immortality of the individual soul is thus grounded in the correlation between God and man, in the holy spirit. It is a correlation for which material conditions only constitute a negative presupposition, guaranteed as conservation of the nature of God's creative providence. The true positive condition of the individual's immortality consists in the historical evolution of mankind, into which the infinite task of the individual soul flows. The historical evolution of mankind is thus the process of realization of the immortality of the soul, seen as the process of a return to God in the spirit of holiness which stimulates the moral individual (cf. *RV* 351f.; Eng. trans. 302f.).

The relationship between individual and mankind in history thus takes shape in a way that is not particularly different, though more detailed and complex in respect of ethics. On the one hand, the messianic evolution of history is not at all conceived on the model of the organic evolution of nature, but in the sense of teleological ethics. This, however, finds its foundation in the correlation between the infinite process of moral purification of man as an individual and divine holiness:

Who could believe that holiness can die! Jewish piety, therefore, had to reject the myth: "For Thou wilt not abandon my soul to the nether-world;

neither wilt Thou suffer Thy godly one to see the pit" (Ps. 16:10). And since, in addition, the concept of God created the messianic future, the soul was also assured of a future. Thus, Messianism, added to the concept of the soul the factor of development, and made the soul the messianic principle of development. To the messianic development the individual's development could and had to be joined. For holiness had been secured in the reconciliation and redemption through God. Thus, man had become not only the symbol of mankind but—as the individual, as the person, as I—the appointed carrier of holiness. (*RV* 389; Eng. trans. 334)

On the other hand, the immortality of the individual soul does not contradict the universal character of the story of mankind, since, seen in the dimension of historical evolution, the moral individual is the "*individual of totality*," the "*individual of mankind*" (*RV* 358; Eng. trans. 308). The individual soul is a "historical soul" (*RV* 391; Eng. trans. 336). In this sense of historical evolution as a place of individual immortality, Cohen interprets the biblical conception of 'death' as reunification of the individual with the people and as a return to the "Fathers" (cf. *RV* 350; Eng. trans. 301). Correlation as origin and end, as revelation and redemption, the sense of monotheism and messianism, are united in the idea of the immortality of the soul and the messianic evolution of mankind:

To the eternity of God corresponds, as an anthropomorphic consequence, the eternity of man. Liberated of the anthropomorphic setting, this eternity of man means only the infinite continuation of the correlation of man and God. Without immortality God's creation, revelation and providence could not have existence. Thus, Messianism is only an analogy of immortality, while monotheism itself in its correlation of God and man has immortality as its necessary consequence. (*RV* 392; Eng. trans. 337)

The problem of the realization of the ideal in history receives further investigation in the religion of reason. The infinite task of moral realization by man is now considered in correlation with divine redemption. The process by which the immortal soul returns to God does not have a mystical meaning of unification with God for Cohen. It "lightly touches" this "limit," but "does not cross over it" (cf. *RV* 389f.; Eng. trans. 335). The process of the individual's nearness to God does not have the eschatological meaning of the final realization of a "kingdom of heaven" outside history, but has the rigorously historical meaning of the social, political, and human realization of the "kingdom of God" on earth (cf. *RV* 357; Eng. trans. 307).

Immortality is therefore a limit concept of the critical philosophy of history. The need to trace the limit of critical thought in respect of mysticism and eschatology gives Cohen the idea of positing hope for immortality as a limit (and only that) of the knowledge (though in the sense of practical knowledge, i.e., of moral action) of the messianic evolution of history:

> Truly profound and of the highest clarity, is this sentence in the Talmud which guided Maimonides: "All the prophets have prophesied for the days of the Messiah only." But about the future world the following words are valid:"neither hath the eye seen a God, beside Thee, who worketh for him that waiteth for Him" (Isa. 64:3). Consequently, according to the above rabbinical statement the world beyond is generally separated from the problem of prophecy. The prophets are only concerned with the Messianic Age, with the historical development of the human race. But immortality belongs to God's secrets; it is an object of human hope. (*RV* 363 f.; Eng. trans. 313)

Consideration of the historical evolution of mankind as the only true dimension of man's return to God and the strong defense of the transcendence of God in respect of history remove Cohen's conception of history from any kind of historicism: both the absolute historicism of romantic idealism, especially of the Hegelian kind, which sees history as a process of realization of the absolute, and historicism that does not recognize any correlation of historical events with the absolute. For Cohen, historical evolution is the evolution of man inasmuch as he is spirit of holiness, and it is founded on the correlation with God the Creator and Revealer. Besides, it moves in the direction of a redemption, which is not the result of historical evolution, since man's process of moral purification is infinite, but it is the correlative act of God the redeemer, who in this sense remains transcendent in respect of history. As I have already mentioned, only in a total conception of the meaning of God as idea is the inadequacy of any ontological interpretation of the idea of God as origin clearly understood, in that it is inextricably tied to the moral, historical function of the messianic idea, and only by keeping in mind the foundation of messianism in the idea of transcendent God can one avoid the risk of an immanentist historical perspective for messianism itself.

Cohen's religious philosophy is also a deepening of the results of ethics concerning the third aspect of the problem of history, which was examined above: the problem of evil and theodicy. Cohen organized these developments in philosophical reflection around the interpretation of the theme of the "merit of the Fathers." The merit of the Fathers has a twofold meaning for him. In a negative sense, it means the negation of a merit of the individual for his effort for moral purification, for his repentance and for his suffering. The moral task of the individual is infinite; in no way can one think of its fulfillment and recognition of merit. The latter is projected on the Fathers as representatives of the whole people or rather of all mankind in its historical evolution. Individual merit is not even required in a critical conception of morality (cf. *RV* 368; Eng. trans. 316). The classical problem of the unhappiness of the just and the happiness of the unjust is posed in a completely new way in the light of the monotheistic and messianic meaning of suffering. Man's good does not consist of happiness, nor does it involve the latter as one of its moments: "The reward for duty is duty" (a maxim taken by Spinoza: *"praemium virtutis virtus"*), repeats Cohen with the Mishnah (cf. *RV* 374; Eng. trans. 321).

But the merit of the Fathers also has a positive meaning. It is the announcement of faith in universal redemption. The Fathers, also, are not the bearers of merit as individuals, inasmuch as they are heroes of the race, but inasmuch as they are symbols of all mankind in its historical evolution. The Messiah, inasmuch as he is a figure of mankind, is called the "Father of men" (cf. *RV* 357; Eng. trans. 308).

> It is the fathers, not the individuals as such, to whom merit is traced back. The fathers are not such in an absolute sense; they are rather the fathers of the development, the standard-bearers of history. In no way are they to be thought of as exceptional individuals, as individual saints. As such they, too, could have no merit. It is only the fact that something begins with them, something that surpasses them, which makes them into starting points for the problem of merit. (*RV* 369; Eng. trans. 317)

Now, if the merit regards mankind and not individuals, it can be thought as a reward for moral improvement, which is a task proper to the individual, and even less as its result. It must, therefore, be thought as a divine gift, as the grace of God the Redeemer: "Here, too, it is possible to see the value of human morality is only patch-work, and can never be meritorious. It always needs the reconciliation with God and, hence, God's grace" (*RV* 375; Eng. trans. 323).

The historical evolution of mankind, which occurs through moral improvement of individuals, that is, that has its principle in the immortality of the soul, is in correlation with God's redemption. God the Good is he who takes away the sins of the world, and only he can do this. Redemption, therefore, is not the reward for moral improvement. It is certainly its fulfillment, but as a presupposition. It is the teleological meaning of God's holiness and goodness: the same unique, holy, good God, who creates moral man in correlation, granting him the commandment of good and the strength to follow it; he will grant man final redemption, also in correlation that is, the elimination of sin: "No condition is attached to immortality. Even redemption cannot be made the condition for immortality. And to redemption itself no other condition is attached but the self-redemption of the human soul in its correlation with God and, consequently, in its confidence in God" (*RV* 391; Eng. trans. 336).

Redemption as the ultimate end of history completes and clarifies the meaning of correlation between man's penitence and God's forgiveness. The forgiveness of individual sin has a provisional meaning, which can only be overcome in the final perspective of redemption. The individual, in his or her earthly life, is always forgiven for his or her sin, but is always a sinner again. And yet this infinite process is not an empty, senseless game, since it is a process that enters the historical evolution of mankind and that receives from God its fulfillment with redemption, with the elimination of sin (cf. *RV* 369f.; Eng. trans. 318).

Cohen, after removing pain and suffering from the meaning of punishment and having placed them in correlation with divine forgiveness now places this correlation in the universal picture of correlation between the messianic evolution of history and God's redemption. This is possible for him by means of the idea of immorality, which joins the individual's infinite task with the history of mankind. In this way the problem of the judgment of the good and the bad is overcome. Not in the sense that this difference is eliminated or that evil is justified, but in the sense that redemption takes the shape of elimination of mankind's sin, not as a reward for virtue, but as the product of divine holiness and goodness: God will take away the sin of the world independently of the merits of individual men, because of his goodness. "There is no other compensation for sin but the one which one's own self-sanctification can achieve" (*RV* 371; Eng. trans. 319). Man as a historical individual, responsible for his moral self-purification and the purification of mankind, through vicarious suffering, can hope and believe in final redemption of sins, not through his own merits, but because of that radical good in him which is the fruit of revelation, since he was constituted by God as a spirit of holiness in correlation with God and "the loss of moral dignity is therefore generally impossible" (*RV* 380; Eng. trans. 327). God the Redeemer is nothing more than the final sense of God the Creator and Revealer.

Between the messianic evolution of mankind and redemption, just as between the individual's penitence and forgiveness, there is no consequential relationship; neither are these two terms independent of each other (which would make morality and history useless). Correlation between the two terms must be recognized, for which divine revelation is the ground of the historical evolution of immortality and divine redemption is the fulfillment, without God being identified with history:

> In the presence of the concept of immortality, sin disappears from the concept of the soul of man. Man is immortal, he has an equal share with all men in eternal life—this thesis effaces the moment of sin from the concept of the human soul. The latter is not thereby betrayed into indifference with regard to good and bad, but is only exempted from the indelibility of sin. This condemns as false the idea that sin is an essential part of man. Sin only presses its way to man as long as he lives. But his sin is only *shegagah* in God's eyes. And God forgives it, because man in his confidence in God is able to achieve his self-sanctification and self-purification. Therefore, he does not die with the death of his body, but the messianic God also gives his individual soul in infinite development, an eternal existence. Thus all the fundamental concepts of religion radiate in the direction of the immortality of the soul, and from it the rays shine back to the center—God. And this radiation evolves in its entirety from the correlation of God and man. (*RV* 391f.; Eng. trans. 336f.)

The theodicy of *Ethik des reinen Willens* is thus substantially revived and not abandoned. However, it is deepened in its meaning and cleansed of the apparent frustration of evil characterizing it. Man's sin is not justified. It is recognized as the origin of the suffering of mankind; and this suffering is not abandoned to the mockery of chance and uselessness but regained in the supreme messianic meaning. However the certainty of the triumph of good is also confirmed in *Religion der Vernunft*, not as the result of a necessary historical process, but as the well founded certainty of correlation between God and man, between redemption and history, monotheism and messianism:

> Messianism offered the main conditions for the concept of man; all these conditions culminate in the concept of the pious of the peoples of the world. On the other hand, for the concept of God, monotheism in itself disclosed the idea of immortality; for this goal, all of its fundamental concepts culminate in the concept of reconciliation. Man does attain reconciliation with God. Sin does not possess with him an indestructible character. His soul is pure and therefore immortal. God gave it to him; therefore sin is never his inheritance; his inheritance is rather only and exclusively his soul; it is as a human soul that the soul is immortal, not as the soul of a faith, not even of the faith in the unique God. If the soul has not yet found God, it always may: it is immortal. (*RV* 392; Eng. trans. 337)[8]

6. The Anti-Eudemonist Conception of History

The eudemonist conception of ethics, through the analysis of man and his correlation with God, means an anti-eudemonist conception of history:

The religion of reason protests against all the alleged powers of the self, against all those pretended powers of the *I*, which are rooted in pleasure and pain. All animal selfishness and self-love, all eudemonism, which recognizes only pleasure as a legitimate criterion, all materialism, which honors only debit and credit and considers give and take as the essence of man, are eliminated by reason. The subjective basis of materialism lies in the principle of pleasure. What matter means to the nature of the world, pleasure means to human nature. It is the consciousness of animal sensuality. *Naturalness in its primitive historical form* is also rejected together with sensuality as a source of religion, insofar as its factual reality is, properly speaking, merely contingent. It is reason alone that elevates historical actuality to necessity, the meaning of which is the abolition of contingency. (*RV* 7; Eng. trans. 6)

This position is the result of the religious elaboration of the meaning of suffering, as the essential moment of messianic history. The value of suffering in the redemptive process of mankind and the recognition of the value of suffering only as a means and not as an end, and of redemption as the final gift of God, for which suffering will be eliminated, determine a precise relationship between Cohen's anti-eudemonism and historical optimism. Certainly, Cohen is convinced that one can have faith in historical progress of the material conditions of mankind, and that one must operate to this end, so as to alleviate the suffering caused by social injustice, death, disease and war. His militancy in favor of socialism bears witness to this. But it would be a mistake to link his historical optimism to this concern for justice and social welfare, thus turning it into mere trust in progress. Cohen's optimism is rather grounded in his faith in man's basic goodness, in turn grounded in correlation with God, and in the historical nature of evil as sin, which cannot be considered as man's tragic destiny. Besides, Cohen's optimism is grounded in the recognition of the redemptive meaning of suffering and the irrelevance of pleasure and reward for man's virtue and dignity. Man's suffering in history is not thus undervalued or removed by philosophical irenism, but seriously considered in messianic idealism. It is rather pessimism that reveals disappointed eudemonism, while optimism is the religious anti-eudemonist taking up of suffering and guilt as dramatic dimensions, but not tragic ones, of history. It is the active collaboration in historical evolution and trust in the redemption of mankind by God. (cf. *RV* 20f.; Eng. trans. 18).

Faith in the salvational value of suffering saves monotheism from gnostic dualism between good and evil. Evil, seen as suffering, is restored to God, not in the economy of trial and punishment, but in that of redemption and perfection:

The intellectual restriction brought about the maturity of *ethical rigor*. In it monotheism fulfills its opposition to *eudemonism*. We have already recognized (cf. p. 21) that only Isaiah could have said about his God: "He makes peace and creates evil." In this brave surpassing of Zoroastrianism, evil rather means ill. God cannot be the creator of evil, yet he makes the ill, which men, in their delusion, consider evil. But God is the creator of peace, and in peace, according to the Hebrew root of the word, the creator of perfection transforms the seemingly unsuitable ill into its highest end. (*RV* 302; Eng. trans. 259)

Cohen's historical optimism is none other than the humility of the messianic man mentioned previously: "Humility is the positive power which defeats all eudemonism" (*RV* 310; Eng. trans. 266). The humble man does not close his eyes before human suffering but takes it upon himself, willingly, without expecting any reward (cf. *RV* 361; Eng. trans. 310). He does not seek refuge in illusory theodicy, but makes himself the living theodicy of history, bearing witness to the vanity of earthly happiness as man's end, and the supreme value of suffering for the historical evolution of mankind toward redemption. This is the anti-eudemonist meaning of the virtue of contentment (*Zufriedenheit*), to which we shall return:

> Peace of the soul manifests itself in contentment, which is preeminently a religious virtue, for it is concerned with the acknowledgment of God's providence and rule over the world. In face of contentment all the assaults of eudemonism are shattered, as are also all the doubts that the deepest suffering of the soul might stir up. "As one praises God for the good, so also for the bad." This is the general talmudic instruction with regard to benedictions. (*RV* 518; Eng. trans. 449)

7. TRUTH AND PEACE

The idea of God as a principle of truth, which, as we have seen, had already been the object of reflection in Cohen's ethics, also receives deeper treatment in the philosophy of religion. This greater attention occurs in the specific direction of religion, in the God-man correlation: the meaning of truth which is God is developed in relation to man; not only man as the subject of the scientific knowledge of nature, or the self of the humanity of juridical and moral law, but man of religion, as an individual and subject of history. Here I shall restrict myself to a few remarks on truth as the ground in the correlation with the individual, to show, especially, the meaning of truth for history.[9]

The very fact that systematic philosophy recognizes the principle of truth in the idea of God, and that this principle is the "original problem of systematic philosophy" (*RV* 476; Eng. trans. 410), confirms the participation of religion in reason (cf. *RV* 476; Eng. trans. 410). Thus Cohen rejects once again any irrationalist interpretation of religion as feeling or *Erlebnis*. If a rationalist conception of religion is not accepted, the possibility of religious truth also falls with it, which certainly cannot be different and contradictory in respect of the truth of science and morality. Even in this partaking of rational truth, religion is the bearer of a peculiarity, for which it does not depend on the logical-scientific or ethical-moral sense of truth, but actually claims primacy and particular authority in respect of the meaning of truth (cf. *RV* 476f.; Eng. trans. 410f).

For religion truth is God himself in correlation with man. The meaning of truth is, also for religion, near to that of unity: both are essential attributes of God (cf. *RV* 441; Eng. trans. 379f.). But truth does not only mean the ideal unity of the methods of the sciences of nature and the moral sciences, nor simply the ideal of the final unity of nature and morality, which is already a further development of the meaning of unity (as we saw announced in *Ethik des reinen Willens*), but is still too abstract. Truth is the unity of God in correlation with the unification of man. And the meaning of correlation, as we have already seen, does not only consist in positing God as the teleological reference for man's task, but also as the transcendent ground, as a force that makes it possible for man to continue with his task and as transcendent author of the final task.

God as truth is placed in correlation with truthfulness (*Wahrhaftigkeit*) as man's "absolute virtue" (*RV* 492; Eng. trans. 424), in his relations with the individual ("*Unwahrhaftigkeit*" is considered by Cohen as "absolute sin" [*RV* 491; Eng. trans. 423]). Cohen takes the biblical example of a pure heart, to indicate truthfulness as an essential virtue for the individual. Pure heart means man's inner unification, the overcoming of division due to the passions, the unity of the individual's consciousness turned to God, which is, at the same time, condition and content of prayer and worship. Unity and purity of heart do not mean fulfillment reached at last for man, but rather the simplicity of his spirit entirely turned to God:

> Therefore the prophets determine the true worship through the connection of the truth not with the spirit—what is the spirit if not heart?—but indeed with the heart and its moral power. "Serve him in wholeness and in truth" (Josh. 24:14); Wholeness (*t^emimûth*) is simplicity. To translate it as perfection is misleading; "Thou shalt be whole-hearted with the Eternal thy God" (Deut. 18: 13). Man should not and could not be perfect along-

> side God, but he ought to be whole, that is, unified and simple. Hence, this simplicity, this freedom from discord, becomes the expression for truth-fulness in human life. In the same way: "Serve Him in truth with all your heart" (I Sam. 12:24; cf. Jer. 32:41). (*RV* 483; Eng. trans. 416f.)[10]

The full authentic meaning of religious correlation must be remem-bered so as not to reduce the truth-truthfulness correlation to the ethical relationship between task and effort for improvement. God, as truth, is certainly the end to which the effort for improving and unifying his heart on the part of man must incline, but he is much else besides. The pure heart is one of man's virtues, but he cannot obtain it except from God. This is the reason for prayer:

> In truthfulness, God appears as the other link of the correlation. God is the God of truth, and man is to become the man of truthfulness. Therefore, man prays to God. Man would be perfect, and he would be able to redeem himself without looking to God, if he were able to establish and accomplish his truthfulness without praying to God. This is the main prayer, as the psalm expresses it: "Create me a clean heart, O God; and renew an established spirit within me (Ps. 51:12). (*RV* 443; Eng. trans. 381)

God's truth then is above all the presupposition, the condition of the possibility of man's truthfulness. Despite his inclination to lie, his disper-sion in pursuit of passions, man is capable of truthfulness, since God granted him and continually renews a pure heart, a holy spirit which keeps him, despite everything, in correlation with God's truth (cf. *RV* 443; Eng. trans. 381). God's truth places man's moral improvement in the final perspective of the fulfillment of redemption.

As we have seen, an essential moment in man's work of self-purifica-tion consists of the confession of his sins. It is a necessary moment of the purification of the heart; but since God is the redeemer, since God's truth is the promise of the elimination of sin, man's truthfulness does not only consist of contrite confession of his guilt, but also of the joyous confession of God the Redeemer's truth and of the elimination of guilt: "Confession is not merely a condition for true repentance; it is not merely the confession of sin, but also the confession of truth. The con-fession, too, is the duty of man. . . . Purity of the heart distinguishes the confession of truth from the confession of sin. The soul of man is pure; it is capable of truthfulness. God gave me a pure soul: man has the task of confessing the truth" (*RV* 443f.; Eng. trans. 381f.).

Therefore, truthfulness is the essential virtue of man as an individual, but it is also the virtue that gives the individual meaning and dignity as a historical man, since, as we have seen, the individual's historical task is

precisely the testimony of truth, even with suffering including martyr-
dom, that links him actively to mankind and places him as a protagonist
in historical evolution: "Truth establishes truthfulness, and truthfulness
is the backbone of the moral man. Thanks to the power of religious
truthfulness the moral man is the religious man. And the religious man
is the historical man" (*RV* 485; Eng. trans. 418).

Historically, God, as the principle of truth, does not place himself
simply in the ethical relationship of the ideal, of the task, in respect of
human effort. Man cannot be under the illusion that the process of historical evolution that has been entrusted to him is achieved by itself in
the universal unification of mankind and in perpetual peace. However,
he can believe and hope that God the redeemer will realize peace as the
fulfillment of his messianic operation. Peace is the historical realization
of truth; it comes from God and carries out the messianic work of the historical man:

> Therefore it is possible to consider peace the principle of finality. God
> makes peace, this means that he is the highest end of all existence and of
> all moral actions. God, as the originator of peace, is equal to the principle
> of finality. The latter, in turn, is identical with the principle of truth, inso-
> far as it unites both finalities, that of nature and that of morality, in a new
> finality. God as finality is equivalent to God as peace. From this point of
> view, too, one may recognize the inner opposition of monotheism to the
> principle of all sophistry,which lies in the Heraclitan saying that war is the
> father of all things. War is not the original cause of the moral universe; the
> end of peace becomes the cause. Peace, which is the goal of the moral
> world, must also be valid as its originating power. God is peace. God stands
> for the harmony between the moral powers of the universe and their nat-
> ural conditions. (*RV* 517; Eng. trans. 447f.)

The kingdom of God is the task of the historical evolution of
mankind. It is, however, not the result of man's messianic action, but the
realization of divine creation in "God's government of the world" (*RV*
460; Eng. trans. 396). God created the spirit of holiness in man and has
continually renewed it in him, making him capable of the messianic
operation. In the end, God as the Lord of the world fulfills the historical
evolution of mankind, with the realization of the kingdom: "Government of the world, as a position and fulfillment of the end of the world is
the sense and content of monotheism. . . . The kingdom of God is the
creation and providence, that is the lordship of God. Insofar as he is
Lord of the world he is the 'God of truth.' And he is praised as 'King of
all the earth' " (*RV* 460; Eng. trans. 396).

'Peace' is the biblical concept which Cohen used to work through the further religious investigation of the ethical concept of 'humanitarianism' (cf. *RV* 515 f.; Eng. trans. 446). Peace, however, is a further investigation, but it is also enrichment of humanitarianism,[11] since it does not only consist in the "harmonization of the whole of morality peace" (*RV* 516; Eng. trans. 446), but also in "harmony between the moral powers of the universe and their natural conditions" (*RV* 517; Eng. trans. 448). God's peace is certainly the ideal of messianic man, the end of his moral labor and suffering: "Thus the suffering of the Messiah becomes a chastisement of peace, it becomes a means to the end of peace. Peace is the ideal of the messianic man. Only in peace is the spiritual welfare of man completed" (*RV* 517; Eng. trans. 448). Peace is the "final step in the development of man" (*RV* 518; Eng. trans. 449). But the peace of God, according to the general sense of correlation, is also ground and strength that makes possible man's messianic resolution, inasmuch as it is grounded in contentment, the specific attitude of the religious man, of the messianic man, suffering for humanity. I have already mentioned the virtue of contentment. Here it is enough to add that this virtue draws its sense and justification from the solid correlation of the historic man with the God of peace.

In the religious attitude of contentment, suffering, as compassion toward mankind, is certainly not removed nor reduced in its dramatic meaning, since contentment has nothing to do with quietism (cf. *RV* 519, 520; Eng. trans. 449). However, it is born in the light of "joy" (*Freude*), which is a "sign of peace" (*RV* 526; Eng. trans. 456): "To think that shared joy is not as immediate a vital power of the human mind as is compassion or shared suffering is a psychologically false view, a mistake of pessimism and of the common view of the radical evil in men which Kant, to be sure, idealized both correctly and profoundly. If this were true, then peace would not be genuine peace or an unambiguous view of virtue" (*RV* 527; Eng. trans. 456f.).

The joy characterizing a holy day is a messianic symbol of the joy accompanying the final realization of messianic peace in the kingdom of God, but is also a real anticipation in the historical present of that future peace, which is stronger than any contingent privation that man must bear:

> Peace in the joy of the feast is a characteristic of the Jewish mentality. Considering the suffering that pervades the whole historical life of the Jew, it is surely a wonder that he could continually maintain such equanimity, such a genuine humor, without which he would never have been able to lift himself again and again from the deepest humiliation to proud heights. The Jewish holidays have brought about this wonder for him. On

the Sabbath and on the feasts, joy governed the Ghetto no matter how much suffering had embittered the days of the week. Joy on a holiday was a religious duty, and hence it became an inviolable and vital power in the Jewish consciousness. But it could not have been established and preserved as such a power if peace had not been, and remained, such a strong magic power in the Jewish spirit. "Peace, peace to him that is far off, and to him that is near, saith the Eternal . . . and I will heal him" (Isa. 57:19). Peace was the healing power of the prophets, peace first of all in opposition to war, but then also in opposition to human passion. Peace has the same significance as reconciliation and redemption. (RV 529f.; Eng. trans. 458f.)

Abbreviations

Following is a list of abbreviations with explanations and some essential bibliographical references.

W   =   *Werke*, hg. vom Hermann-Cohen-Archiv am Philosophischen Seminar Zürich unter der Leitung von Helmut Holzhey, Hildesheim, G. Olms. The following volumes have been published so far: vol. 6; *Logik der reinen Erkenntnis*, Einleitung von Helmut Holzhey, 1977; vol. 4; *Kommentar zu Immanuel Kants Kritik der reinen Vernunft*, Einleitung von Helmut Holzhey, 1978; vol. 7; *Ethik des reinen Willens*, introduction by Steven S. Schwarzschild, 1981; vol. 8/9; *Ästhetik des reinen Gefühls*, Einleitung von Gerd Wolandt, 1982; vol. 5; I, *Das Prinzip der Infinitesimal-Methode und seine Geschichte*, Einleitung von Peter Schulthess; II, *Einleitung mit kritischem Nachtrag zur 'Geschichte des Materialismus' von F. A. Lange*, Einführung von Helmut Holzhey, 1984; vol. 1, I–III, *Kants Theorie der Erfahrung*, Einleitung von Geert Edel, 1987.

KTE = *Kants Theorie der Erfahrung*, Berlin, Dümmler, 1871, 1885²; Berlin, Bruno Cassirer, 1918³; repr. in *W1/I–III*. Quotations normally come from the third edition. When it is necessary to specify edition, the abbreviation will be accompanied by a superscript.

KBE = *Kants Begründung der Ethik*, Berlin, Dümmler, 1877; Berlin, Bruno Cassirer, 1910².
Where there are unimportant differences between the first and second editions, considering that the first edition is not

263

easy to find, for the reader's convenience, quotations throughout are taken from the second edition, even when the context refers to the first edition. When required, important variations between editions will be mentioned in the notes.

KBA   = *Kants Begründung der Ästhetik,* Berlin, Dümmler, 1889.

PIM   = *Das Prinzip der Infinitesimal-Methode und seine Geschichte. Ein Kapitel zur Grundlegung der Erkenntnisskritik,* Berlin, Dümmler, 1883; repr. Frankfurt, Suhrkamp, 1968; repr. in *S* II: 1–170 and in *W* 5/I from which quotations are taken.

E   = *Einleitung mit kritischem Nachtrag zu F. A. Langes Geschichte des Materialismus,* Leipzig, Baedeker, 1896, 1902^2; Leipzig, Brandstetter, 1914^3. The last of the three editions, published with the ninth edition of Lange's works, was reprinted in *S* II: 171–302 and in *W* 5/II (with variations from other editions), from which quotations are taken.

LRE   = *System der Philosophie. Erster Teil: Logik der reinen Erkenntnis,* Berlin, Bruno Cassirer, 1902, 1914^2; the latter edition was reprinted in *W* 6 (with variations from the first edition), from which quotations are taken.

ERW   = *System der Philosophie. Zweiter Teil: Ethik des reinen Willens,* Berlin, Bruno Cassirer, 1904, 1907^2; the latter edition was reprinted in *W* 7 (with variations from the first edition), from which quotations are taken.

ARG   = *System der Philosophie. Dritter Teil: Ästhetik des reinen Gefühls,* 2 Bde., Berlin, Bruno Cassirer, 1912; repr. in *W* 8/9, from which quotations are taken.

BR   = *Der Begriff der Religion im System der Philosophie,* Giessen, Töpelmann, 1915.

RV   = *Religion der Vernunft aus den Quellen des Judentums,* hg. von Benzion Kellerman, Leipzig, Fock, 1919: hg. von Bruno Strauss, Frankfurt, J. Kaufmann, 1929; repr. Cologne, J. Melzer, 1959 from which quotations are taken; repr. Wiesbaden, Fourier, 1978. English translation, with an introduction by Simon Kaplan, introductory essay by Leo Strauss, New York, Frederick Ungar, 1972.

S   = *Schriften zur Philosophie und Zeitgeschichte*, 2 Bde., hg. von Albert Görland and Ernst Cassirer, Berlin, Akademie Verlag, 1928. The essays in this collection will be cited in the first instance with the date of the first edition or composition (in the case of unpublished essays) in brackets after the title.

J   = *Jüdische Schriften*, 3 Bde., hg. von Bruno Strauss, mit einer einleitung von Franz Rosenzweig, Berlin, Schwetschke, 1924. The essays in this collection will be cited in the first instance with the date of the first edition or composition (in the case of unpublished essays) in brackets after the title.

Extensive bibliographies of secondary work on Cohen can be found in H.-L. Ollig, *Religion und Freiheitsglaube. Zur Problematik von Hermann Cohens später Religionsphilosophie*, Königstein/Ts., Forum Academicum, 1979; E. Winter, *Ethik und Rechtswissenschaft. Eine historisch-systematische Untersuchung zur Ethik-Konzeption des Marburger Neukantianismus im Werke Hermann Cohens*, Berlin, Duncker & Humblot, 1980; H. Holzhey, *Cohen und Natorp*, 2 Bde., Basle/Stuttgart, Schwabe & Co. - AG Verlag, 1986.

Notes

CHAPTER ONE. THE INTERPRETATION OF KANT

1. For the history of the term and its historiographical use cf. H. Holzhey, "*Neukantismus*," in *Historisches Wörterbuch der Philosophie*, Bd. 6, Basle/Stuttgart, Schwabe, 1984, col. 747–54.

2. E. Zeller, *Ueber Bedeutung und Aufgabe der Erkenntnistheorie. Vortrag bei Eröffnung der Vorlesungen über Logik und Erkenntnistheorie, den 22. Oktober 1862 in Heidelberg gehalten*, in *Vorträge und Abhandlungen*, Leipzig, Fries, 1877, 2. Sammlung, p. 490.

3. O. Liebmann, *Kant und die Epigonen. Eine kritsche Abhandlung*, Stuttgart, C. Schober, 1865, pp. 85, 109, 138, 156, 204, 216.

4. E. Winter, op. cit., p. 60. For this historical judgment Winter quotes, E. Troeltsch, *Das logische Problem der Geschichtsphilosophie*, in *Die Entstehung des Historismus*, in *Gesammelte Schriften*, Bd. 3, Tübingen, Mohr, 1922, p. 314; K. Schilling, *Geschichte der Philosophie*, Munich, E. Reinhardt, 1953², Bd. 2, p. 342; J. Hirschberger, *Geschichte der Philosophie*, Teil II, *Neuzeit und Gegenwart*, Freiburg, Herder, 1952, p. 395.

5. H. von Treitschke, *Deutsche Geschichte im neunzehnten Jahrhundert*, Leipzig, S. Hirzel, 1907, Bd. 5, p. 425: "The country was sick and tired of philosophy up to the point of nausea"; quoted by E. Winter, op. cit., p. 66.

6. Cf. H.-M. Sass, *Daseinsbedeutende Funktionen von Wissen und Glauben im Jahrzehnt 1860–1870*, in "Zeitschrift für Religions- und Geistesgeschichte," xx (1968), pp. 113–38.

7. K. Vogt, *Köhlerglaube und Wissenschaft*, Giessen, J. Ricker 1854.

8. L. Büchner, *Kraft und Stoff, oder Grundzüge der natürlichen Weltordnung. Nebst einer darauf gebauten Moral- oder Sittenlehre. In allgemein verstänlicher Darstellung*, Frankfurt, Meidinger Sohn & Cie, 1855.

267

9. Cf., for example, F. E. Beneke, *Kant und die philosophische Aufgabe unserer Zeit. Eine Jubeldenkschrift auf die Kritik der reinen Vernunft*, Berlin, E. S. Mittler, 1832, p. 43.

10. Cf., for example, Ch. H. Weisse, *In welchem Sinn die deutsche Philosophie jetzt wieder an Kant sich zu orientiren hat*, Leipzig, Dyk, 1847, p. 22.

11. Cf., for example, R. Haym, *Hegel und seine Zeit*, Berlin, R. Gaertner, 1857, p. 468.

12. Cf., for example, E. Zeller, *Ueber Bedeutung und Aufgabe der Erkenntnistheorie*, cit., 2. Sammlung, p. 490.

13. M. Campo, *Schizzo storico della esegesi e critica kantiana. Dal "ritorno a Kant" alla fine dell'Ottocento*, Varese, Ed. Magenta, 1959, p. 16.

14. J. E. Erdmann, *Grundriss der Geschichte der Philosophie*, Berlin, W. Hertz, 1896, Bd. 2, p. 728.

15. P. Natorp, *Kant und die Marburger Schule*, in "Kant-Studien," xvii (1912), p. 194. The statement by Wilhelm Windelband "Understanding Kant means going beyond him," which the Neo-Kantians were fond of repeating, is well known (*Präludien. Aufsätze und Reden zur Philosophie und ihrer Geschichte*, Tübingen, 1921[7], J. C. B. Mohr/Paul Siebeck, Bd. 1, p. iv).

16. H. Helmholtz, *Ueber das Sehen des Menschen* (1855), in *Vorträge und Reden*, Brunswick, Vierweg, 1896[4], Bd. 1, pp. 85–117.

17. F. A. Lange, *Geschichte des Materialismus und Kritik seiner Bedeutung in der Gegenwart*, Iserlohn, Baedeker, 1866; quotations come from the fourth edition, Iserlohn/Leipzig, 1887.

18. O. Liebmann, *Kant und die Epigonen*, cit. See also Idem, *Ueber den objectiven Anblick*, Stuttgart, C. Schober, 1869.

19. H. Helmholtz, *Ueber das Sehen des Menschen*, cit., p. 116.

20. Cf. *ibid.*

21. Cf. E. Cassirer, *Hermann Cohen und die Erneuerung der Kantischen Philosophie*, in "Kant-Studien," xvii (1912), p. 257.

22. J. Ebbinghaus, *Hermann Cohen als Philosoph und Publizist*, in "Archiv für Philosophie," vi (1956), p. 110.

23. The dispute between Trendelenburg and Fischer broke out over the former's theses in his *Logische Untersuchungen*, Berlin 1840, Leipzig 1862[2], and was carried on in the following works: K. Fischer, *System der Logik und Metaphysik oder Wissenschaftslehre*, Heidelberg, F. Bassermann, 1865[2]; A. Trendelenburg, *Über eine Lücke in Kants Beweis von der ausschliessenden Subjektivität des Raumes und der Zeit*, in *Historische Beiträge zur Philosophie*, 3 (1867), pp. 215–76; K. Fischer, *Geschichte der neueren Philosophie*, Heidelberg, F. Bassermann, 1854–1877, Bd. 3 and 4, 1869[2]; A. Trendelenburg, *Kuno Fischer und sein Kant: Eine Entgegnung*,

Leipzig, S. Hirzel, 1869; K. Fischer, *Anti-Trendelenburg. Eine Duplik,* Jena, H. Dabis, 1870. Among those who intervened in the dispute, Cohen cites the following (cf. *S I:* 230): R. Quäbiker, *Rezension der Trendelenburgschen Broschüre,* in "Philosophische Monatshefte," iv (1869), pp. 236–49, 408–14; C. Grapengiesser, *Kants Lehre von Raum und Zeit; Kuno Fischer und Adolf Trendelenburg,* Jena 1870; Bergmann, *Rezension der Grapengiesserschen Schrift,* in "Philosophische Monatshefte," v (1870), n. 3, pp. 273–8; E. Bratuschek, *Kuno Fischer und Trendelenburg,* in "Philosophische Monatshefte," v (1870), pp. 279–323. In Italy, the dispute was discussed by F. Masci, *Una polemica su Kant,* Naples, Morano, 1873, and P. Ragnisco, *La critica della ragion pura di Kant: studi,* Naples, Perrotti, 1873. For a more detailed and complete bibliography of the Trendelenburg-Fischer dispute, cf. H. Vaihinger, *Kommentar zu Kants Kritik der reinen Vernunft,* Stuttgart, Union deutsche Verlagsgesellschaft, 1922²; repr. Aalen, Scientia Verlag, 1970, Bd. 2, pp. 545–48.

24. Cf. Cohen's letter to H. Lewandowsky October 3, 1870, in H. Cohen, *Briefe,* ausgewählt und herausgegeben von Bertha und Bruno Strauss, Berlin, Schocken Verlag/Jüdischer Buchverlag, 1939, p. 28.

25. In his essay Cohen provides the following summary of Trendelenburg's well known thesis: "Kant claims to have demonstrated not only the pure subjectivity, but, at the same time, the *exclusive* subjectivity of space and time. Space and time must not be simply pure, a priori intuitions, in as much as they precede every experience, but representations grounded *solely and exclusively in the forms of our sensibility.* Thus they must not only *precede* every experience, but also be *modifications of our sensibility, which take place solely within us.* Here Trendelenburg exclaims: Stop! Where did Kant demonstrate *this* meaning of the subjective, *exclusive* subjectivity? So he puts the demonstrations which should allegedly establish this *exclusive* subjectivity to the test, but discovers that they are without foundation. He only finds that *pure* subjectivity has been demonstrated, while nowhere is the same true for *simple* subjectivity" (*S I:* 234). Cohen was to point out later that these criticisms of Kant by Trendelenburg grew out of a mistaken conception in the latter of "constructive motion"; cf. *LRE* 226.

26 Cf. H.-L. Ollig, op. cit., p. 37. This is also Ollig's interpretation of a passage in H. Liebeschütz, *Von Georg Simmel zu Franz Rosenzweig. Studien zum Jüdischen Denken im deutschen Kulturbereich,* Tübingen, J. C. B. Mohr (Paul Siebeck), 1970, p. 17, which seems to me, however, to be less obvious.

27. Trendelenburg's influence on Cohen, which is still awaiting detailed study, is pointed out by G. Lehmann, *Geschichte der Philosophie,* Bd. 9: *Die Philosophie des neunzehnten Jahrhunderts II,* Berlin, de Gruyter,

1953, p. 75, and by P. Schulthess, *Einleitung*, in *W 5/I*, pp. 10* n. 5, 25* n. 56, 27* n. 64. Some brief references to this influence can be found in G. Gigliotti, *Hermann Cohen e la fondazione kantiana dell'etica*, Florence, Sansoni, 1977, pp. 57 ff.

28. Cf. Cohen's letter to Hermann Lewandowsky dated November 8, 1865, in H. Cohen, *Briefe*, cit., p. 19.

29. Cf. F. A. Lange's letter dated September 5, 1874, in F. A. Lange, *Über Politik und Philosophie. Briefe und Leitartikel 1862 bis 1875*, hg. von Georg Eckert, Duisburg, Walter Braun Verlag, 1968, p. 377.

30. On Cohen's conception of the history of philosophy cf. E. Winter, op. cit., pp. 86ff. Among other things, Winter clearly shows that Cohen's acceptance of the psychological method of Lazarus and Steinthal was more apparent than real, and makes an interesting comparison between Cohen's hermeneutic method and that of Gadamer.

31. Cohen states that the discovery of Kant's "fundamental thought" must be guided by a "psychological method" (*S I:* 271). However, the extent to which this statement is only a left over from his acceptance of the *Völkerpsychologie* of Lazarus and Steinthal, which he was largely leaving behind him, clearly comes out from comparison between the truly psychological method he had used for interpreting Plato in the 1866 essay *Die platonische Ideenlehre psychologisch entwickelt*, and the method he was about to use for the interpretation of Kant (cf. *KTE*[1]), which is already philosophical rather than psychological. Kant's fundamental thought was to be discovered by means of the interpreter's philosophical hypothesis, and not through a reconstruction of the psychic process of the author under study. What remains as a common feature both of the earlier psychological method and "the subsequent philosophical method," is the approach required of the interpreter. Far from taking on a neutral, detached standpoint as regards the object of his interpretation, he must immerse himself (*sich versenken*) in the author he is interpreting, so as to be able to understand him. This need for "immersion," which had been mentioned regarding the interpretation of Plato in *Die platonische Ideenlehre psychologisch entwickelt* (cf. *S I:* 33), when Cohen was still explicitly using a psychological interpretive method, was newly emphasized, in the same terms, regarding the interpretation of Kant, in a lecture given in 1904, *Rede bei der Gedankfeier der Universität Marburg zur 100 Wiederkehr des Todestages von Immanuel Kant*, in *S I:* 488.

32. K. Fischer, *Geschichte der neueren Philosophie*, cit., Bd. 1, p. XVI; quoted by Cohen in *S I:* 231.

33. H. Dussort, *L'école de Marbourg*, Paris, P.U.F., 1963, p. 87 n. 1, makes the following comment: "The reader will certainly be struck by

this observation on the danger of historical studies, published three years before Nietzsche made it the theme of the second of his *Unzeitgemässe Betrachtungen.*"

34. E. Winter, op. cit., p. 98.

35. Cf. H.-M. Sass, op. cit., pp. 113ff.

36. K. Fischer, *Geschichte der neueren Philosophie*, cit., Bd. 1, p. xvi; quoted by Cohen in *S I:* 274, also thought of "the history of philosophy as, at the present time, the most important of the philosophical sciences."

37. Letter quoted by W. Kinkel, *Hermann Cohen. Eine Einführung in sein Werk*, Stuttgart, Strecker und Schröder, 1924, p. 46.

38. H. Cohen, *Briefe*, cit., p. 24.

39. In July 1870, Cohen wrote: "I must severely criticize Trendelenburg. I am of the opinion that he has completely misunderstood Kant. To such an extent that Fischer is right to be surprised that, after such a short time, Kant is so little known by colleagues" (letter quoted by W. Kinkel, op. cit., p. 46). Furthermore, in a letter to Hermann Lewandowsky dated August 15 1871, Cohen wrote: The progress of German philosophy consists, unfortunately, in the fact that, with the exception of Herbart the psychologist, they are developing Kant's mistakes. The Great Man is linked to the century that followed him by his own weak points! Thus, even Schopenhauer, as a constructor, as a metaphysician and poet, as compared with his Kant is on the wane. The result is that Kant is misunderstood by him precisely where he should be disparaged. Nevertheless, I am learning a great deal from him for the comprehension of Kant, even in the points where he is wrong. . . . Having seen how one can be mistaken, I have gone further, in order to understand the profound wisdom and art in the writing of Kant, who rejected all that; but I have certainly gained very much" (H. Cohen, *Briefe*, cit. p. 31).

40. Cf. W. Kinkel, op. cit., p. 47.

41. Cf. the letter from Cohen to Hermann Lewandowsky dated August 2, 1870, in H. Cohen, *Briefe*, cit., p. 25.

42. M. Campo., op. cit., p. 61.

43. I. Kant, *Kritik der reinen Vernunft*, 2. Auflage, Akademie Ausgabe, Bd. 3, p. 27; English trans. N. Kemp Smith, London, Macmillan, 1929, p. 41.

44. *Ibid.*, p. 13; English trans. cit., p. 23.

45. *Ibid.*, p. 54; English trans. cit., pp. 70–71.

46. Cf. J. F. Herbart, *Psychologie als Wissenschaft neu gegründet auf Erfahrung, Metaphysik und Mathematik. Erster synthetischer Teil (1824)*, in Idem, *Sämtliche Werke*, hg. von Karl Kehrbach und Otto Flügel, Bd. 5,

Langensalza, H. Beyer & Söhne, 1890; repr. Aalen, Scientia Verlag, 1964, pp. 427ff.

47. At this stage in the development of his thought, Cohen regarded "formal logic" and empirical psychology as comparable: cf. *KTE*[1] 205f. A detailed analysis of the metaphysical deduction of the a priori and of its role in Cohen's interpretation of Kant was carried out by W. De Schmidt, *Psychologie und Transzendentalphilosophie. Zur Psychologie-Rezeption bei Hermann Cohen und Paul Natorp*, Bonn, Bouvier (Herbert Grundmann), 1976, pp. 39ff.

48. Cf. I. Kant, *Kritik der reinen Vernunft*, 2. Auflage, cit., p. 94; English trans. cit., p. 114.

49. A.Trendelenburg, *Logische Untersuchungen*, cit., Bd. 1, p. 163.

50. I. Kant, *Kritik der reinen Vernunft*, 2. Auflage, cit., p. 145; English trans. cit., p. 194.

51. *Ibid.*, p. 13; English trans. cit., p. 23.

52. As we have seen (cf. note 23 above), Trendelenburg published an essay entitled *Über eine Lücke in Kants Beweis von der ausschliessenden Subjektivität des Raumes und der Zeit*, cit.

53. Berlin, W. Hertz, 1870.

54. Cf. K. Fischer, *System der Logik und Metaphysik oder Wissenschaftslehre*, Heidelberg, F. Bassermann, 1865[2], p. 112; cit. in *KTE*[1] 106n.

55. Cf. I. Kant, *Kritik der reinen Vernunft*, 2 Auflage, cit., p. 263; English trans. cit., p. 330.

56. Cf. J. B. Meyer, op. cit., p. 174; cit. in *KTE*[1] 124.

57. H. Cohen, *Briefe*, cit., pp. 28–29.

58. It is interesting to note how Spinoza is still included in this list of the principal idealist thinkers. Cohen's attitude to him was soon to become very hostile. It is also interesting that Leibniz's name is missing. His philosophy was to influence Cohen's idealism profoundly.

59. As further proof of this, Cohen wrote to Hermann Lewandowsky, nearly a year later in the following terms: "I am only now able to deal with your favorite theme: idealism in the natural sciences. Able from the philosophical viewpoint. If I now make further progress from the other viewpoint, then it could happen soon," (letter dated August 15, 1871, in H. Cohen, *Briefe*, cit., p. 31).

60. Cf. P. Natorp, *Kant und die Marburger Schule*, cit., pp. 194ff.; A. Görland, *Hermann Cohens systematische Arbeit im Dienste des kritischen Idealismus*, in "Kant-Studien," xvii (1912), pp. 250ff.; E. Cassirer, *Kants Leben und Lehre*, Berlin, Bruno Cassirer, 1921, p. viii. Many other similar quotations could be drawn from other members of the Marburg school.

61. G. Edel, *Einleitung,* in *W 1/I*: p. 20*. Cf. also H. Dussort, op. cit., pp. 96f. Dussort sees the crucial difference between Neo-Kantianism and phenomenology in the interpretation of experience either in a limited sense as science, or in a wider sense as the set of "all experiences, be they affective or cognitive."

62. Cf., for example, *KTE*[1] 206, 208.

63. "This is exactly the change we owe to the Marburg school: the capacity to raise transcendental from its former role as a simple adjective to that of a fundamental method, and to have brought to light a reverse dependency relationship between the two terms: the raison d'être of the *a priori* only holds through the transcendental method": A. Stériad, *L'interprétation de la doctrine de Kant par l'école de Marbourg (Etude sur l'Idéalisme critique)*, Paris, M. Giard & E. Brière, 1913, p. 31.

64. I. Kant, *Kritik der reinen Vernunft,* 2. Auflage, cit., p. 338n.; English trans. cit., p. 439n.

CHAPTER TWO. THE INTERPRETATION OF PLATO

1. Cf. P. Natorp, *Kant und die Marburger Schule,* cit., p. 219.

2. Cf. Cohen's letter to Hermann Lewandowsky, November 8, 1865, in H. Cohen, *Briefe,* cit., p. 19.

3. *Philosophorum de antinomia necessitatis et contingentiae doctrinae* (1865), in *SI:* 1-29.

4. Cf. the anonymous review of H. Cohen, *Platons Ideenlehre und die Mathematik,* in "Jahresbericht über die Fortschritte in die klass: Altertumswissenschaft" vii (1879), pp. 198-9; E. Hohmann, *Plato ein Vorgänger Kants? Kritische Bemerkungen zu P. Natorps "Platos Ideenlehre. Eine Einführung in den Idealismus,"* Progr. Nr. 16 des Königl. Gymnasium zu Rössel, 1906; A. Stériad, *L'interprétation de la doctrine de Kant par l'école de Marbourg (Étude sur l'idéalisme critique)* cit.; F. Sirchia, *L'idealismo di Hermann Cohen,* in *Contributi dell'Istituto di Filosofia; Pubblicazioni dell'Università del Sacro Cuore,* Milan, Vita e Pensiero, 1969, pp. 115ff. Alice Stériad (cf. p. 24) is right in her opinion that criticism of Cohen for interpreting Plato through Kant should be reversed when recognizing the crucial importance for Cohen's interpretation of Kant of his reading of Plato. However, she believes that Cohen's ideas on Plato being a forerunner of Kant in the transcendental method were already "firm and very clear" (p. 24) by the time the 1866 work appeared. This historiographical judgment has its importance in Stériad's interpretation of Cohen. It is indeed a premise to the conviction she expresses later on in her book (pp. 55ff.) that the reduction of intuition to thought is not the result of a development in Cohen's interpretation of Kant, but an idea

that was already part of his future plans right from the beginning. He simply had not taken it further because of a certain caution in "preparing the ground." Stériad does, admittedly, add that this "clear vision of consequent idealism" can certainly be attributed to Cohen "*at least* from 1883 onwards" [my italics]. In my view, two aspects of Stériad's position can be unconditionally accepted: the importance given to Plato in Cohen's interpretation of Kant, and the, admittedly indirect, connection between Cohen's interpretation of Plato and the reduction of intuition to thought in his development and modification of Kant's gnoseology. Nevertheless, I believe that Cohen's conception of these matters does not antedate 1878, the year *Platons Ideenlehre und die Mathematik* was published. In his 1866 work he was a long way from considering Plato to be the originator of the "method of purity," and, even though he explicitly aligned Plato with Kant, he considered this alignment as evolving in the direction of Fichte and the importance attributed to the theme of intellectual intuition by the latter.

5. Cf. E. Hohmann, op. cit., p. 3.

6. On the contrary, this position received passing confirmation in *Platons Ideenlehre und die Mathematik* (cf. *S I*: 347).

7. In his *Philosophorum de antinomia necessitatis et contingentiae*, in *S I*: 29, Cohen posited the following thesis: "*Omnem philisophiae progressum in psychologia constitutum esse.*"

8. Cohen refers to K. F. Hermann's chronology of the Platonic dialogues (cf. *S I*: 60). For an outline of this chronological scheme, see E. Zeller, *Die Philosophie der Griechen in ihrer geschichtlichen Entwicklung*, Teil 2, Abteilung I, Leipzig, O. R. Reisland, 1922[5], p. 501, n. 2.

9. Cf. *KBA* 7; *ARG I*: 243; *Der deutsche Idealismus und die Antike* (1916), in *S II*: 306.

10. Cf., for example, *Charakteristik der Ethik Maimunis* (1908), in *J III*: 223.

11. Cf. *KTE* 643; *LRE* 21; *BR* 30; *Der deutsche Idealismus und die Antike*, in *S II*: 306.

12. The bias toward Fichte of this essay was also recognized in A. Levi, *Sulle interpretazioni immanentistiche della filosofia di Platone*, Turin, Paravia, no date (1920?), p. 88. H. Dussort, op. cit., p. 76 uses the expression *Fichtean interpretation* of Plato.

13. Comparison is invited between *Platons Ideenlehre und die Mathematik* and the reconstruction of ancient philosophy in F. A. Lange, *Geschichte des Materialismus und Kritik seiner Bedeutung in der Gegenwart*, cit. regarding several important themes, e.g., apart from the interpretation of Democritus (pp. 9ff.), the relationship between Socrates and Plato (pp. 54f.) and Heraclitus' influence on Plato (p. 55), the substantialist

interpretation of Platonic ideas, (p. 56) the separation between reason and sensibility (p. 59), the nonscientific nature of Platonic philosophy (pp. 60f.), the relationship between Plato and Aristotle (p. 61).

14. "It was Socrates who originated the new tendency. Plato sealed it with idealism, and Aristotle, combining it with empirical elements, created the encyclopedic system which was to keep thought in chains for centuries" (*Ibid.*, p. 44).

15. Cf. also pp. 30, 53f.

16. Cohen's conviction that Plato's theory of ideas established idealism, *inasmuch as* it consists of a theory of knowledge, is evident right from the beginning of *Platons Ideenlehre und die Mathematik* and is the fundamental perspective of his interpretation of Plato (cf. *S I:* 336). This crucial point in Cohen's interpretation of Plato, and in that of the Marburg school after him, has been underestimated by critics. Admittedly, Cohen and his school are partly to blame for this, since the title *Platons Ideenlehre . . .* , which Cohen chose for his essay, and to which his school gave classic status (A. Auffarth, *Die platonische Ideenlehre*, Inaugural-Dissertation, Marburg 1883; P. Natorp, *Platos Ideenlehre: Eine Einführung in den Idealismus*, Leipzig, Dürr, 1903, 1921²; Darmstadt, F. Meiner, Wissenschaftliche Buchgesellschaft, 1961³; Idem, *Über Platos Ideenlehre*, Berlin, Reuther & Reichard, 1914) is not explicit concerning the methodological or gnoseological perspective of the school's interpretation of Plato. Nevertheless, even though many of the critics' views, in their overall objection to the Marburg school's not having provided an objective, comprehensive interpretation of Plato's ideas, are well founded, they do not appear to me to have a really firm grasp of this interpretation, when considering it in the light of the question: What are ideas? Viewed in such a way, the problem has already taken an ontological turn. The originality of Cohen and his school, in this respect, consists in their having conceived Plato's ideas bearing in mind the question: Why are ideas (=true) while being (=sensible reality) is not? Thus the problem is really to be seen in the sense of ideas being true, i.e. in their foundation. The meaning of the Platonic dialectic is recognized in the identification of ideas with the groundbreaking activity of reason. The mistaken perspective I have already mentioned can be seen, for example, in H. Gomperz, *Review* of P. Natorp, *Platos Ideenlehre*, in "Archiv für Philosophie; I Abteilung: Archiv für Geschichte der Philosophie," 18, Neue Folge 11 (1905), pp. 441–95. A. Levi, op. cit., p. 223, appears to have realized that Cohen had a special perspective, but he rejected it without discussing it adequately and noting its considerable philosophical significance. What he sees as a simple "substitution of the hypothetical nature of the method of searching for Idea for that of Idea itself" is in

fact a conscious identification in Cohen. A clear example of the perspective adopted by the Marburg school is provided by G. Falter, *Platos Ideenlehre*, in "Archiv für Geschichte der Philosophie, "21, Neue Folge 14 (1908), p. 364, who, in reply to Gomperz's objection to Natorp: "Is the ox a method?" (H. Gomperz, op. cit., p. 444), explains: "Of course "the ox" is not a method in the sense Herr Gomperz means. However, a method is needed to formulate the concept of ox and to objectify a new phenomenon such as "the ox"; a method, or hypothesis of 'the ox.' Do you understand, Herr Gomperz? Idea for Plato, as for Kepler and Plotinus before him, is the expression for the law in which we objectify nature. The intellect produces being by means of foundations. To quote Plotinus, "the intellect is the legislator of being" (Enneads V 8.5)."

17. This radical criticism of Aristotle's interpretation of Plato is evidence of a further contrast between *Platons Ideenlehre und die Mathematik* and *Die platonische Ideenlehre psychologisch entwickelt*. Not only does Cohen refrain from criticizing Aristotle's interpretation in his 1866 essay, but he even fully accepts its validity (cf. *S I:* 87).

18. Cf. I. Kant, *Prolegomena zu einer jeden künftigen Metaphysik die als Wissenschaft wird auftreten können*, Akademie Ausgabe, Bd. 4, p. 375.

19. Cf. Plato, *Republic*, 510f.

20. Here Cohen quotes (*S I:* 361) H. Hankel, *Zur Geschichte der Mathematik im Altertum und Mittelalter*, Leipzig, B.G. Teubner, 1874, p. 149.

21. Plato, *Republic*, 511 b.

22. Plato, *Phaedo*, 101 e.

23. Here Cohen is no longer referring to *Republic* 511, where a distinction is made between νόησις and διάνοια, but to *Republic* 533 e–534 a, where ἐπιστήμη and διάνοια are subsumed by νόησις.

24. It has already been noted (see the beginning of section 1) that P. Natorp, *Kant und die Marburger Schule*, cit., p. 219 refers to Cohen's further investigation of Kant by way of Plato, and A. Stériad, op. cit., p. 24, believes the influence of Plato on Cohen's reading of Kant to be even more important, though her argument does not entirely convince me (see note 4 above). Interestingly, G. de Ruggiero, *La filosofia contemporanea. Germania—Francia—Inghilterra—America—Italia*, Bari, Laterza, 1951[6], p. 74, goes even further in his insistence on Plato's influence on Cohen. He writes that Cohen was "a Platonist with reminiscences of Kantism entirely alien to his philosophical teaching"! However, for De Ruggiero Platonism and Kantianism have different, and in some respects opposite, meanings to those intended by Cohen. For this reason De Ruggiero's criticism appears extrinsic.

25. In defending the Marburg school's interpretation of Plato against H. Gomperz (cf. op. cit.), G. Falter, op. cit., p. 364, writes: "Thought and event cannot be separated. The fact that Herr Gomperz does just this shows that he identifies thinking with representing. Scientific thought, thought in scientific concepts, is not representation. Concepts preserve thought from the subjectivity of representation. Truth would be illusory, if thinking and representing could not be separated."

26. Cf. chapter 9, sections 4 and 7 in this book.

27. However, only passing reference is made, to these developments in the subsequent editions of *Kants Theorie der Erfahrung*, where Cohen substantially repeats the interpretation of Plato's theory of ideas to be found in *Platons Ideenlehre und die Mathematik* (cf. *KTE* 13ff.).

28. On the Platonic Idea as a development of the Socratic concept cf. *KBE* 91f.; *LRE* 15, 30, 211, 311, 316f., 344, 374, 376, 502f., 528; *E* 16ff.; *ERW* 209 f.; *Charakteristik der Ethik Maimunis*, in *J III*: 222f.; *Über das Eigentümliche des deutschen Geistes* (1914), in *S I:* 541; *BR* 34, 48; *Der deutsche Idealismus und die Antike*, in *S II:* 306; *Das soziale Ideal bei Platon und den Propheten* (a lecture given for the first time in 1916, published posthumously in 1924), in *J I*: 308; *RV* 464; Eng. trans. 400. On Idea as "foundation" cf. *KTE* 22; *LRE* 20, 30, 94, 211; *E* 18, 31; *ERW* 429, 512; *Charakteristik der Ethik Maimunis*, in *J III:* 224; *ARG I:* 22, 73, 88, 243; *Über das Eigentümliche des deutschen Geistes*, in *S I:* 540; *BR* 28; *Der deutsche Idealismus und die Antike*, in *S II:* 308 f.; *Das soziale Ideal bei Platon und den Propheten*, in *J I:* 308 f.

29. Cf. *E* 17f.; *ARG I:* 73; *BR* 48; *Über das Eigentümliche des deutschen Geistes*, in *S I:* 540.

30. Cf. also *Das soziale Ideal bei Platon und den Propheten*, in *J I:* 309.

31. *Jubiläums-Betrachtungen. Rezension von: Philosophische Aufsätze. Eduard Zeller zu seinem fünfzigjährigen Doctor-Jubiläum gewidmet* (1888), in *S I:* 404.

32. Cf. *Über das Eigentümliche des deutschen Geistes*, in *S I:* 541.

CHAPTER THREE. THE NEW INTERPRETATION OF KANT
AND THE DEFINITION OF CRITICAL IDEALISM

1. F. Staudinger, *Review* of H. Cohen, *Kants Theorie der Erfahrung*, 2. Auflage, in "Philosophische Monatshefte," xxii (1886), pp. 402–3.

2. A list of the main differences between the first and second editions of *Kants Theorie der Erfahrung* can be found in H. Dussort, op. cit., p. 121 n. 6 and in G. Edel, *Einleitung*, in *W1/I:* 26* f. n. 22.

3. Cohen sees the distinction between the Plato-Kant and Aristotelian-empiricist traditions as grounded in the recognition of the fundamental relationship between mathematics and science: cf. *KTE* 35f. On Aristotle cf. *KTE* 25–31; on the empiricists cf. *KTE* 60–79.

4. However, Cohen does mention many other thinkers in his reconstruction of the history of critical idealism, among whom are Nicholas of Cusa, Galileo, Descartes and Newton. Even before the appearance of *Das Prinzip der Infinitesimal-Methode und seine Geschichte* and the second edition of *Kants Theorie der Erfahrung* this history had been outlined in *Von Kants Einfluss auf die deutsche Kultur. Rede bei der Marburger Universitäts-feier des Geburtstages Sr. Majestät des Kaisers und Königs am 17. März 1883*, in *S I: 371*.

5. On Cohen's interpretation of Leibniz see W. Marx, *Transzendentale Logik als Wissenschaftstheorie. Systematisch-kritische Untersuchungen zur philosophischen Grundlegungsproblematik in Cohens "Logik der reinen Erkenntnis,"* Frankfurt, Klostermann, 1977, pp. 82 ff.; V. Zeman, *Leibniz's Influence on the Marburg School, in particular on Hermann Cohen's conception of Reality and of the "Infinitesimal-Methode,"* in *Akten des Internationalen Leibniz-Kongresses,* Hannover 1977, in "Studia Leibnitiana," suppl. vol. 21, Wiesbaden 1980, pp. 145–52; P. Schulthess, *Einleitung* in *W 5/I*; H. Holzey, *Die Leibniz-Rezeption im "Neukantianismus" der Marburger Schule,* in *Leibniz. Werk und Wirkung. IV Intern. Leibniz-Kongress. Vorträge,* Hannover 1983, pp. 287–95.

6. For this distinction, the presence of both conceptions in Leibniz, their development in the history of philosophical and scientific thought up to Cohen, and Cohen's own position, see P. Schulthess, *Einleitung* in *W 5/I*: 14*ff.

7. In this passage it is clear how Cohen interprets Leibniz in relation to his formulation of the problem of Platonic idealism.

8. This is, to all intents and purposes, the essence of Leibniz's fidelity to the teaching of Plato and of his advance on the position of Descartes: "The incalculable value of Leibniz's idealism lies in the fact that he, more sharply and more clearly than Descartes, gave new life to the originary thought of Platonism, in thought and reason in the face of sensation and sensibility, i.e. that nature must be discovered in consciousness, matter must be constituted in thought" (*KTE* 57–8).

9. "Since Leibniz does not take a specific *concept of knowledge* as his starting point, as Kant does with the *mathematical science of nature,* or else from experience, consequently, he makes no exact distinction between *infinity as a fundamental law of the production of reality (realisierender Grundsatz)* and the *simple as a regulative principle (regulatives Prinzip);*

rather, he confuses the two meanings of the monad *or else* of substance, which he in conformity calls *atom* (*PIM* 55–6).

10. Friedrich Kuntze, in his substantial monograph, *Die Philosophie Salomon Maimons*, Heidelberg, Carl Winter, 1912, p. 339, notes that "*Cohen* in his *Das Prinzip der Infinitesimal-Methode und seine Geschichte* (Berlin 1883) transformed the Kantian principle of anticipations in exactly the same way, using the same means, and with the same systematic purpose as Maimon. But is striking is that Cohen appears not to have been acquainted with Maimon's work on this matter. He does not quote Maimon, even though he is well acquainted with the ideas of *Bendavid*." G. Lehman, op. cit., p. 76, takes up this opinion again and enlarges on it: "One should understand *Cohen's* Neo-Kantianism starting out more from *Maimon* than *Kant.* Just as Maimon places transcendental logic before the transcendental aesthetic, conceives the given as infinitesimal reality, establishes the thing-in-itself as idea, Cohen does likewise." It is true that Maimon's name is curiously missing from Cohen's works (as far as I know, apart from the note in *KTE²/KTE³*, to which I shall refer, the name is mentioned only once in Cohen's works, in *Innere Beziehungen der kantischen Philosophie zum Judentum* (1910), in *J I:* 302). In a note in *KTE²* 424, Cohen writes: "Salomon Maimon cogently argued for the connection between consciousness and differential in his investigations of transcendental philosophy." In an addition to the same note, in *KTE³* 540, Cohen criticizes Kuntze: "*Kuntze* ignored the addition to this note, in the second edition, in his criticism of me. It extends my links with Maimon beyond the above mentioned limits." Cohen's words are certainly not a sufficient acknowledgment of Maimon's earlier contribution to the interpretation of the infinitesimal in Kant. Thus Kuntze's doubts maintain their validity, at least on this point. Simply in order to provide some further details for anyone who wishes to explore the problem of Cohen's lack of attention to Maimon further, I shall just mention the fact here that Cohen's failure to mention this writer forms part of his general lack of interest in the whole group of the initial interpreters of the theory of knowledge in Kant (with the partial exception of *Bendavid*); perhaps, then, the problem should be dealt with in these general terms. On the relationship between Cohen and Maimon: J. Gordin, *Untersuchungen zur Theorie des Unendlichen Urteils*, Berlin, Akademie Verlag, 1929 (in particular on the concept of 'differential' see pp. 31ff.); H. Bergmann, *Maimon und Cohen*, in "Monatsschrift für Geschichte und Wissenschaft des Judentums," lxxxiii (1939), pp. 548–61.

11. It will be recalled that the presence in Plato of the role of sensation as a stimulus to pure thought had already been foregrounded by Cohen.

12. I. Kant, *Kritik der reinen Vernunft*, 1. Auflage, Akademie Ausgabe, Bd. 4 p. 115; Eng. trans. cit., p. 201n.

13. I. Kant, *Kritik der reinen Vernunft*, 2. Auflage, cit., p. 151; Eng. trans. cit., p. 201.

14. Cf. G. Martin, *Immanuel Kant, Ontologie und Wissenschaftstheorie*, Berlin, de Gruyter, 1969⁴, p. 160.

15. In the first edition of *Kants Theorie der Erfahrung* Cohen had devoted little attention to the problem of the thing-in-itself, and had only accepted a negative meaning for it in Kant's writings. This was no doubt due to Cohen's concentrating, as we have already seen, on other problems in the interpretation of Kant. Nevertheless, one reason for this attitude can be sought in Cohen's acceptance of the Neo-Kantians' exclusive concentration on, and recognition of, the validity of Kant's philosophy in the transcendental method, underestimating the thing-in-itself theme, because they considered it ephemeral, incoherent with the rest of Kant's thought, and irretrievable. In the second edition of the same work, however, Cohen takes his distance from this attitude and, though continuing to maintain a central position for the transcendental method, attempts a recovery of the meaning of the thing-in-itself.

16. Cf. also *KBE* 36. The most significant variants in the 1st edition are "that designate and guarantee that real..."; 1st. edition: "...that designate the real" "in which the flux of phenomena takes on subsistence"; 1st. edition: "in which the reality of phenomena is grounded, in which it *holds good.*"

17. I. Kant, *Kritik der reinen Vernunft*, 2. Auflage, cit., p. 483; Eng. trans. cit., p. 420. For the difference between empirical contingency and intelligible contingency cf. Ibid. p. 318; Eng. trans. cit. p. 277.

18. Ibid., p. 82; Eng. trans. cit., pp. 100–101.

19. The most significant variants in the 1st edition are "*critical-cognitive*"; 1st. edition: "*theoretical-cognitive.*"

20. Subsequently, Cohen revised and corrected his point of view on the relationship between logic and ethics, in the direction of a greater independence of the latter from the former. However, his thesis of the need, within the theory of experience, for an extension of this theme to the world of ethics is still valid and is in fact one of the kernels of Cohen's critical idealism. On this development in Cohen's thought, see E. Winter, op. cit., pp. 224ff.

21. I. Kant, *Kritik der Urteilskraft*, Akademie Ausgabe, Bd. 5, p. 170; Eng; trans. by James Creed Meredith, Oxford, Clarendon Press, 1952, p. 6. As confirmation of Cohen's integration of Kant's theory of teleological judgment into the "theoretical part of philosophy" in the second edition of *Kants Theorie der Erfahrung*, it should be noted that Cohen never

published a complete interpretation of Kant's *Critique of Judgment*, as he did for Kant's two other *Critiques*, but only a discussion, in 1889, of Kant's theory of aesthetic judgment, entitled: *Kants Begründung der Ästhetik*, where only brief mention is made of teleological judgment in a chapter of the *Systematische Einleitung* (cf. *KBA* 102–27), which rapidly returns essentially to what he had written in *Kants Theorie der Erfahrung*, adding only a few references to aesthetic judgment and art.

22. Admittedly, I have not covered other, equally essential, aspects, such as the interpretation of Kant's ethics, carried out by Cohen in *Kants Begründung der Ethik*, Cohen's interpretation of Kant's aesthetics in his *Kants Begründung der Ästhetik*, and the conception of the philosophical system in the area of Kant's critical philosophy, to which Cohen devoted substantial attention in the last chapter of the second edition of *Kants Theorie der Erfahrung. Das System des kritischen Idealismus*. These important aspects, which have not yet been dealt with, will be analyzed later, in accordance with a strategy that requires step by step investigation of the meaning of critical philosophy in Cohen.

23. The perfect collaboration between Cohen and August Stadler and their influence on each other was decisive for the further investigation of the meaning of experience in Kant and its identification with science, as it was for several other aspects of Cohen's interpretation of Kant. Stadler (1850–1910) was a pupil of Lange, who suggested he contact Cohen in 1872, when the latter was lecturing in Berlin, to continue his philosophical studies with him. He attended Cohen's lectures on the *Critique of Pure Reason*. The two soon began to respect one another and became close friends (see the many letters written to Lange both by Cohen and by Stadler in F. A. Lange, *Über Politik und Philosophie. Briefe und Leitartikel 1862 bis 1875*, cit., pp. 360 ff.). It was precisely in the years between 1871 and 1885, when Cohen was working on his new interpretation of Kant, that Stadler demonstrated how brilliant he was at assimilating, developing, and giving new insights to what he had been taught, in a series of publications on the interpretation of Kant, including *Kants Theleologie und ihre erkenntnistheoretische Bedeutung*, Berlin, F. Dümmler, 1874; *Die Grundsätze der reinen Erkenntnistheorie in der Kantischen Philosophie*, Leipzig, S. Hirzel, 1876; *Kants Theorie der Materie*, Leipzig, S. Hirzel, 1883. In these works Stadler developed several interpretative insights such as the identification of experience with science, the priority of principles in respect of categories, the themes of the contingency of experience and of the regulative function of ideas, the meaning of the idea of end etc., all of which were to have a profound influence on Cohen. Therefore one can agree with H. Dussort, op. cit., p. 97, that Stadler was "the first member of the Marburg school *ante litteram*,"

adding, though, that the relationship between Stadler and Cohen did not only follow one direction, but was rather a "remarkable example of mutual emulation." Unfortunately, owing to lack of space, I am unable to go further into the fascinating Cohen-Stadler relationship. The first reference for a further investigation of this relationship is the obituary written by Cohen, *August Stadler. Ein Nachruf* (1910), in *S II:* 440–58; see also H. Dussort, op. cit., pp. 97 ff.; G. Gigliotti, op. cit., pp. 37 ff.; G. Edel, *Einleitung,* in *W 1/I:* 43*.

24. G. Edel, *Einleitung,* in *W 1/I:* 23*.

25. G. Lehmann, op. cit., p. 74.

26. Cf. E. Cassirer, *Hermann Cohen und die Erneuerung der Kantischen Philosophie,* cit., p. 261; P. Natorp, *Herman Cohens philosophische Leistung unter dem Gesichtspunkte des Systems,* Philosophische Vorträge veröffentlicht von der Kant-Gesellschaft Nr. 21, Berlin, Reuther & Reichard, 1918, p. 16.

27. W. Flach, *Einleitung,* in H. Cohen, *Das Prinzip der Infinitesimal-Methode und seine Geschichte. Ein Kapitel zur Grundlegung der Erkenntniskritik,* Frankfurt, M. Suhrkamp, 1968, p. 14.

28. See chapter 1, section 3.

29. Cf. G. Edel, *Einleitung,* in *W 1/I:* 30*; H. Holzhey, *Cohen und Natorp,* Bd. 1 cit., pp. 75f. provides a brief presentation of the main views on this problem.

30. In *KTE*[1] 134 Cohen wrote: "Transcendental apperception must explain the psychological fact that those phenomena are connected in 'functional identity' with an identical concept." In the second edition (*KTE*[2] 307), Cohen corrected himself: "Transcendental apperception does not merely have to explain a psychological fact, but the most fundamental fact of consciousness: that we objectify the content of inner sense, we shape it as an object of representation and knowledge. This objectification is ultimately grounded in transcendental of apperception, in a 'subjective condition,' which, as such, allows those inner sense phenomena to be connected in 'functional identity' with an identical concept." In *KTE*[3] 395, the passage remains unchanged except for the following variant: "the fundamental fact of consciousness."

31. H. Cohen, *Briefe,* cit., p. 44.

Chapter Four. Critical Idealism

1. Cf. J. Klein, *Die Grundlegung der Ethik in der Philosophie Hermann Cohens und Paul Natorps: Eine Kritik des Neokantianismus,* Göttingen, Vandenhoeck & Ruprecht, 1976.

2. J. Klatzkin, *Hermann Cohen*, Berlin, Jüdischer Verlag, 1919, p. 26.

3. By saying this I do not mean to give the impression that, as a preliminary point without further discussion, Cohen's idealism was not affected by the objections and criticisms directed against idealism in general by the adherents to the the the new philosophical trends. This problem can only be dealt with after Cohen's critical idealism has been subjected to detailed analysis, as regards its principles, content, and results. My intention here is to point out that this kind of idealism cannot merely be seen as an analogue, and even less as a development, of the idealism he calls "romantic." It cannot, therefore, be assimilated to the latter when idealism is under attack.

4. *Der deutsche Idealismus und die Antike*, in *S II:* 305.

5. Cf. *Der deutsche Idealismus und die Antike*, in *S II:* 309.

6. In this connection, it is worthwhile to recall the definition of idealism in *Platons Ideenlehre und die Mathematik*, in *S II:* 382f.; see also chapter 2, section 2.

7. *Der deutsche Idealismus und die Antike*, in *S II:* 313.

8. Cf. *Ibid.*, in *S II:* 313.

9. See chapter 2, section 2.

10. Cf. *Friedrich Albert Lange* (in "Preussische Jahrbücher" 1876), in *S II:* 374ff.

11. *Ibid.*, in *S II:* 382.

12. Cf. *Ibid.*, in *S II:* 382f.

13. Cf. I. Kant, *Preisschrift über die Fortschritte der Metaphisik*, Akademie Ausgabe, Bd. 20, 7, p. 263. Cf. also *KBE* 37; *KBA* 105.

14. Cf. I. Kant, *Kritik der reinen Vernunft*, 2. Auflage, cit., pp. 495ff.; Eng. trans. cit. pp. 436 ff.

15. *Platons Ideenlehre und die Mathematik*, in *S I:* 342.

16. M. Brelage, *Studien zur Transzendentalphilosophie*, Berlin, de Gruyter, 1965, p. 97.

17. *Ibid.*, p. 94.

18. S. Marck, *Die Lehre vom erkennenden Subjekt in der Marburger Schule*, in "Logos," iv (1913), pp. 364–86.

19. Cf. *Ibid.*, p. 370. On the basis of this and other considerations, Marck held that there was also an objective meeting of the Marburg school's philosophy of correlation with Hegel's philosophy of identity. Therefore, he placed the Marburg school in an instable position between Kant and Hegel.

20. *Ibid.*, p. 379.

21. N. Hartmann, *Grundzüge einer Metaphysik der Erkenntnis*, Berlin, de Gruyter, 1965^5, pp. 160ff.

22. *Ibid.*, p. 160.

23. *Ibid.*

24. Hartmann sees this as a case of panlogism, and thus, like Marck, though for different reasons, acknowledges substantial convergence between the Marburg school and Hegel.

25. *Ibid.*, p. 163.

26. Actually Brelage was dealing with critical philosophy in general, both that of the Marburg and that of the Baden schools. For this reason his views are relevant in both instances.

27. M. Brelage, op. cit., pp. 94–5.

28. *Ibid.*, p. 97.

29. *Ibid.*, pp. 103–4. A further interpretation of Cohen's philosophy as subjectivism can be found in F. Heinemann, *Neue Wege der Philosophie: Geist-Leben-Existenz. Eine Einführung in die Philosophie der Gegenwart*, Leipzig, Quelle & Meyer, 1929, pp. 62ff. On the problem of the interpretation of Cohen's philosophy as idealism without a subject, cf. also E. Winter, op. cit., pp. 202ff.

30. Cf. *KBE* 176; *Der deutsche Idealismus und die Antike*, in *S II*: 311; *Das soziale Ideal bei Platon und den Propheten*, in *J I*: 309.

31. Natorp also saw ethics as an expansion in respect of the theoretics of the Marburg school; cf. P. Natorp, *Kant und die Marburger Schule*, cit., p. 217.

32. Cf. *KTE* 783; *Der deutsche Idealismus und die Antike*, in *S II*: 311.

33. Similar remarks are also made about aesthetics, cf. *KTE* 736.

34. For the distinction between 'knowledge' and 'learning' cf. *KBE* 171ff.

35. Cf. *ERW* 328; *Das soziale Ideal bei Platon und den Propheten*, in *J I*: 309.

36. The passage from Kant, quoted by Cohen, comes from *Grundlegung zur Metaphysik der Sitten*, Akademie Ausgabe, Bd. 4, p. 427.

37. Cohen had already seen this in Kant's philosophy: cf. *Rede bei der Gedenkfeier der Universität Marburg zur 100 Wiederkehr des Todestages von Immanuel Kant*, in *S I*: 477. Cohen's certainty about the foundation of a new kind of metaphysics on a critical ground in Kant's practical, rather than in his theoretical, philosophy was to be a constant in the Marburg school. It was one of the fundamental themes in Cassirer's critique of Heidegger's interpretation of Kant at the Davos seminar: cf. E. Cassirer-M. Heidegger, *Davoser Disputation*, in M. Heidegger, *Kant und das Problem der Metaphysik*, Frankfurt, Klostermann, 1973⁴.

38. Cf. E. Fackenheim, *Hermann Cohen—After Fifty Years*, Leo Baeck Memorial Lecture 12, New York, Leo Baeck Institute, 1969, pp. 9f. Correct understanding of Cohen's ethical idealism as a principle of the

understanding of history clearly does not protect Cohen from possible criticism of his analyses of the historical facts and circumstances he had to evaluate. Such understanding only prevents the abstract nature of his idealism being held responsible for any errors in his historical judgment. I shall return to Cohen's philosophy of history in the last chapter. On the specific question of the idealist interpretation of the relationship between Judaism and Germanism, to which Fackenheim devotes particular attention, my views can be found in *La risposta di Hermann Cohen all'antigiudaismo*, in *Atti del secondo Convegno dell'Associazione Italiana per lo Studio del Giudaismo* (Bologna, November 4–5 1981), Rome, Carucci, 1983, pp. 59–75.

39. *Vom ewigen Frieden* (1914), in *S II*: 343.

40. *Religion und Sittlichkeit. Eine Betrachtung zur Grundlegung der Religionsphilosophie* (1907), in *J III*: 142.

41. *Ibid.*, in *J III*: 148.

42. Cf. *Der deutsche Idealismus und die Antike*, in *S II*: 319.

43. *Ibid.*, in *S II*: 314.

44. *Der Prophetismus und die Soziologie* (1917), in *J II*: 398.

45. *Der deutsche Idealismus und die Antike*, in *S II*: 317.

46. Cf. *Deutschtum und Judentum mit grundlegenden Betrachtungen über Staat und Internationalismus* (1916), in *J II*: 291. In the final part of chapter 4 and in chapter 6, section 2, it is shown how Cohen drew together all the positions in direct contrast with ethical idealism: eudemonism, materialism, Spinoza's pantheism, Hegel's philosophy of identity, and placed them in the category of naturalism.

47. The essence of pantheism had been present since its beginnings in Greek thought; cf. *BR* 24ff.

48. Cohen considered Spinoza's philosophy the classical model of pantheism, toward which he had only shown an inclination in one of his youthful works: *Heinrich Heine und das Judentum* (1867), in *J II*: 2–44. Subsequently, his opinion of Spinoza was to take a radically negative turn. Cohen specifically dealt with Spinoza in the essay: *Spinoza über Staat und Religion, Judentum und Christentum* (1915), in *J II*: 290–372. In 1910, he also gave a lecture entitled *Spinozas Verhältnis zum Judentum*, which was published, with an introduction by Franz Rosenzweig, in *Festgabe zum 10 jährigen Bestehen der Akademie für die Wissenschaft des Judentums 1919–29*, Berlin, Akademie-Verlag, 1929, pp. 42–68. See also Cohen's *review* of the book by J. Freudenthal, *Spinoza: Sein Leben und seine Lehre* (1904), in *S II*: 501–3. On Cohen and Spinoza see F. Rosenzweig, *Einleitung*, in *J I*: lv f.; L. Strauss, *Cohens Analyse der Bibelwissenschaft Spinozas*, in "Der Jude," viii (1924), pp. 905–811, C. Simon, *Zu Hermann Cohens Spinoza-Auffassung*, in "Monatsschrift für Geschichte und Wissenschaft des Judentums," lxxix

(1935), pp. 181–94, reprinted in Idem, *Brücken Gesammelte Aufsätze*, Heidelberg, Lambert Schneider, 1965, pp. 205–14, and in *Wissenschaft des Judentums im deutschen Sprachbereich. Ein Querschnitt*, Bd. 2, Tübingen, Mohr, 1967, pp. 539–49; H. Liebeschütz, *Hermann Cohen und Spinoza*, Bulletin No. 9 of the Leo Baeck Institute, Tel Aviv 1960, pp. 225–38; F. Nauen, *Hermann Cohen's Perception of Spinoza: A Reappraisal*, in "AJS Review" iv (1979), pp. 111–24.

49. Cf. *Religiöse Postulate* (1907), in *J I:* 5; *Die religiösen Bewegungen der Gegenwart* (1914), in *J I:* 57; *Deutschtum und Judentum* (1916), in *J II:* 312.

50. *Innere Beziehungen der Kantischen Philosophie zum Judentum*, in *J I:* 296.

51. Cf. *E* 115f.; *Charakteristik der Ethik Maimunis*, in *J III:* 284; *Der deutsche Idealismus und die Antike*, in *S II:* 318f.

52. *Der deutsche Idealismus und die Antike*, in *S II:* 321–22.

53. *Ibid.*, in *S II:* 322–23. On the concept of 'humor,' see chapter 7, section 1.

54. Just as Cohen had identified the origin of critical idealism in Plato, so he attributed the origin of eclecticism to Aristotle (cf. *LRE* 595). Concerning the mixture of sensualism, psychologism, and metaphysics in Aristotle, cf. *KTE* 25ff.

55. *Über das Eigentümliche des deutschen Geistes*, in *S I:* 546. Cf. also, *Eduard Zeller. Zu seinem 100. Geburtstag am 22. 1. 1914* (1914), in *S II:* 465.

56. Cf. *Innere Beziehungen der Kantischen Philosophie zum Judentum*, in *J I:* 288.

57. Cf., for example, *ARG I:* 12.

58. Cf. *KBA* 338ff.; *ARG I:* 10f., 34; *Spinoza über Staat und Religion, Judentum und Christentum*, in *J III:* 362.

59. Cf. *KBA* 340ff.; *ERW* 16; *Was einigt die Konfessionen?* (1917), in *J I:* 80.

60. On Cohen and Fichte see J. Solowiejczyk, *Das reine Denken und die Seinskonstituierung bei H. Cohen*, Diss., Berlin 1932, pp. 51 f.; J. Vuillemin, *L'héritage kantien et la révolution copernicienne. Fichte—Cohen - Heidegger*, Paris, P.U.F., 1954; H. Dussort, op. cit., pp. 78, 104 n. 2; G. Gigliotti, op. cit., pp. 50ff., 115ff.

61. H. Dussort, op. cit. p. 104 n. 2, disagrees with J. Vuillemin, op. cit., who attributed great importance to Cohen's critique of Fichte in the formation of the former's philosophy, considering it merely ancillary. I am not convinced by Dussort, and, though not having found absolutely watertight historical evidence to support my view, believe that Cohen made use of his critique of Fichte to clarify some essential aspects of his critical idealism. It is worth considering how Cohen adopted a partially

Fichte-like approach in *Die platonische Ideenlehre psychologisch entwickelt* (also acknowledged by Dussort, op. cit., p. 78), which was put aside entirely in his subsequent works. Furthermore, it should be noted that in Cohen's ethics the distinction between logic and ethics became increasingly clear-cut (cf. E. Winter, op. cit., pp. 220ff.). This can surely be seen as avoidance of the risk of committing the same error as Fichte.

62. Cf. *KBE* 368; *ERW* 319; *E* 123; *Religion und Sittlichkeit. Eine Betrachtung zur Grundlegung der Religionsphilosophie,* in *J III:* 109; *Der deutsche Idealismus und die Antike,* in *S II:* 321, 326; *Deutschtum und Judentum mit grundlegenden Betrachtungen über Staat und Internationalismus,* in *J II:* 282f.; *Die Messiasidee* (probably written in 1892, published posthumously in 1924), in *J I:* 122.

63. J. Vuillemin, op. cit., p. 143.

64. J. Vuillemin, op. cit., pp. 132ff. appropriately highlights this aspect of Cohen's criticism of Fichte. Vuillemin's book contains an extremely interesting analysis of this criticism, even though it forms part of a more general interpretative scheme, that is not entirely convincing. In Fichte, Cohen, and Heidegger, Vuillemin saw three successive attempts at further investigation of the concept of the finite from Kant onward, in order to avoid the metaphysics of infinity. He argues that each attempt rejected the previous one and that they constitute a retrospective reading of the *Critique of Pure Reason,* inasmuch as Fichte began with the *transcendental dialectic,* Cohen with the *transcendental analytic,* and Heidegger with the *transcendental aesthetic.* The most debatable part of this admittedly highly interesting and acute interpretation seems to me to be Vuillemin's view of Cohen's philosophy as an attempt at restoring the philosophy of infinity to the finite. This approach does not sufficiently bring out the need in Cohen's critical thought to hold the finite and infinity together, and cause the one to act critically on the other, though from the viewpoint of the finite.

65. For Descartes's influence on Fichte cf. *KBE* 291; *KTE* 750; *LRE* 417. As often happens to philosophers, Cohen himself was also accused of being influenced by Descartes by F. Heinemann, op. cit., pp. 70, 74, 77.

66. Cf. *Charakteristik der Ethik Maimunis,* in *J III:* 226f.

67. *Jubiläums-Betrachtungen. Rezension von: Philosophische Aufsätze. Eduard Zeller su seinem fünfzigjährigen Doctor-Jubiläum gewidmet,* in *S I:* 430.

68. Cf. *Die dichterische Phantasie und der Mechanismus des Bewusstseins* (1869), in *S I:* 165; *E* 39f.; *ERW* 460f.

69. Here I have limited myself to analyzing Cohen's explicit judgment of Hegel, without facing the interesting problem of the objective similarity or difference between Hegel's and Cohen's philosophies. E.

von Aster, *Neukantianismus und Hegelismus. Eine philosophie-geschichtliche Parallele*, in *Münchener Philosophische Abhandlungen. Theodor Lipps zu seinem 60. Geburtstag*, Leipzig, Johann Ambrosius Barth, 1911, argues for substantial similarity between Marburg philosophy and that of Hegel. In fact, von Aster, in this essay, means Natorp's philosophy, but, in 1935, he extended this similarity to Cohen, in *Die Philosophie der Gegenwart*, Leiden, A. W. Sijthoff's Vitgeversmaatschappij, 1935, pp. 24ff. As has already been noted, S. Marck, op. cit., 1913, suggests that Cohen was near to Hegel's philosophy of identity. N. Hartmann also identifies important similarities between Cohen and Hegel, not so much in *Systhematische Methode*, in "Logos," iii (1912), pp. 121–63, where he sees more of a Platonic and Hegelian dialectic in Cohen's philosophy, as in 1921, in *Grundzüge einer Metaphysik der Erkenntnis*, cit., pp. 161f., where he asserts there is a Hegelian-type panlogism in Cohen. Such an inclination to reduce Cohen to Hegel can also be observed in E. Troeltsch, op. cit., pp. 541ff., though the author does point out important differences between the two philosophies; in H. Levy, *Die Hegel-Renaissance in der deutschen Philosophie, mit besonderer Berüksichtigung des Neukantianismus*, Charlottenburg, Pan-Verlag Rolf Heise, 1927, pp. 30ff., who places Cohen and the Marburg school in the area of the *Hegel-Renaissance*; G. Körber, *Die Marburger Logismus und sein Verhältnis zu Hegel*, in "Archiv für Philosophie. 1 Abteilung Archiv für Geschichte der Philosophie," Neue Folge, xxiii (1910), Heft 3, pp. 189–202; F. Heinemann, op. cit., pp. 77f.; more recently in G. Lehmann, op. cit., p. 81, who even states that, if the relationship between the Marburg school and Hegel had been brought to light at the right moment, there would not have been any need for Neo-Hegelianism; in H.-G. Gadamer, *Die philosophische Bedeutung Paul Natorps*, in "Kant-Studien," xlvi (1954–55), pp. 129–34, reprinted as *Vorwort* in P. Natorp, *Philosophische Systematik*, Hamburg, Meiner, 1958, pp. xi–xvii, who writes of unacknowledged Hegelianism in Cohen and explicit Hegelianism in Natorp (cf. p. xvi). The representatives of the Marburg school did not accept this relationship and reacted by under-stating it, like P. Natorp, who, in reply to von Aster in *Kant und die Marburger Schule*, cit., maintains that all the Marburg school has in common with Fichte and Hegel is the inheritance of Platonic and Kantian philosophy (cf. pp; 210f.), and is sarcastic about the presumed similarity of the Marburg school's philosophy with that of Hegel; after underlining the numerous, fundamental differences, he writes: "We agree with Hegel on many points. One could almost say that he accepts all the essential features of 'critical idealism,' as understood and developed by us, with one exception: its absolutism. But this would be, more or less, like saying that Tycho Brahe agreed with Copernicus, apart from the inertia of the denial of the Earth's movement" (p. 213). A. Görland, op. cit. p. 226, is even more radically inclined to reject comparison as uninteresting (M. Brelage, op. cit. pp. 86f., additionally provided a historical justification for this lack of interest in comparison). The 1920s saw the beginning of a tendency, in contrast to that described above, to highlight the differences between Cohen and Hegel, up to the point of seeing the former's philosophy as an alternative to the latter's: J. Gordon, *Der Ichbegriff bei Hegel, bei Cohen und in der Südwestdeutschen Schule hinsichtlich der Kategorienlehre untersucht. Erster Teil: Der Begriff des Denkens bei Hegel und Cohen*, Diss., Hamburg 1926; J. Gordin, op. cit.; and, more recently, W. Marx, op. cit. pp. 133 ff. (while in idem, *Hegels Theorie logischer Vermittlung. Kritik der dialektischen Begriffskonstruktionen in der "Wissenschaft der Logik,"* Stuttgart/Bad Cannstatt, Frommann-Holzboog, 1972, pp. 22ff., there is no mention of Cohen's philosophy being an alternative to Hegel's). There is an interesting recent discussion of the question in H. Holzhey, *Cohen und Natorp*, cit., Bd. 1, pp. 65ff.

CHAPTER FIVE. LOGIC

1. An undated letter from Cohen to Natorp (written after March 21, 1902, and therefore shortly before the book's publication) is evidence that the idea of making *Logik der reinen Erkenntnis* the first part of the system in the book's title was not Cohen's, but his publisher's: "One other thing. The publisher of my Logic wants a comprehensive title: System of Philosophy. Part 1. What do you think about it? Isn't it a little arrogant?" (original letter in Marburg University Library, Hs 831:68, quoted by H. Holzhey, *Einleitung*, in *W 6*: vii*). Cohen planned a second volume of his *Logik*, which would cover historical aspects, on the relationship between his theories and philosophical tradition, and systematic aspects, on the relationship with the specific problems of the mathematical science of nature, and debate with his contemporaries (cf. *LRE* x f.). He never wrote this second volume, but, as H. Holzhey, *Einleitung*, in *W 6*: xvii*-xviii*, rightly remarks: "we can find a kind of substitute in *Einleitung mit kritischem Nachtrag zu F.A. Langes 'Geschichte des Materialismus'*—also published in 1902 in a second edition with additions in the third 1914 edition—which further investigates and defines the meaning of the philosophical 'classics' and expresses views on issues of the time concerning conceptions of scientists of nature (Hertz, Planck, Boltzmann, Einstein) and philosophers (Bergson)."

2. In the *Nachwort* to the third edition of *Kants Theorie der Erfahrung* (cf. *KTE* 784ff.), Cohen attempts to show that loyalty to Kant is compatible with going beyond him.

3. Cf., for example, W. Kinkel, op. cit., pp. 81ff. On the shift from the critique of knowledge to the logic of pure knowledge, cf. A. Görland, op. cit., pp. 224f.

4. H. Holzhey, *Einleitung*, in *W 6*: ix*.

5. For the moment I shall not consider the third meaning of critical philosophy as the philosophy of idea, understood both as limit and as task.

6. Cf. F. Rosenzweig, *Einleitung*, in *J I*: xviii f.; W. Kinkel, op. cit., pp. 100f.; J. Solowiejczyk, op. cit., p. 51; K. Löwith, *Philosophie der Vernunft und Religion der Offenbarung in H. Cohens Religionsphilosophie*, Heidelberg, Carl Winter-Universitätsverlag, 1968, p. 6; W. Marx, *Transzendentale Logik als Wissenschaftstheorie etc.*, cit., pp. 43ff., 85ff.; E. Winter, op. cit., pp. 178ff. H. Holzhey, *Cohen und Natorp*, Bd. 1, cit., pp. 175ff., provides a balanced, comprehensive examination of the question.

7. Cf. H. Holzhey, *Cohen und Natorp*, Bd. 1, cit., p. 175. Cf. *ERW* 29.

8. Cf. W. Kinkel, op. cit., p. 101.

9. Cohen deals with both in the second class of judgments, those of mathematics: with time in the judgment of manifoldness (cf. *LRE* 149 ff.), with space in the judgment of universality (cf. *LRE* 188 ff.). I use the term universality rather than totality to translate Cohen's term *Allheit* since it always has an open sense in his use, and he explicitly contrasts it with the conclusive character of totality (*Totalität, Ganze*): cf. *LRE* 175f., 205, 326.

10. Cf. *LRE* 78, 403. The section on judgments of method is to be found in *LRE* 404ff.

11. Cohen believed that even Plato, though being the "creator of classical logic" (*LRE* 22), was not immune to this risk (cf. *LRE* 21f.).

12. There is unanimity on this point: cf. W. Kinkel, op. cit., pp. 81f.; E. Winter, op. cit., p. 193; H. Holzhey, *Einleitung*, in *W 6*: ix*f.

13. Cf. chapter 3, section 4.

14. J. Gordin, op. cit., p. 131. As confirmation Gordin also quotes a similar opinion from Görland: "Logical clarification of idealism made great progress. For this we must thank Hermann Cohen, who placed the 'law-of-thought (*Denkgesetz*) of origin' at the beginning of his 'Logic. . . .' Thus a concept was created that is a presupposition of Kant's transcendental concept. A concept is transcendental if it is a condition of the possibility of experience, i.e. of the unity of experience. Experience is therefore always presupposed as a yardstick. In the concept of origin there are no risks of colliding with a fact of experience and the concept of idealism is eminently purified" (A. Görland, *Ethik als Kritik der*

Weltgeschichte, Leipzig/Berlin, B.G. Teubner, 1914, p. 52, quoted by J. Gordin, op. cit., p. 131n.).

15. Here I shall not deal with the admittedly interesting problem of the radical difference between the dialectic of Cohen and that of Hegel. J. Gordin, in op. cit., pp. 142ff. *Die Dialektik des Ursprungs (Cohen) und die Dialektik des Systems (Hegel)* is very clear on the matter.

16. N. Hartmann, *Systematische Methode*, cit. I cannot follow Hartmann, however, when he states that Cohen is an example of a philosopher who applied the dialectical method without being conscious of it (cf. *Ibid.*, pp. 150ff.). Cohen's detailed analyses of Plato's dialectic and his explicit identification of logic with dialectic in *LRE* 20 are sufficient evidence of Cohen's awareness. Hartmann himself should have been conscious of the fact that he took his interpretation of the dialectical method, in the Platonic sense to which he refers here, from Cohen. This is shown by his essay on Plato (*Platos Logik des Seins*, Giessen, A. Töpelmann, 1909), which is strictly in line with Cohen's approach. If Cohen is not particularly partial to the term dialectic for the process of pure thought, this is probably due to his being conscious of the fact that his readers would have understood the term in Hegel's sense of the collapse of opposites, which is very far from his approach; cf. *LRE* 112ff.

17. N. Hartmann, *Systematische Methode*, cit., p. 159. The relationship between the transcendental and dialectical methods was later highlighted by H. Wagner, *Über den Begriff des Idealismus und die Stufen der theoretischen Apriorität*, in "Philosophia Naturalis," ii (1952), pp. 178–99, reprinted in Idem, *Kritische Philosophie*, Würzburg, Königshausen/Neumann, 1980, pp. 28–41, who uses the terms *categorial-analytical method* and *categorial-architectural method* for the transcendental and dialectical methods respectively (cf. *ibid.*, p. 38).

18. Cf. Plato, *Republic*, 511.

19. *Ibid.*, 511 b–c; English trans. by P. Shorey, vol. 2, Cambridge (Mass.), Harvard University Press (Loeb Classical Library), 1935, p. 115; also cf. N. Hartmann, *Systematische Methode*, cit., pp. 142f.

20. Here I shall quote the well-known passage from Plato's *Sophist* (253 b–d; English trans. by B. Jowett, New York, Scribner's, 1911, p. 491f.), which is also significant because of the close, no doubt deliberate, terminologically similarity with Cohen's discourse (italics are mine): "Stranger—And as classes are admitted by us in like manner to be some of them capable and others incapable of admixture, must not he who would rightly show what kinds *will unite* and what *will not*, proceed rationally by the help of some science? And will he not ask whether there are any universal classes which *bind them together* and make them capable of admixture; and others, again, which are necessary in all *division*?

Theaetetus—To be sure he will require science, and perhaps the very greatest of all sciences. Stranger—And what is the name of this science? . . . Should we not say that the *division* according to classes, which neither *makes the same other, nor makes other the same*, is the business of the dialectical science? Theaetetus—That is what we should say."

21. N. Hartmann, *Systematische Methode*, cit., p. 159.

22. This principle was formulated for the first time in *LRE* 29.

23. However, this does not mean that thought as activity and thought as content are identical. There is *correlation*, which protects distinction in unity. H. Holzhey, *Cohen und Natorp*, cit., Bd. 1, p. 180 n. 15, notes that in order to understand Cohen's terminology the reader sometimes needs the guidance of his entire philosophical perspective: "Understanding of Cohen's logic can only be aided by taking its author's intentions and viewpoint from his formulations, which are undoubtedly often very debatable and imprecise, such as, in the case in point, hurriedly taking propositions with 'is' to be precise expressions of identity."

24. This is why Cohen did not see unity as one category among others, but developed its meaning through all the mathematical categories: reality (*Realität*), plurality (*Mehrheit*), universality (*Allheit*), showing its complex meaning as a fundamental characteristic of judgment, and not as a specific category.

25. Here, too, as in the case of continuity and origin, Cohen elaborates the categories of pure thought on the basis of reflection on the concepts of science. In this case the model is the law of conservation of energy (cf. *LRE* 70ff.; for treatment of the category of energy, cf. *LRE* 288ff.). From Cohen's point of view this was a legitimate operation, since, if the principles of thought in general are the immanent a priori conditions of the principles of science, in accordance with the transcendental method they must be discovered in the fact of science, so as to constitute, in turn, the principle of its deduction.

26. H. Holzhey, *Cohen und Natorp*, cit., Bd. 1, p. 180.

27. Though Cohen preferred the term origin to idea, we can give the same meaning to the latter that Cohen gave to the Platonic Idea, as "giving account" of concept (cf. *LRE* 601). Cohen's distrust of the term idea, when it is not in an explicitly Platonic context, can probably be explained, as with the case of the term dialectic, by his being worried about possible misunderstanding on the part of his readers. Cohen notes that Kant had corrected the defect in the Platonic Idea when it claimed to refer both to ethics and to the mathematical science of nature, by distinguishing between ideas and concepts and restricting the former to the ethical and biological contexts, which are the moment in which the science of nature passes over to ethics. Though Cohen did not

accept the limited clarity of this distinction of Kant, he did fully agree with Kant's intention to distinguish the context of ethics from that of the mathematical science of nature, a crucial distinction for critical philosophy. However, romantic idealism abandoned this distinction, and this resulted in Hegel's identification of idea with concept (cf. *LRE* 313ff.). The meaning of idea in Hegel's philosophy of identity and its abandonment of the critical requirement, which is what had made Kant separate idea and concept, are probably important reasons for Cohen's inclination to use the term idea in *Logik der reinen Erkenntnis* with great care.

28. Cf. W. Kinkel, op. cit., pp. 107f.

29. H. Holzhey, *Cohen und Natorp*, cit., Bd. 1, pp. 184–85.

30. It was precisely Nicholas of Cusa's emphasis on the problem of origin as a problem of infinity and on the certainty of mathematical knowledge that induced Cohen to consider him the first modern philosopher (cf. *LRE* 31f.; *Rede bei der Gedenkfeier der Universität Marburg zur 100 Wiederkehr des Todestages von Immanuel Kant*, in *S I:* 473 f.; *E* 20; *Über das Eigentümliche des deutschen Geistes*, in *S I:* 531; *Was einigt die Konfessionen?*, in *J I:* 75), thus initiating a historiographical approach that was to be taken up by E. Cassirer in *Das Erkenntnisproblem in der Philosophie und Wissenschaft der neueren Zeit*, Bd. 1, Berlin, Bruno Cassirer, 1906.

31. H. Holzhey, *Cohen und Natorp*, cit., Bd. 1, pp. 183–84. Cf. also J. Gordin, op. cit., pp. 94ff.

32. For these terms, cf. *LRE* 118ff.

33. W. Marx, *Cassirers Symboltheorie als Entwicklung und Kritik der Neukantianischen Grundlagen einer Theorie des Denkens und Erkennens. Überlegungen zur Struktur transzendentaler Logik als Wissenschaftstheorie*, in "Archiv für Geschichte der Philosophie," lii (1975), pp. 188–206, 304–39, and Idem, *Transzendentale Logik als Wissenschaftstheorie etc.*, cit. emphasizes the purely methodical character of Cohen's principle of origin, which cannot thus be mistaken for a principle of deduction of being from thought, characteristic of panlogism. H. Holzhey, *Cohen und Natorp*, cit., Bd. 1, pp. 184f. gives a more subtle picture, arguing, in my view rightly, that the principle of origin is not to be understood merely as a methodical principle, but as the ground of the method, and, though with new meaning, also as an ontological principle.

34. Cohen criticized the interpretation of Aristotle (cf. *LRE* 86 f.), and those of Hegel and Lotze (cf. *LRE* 89f.). For the history of the interpretation of infinite judgment see J. Gordin, op. cit., pp. 1ff. For Gordin one of the crucial points in the difference between Hegel's and Cohen's philosophical systems is the contrast in their interpretations of infinite judgment.

35. On the theme of limitative judgment, cf. *PIM* 35ff.

36. Cohen had already dealt, in detail, with the law of continuity, and the decisive part played by Leibniz in the foundation of infinitesimal calculus and modern science and philosophy in *Das Prinzip der Infinitesimal-Methode und seine Geschichte*. cf. especially *PIM* 34ff., 56ff.

37. Here Cohen is referring to the following words of Democritus: μὴ μᾶλλον τὸ δὲν ἢ τὸ μηδὲν εἶναι (Fr. B 156, Diels-Kranz), cit. in *LRE* 85.

38. H. Dussort, op. cit., p. 139 defines Cohen's logic as "the systematic study of the presuppositions of truth and, more exactly, of scientific truth." F. Heinemann, op. cit., pp. 62ff., in his treatment of Neo-Kantianism (in which he concentrates on the Marburg school), deals exclusively with the problem of truth.

39. Cohen was accused of this by, for example, J. Ebbinghaus, op. cit., pp. 114f., 121; Idem, *Hermann Cohen*, in *Neue Deutsche Biographie*, Bd. 3, Berlin, Duncker & Humblot, 1957, p. 312.

40. On the difference between *B*, as "it is not *A*," and non-*A*, as "*A* is not," cf. J. Gordin, op. cit., pp. 64ff.

41. Cf. *Platons Ideenlehre und die Mathematik*, in *S I*: 343, 363.

42. Cohen makes a clear distinction between his interpretation of contradiction and any restriction of it to mere 'opposition' (*Gegensatz*), since the latter concept is linked with that of 'change' (*Veränderung*) and thus allows conciliation between opposites, which is out of the question with contradiction. In this he differs from Hegel (cf. *LRE* 111ff.).

43. The laws-of-thought of "universality" (cf. *LRE* 205 f.), "sufficient reason" (cf. *LRE* 304ff.), the "excluded middle" (*LRE* 392ff.), "equality" and "consciousness" (cf. *LRE* 482ff.).

44. E. von Aster, *Die Philosophie der Gegenwart*, cit., pp. 14–15, with reference to the relationship between truth and being in Neo-Kantianism, writes: "Truth is not the derived concept, and being the fundamental one; the opposite is true. Objective being and, in an even narrower sense, 'existing reality' as the being of the sensible phenomenon, in the guise of the manifold of intuition, appears as a sphere of truth. It is this whole complex that is constituted in true judgments of existence, posited one by one by thought, corresponding to the norms of logic, solid in respect of the flux of perception. The truth of thoughts is the measure of 'what is.'"

45. On the meaning of disjunctive judgment in Cohen, cf. J. Gordin, op. cit., pp. 75ff.

46. Cohen refers to Aristotle and Leibniz: cf. *LRE* 393.

47. This is how K. Kinkel, op. cit., p. 145, presents Cohen's interpretation of the excluded middle: "Cohen explains it in the sense of that which contains the guarantee of the feasibility of the system. *It must be possible* to articulate nature in accordance with the system of concept,

otherwise every scientific effort is useless. Thus, this law-of-thought, like that of contradiction, is a bulwark against sophistry and skepticism."

CHAPTER SIX. ETHICS

1. Cf. E. Winter, op. cit., pp. 212ff. (especially pp. 238ff.).
2. The most important variations in the first edition: "*is to be deduced from the analytical concept*"; Ist. ed.: "*is to be deduced from concept.*" It should be noticed that despite profound differences, the theme of the deduction of moral law from pure will, characteristic of *Ethik des reinen Willens* is already present here. This is a sign of continuity in the evolution of Cohen's reflections on ethics from his interpretation of Kant to the formulation of his own, original theory, even if this should not obscure the fundamental differences between the first edition of *Kants Begründung der Ethik* and *Ethik des reinen Willens* even in this case.
3. I. Kant, *Kritik der reinen Vernunft*, 2. Auflage, cit., p. 377; Eng. trans. cit., p. 479.
4. The most significant variants in the first edition are: "its premisses, and its grounds makes"; 1st. edition: "its premisses makes"/"of another kind of reality"; Ist. edition: "of another reality"/"methodological conditions"; Ist. edition: "conditions."
5. For this see chapter 3, section 4, as well as E. Winter, op. cit. (especially pp. 220ff.).
6. For a critical analysis of the differences between the two editions of *Kants Begründung der Ethik* regarding this point see E. Winter, op. cit., pp. 224ff.
7. Cf. E. Winter, op. cit., pp. 223f.
8. G. Gigliotti, op. cit., p. 116.
9. A glimpse of this can be had, for example, in *ERW* 23, where Cohen first categorically states that logic and ethics are distinct and the former takes precedence over the latter, attributing this formulation to Kant, and then immediately goes on to criticize Fichte for overturning this relationship and thus confusing the two fields.
10. For detailed treatment readers are once again referred to E. Winter, op. cit., pp. 238ff.
11. J. Guttmann, *Hermann Cohens Ethik*, in "Monatschrift für Geschichte und Wissenschaft des Judentums", il (1905), also sees a foundation of law in Cohen's work and argues for the inadequacy of a foundation of morality: cf., for example, pp. 388ff.
12. Cf. F. Jodl, review of H. Cohen, *Ethik des reinen Willens*, in "Neue Presse" (Vienna), Literaturblatt vom 10 September 1905.
13. Cf. chapter 4, Excursus, section c.

14. *Religion und Sittlichkeit etc.*, in *J* III: 114–15.

15. On the importance of reference to this formulation of Kant's categorical imperative in German socialist discussion, see the texts collected by H. J. Sandkühler, in *Marxismus und Ethik: Texte zum neukantianischen Sozialismus*, Frankfurt, Suhrkamp, 1970.

16. On this question, cf. E. Cassirer, *Hermann Cohen und die Erneuerung der Kantischen Philosophie*, cit., pp. 266ff.

17. On the problem of self-consciousness in Kant, cf. *ERW* 95, 204. In *Religion und Sittlichkeit etc.*, in *J* III 149f., Cohen posits an interesting relationship between failure to fully, unambiguously recognize the self as a task and Kant's consideration of the idea of God as a postulate, which he rejects, in this case, considering it to be too limited in the light of the reality of the idea of God.

18. This theme is also touched on in *ERW* 468.

19. Cf. P. Natorp, *Allgemeine Logik*, in W. Flach and H. Holzhey, *Erkenntnistheorie und Logik im Neukantianismus. Texte von Cohen, Natorp, Cassirer, Windelband, Rickert, Lask, Bauch*, Hildesheim, Gerstenberg Verlag, 1980, pp. 227ff. This distinction is also treated critically, though not exactly in the same terms, in the essay on Cohen by P. Natorp, *Hermann Cohens philosophische Leistung unter dem Gesichtspunkte des Systems*, cit., pp. 24ff., 29f.

20. Cf., for example, E. Winter, op. cit., pp. 247ff.

21. On Cohen's socialism see S. S. Schwarzschild, *The Democratic Socialism of H. Cohen*, in "Hebrew Union College Annual," xxvii (1956), pp. 417–38; H. Lübbe, *Politische Philosophie in Deutschland. Studien zu ihrer Geschichte*, Basel/Stuttgart, Schwabe & Co., 1963, pp. 102ff.; G. L. Mosse, "*Left-Wing Intellectuals in the Weimar Republic." Germans and Jews: The Right, the Left and the Search for a "Third Force" in Pre-Nazi Germany*, New York, Grosset and Dunlap, 1970, pp. 171–228; A. Zanardo, *Filosofia e socialismo*, Roma, Editori Riuniti, 1974, pp. 73ff.; T. Keck, *Kant and Socialism: The Marburg School in Wihelmian Germany*, Diss., Madison 1975; Th. E. Willey, *Back to Kant—The Revival of Kantianism in German Social and Historical Thought 1860–1914*, Detroit,Wayne State University Press, 1978, pp. 103ff.

22. On Cohen's attitude to the political situation of his time see, apart from the chapter in H. Lübbe's book quoted in the previous note, R. A. Fritzsche, *Hermann Cohen aus persönlicher Erinnerung*, Berlin, Bruno Cassirer, 1922, pp. 30ff.

23. Cf., for example, the letters from Cohen to Natorp dated December 12, 1914, and December 21, 1914, published in H. Holzhey, *Cohen und Natorp*, cit., Bd. 2, pp. 438–40.

24. V. H. Günter, *Philosophie des Fortschritts: Hermann Cohens Rechtsfertigung der bürgerlichen Gesellschaft,* Munich, Wilhelm Goldmann Verlag, 1972. On the theme of progress see also J. Ebbinghaus, *Hermann Cohen als Philosoph und Publizist,* cit., p. 116, and Idem, *Hermann Cohen,* cit., p. 312. Ebbinghaus, however, includes this characteristic of Cohen's ethics among his defects.

25. "Every man, who is not stubborn in his way of life, has his own motto, just as every Jew receives a Biblical verse from his father, which he always says before the conclusion of the great prayer of the eighteen blessings. Should I quote mine? It says: 'The right hand of the Lord is lifted up, the right hand of the Lord is a fortress' " (letter from Cohen to Frau Mathilde Burg [presumably written in 1886], quoted in H. Cohen, *Briefe,* cit., p. 62). The verse comes from *Psalm* 118, 16.

26. This itinerary from pure principles to their application as the linking thread of the book, after the formulation of the pure principles themselves, is highlighted by Cohen at the beginning of the eighth chapter, Das Ideal, in a concise summary of the argument carried on up to that point (cf. *ERW* 389ff.).

27. Cf. especially *ERW* 591f., 616ff. "Humanitarianism" is used to translate the German words *Humanität* and *Menschlichkeit* so as to distinguish them from the completely different word *Menschheit* (cf. *ERW* 625ff.).

28. Cf. W. Herrmann, *Hermann Cohens Ethik,* in "Die Christliche Welt," xxi (1907), n. 3, columns 51–9; N. 10, columns 222–8; reprinted in Idem, *Schriften zur Grundlegung der Theologie,* Munich, Kaiser, 1966–1967, Teil 2, pp. 88–113 (cf., especially, pp. 99f., 112f.). On the discussion between Cohen and Herrmann (on which see also chapter 8, section 4, and chapter 10, sections 1 and 9): S. S. Schwarzschild, *Introduction,* in *W 7:* xxviii*; W. Kluback, *Friendship without communication: Wilhelm Herrmann and Hermann Cohen,* in "Leo Baeck Institute—Year Book," xxi (1986), pp. 317–38; reprinted with very few variants in Idem, *The Idea of Humanity: Hermann Cohen's Legacy to Philosophy and Theology,* Lanham/New York/London, University Press of America, 1987, pp. 163–86.

29. Explicit recognition of this can be found in *BR* 56ff.

30. Even though, as R. A. Fritzsche, op. cit., p. 25, tells us, Cohen showed surprise that his books were considered difficult to understand.

31. Cf., for example, E. Winter, op. cit., pp. 263ff. (who also quotes the opinions of F. Tönnies, H. Kantorowicz, W. Windelband, and M. Scheler).

32. E. Winter, op. cit., pp. 252–53.

33. Cf. *Leopold Schmidt* (1896), in *S II:* 415ff.

34. Cf., for example, *ERW* 53f.

35. E. Winter, op. cit., p. 262.

36. I can find no justification for the opinion expressed by J. Weise, *Die Begründung der Ethik bei Hermann Cohen*, Diss., Erlangen 1911, p. 18, that "the first part of ethics in Cohen's system was a useless deviation."

37. For the logical determination of the concepts of 'plurality' (*Mehrheit*) and "universality" (*Allheit*), cf. *LRE* 144ff., 174ff.

38. Often, in *Ethik des reinen Willens*, Cohen uses the word *self* (*Selbst*) as a synonym of *self-consciousness* (*Selbstbewusstsein*).

39. *Die Nächstenliebe im Talmud. Ein Gutachten dem Königlichen Landgerichte zu Marburg erstattet* (1888), in *J I:* 174. Cohen had already written the following, in a letter to Louis and Helene Lewandowsky dated June 24 1873: "And yet I am able to honestly devote my labours to the supreme human activity and I am confident that, as long as I am in good health, I shall search for what I believe to be the truth, without being distracted by irrelevant temptations."

40. Cf. G. E. Lessing, *Eine Duplik*, in *Werke*, Bd. 8, Munich, Carl Hanser, 1979, p. 33; cf. also *ERW* 91.

41. Cf. S. S. Schwarzschild, *Introduction*, in *W 7:* viii*.

42. The meaning of truth in Cohen's ethics, not restricted to methodology, has already been thoroughly foregrounded and analyzed by S. Kaplan, *Das Geschichtsproblem in der Philosophie Hermann Cohens*, Berlin, Reuther & Reichard, 1930, pp. 65–87.

43. In *Kant und die Marburger Schule*, cit., p. 216, Natorp answers and rejects the accusations made against Cohen by Windelband and by von Aster that he restricted ethics to logic.

44. *Vom ewigen Frieden*, in *S II:* 343. Cohen had already written to Louis and Helene Lewandowsky in a letter dated August 19 1871 as follows: "The idealist conception of the world does not consist of the fact that things are believed *to become* as they should be, but of the fact that they are believed *to have* to become as they should be" (H. Cohen, *Briefe*, cit., pp. 32–33).

CHAPTER SEVEN. AESTHETICS, PSYCHOLOGY, AND CRITICAL SYSTEM

1. This double aspect is also present in the other parts of the system, as we have already seen, since both logic and ethics, besides being parts of the system of philosophy, and precisely because they are, are also

considered to be the systematic ground, the one of the sciences of nature, the other of the moral sciences.

2. On the development, problems and major representatives of *Kunstwissenschaft*, see D. Formaggio, *L'arte come comunicazione: I-Fenomenologia della tecnica artistica*, Milan, Nuvoletti, 1953, pp. 279–311.

3. Cf. P. Natorp, *Hermann Cohens philosophische Leistung unter dem Gesichtspunkte des Systems*, cit., pp. 20 f.; E. Cassirer, *Paul Natorp*, in "Kant-Studien," xxx (1925), pp. 288f.; H.-L. Ollig, op. cit., p. 172.

4. Ernst Cassirer, a member of the Marburg school and follower of Cohen, was to formulate a different division of the branches of culture, in his cultural philosophy.

5. Cf. H. Heinemann, op. cit., p. 83; G. Wolandt, *Einleitung*, in *W* 8/9: xii*.

6. I shall not deal with the specific characteristics of the aesthetic object here, as I did above, to return to it later. Cohen had no doubts, however, about the need to be able to define an aesthetic object, since *"there is no purity without the object"* (*ARG I: 78*).

7. The meaning of the Platonic hypothesis as pure foundation is repeated by Cohen in *ARG I:* 22.

8. Cf. *Mythologische Vorstellungen von Gott und Seele pyschologisch entwickelt* (1869), in *S I:* 88–140, and *Die dichterische Phantasie und der Mechanismus des Bewusstseins*, in *S I:* 141–228.

9. Cf., especially, the first chapter: *Die Gesetzlichkeit des ästhetischen Bewusstseins*, in *KBA* 144ff. Unlike the case of ethics, where, as we have already seen in the previous chapter, the organization of the work commenting critically on Kant and the book in the system dealing with ethics are very different, in the case of aesthetics, there is considerable continuity between *Kants Begründung der Ästhetik* and *Ästhetik des reinen Gefühls*. There are even cases where the former provides a more detailed and more thoroughly argued treatment than the latter, for example, in the analysis of the historical development of aesthetics in Ancient Greek culture (mostly in Plato, but also in Aristotle and Plotinus) and in modern Germany (Leibniz, Baumgarten, Winckelmann, Mendelssohn, Lessing, Herder, and, naturally, Kant), and also in the case of reference to the history of the meaning of a number of central concepts in Cohen's aesthetics (an essential reference to understand the meaning given to them by Cohen in his philosophy), such as 'love' (referring to the Platonic meaning) and 'humanitarianism' (*Humanität*) (with reference to the German tradition). The reader needs to refer to the earlier work on these questions, since Cohen appears to treat the considerations expressed there as presuppositions for the later work. There is, as we shall see, nevertheless, considerable difference concerning the concept

'sublime.' On their fundamental unity, but also on the differences between the two works, see G. Wolandt, *Einleitung*, in *W8/9*: x*f.

10. Cf. chapter 4 in *ARG I*: 135ff.

11. This expression is only present in *ARG I*: 363f., but the explanation of its meaning can already be found in *ARG I*: 152ff. (cf., especially, *ARG I*: 160).

12. Cohen is following Herder's considerations on touch as an originary feeling (cf. *ARG I*: 132; also *KBA* 84), corrected in accordance with the psychophysiological studies by Johannes Müller on necessary preconceptions (*notwendige Vorbegriffe*) (cf. *ARG I*: 133; also *ERW* 156).

13. On the 'criterion of fulfillment,' cf. *ARG I*: 189ff.

14. See Cohen's interesting considerations on the nude as a theme in art, in *ARG I*: 176ff.

15. These very well-known lines of Goethe are quoted on p. 209 of *ARG* I (there is also a reference to them on p. 199). Cf. also *KBA* 420; *ERW* 637.

16. "*The production of feeling has the production of the individual as its sole purpose*" (*ARG I*: 200).

17. Cf., for example, P. Stern, *Review of H. Cohen, Ästhetik des reinen Gefühls*, in "Zeitschrift für Ästhetik und Kunstwissenschaft," viii (1913), p. 300; W. Kinkel, op. cit., p. 291; H.-L. Ollig, op. cit., p. 188; G. Wolandt, *Einleitung*, in *W8/9*: x*.

18. It is probable that in this opinion of Cohen in favor of impressionism, against symbolism, there also is a reflection of his interest in the debate between these two artistic movements, which took place above all in France, at the end of the ninteenth; century. However, I have been unable, to find any explicit evidence of this in Cohen's writings, except for his open appreciation of French impressionism (Monet) and its precursors (Millet, Rousseau, Corot, Courbet) and German adherents (Joseph Israëls, Max Liebermann) (cf. *ARG II*: 407ff.).

19. The smile is seen by Cohen as a characteristic revealing attitude of humor (cf. *ARG I*: 286f., 305ff.; *II*: 280, 344ff.).

20. On humanitarianism as a dimension of art, cf. *ARG I*: 229ff.; 298f. *ARG II*: 41 ff., 304, 414f. The relationship between love and humanitarianism necessarily recalls the role of love in the theory of the virtues, formulated by Cohen in *Ethik des reinen Willens*, and consequently gives rise to doubts about possible confusion and mutual penetration between ethics and aesthetics. Cohen was careful to clarify this problem in such a way as to highlight the dense network of reciprocity between ethics and aesthetics, even if he did not entirely resolve the difficulties (cf. *ARG I*: 178f.; *II*: 127). On the relationship between ethics and aesthetics, with reference to the virtue of humanitarianism, cf. *ERW* 636f. The problem becomes more complex owing to the need for confrontation of the aes-

thetic meaning of love with the religious one. This need had also emerged in *Ästhetik des reinen Gefühls* (cf. *ARG I:* 179), but was to be treated more thoroughly in his writings on the philosophy of religion (cf. *BR* 87ff.; *RV* 186ff., 433f.; Eng. trans. 160ff., 373f.).

21. Reproduced in H. Holzhey, *Das Hermann-Cohen-Archiv in Zürich*, in "Zeitschrift für philosophische Forschung," xxxi (1977), Heft 3, pp. 444ff. (the passage referred to here is on p. 445).

22. This, and other information can be found *ibid.* p. 451.

23. For a more thorough analysis of all these aspects of Cohen's psychology see A. Stériad, op. cit., pp. 229ff.; W. de Schmidt, *Psychologie und Transzdentalphilosophie. Zur Psychologie-Rezeption bei Hermann Cohen und Paul Natorp*, cit.; H. L. Ollig, op. cit., pp. 204ff.; H. Holzhey, *Cohen und Natorp*, cit., Bd. 1, pp. 337ff.

24. W. Moog, *Logik, Psychologie und Psychologismus*, Halle, M. Niemeyer, 1919, p. 55. W. de Schmidt, op. cit., p. 103, quotes, and accepts, this criticism by Moog.

25. Cf. G. W. Leibniz's letter to Louis Bourget written in December 1714, in *Die philosophische Schriften von Gottfried Wilhelm Leibniz*, hg. von C. I. Gerhardt, Bd. 3, Leipzig, Alfred Lorentz Buchandlung, 1931, p. 572; cit. by Cohen in *LRE* 409.

26. Cf. *ibid.*

27. Cf. *LRE* 63, 435, 469; *E* 54ff.; *ERW* xii f., 136, 153, 172, 327, 340; *ARG I:* 94, 99f.,127, 129, 146.

28. This contrast with romantic metaphysics and its heirs, which is essential for correct understanding of the meaning of Cohen's psychology, very clearly emerges in the second chapter of *Einleitung mit kritischem Nachtrag zu F.A. Langes Geschichte des Materialismus etc.*, even in the 1902 edition (only the last pages, dealing with the arguments against empirical, experimental psychology, were added later, in the 1914 edition). In these pages, significantly entitled "Das Verhältnis der Psychologie zur Metaphysik," Cohen presents his conception of psychology as the concluding part of the system of critical philosophy, against the identification of psychology with the romantic metaphysics of the absolute (cf. *E* 29ff.). See also H. Holzhey, *Einführung*, in *W* 5/II: 15*ff.

29. It is true that, in *LRE* 610ff., Cohen insists that culture is not a fact, but a task (an "ideal concept," as it is called in *ARG II:* 429), but this task is "the climax of human development" (*LRE* 610). Therefore, if culture, as the complete realization of the spirit, is an infinite task, the development of the human spirit towards this task, in the various directions of science, morality and art, is already a fact (in *ARG I:* 18, Cohen writes of "the fact of culture" [*Kulturfaktum*]). For Cohen there is no antithesis or break between reality and idea, between fact and task, but continuity and correlation. Since psychology, though dealing with the

unity of the consciousness of culture as a task, follows this purpose through "presentation" (*Darstellung*) (*LRE* 610), not only of the unity of culture, but also of development towards the latter, there is basic correlation between culture as a task and as a fact.

    30. Cf. *LRE* 17, 427, 609ff.; *ERW* 637; *ARG II:* 432.

    31. Thus Cohen is far from any temptation of pantheism.

    32. Cf. *LRE* 609; *ERW* 637; *ARG I:* 88; *II:* 428.

    33. On the relationships and differences between the psychology of Cohen and that of Natorp, see W. de Schmidt, op. cit., pp. 109ff.; H. Holzhey, *Cohen und Natorp*, cit., Bd. 1, p. 225.

    34. H. Holzhey, *Cohen und Natorp*, cit., Bd. 1, p. 225.

    35. F. Rosenzweig, *Einleitung*, in *J I:* xlii–xliii.

    36. *Ibid,* xliii.

CHAPTER EIGHT. THE PHILOSOPHY OF RELIGION AND THE SYSTEM OF PHILOSOPHY

    1. Cf. J. Klein, *Der Mensch im System des Marburger Idealismus*, in the collective study: *Das Bild vom Mensch. Beitrag zur theologischen und philosophischen Anthropologie. Fritz Tillmann zum 60. Geb. (I.II.1934)*, hg. by Th. Steinbüchel und Th. Müncker, Düsseldorf, Schwann, 1934, pp. 122, 130; Idem, *Die Grundlegung der Ethik in der Philosophie Hermann Cohens und Paul Natorps. Eine Kritik des Marburger Neukantianismus*, cit., p. 134.

    2. The opinions of J. Guttmann, *Die Philosophie des Judentums (Geschichte der Philosophie in Einzeldarstellungen. Abt. I: Das Weltbild der Primitiven und die Philosophie des Morgenlandes*, Bd. 3), Munich, Ernst Reinhardt, 1933, are especially interesting and reliable as a balanced view both of the continuity and of the novelty in Cohen's late religious philosophy in respect of his system. If this view is not further discussed here, it is precisely due to its characteristics, making it, in my opinion, one of the most valid interpretations of the problem. Here I decided only to quote those views that best represent the extremes of the debate. For a general treatment of the positions adopted by critics of Cohen see E. L. Fackenheim, op. cit., p. 21; H.-L. Ollig, op. cit., pp. 331ff.

    3. In the *Einleitung* to the collection of Cohen's *Jüdische Schriften*, Rosenzweig, though proposing a unified reading of Cohen's religious thought (cf. *J I:* xxi), interprets it as a gradual conversion and return (*Umkehr/Heimkehr*) (cf. *J I:* xxf.) to Judaism, culminating in the turning point represented in his last writings on the philosophy of religion. Paradoxically, it was precisely Cohen's desire to find a place for religion in the system of culture—which is particularly explicit in *Der Begriff der Religion im System der Philosophie*, being resolved in the denial of the inde-

pendence of religion, as an independent branch of culture, beside logic, ethics, and aesthetics, and in the recognition of a simple *specificity* (*Eigenart*) of religion in respect of the three fundamental areas of culture—that endows it with a "systematic ubiquitousness" (*J I:* xlvii), actually placing it outside the system. The fundamental concept, in which Cohen's entire philosophy of religion is grounded, and which is the cause of the turning point in respect of his previous thought, is that of correlation. This concept, which he had already used, though marginally, in the system, defines the fundamental relationship between man and God, and God and the world. The implications of this new concept and of Cohen's use of it in his last works are decisive. First, the correlation between God and man and that between God and the world imply that the difference cannot be overcome, and thus break "the magic circle of idealism," in which Cohen had been up to that moment (cf. *J I:* xlviiif.). (In this interpretation of Cohen's last works as a break with idealism, Rosenzweig's recognition of the later Cohen as a herald of the new thought, in which he believed is already implicit. It is well known that Rosenzweig formulated this thought as a break with idealism. He saw this break as already being potentially present in Cohen's concept of origin, although it is not clearly developed by him: cf. F. Rosenweig, *Der Stern der Erlösung*, The Hague, Martinus Nijhoff, 1976, p. 23). Cohen went beyond idealism, denying the absolute nature of reason, the fundamental principle of idealism, which he had never doubted. In *Religion der Vernunft*, reason is acknowledged as the creation of God, and the barriers of idealism are overcome by its last great offspring (cf. *J I:* xlix–l). Second, the overcoming of idealism in the later Cohen means the need for understanding man as a concrete individual and God as his interlocutor, and thus follows the direction of existentialist, dialogic thought (cf. *J I:* xlvf.). Overcoming idealism and understanding man as a concrete individual, in his unequalled difference and in his fundamental relationship with God, are, in Rosenzweig's view, the fundamental aspects of the new thought in Cohen's last period (cf. *J I:* xlix).

4. Ucko does not mainly consider the concept of correlation, which is definitely central to Cohen's thought, but only for his "philosophy of religion in the strictest sense" (*Der Gottesbegriff in der Philosophie Hermann Cohens*, Berlin, Siegfried Scholem, 1927, p. 50), but rather more the concept of God. Cohen's originality in respect of his contemporaries among philosophers of religion, not only the phenomenologists, but also critical philosophers such as Natorp, consists in not starting out from man's religious experience to arrive at consideration of the concept of God, but actually beginning with the latter (cf. *ibid.*, pp. 22, 35. W. S. Dietrich, *Cohen and Troeltsch. Ethical Monotheistic Religion and Theory of Culture*, Atlanta, Scholars Press, 1986, p. 1, has recently fore-

grounded this primacy of God as the object of attention of ethical monotheism, not only Cohen's, but also Troeltsch's). This is why the problem of the philosophy of religion follows that of theology in the evolution of Cohen's thought and in the conceptual order of problems (cf. *Der Gottesbegriff*, p. 6). Admittedly, the possibility of a philosophy of religion was opened up for Cohen with the discovery of the inadequacy of ethics, owing to its inability to understand man as an absolute individual. This gap is filled by the philosophy of religion, which establishes the uniqueness of man in correlation with the uniqueness of God (cf. *ibid.*, p. 34). This correlation, therefore, is certainly fundamental for the philosophy of religion, but the meaning of its terms is not exhausted in correlation. These terms are independent in their origin and emerge from different problems. The concept of the concrete individual emerges from "a modification within the area of ethics" (*ibid.*, p. 36): its meaning is therefore fundamentally ethical. The other, the concept of God, is linked to a problem which, though being placed by Cohen in ethics, precedes the latter. Its meaning concerns ontology (cf. *ibid.*, p. 16). The concept of God as the guarantee of the eternal conservation of nature for the realization of morality is not only a methodological principle, however wide the meaning given to this expression, nor a moral postulate, that is, a necessary ground of the possibility of morality in its subjective aspect, as Kant would have it (cf. *ibid.*, pp. 19 f.), but idea, the hypothesis establishing the unity of the two objective orders of being, that of nature, and that of morality. It thus takes on an ontological valence (cf. *ibid.*, p. 18). Cohen's concept of God reaches its full meaning in the concept of the uniqueness of God, which is typical of his last works. At least two aspects of Ucko's position regarding the issue of change or continuity in the phases of Cohen's thought must be evaluated. Concerning its idealist nature, the overcoming of which constitutes one of the essential features of the turning point, in Rosenzweig's view, we find two apparently conflicting statements in Ucko's essay. On the one hand, he states that he wishes to "situate Cohen's general spiritual direction in an intimate connection with the thought of German idealism" (*ibid.*, p. 11); on the other, he believes that the concept of the uniqueness of God, owing to its ontological valence, breaks off from Cohen's previous rationalist approach, and that this explains Cohen's reluctance to take it up and develop it (cf. *ibid.*, p. 33). The cause of the difficulty arising from the juxtaposition of these two statements lies in the completely different meanings of the category of idealism for Cohen and Ucko. The latter treated it as part of classical German idealism, and saw Cohen as part of this tradition, without seeing the abandonment of rationalism and the taking up of an ontological principle preventing this: for Ucko, Cohen's rationalism is not an essential feature of his idealism, but only the product of a synthesis including idealism and positivism (cf. *ibid.*, p. 33), that he is alleged to have put together. For Cohen, on the other hand, as we have seen, the only true idealism was critical, rationalist idealism which he contrasts with false romantic idealism. Thus, the real problem is whether, in Ucko's view, Cohen's last developments of his concept of God can be reconciled with idealism *in Cohen's meaning*. Here Ucko's answer must be in the negative. He did believe that the last developments of the ontological concept of God were a turning point in respect of the methodological character of Cohen's previous philosophy, but, on the other hand, he underlines the fact that many of Cohen's fundamental concepts, such as those of origin, truth, and transcendence, had metaphysical implications, even though he had not developed them (cf., for example, *ibid.*, p. 48). These considerations could lead one to believe that Ucko favored the view that there was radical novelty in the last phase of Cohen's thought. As a matter of fact, this impression needs revising, if one remembers his conviction that, right from the start, this metaphysical approach was already present, though hidden, in Cohen's thought (cf. *ibid.*, p. 49). Cohen's attempt to place his religious philosophy in the system is thus significant for Ucko, not so much because he was successful, but, on the contrary, because, though he was unsuccessful, he uncovered the metaphysical implications hidden in the system itself (cf. *ibid.*, p. 38).

     5. H. Graupe, *Die Stellung der Religion im Systematischen Denken der Marburger Schule*, Diss., Berlin 1930, mostly argues against the theses presented by Ucko on the metaphysical character of the concept of God in Cohen's later works. He also looks at Rosenzweig's position, but considers it to be "a question *of principle*, and thus, in the end, unimportant" *ibid.*, p. 55). The question posed by Ucko is, on the other hand, "the really *methodical* one" *ibid.*, p. 55), and is thus more serious. Graupe acknowledges the value of Ucko's considerations (cf. *ibid.*, p. 22) and accepts many of his arguments, but criticizes the final result of his interpretation, since, although agreeing on the "*structural difference* in Cohen's concept of origin," in contrast with Ucko, he believes "that this structural difference certainly impinges upon 'the merely *logical* formulations of the issue,' but not unlike how, in general, the concepts of Cohen's logic, on their journey towards ethics, in the process of this experimental thought of his, had to submit to a *structural enlargement*" *ibid.*, p. 55). By means of an analysis of the fundamental concepts of Cohen's philosophy of religion and the whole Marburg school: the concept of God and man, Graupe intended to show that they make up an "enlargement" in respect of the system, but not in the sense of a move to a new ontological position, but rather, in that of a further investigation of the methodical problems, which he identifies with the problem of the

limit (a problem which he neither establishes nor clarifies sufficiently in his essay). The problem of the limit is the distinguishing feature of Cohen's entire thought, which could be defined as *"thought of the limit"* rather than "logic of origin" (cf. *ibid.*, p. 11). The methodical character of the limit concepts of God and man ensures the continuity of Cohen's thought, even in its last phase.

6. A. Altmann, *Hermann Cohens Begriff der Korrelation*, in *In zwei Welten. Siegfried Moses zum 75. Geburtstag*, hg. von H. Tramer, Tel Aviv, Verlag Bitaon,1962, pp. 377–99, concentrating on the concept of correlation, argues against Rosenzweig, though his position is also implicitly in contrast with that of Ucko. By means of an analysis of the concept of correlation and the relationship between religion and the four parts of the system in Cohen's philosophy, Altmann intends to show that the concept of correlation and Cohen's philosophy of religion never go beyond the limits of of his idealist, formalist, methodological thought and do not imply, as Rosenzweig argues, an opening to dialogistic thought and the conception of the relationship between God and man as interpersonal.

7. H. Cohen, *Briefe*, cit., p. 82.

8. J. Guttmann, op. cit., p. 353.

9. Cf. F. Rosenzweig, *Einleitung*, in *J I:* xxiif.; 'H. Riegner, *Hermann Cohen. Der Mensch*, in "Bulletin für die Mitglieder der Gesellschaft der Freunde des Leo Baeck Institute,'" n. 7, Juni 1959, pp. 117f. Cf. also Cohen's letter to Louis and Helene Lewandowsky, probably written at *Pesach* 1872, in H. Cohen, *Briefe*, cit., pp. 38ff., to which the authors quoted here refer.

10. Letter from Cohen to Leo Munk dated March 27 1907, *Ibid* p. 77. The Italian words *sacrificio dell'intelletto* (. . .) *del sentimento* are used in the text.

11. U. Ucko, op. cit., pp. 8ff., who, among other things, insists on the irrational character of the concept of the uniqueness of God, which he considers the focal point of Cohen's later religious philosophy, acknowledges the rationalist character of Cohen's formulation, defining it, using terms taken from Heinrich Scholz, *Religionsphilosophie*, Berlin, Reuther & Reichard, 1921: *constructive method*, contrasted with the *receptive method*, i.e. with the descriptive-phenomenological formulation, which came to the fore at the same time. H. Graupe, op. cit., p. 7, also returns to Ucko's approach to this issue.

12. Cf. S. Ucko, op. cit., p. 10; H. Graupe, op. cit., p. 63.

13. On Cohen's conviction of the need for a "deductive" stage in the philosophy of religion, arguing against the purely "inductive" research of *Religionsgeschichte*, cf. *BR* 1ff.; *RV* If.; Eng. trans. 1f.

14. Cf. S. Ucko, op. cit., p. 10.

15. Cf. H. Graupe, op. cit., p. 7.

16. E. Bréhier, *Le concept de religion d'après Hermann Cohen,* in "Revue de métaphysique et de morale," xxxii (1925), pp. 359–72.

17. Cf., *ibid.*, p. 163.

18. *Ibid.*, pp. 370–71.

19. In *E* 106, Cohen writes of "*reception (Aufnahme) of religion in ethics,*" but in the first (1896) and second (1902) editions of the same work the expression was more extreme: "*solution (Auflösung) of religion in ethics.*" In *ERW* 586, Cohen states: "*Ethics cannot in any way acknowledge the independence of religion. . . . Thus it can only acknowledge religion as a natural situation, whose cultural maturity appears in ethics.*" In *Religion und Sittlichkeit etc.*, in *J III: 151,* Cohen writes: "*The direction of religion is resolved (aufgehoben) in that of ethics.*" The Italian scholar P. de Vitiis studied the relationship between religion and ethics in Cohen in *Filosofia della religione e preghiera in Hermann Cohen,* in *Preghiera e filosofia della religione,* ed. by Albino Babolin, Perugia, Benucci, 1978, pp. 109–40.

20. Cf. W. Hermann, *Hermann Cohens Ethik,* cit., in Idem, *Schriften zur Grundlegung der Theologie,* cit., II Teil, pp. 88–113; Idem, *Die Auffassung der Religion in Cohens und Natorps Ethik,* in "Zeitschrift für Theologie und Kirche," xix (1909), n. 1, pp. 57–69, n. 2, 162–75; reprinted in Idem, *Schriften zur Grundlegung der Theologie,* cit., II Teil, pp. 206–32. This relationship of religion with the individual's existential experience, incomprehensible for any type of rational, universal knowledge, is a constant theme in the thought of Wilhelm Herrmann and also appears in his writings, such as *Die Lage und Aufgabe der evangelischen Dogmatik in der Gegenwart,* in "Zeitschrift für Theologie und Kirche," xvii (1907), n. 1, pp. 1–33, n. 3, pp. 172–201, n. 5, pp. 315–51; reprinted in Idem, *Schriften zur Grundlegung der Theologie,* cit., II Teil, pp. 1–87, and *Der Begriff der Religion nach Hermann Cohen,* in "Die Christliche Welt," xxx (1916), n. 44, columns 839–42; reprinted in Idem, *Schriften zur Grundlegung der Theologie,* cit., II Teil, pp. 318–23. In this last essay Herrmann repeats his criticisms of Cohen on this point, despite the latter's corrections of his position in *Der Begriff der Religion im System der Philosophie.* This is significant for my position on the Cohen-Herrmann relationship.

21. Actually, already in the *Vorrede* to the second edition of *Ethik des reinen Willens,* Cohen maintains that he had considered Herrmann's objections (cf. *ERW* xiii). However, he is less convincing here, since he tries to oppose rather than to accept these objections (cf. *ERW* 220, 351, 502).

22. But cf. *RV* 186; Eng. trans. 160.

23. S. Ucko, op. cit., p. 19.

24. Both Ucko and Graupe recognize the connection between these two concepts, though from opposing viewpoints. The former high-

lights the novelty of the theme of the uniqueness of God in respect of that of his transcendence (cf. S. Ucko, op. cit., pp. 31ff.), while the latter highlights its continuity (cf. H. Graupe, op. cit., p. 22).

25. The words in the German text are "(. . .)*dass er unbefriedigend bleibt.*" As it stands, this makes no sense. In my view, the masculine pronoun must be a printer's error. This hypothesis is confirmed by the fact that the first edition, at this point, has the feminine pronoun *sie*.

26. I. Kant, *Die Religion innerhalb den Grenzen der blossen Vernunft,* Akademie Ausgabe, Bd. 6, pp. 3–5; Eng. trans. (*Religion within the Limits of Reason Alone*) by Theodore M. Greene & Hoyt H. Hudson, New York, Harpur Torchbooks, 1960, pp. 3–5. The present study, as it concentrates on the development of critical philosophy in Cohen, will not analyze the numerous, profound relationships (of similarity and difference) between Cohen's philosophy of religion and that of Kant, which deserves separate treatment. To my knowledge, such a detailed study has not appeared, though it would be of great interest, not only for the understanding of Cohen's philosophy of religion, but in general for the development of the critical philosophy of religion.

27. Cf. *KBE* 364ff.; *ERW* 440; *Religion und Sittlichkeit etc.*, in *J III:* 147ff. Cohen had already supported this view in *KBE*[1] in order to foreground the continuity of his thought, both in affirming the function of the idea of God for the philosophical foundation of the objective unity between the being of nature and moral what ought to be, and in the relationship between the contingency of nature, present in *KBE*[1], the idea of God as truth, developed in his ethics, and the theme of creation, as the foundation of the idea of God in the everlasting world, which appears in the late works on religion.

28. As has already been noted, Ucko is right to point out this important specific feature of Cohen's religious philosophy as compared with the phenomenologists' formulation, but also that of certain of his contemporaries among critical philosophers.

29. Published with the title: *Der Sabbath in seiner kulturgeschichtlichen Bedeutung.* Vortrag gehalten zu Berlin im Januar 1869 nebst einem Nachwort (1881), in *J II:* 45–72.

30. *Mahnung des Alters an die Jugend* (1917), in *J II:* 176.

31. The italics are mine, to highlight the expression *jenseits,* a deliberate reference to Plato's ἐπέκεινα, to which I shall refer later.

32. In *Religiöse Postulate*, in *J I:* 2, Cohen defined the idea of the unique God as the "foundation stone of our religion," and continued: "*A religion must preserve and develop for ever the ground of its existence in its concept of God.*" Further on, in the same work, he highlights the religious perspective that establishes the unity of nature and morality in the idea of the unique God: "Nature and morality are different and remain so, but

the originary ground of their connection is unitary, it is guaranteed in the unity of God. Inasmuch as I live for the idea of morality, I am not an animal, but a natural being, though I present myself as a member of a moral world. But the conviction that morality becomes reality on the earth is given to me by the idea of God. Since I cannot live without this trust, therefore, I cannot live without God. Fill your heart with this, large as it is, but we accept no other name than that of the unique God for this" (*JI:* 5).

33. Cf. H. Graupe, op. cit., p. 11. However, Graupe developed the theme in a purely methodological, over-restricted and incorrect sense, since in Cohen's as in Kant's critical philosophy, the problem of the limit, though having a methodological aspect, is not limited to this. The identity of critical philosophy and philosophy of method was incorrect both for Kant and for Cohen, in religious philosophy, and also in ethics, at least for the problems it raises, if not for the solutions offered.

CHAPTER NINE. THE UNIQUENESS OF GOD AND CORRELATION

1. For the transition from one concept to the other in Cohen's thought, see S. Ucko, op. cit., pp. 30ff.

2. The identification of being, God, and cosmos through the concept of unity was mainly attributed to Xenophanes by Cohen. Concerning Parmenides, Cohen's interpretation saw a difference from pantheism. Nevertheless, is not entirely unambiguous. It is not necessary here to examine the development and discrepancies on this issue throughout his work, because the "history of his philosophy" as a set of detailed, organic historical judgments begins with Democritus and Plato (the reason for this being both his exclusive interest in the reconstruction of critical idealism and the influence over him of Lange's *Geschichte des Materialismus,* a work to which Cohen had frequent recourse when formulating his historical judgments, and which also begins its historical reconstruction with Democritus). Cohen's references to writers prior to Democritus are to be seen more as serving his theoretical interests than forming part of his detailed historical judgments.

3. On the evolution of Cohen's thought on pantheism, see S. Ucko, op. cit., pp. 23ff.

4. Here Cohen uses the Platonic expression ὄντως ὄν, with reference to the idea of God. This was a deliberate choice, as we shall see.

5. With the same meaning Cohen had already used the term correlation to indicate the relationship between separation and unification, the two fundamental movements of pure thought: (cf. *LRE* 60; cf. also chapter 5, section 7).

6. Cf. *BR* 45; *Einheit oder Einzigkeit Gottes* (1917–18), in *J I:* 93f.; *RV* 79, 81; Eng. trans. 68f. 70.

7. Cf. *Charakteristik der Ethik Maimunis,* in *J III:* 248ff.; *RV* 70ff.; Eng. trans. 61ff. There are also some remarks in *BR* 46f. Cohen gave his most thorough interpretation and evaluation of Maimonides's thought in his work entitled *Charakteristik der Ethik Maimunis.* The influence of this philosopher on Cohen was of the foremost importance, especially for his philosophy of religion and interpretation of Judaism, but also for his conception of the history of philosophy, given the importance he attributed to Maimonides's thought for modern philosophy, starting with Nicholas of Cusa. This is not the place for a detailed analysis of Cohen's interpretation of Maimonides. Information on their relationship can be found in J. Melber, *Hermann Cohen's Philosophy of Judaism,* New York, Jonathan David Publishers, 1968, and S. Zac, *La philosophie religieuse de Hermann Cohen,* Paris, J. Vrin, 1984.

8. Plato, *Republic,* 509b. See *Autonomie und Freiheit* (1900), in *J III:* 36; *Charakteristik der Ethik Maimunis,* in *J III:* 224ff.; *E* 32; *Die religiösen Bewegungen der Gegenwart,* in *J I:* 56; *BR* 35ff.; *Der deutsche Idealismus und die Antike,* in *S II:* 311 f.; *Das soziale Ideal bei Platon und die Propheten,* in *J I:* 309f.

9. Plato, *Phaedo,* 101d. Cf. also *Charakteristik der Ethik Maimunis,* in *J III:* 225f.

10. Cf. *Die platonische Ideenlehre psychologisch entwickelt,* in *S I:* 74ff.; *Platons Ideenlehre und die Mathematik,* in *S I:* 363; *KTE* 24; *KBE* 175f.; *KBA* 127; *ERW* 429; *Charakteristik der Ethik Maimunis,* in *J III:* 224ff.; *E* 32f.; *BR* 35ff.

11. Cf. *KBE* 3, 176, 300; *LRE* 88, 212; *E* 33; *BR* 37.

12. Cf. *Die religiösen Bewegungen der Gegenwart,* in *J I:* 56; *Der deutsche Idealismus und die Antike,* in *S II:* 311; *Das soziale Ideal bei Platon und den Propheten,* in *J I:* 309.

13. Though this work is a transitional stage in the evolution of Cohen's thought, and thus is still strongly influenced by an inclination to ethicize religion, characteristic of his previous phase, it is, nevertheless, a very interesting point of reference, from many points of view, for the understanding of Cohen's later, religious philosophy. If, then, as a correct, faithful historical interpretation of Maimonides's thought, it has, nonetheless, puzzled critics, it should be read with greater interest and more highly valued as a stage in the development of Cohen's philosophy.

14. *Charakteristik der Ethik Maimunis,* in *J III:* 224–25.

15. *Ibid.,* 225-27.

16. *Ibid.,* 250.

17. *Ibid.*, 257f.

18. *Ibid.*, 289.

19. *Ibid.*, 225.

20. The fact that reason is conceived here as a "creature" of God can be a problem, if compared with the fundamental principle of Cohen's logic of origin, for which thought has no other origin beyond itself. (cf. *LRE* 13). F. Rosenzweig, *Einleitung*, in *J I:* 1, argues that, in this way, Cohen made a radical break with idealism, by rejecting reason as a principle. However, it has already been seen that the creator-creature relationship was not conceived by Cohen metaphysically, as a cause-effect relationship, but critically, as correlation. Thus, what happens here is rather an aspect of the specific perspective of religion in respect of the system, which has been mentioned above, and, in my view, it does not deny the rationalist formulation, which is actually the essence of Cohen's idealism, but only the scientific perspective, admittedly carrying out a shift in respect of scientific idealism, but not abandoning the context of critical idealism. On this important evolution in the last phase of Cohen's thought, from the identification of critical idealism with scientific idealism to the consideration of religious idealism as the necessary *systematic* complement to scientific idealism in the context of critical idealism, which, in my view, is the most important methodological meaning of the peculiarity of religion in Cohen's conception of critical philosophy, see, especially, chapter 9, sections 7 and 9, and chapter 10, section 1.

21. Cohen did devote a short essay to the theme of the holy spirit (*Der heilige Geist* [1915] in *J III:* 176–96). Though having been published earlier than *Der Religion der Vernunft*, it contains no substantial differences. The holy spirit is briefly referred to in other works dating from the same period: cf., for example, *Deutschtum und Judentum mit grundlegenden Betrachtungen über Staat und Internationalismus*, in *J II:* 237, 245; *Der Jude in der christlichen Kultur* (1917), in *J II:* 201; *Einheit oder Einzigkeit Gottes*, in *J I:* 98ff.

22. Those who did actually point out the importance of this concept for Cohen's religious philosophy include H. Knittermeyer, *Hermann Cohens Religion der Vernunft*, in "Die Christliche Welt," xxxvi (1922), columns. 795f.; H. van Oyen, *Ethik en Religie*, Amsterdam, H. J. Paris, 1929, p. 28; K. H. Miskotte, *Het wezen der Joodse religie*, Harlem 1964², p. 166; H.-L. Ollig, op. cit., p. 292.

23. Cf. *Charakteristik der Ethik Maimunis*, in *J III:* 227ff.; *BR* 11ff. On the influence of Aristotelian eudemonism on subsequent philosophy, cf. *RV* 467f.; Eng. trans. 403. The judgment on the complementarity between metaphysical thought and ethical sensualism in Aristotle revives the scheme of Cohen's judgment on the complementarity between

metaphysics and gnoseological sensualism in the same philosopher (cf. *KTE* 25ff.).

24. Cf., for example, *RV* 39, 93, 243f.; Eng. trans. 22, 80, 208f.

25. *Der heilige Geist*, in *J III*: 194.

26. A collection of these ideas is to be found in *Das soziale Ideal bei Platon und den Propheten*.

27. Kant's concept of 'causality' is interpreted by Cohen, and the Marburg school in general, in the sense of the scientific concept of 'function' (cf. *KTE* 572ff.; *LRE* 276ff.). The concept of 'substance' is therefore considered as the correlate of function, in the sense of its logical precondition (cf. *KTE* 563ff.; *LRE* 254).

CHAPTER TEN. MAN IN CORRELATION WITH GOD

1. Cf. W. Herrmann, *Die Auffassung der Religion in Cohens und Natorps Ethik*, cit., pp. 212ff. Cf. also Idem, *Hermann Cohens Ethik*, cit., pp. 97ff., 104f. Herrmann's debate with Cohen continued, as can be seen by the former's review of *Der Begriff der Religion im system der Philosophie*. Idem, *Der Begriff der Religion nach Hermann Cohen*, cit.

2. W. Herrmann, *Die Auffassung der Religion in Cohens und Natorps Ethik*, cit., pp. 218.

3. The two terms are equivalent. Cohen uses the first in the *Einleitung* to *Religion der Vernunft* (cf. 17ff.; Eng. trans. 14ff.), and the second in the body of the text. For the concept of *'Nebenmensch'* in Cohen's ethics, cf. *ERW* 211ff. In *ERW* 248f. he considers the I-You relationship as the result of overcoming the other man's otherness. In *Religion der Vernunft*, however, he emphasizes the otherness of You and consequently considers ethics unable to understand it.

4. Cf. especially *BR* 72ff.; *RV* 131ff.; Eng. trans. 113ff. Here he innovatively (especially concerning the conception of the stranger as fellowman) works through previously treated themes, starting with an expert opinion given before the law court in Marburg, in 1888, concerning an accusation against Judaism for discrimination against non-Jews (see: *Die Nächstenliebe im Talmud. Ein Gutachten dem Königlichen Landgerichte zu Marburg erstattet*, in *J I*: 145–74).

5. H. Scholz, op. cit., p. 279: "Religion for Hermann Cohen means a relationship between man and man. In Cohen's view, the originative factor of religious consciousness is not love of God, but love for suffering man. Cohen only sees love of God entering under manifold interpretations, when God is recognized as the protector of those who suffer." T. Weiss-Rosmarin, *Hermann Cohen: On the 50th. Anniversary of his Death*, in

"Jewish Book Annual," xxvi (1968–69), p. 91: "Cohen's religious philosophy is not centered in God but in fellowman."

6. L. Strauss, *Introductory Essay*, in H. Cohen, *Religion of Reason of the Sources of Judaism*, New York, Frederick Ungar Publishing Co., 1972, pp. xxix–xxx.

7. On compassion cf. *ERW* 99, 306, 624.

8. The religious theme of the foundation of equality and unity among men in the unity of God the creator was often quoted by Cohen, even before *Religion der Vernunft*: cf., for example, *ERW* 55, 214.

9. For the evolution of Cohen's interpretation of the Sabbath, see, apart from *Der Begriff der Religion im System der Philosophie* and *Religion der Vernunft, Der Sabbath in seiner kulturgeschichlichen Bedeutung*, in *J II*: 45–72; *Liebe und Gerechtigkeit in den Begriffen Gott und Mensch* (1900), in *J III*: 43–97; *Der Stil der Propheten* (lecture delivered in 1901), in *J I*: 262–83: *Innere Beziehungen der Kantischen Philosophie zum Judentum*, in *J I*: 301; *Die Bedeutung des Judentums für den religiösen Fortschritt der Menschheit* (1910), in *J I*: 25ff.; *Gesinnung* (1910), in *J I*: 197, 205; *Das Gottesreich* (1914), in *J III*: 172; *Der heilige Geist*, in *J III*: 184; *Spinoza über Staat und Religion, Judentum und Christentum*, in *J III*: 340.

10. Here I cannot examine Cohen's analysis of the points of contact between religion and aesthetics, and, above all, of the differences and peculiarity of the former in respect of the latter. For this, see, particularly, *BR* 85ff., 121ff. The various different and peculiar features of religion in respect of aesthetics which Cohen highlights can be situated in the general character of the peculiarity of religion, in the perspective of the limit, which is specific to it in respect of each area of the system. Thus, man's nature and man in nature, the God-man correlation, the object of religion also involve a higher, unifying perspective toward pure aesthetic feeling and its object. For this perspective feeling is not an exclusively aesthetic reality, but is united to moral action and resolved in it, and the individual is not transfigured and contemplated in an aesthetic type, but actively loved in his concrete individuality, which is only accessible in correlation with God.

11. Cf. in general *RV* 194ff.; Eng. trans. 167ff. For the problem of guilt in ethics, cf. the sections on self-responsibility and self preservation, in *ERW* 357ff.

12. The concept of 'absolute individual' obviously does not indicate unconditionedness of the individual in respect of God but, in contrast with the other concepts of man, such as plurality and universality, indicates unconditionedness in respect of other men, which only in correlation of the individual with God is conceptually determinable: the absolute individual is the individual only in relation to God. For this rea-

son, this concept takes on neither a metaphyscal nor an empirical meaning, but by rights remains within critical idealism.

13. In considering the particular importance Cohen attributes to Ezekiel in his history of Jewish prophetism, we must recall the special biographical tie with this prophet; Ezekiel was Cohen's Hebrew name. An episode in the life of Cohen, reported by F. Rosenzweig, *Einleitung*, in *J I:* lii, is particularly illuminating on this point: "I can see him, after recovery from his illness, lying on the sofa, saying happily: 'That I, Ezekiel the thirty-sixth'—it was his name in Hebrew—'should come to carry in honor Ezekiel the first!,' and then to himself, in Hebrew: 'Send away all you sins. . . . And make yourselves a new heart and a new spirit,' and again, in an almost inaudible voice, 'send away . . . make yourselves . . . make'" (cf. *RV* 226; Eng. trans. 194).

14. Cohen's terminology is varied on this point. Sometimes he uses the expression *sin against God*, contrasted with *sin against men* ("sin against God" must not be understood in the sense of sin against rites, which Cohen called "sins specially called against God," and which he did not consider very important: cf. *RV* 255; Eng. trans. 219). More frequently, Cohen prefers the expression *sin before God*. My view is that the latter expression is the more accurate (and I use it for this reason), since Cohen's distinction does not really concern he against whom the sin is committed (in this sense, from Cohen's point of view, how could man commit a sin against God?) but the correlation in which man puts himself when becoming aware of his sin. The distinction is methodical, not contingent.

15. For Cohen's interpretation of "radical evil" in Kant, cf. *KBE* 335ff.; also *Innere Beziehungen der Kantischen Philosophie zum Judentum*, in *J I:* 298f.

16. Cohen also reworks material from previous reflections in this case. These date back to the early 1890s when he wrote an essay entitled *Die Versöhnungsidee*, in *J I:* 125–39. On the theme of reconciliation see also *Liebe und Gerechtigkeit in den Begriffen Gott und Mensch*, in *J III:* 43–97, and *Der Tag der Versöhnung* (1917), in *J I:* 140–44.

17. On the irreconcilability of religion with pessimism cf. *BR* 54, 59, 65, 69, 79, 139; *RV* 20f., 170, 263, 503, 524, 527; Eng. trans. 18, 146f., 226, 434, 454, 456f.

18. Cf. Ez. 18, 30, which in Cohen's version reads: "And guilt must not be an offense for you."

19. Cf. Ez. 18, 21–23.

20. F. Rosenzweig, *Einleitung*, in *J I:* lx, remembers how, during a discussion with Cohen on Zionism, the latter, no longer accepting what he considered, the excessively tolerant arguments of his pupil "interrupted

me, moving his enormous head, with its soft curls, threateningly, towards me, and said: 'I want to tell you something,' and then, in a sonorous whisper,: 'The vulgar (*die Kerls*) wish to be happy!'"

21. A still-imperfect concept of critical ethics, for which Cohen blames Kant, in connection with the concept of the supreme good (cf. *KBE* 349ff.).

22. Cf. M. Buber, *Gottesfinsternis. Betrachtungen zur Beziehung zwischen Religion und Philosophie* (New York, Harper, 1952, Zurich, Manesse Verlag, 1953), in Idem, *Werke*, Bd. 1, Munich/Heidelberg, Kösel/Lambert Schneider, 1962, p. 547.

23. *Ibid.*, p. 548.

24. *Ibid.*, p. 547.

25. Cf. M. Buber, *Nachwort*, in *Ich und Du* (Heidelberg, Lambert Schneider, 1958), in Idem, *Werke*, Bd. 1, cit., pp. 169f.

CHAPTER ELEVEN. MESSIANISM AND HISTORY

1. The expression comes from *Micah*, 4, 13.

2. Cf. *Die Messiasidee*, in *J I:* 105 ff.; *Liebe und Gerechtigkeit in den Begriffen Gott und Mensch*, in *J III:* 58; *Die Errichtung von Lehrstühlen für Ethik und Religionsphilosophie an den jüdisch-theologischen Lehranstalten* (1904), in *J II:* 116–23; *Religiöse Postulate*, in *J I:* 6; *Religion und Sittlichkeit etc.*, in *J III:* 140ff.; *Charakteristik der Ethik Maimunis*, in *J III:* 281ff.; *Die Bedeutung des Judentums für den religiösen Fortschritt der Menschheit*, in *JI* 30f.; *Gesinnung*, in *J I:* 209; *Innere Beziehungen der Kantischen Philosophie zum Judentum*, in *J I:* 301f.; *E* 109f.; *Die religiösen Bewegungen der Gegenwart*, in *J I:* 48, 58f.; *Die Lyrik der Psalmen* (probably written in 1914, published posthumously in 1924), in *J I:* 241f.; *Das Gottesreich*, in *J III:* 173; *Vom ewigen Frieden*, in *S II:* 345; *Deutschtum und Judentum mit grundlegenden Betrachtungen über Staat und Internationalismus*, in *J II:* 269; *Der heilige Geist*, in *J III:* 184f.; *Das soziale Ideal bei Platon und den Propheten*, in *J I:* 313ff.; *Der Prophetismus und die Soziologie*, in *J II:* 401; *Über den ästhetischen Wert unserer religiösen Bildung* (published posthumously in 1924), in *J I:* 217ff.

3. For a detailed treatment of Cohen's philosophy of history, see S. Kaplan, *Das Geschichtsproblem in der Philosophie Hermann Cohens*, cit., where a thorough overview of the subject is given, on the basis of the interpretation of Kant's philosophy of history in *Kants Begründung der Ethik* and Cohen's original developments in his works on ethics and religious philosophy. In the present chapter I only highlight his original contribution to the subject in his last works on religious philosophy, as an implication of the wider contribution of religion, in its peculiarity, to Cohen's critical philosophy.

4. One of Cohen's criticisms of Christian messianism is precisely that of having attributed the power of bringing upon himself, not only the suffering but also the guilt of men (cf., for example, *RV* 308f.; Eng. trans. 264f.).

5. Cf. chapter 10, section 10.

6. Cf., in general, *LRE* 226 ff.

7. From this point of view *Der Begriff der Religion im System der Philosophie* does not constitute a crucial stage in this investigation, since, though the idea of immortality is no longer rejected as mythical in this work, unlike *Ethik des reinen Willens*, but was accepted positively, however, the meaning Cohen emphasizes is only that of the holiness of the holy spirit as correlation with God and man and as a guarantee of redemption (cf. *BR* 105), an important meaning of immortality, that does not, however, make its consequences for historical evolution explicit.

8. For Maimonides's concept of the 'pious of the peoples of the world,' cf. *RV* 141ff., 383ff.; Eng. trans. 122ff., 329ff.

9. For a more accurate analysis of the theme of truth in *Religion der Vernunft*, see, especially *RV* 441ff., 460f., 475ff., 482; Eng. trans. 379ff., 396f., 410ff., 415.

10. In this interpretation of the biblical ideal of the unity of the heart, Cohen used the reflections of Bachya ibn Paqada, on whom he also wrote a short essay: *Die Einheit des Herzens bei Bachya* (1910), in *J III*: 213–20.

11. In this one could see criticism of Natorp, who, as is well known, considered humanitarianism (*Humanität*) understood as the harmony of human formation (*Bildung*), the object and ideal of religion, thus eliminating the transcendence of God from religious experience (cf. P. Natorp, *Religion innerhalb der Grenzen der Humanität. Ein Kapitel zur Grundlegung der Sozialpädagogik*, Tübingen, J. C. B. Mohr (Paul Siebeck), (1908²) On the discussion betwen Cohen and Natorp on religion, see *Ibid.*, pp. 96ff., 117ff.; *BR* 121f.; and especially Cohen's unpublished notes on the work by Natorp cited here, and Natorp's on that of Cohen, now published in H. Holzhey, *Cohen und Natorp*, cit., Bd. 2, pp. 99ff., 107ff. Concerning the overcoming of humanitarianism in peace, it is interesting that to Natorp's doubts that the conception of religion in Cohen, as expressed in *Ethik des reinenWillens*, could lead to passing over the "limits of mankind" (*Menschheit*) (cf. P. Natorp, *Religion innerhalb der Grenzen der Humanität etc.*, p. 117), Cohen replied "But has he the right to 'pass over the limits of humanitarianism'" (*Doch das Recht des "Hinausschritts über die Grenzen der Humanität"*) (H. Holzhey, *Cohen und Natorp*, cit., Bd. 2, p. 100).

Index of Names